AF304728

THE RETURN
OF CONSCIOUSNESS
A New Science on Old Questions

THE RETURN OF CONSCIOUSNESS

A New Science on Old Questions

EDITED BY

KURT ALMQVIST AND ANDERS HAAG

BOKFÖRLAGET STOLPE   AXEL AND MARGARET AX:SON JOHNSON FOUNDATION FOR PUBLIC BENEFIT

TABLE OF CONTENTS

PREFACE TO THE ORIGINAL 2016 EDITION

The riddle of consciousness continues to fascinate and inspire to debate and has given rise to conflicting perspectives on, among other issues, the classical mind–body problem that has engaged thinkers and scientists for millennia, from Gautama Buddha over Plato, Aristotle, René Descartes, and Immanuel Kant to John Searle, Daniel Dennett and Christof Koch.

The essays in this volume stem from the lectures delivered at the conference *The Return of Consciousness – A New Science on Old Questions*, held at Avesta Manor, Dalarna, Sweden, in the summer of 2015.

Stockholm, August 2016

Kurt Almqvist
President
Axel and Margaret Ax:son Johnson Foundation for Public Benefit

INTRODUCTION

It is no surprise that consciousness is considered a wonder. It is the window to reality, both the inner and outer world. Without consciousness, you would not experience anything. You would actually be nothing, a zombie, the living dead.

In short, consciousness is all about experience: daily familiar experiences – like the smell of coffee in the early morning, being pushed around by other bodies in a crowded commuter train, the sense of anxiety before an important meeting – and your usual muddle of thoughts. But it is also an awareness of grand things – like feeling fully alive, being in love – and encompasses your own musings about the soul, God, the universe and the meaning of the whole thing. There is something it is like to be a conscious organism, as Thomas Nagel has put it.

Why is this? Why should there be an experience, with a typically subjective aspect? And how on earth does it arise from a mushy lump of brain cells, if it does? This is considered the "hard problem" in modern philosophy. The "easy problem" is to explain how intelligent and purposeful behaviour is carried out by different cognitive and emotive functions of the brain, functions that can be analysed in terms of computational and neural mechanism.

When science was young, René Descartes stipulated the existence of two deeply different substances. There is an experiencer – a thinking thing, that has no extension in time and space – and then there is all the lifeless matter which is extended in time and space. Physical stuff can move by itself, in a non-conscious way, and so can the material bodies of beasts. Only cogito, the soul, can wonder why and how. This proposal was in line with earlier Western spiritual and philosophical traditions, but is not accepted in today's science. You've got to be physicalist, to accept physical stuff as the only base, or not be scientific at all.

For a long time, science went along ignoring the existence of experience. Consciousness was considered too evasive an object of study and not a proper object of scientific enquiry. The behaviouristic movement at the beginning of the 20th century turned the inner life of humans into a black box. Only human behaviour should be studied. In the 1950s, the perspective changed slightly. With the invention of the computer, it became fashionable to study human cognitive abilities. A person's inner life was now considered a non-conscious computer. The metaphor today is, as we all know, "you are your brain". There is really no consciousness, only brain states.

What is less known is that consciousness studies has emerged as a new and fast-growing scientific field in recent decades. It is again scientifically legitimate to ask age-old questions: What is consciousness? What is its relation to the self? How does it arise and where does it exist? When does it arise (in evolution, in the development of an embryo, in the recovery from severe brain injuries)? Or could it be like the philosopher Galen Strawson is claiming? Consciousness was always there, and it is everywhere, because consciousness is a property of the physical stuff, the only stuff there is.

In 2015, the Axel and Margaret Ax:son Johnson Foundation gathered the foremost philosophers and researchers in this new field to a seminar. This book is a collection of essays written by the speakers.

Now, seven years later, we are delighted to publish a new edition of *The Return of Consciousness* in which Dr Christof Koch gives us an update of the exciting field of consciousness studies. Dr Christof Koch has been one of the leading figures in this field for decades. For many years, he cooperated in the research with Nobel laurate Francis Crick. He was president of the world-famous Allen Institute for Brain Science and a co-founder of the most heatedly debated theory of consciousness today: the integrated information theory.

Stockholm, May 2022
Anders Haag
Project leader

THE RETURN OF CONSCIOUSNESS
– REDUX

Christof Koch

Consciousness is the only way I know about the sliver of time's wide horizon that I have been granted. For, without being able to experience something, I am nothing to myself, as in deep sleep or during anaesthesia. My conscious experience is the starting point, my omphalos, from which I abduce, that is, infer, everything else, including the existence of an external world populated by stars, trees, people, viruses and elementary particles. After a century or more of either eliding (behaviourism) or outright denying (parts of Anglo-Saxon analytical philosophy) this central fact of our existence, consciousness and its physical substrate are back in the spotlight of academic discourse and public debate. But, this time around, we have science – in particular, neuroscience – at our back. And that has made all the difference.

To highlight the genesis of a genuine science of consciousness, the Axel and Margaret Ax:son Johnson Foundation organised, in 2015, a series of lectures in the glorious Nordic summer in Sweden. The essays you hold in your hand are the outcome of this workshop. My purpose in these introductory comments is to point out developments that have occurred in the seven intervening years. This is necessary, for our tools are now so powerful that progress in the ancient mind–body problem occurs at a faster pace than ever before. In the following, I will refer to advances in locating consciousness in the brain, in biomarkers for detecting consciousness in brain-injured patients, in psychedelics research and in the maturing of scientific theories of consciousness.

Tracking the footprints of consciousness in the brain
The search for the neural correlates of consciousness (NCC), the minimal neuronal mechanisms jointly sufficient for consciousness, that Crick and I advocated a third of a century ago[1] has turned into a vigorous research enterprise, investigated in humans and other mammals, primarily macaque monkeys and mice.[2] While most of this involves correlating

brain activity with phenomenology – that is, experience X activates brain region Y – an increasing fraction of these studies invoke causal manipulations – that is, removing or inactivating region Y prevents experience X, or stimulating area Y gives rise to experience X. Some of the most compelling studies linking bits and pieces of cortical tissue to specific conscious experiences come from intracranial electrical stimulation prior to neurosurgery. Consider two clinical case studies.[3]

The neurosurgeon Fried and colleagues[4] healed a young girl with generalised tonic–clonic seizures associated with feelings of guilt and distress, caused by a tumour bordering the subcallosal cingulate. Stimulation of nearby regions with electrodes evoked intense guilt and distress. Five years on from the removal of the tumour, the patient remained free of guilt episodes or any other seizures. At least in this one patient, regions involving the subgenual cingulate gyrus and the medial-anterior temporal lobe are closely linked to the experience of guilt, a paradigmatic social emotion.

Parvizi and his colleagues treated a high-functioning executive whose frequent partial seizures consistently distorted his sense of self, including awareness of his body's position in space, not being able to tell up from down, and seemingly listening, as an external observer, to his own thoughts.[5] These seizures were localised to the right posteromedial cortex, in Brodmann area 31. Importantly, electrical stimulation of this region or the corresponding region on the left induced the same subjective sense of self-dissociation. The data from this one patient is compatible with studies in volunteers, demonstrating that this region is a posterior node of the *default mode network* involved with the self, autobiographical memory, spontaneous thoughts, day dreaming, internal chatter and so on. Long-term meditators and volunteers that undergo mindfulness training have reduced connectivity within this default mode network,[6] compatible with the hypothesis that aspects of self-consciousness are instantiated within the default node network.

Of course, the underlying atoms of consciousness are not brain regions but far-flung coalitions of highly heterogeneous cortical and thalamic neurons, belonging to hundreds of distinct neuronal cell types.[7] So it is to discrete neuronal assemblies, perhaps as small as a few hundred neurons, perhaps encompassing tens of millions, that are the physical substrate of any one specific experience, such as feeling guilty or hearing one's thoughts. Disentangling the multiplicity of underlying molecular, genetic, cellular and circuit mechanisms to identify those that are specifically and uniquely linked to any one experience, rather than to cognitive operations leading up to or following the phenomenal experience itself (such as attention, reporting, planning, memory and so on), will take a lot of time, effort and ingenuity.

A related development is a clearer delineation between arousal, or wakefulness, and consciousness. As expressed in the well-known graph of Laureys[8] (reproduced in Anil Seth's opening chapter), these can be dissociated. Wakefulness is low (as measured by arousal threshold) during vivid conscious dreaming. Conversely, it can be high during sleepwalking, partial complex seizures and in vegetative-state patients, all of which show little evidence of consciousness.

Three different laboratories have now, independently, demonstrated that deep brain stimulation (DBS), delivered to the intralaminar nuclei, part of the central nucleus of the thalamus, can effectively reverse anaesthesia,[9] a state in which the subject is unarousable even to such a major insult to the integrity of the body as surgical incision. While the monkey is "put to sleep" by the action of the general anaesthesia, stimulating the thalamus wakes the animal up, as assayed by brain-wide haemodynamic signatures, eye opening and EEG evidence of sophisticated auditory processing.

Building a consciousness meter
Searching for the NCC is beginning to pay off in terms of its therapeutic implication for patients with disorders of consciousness (DOC),[10] in particular for vegetative-state patients, also known as patients with behavioural unresponsive syndrome (see the chapter by Nicholas Schiff). Severely brain injured, and often on ventilator support, with daily periods of open eyes and other signs of arousal, but no evidence of voluntary responses during bedside interviews, these patients can remain in this liminal state for months or years. Clinical studies estimate that up to 40 per cent are either covertly conscious or – following careful and time-consuming behavioural examination using the current "gold standard", the JFK Coma Recovery Scale-Revised – should be reclassified as being in a minimally conscious state (MCS), defined by inconsistent but reproducible goal-directed behaviours, such as response to command, utterances or tracking with their eyes.[11] Misdiagnosis can have grave consequences, especially in end-of-life decision-making.[12] Indeed, the question

of whether "anyone is home" is perennially preying upon the minds of family, friends and care givers.

Furthest along the road to answer this is the perturbational complexity index (PCI), in which the brain is probed by a brief magnetic pulse (generated via transcranial magnetic stimulation applied to the skull) and the resulting cortical activity is recorded using a high-density EEG electrode array.[13] A simple algorithm then computes the complexity of the brain's reverberations to this knock, from which the presence of consciousness can be inferred with unprecedented sensitivity – ie, low false-alarm rate – and specificity – ie, low miss rate – at the level of individual patients. This is critical, as biomarkers that only identify a trait (whether that be the presence of consciousness or a tumour in some organ) at the group level are not useful in clinical practice, given the huge heterogeneity in people and their brains (this lack of accuracy is why the bible of psychiatry, the 5th edition of the *Diagnostic and Statistical Manual of Mental Disorders*, does not list a single biomarker for any mental disorder). Attempts to infer consciousness from spontaneous EEG have much lower signal-to-noise and therefore lower performance.[14] Furthermore, preliminary evidence suggests that the PCI method can also stratify these patients into subgroups with higher and lower chances of recovery.

The development of a practical consciousness-meter for the clinic, after more than two millennia of eristic debate that has filled libraries with learned books on the mind–body problem but has achieved little communal convergence upon accepted truths, is a major milestone.

Consciousness and psychedelics
The renaissance of using psychedelics to manipulate conscious experience and derive therapeutic benefits has been nothing short of astonishing.[15] Every day brings new stories in both mainstream and alternative media, by and large with a positive tone. How things have changed!

After artists, intellectuals, political activists and young people in Western countries became enamoured by classical psychedelics, in particular mescaline (the active ingredient in peyote), psilocybin (the active agent in magic mushroom) and the synthetic lysergic acid diethylamide (LSD, aka 'acid') in the late 1950s and 1960s, and psychiatrists studied their beneficial effects on a variety of mental afflictions, conservative forces pushed back and helped pass restrictive laws (eg, the Controlled Substances Act in the US, in 1970). These criminalised psychedelics and lumped them, in the eyes of the public and law enforcement, together with crack, cocaine, heroin and other highly addictive and toxic drugs that have quite different brain biochemistry and neuronal targets.

Research carried out, under difficult conditions, in the intervening years by a few intrepid academics scattered across Europe and the US[16] demonstrated what shamans and healers from indigenous populations in the Americas have known, and practised, for centuries – that a single dose of psilocybin can trigger breathtaking changes in conscious experience.[17] These can include perceptual (shimmering, motion trails, colours), aesthetic (gratefulness, beauty, sacredness), cognitive (ego loss), psychotic (fear, panic, confusion, impairment) and psychodynamic aspects (suppressed emotions). In some cases, in particular with N,N-dimethyltryptamine (DMT, aka the "spirit" molecule, one of the two active components in ayahuasca) and 5-methoxy-N,N-dimethyltryptamine (5-MeO-DMT, aka the "God" molecule or "the toad"), users report full-blown mystical experiences, including feelings of cosmic unity, oceanic boundlessness, radical change in the geometry and even the topology of phenomenally experienced space, cessation of the perceived flow of time, dissociation from the external world and the body, and encountering and conversing with spirits and celestial messengers. Consider this summary by a trained observer and psychologist:

> ...all things imaginable and non-imaginable can be seen with Ayahuasca. One can see all the moments of one's life, all the people and places that one knows, Nature and the Cosmos in all their manifestations, human history and the different cultures that it has and has not produced, and scenes that lead one above the planet to the far reaches of the cosmos, to the heavens. One can see the inner parts of one's body and the deeper strata of one's soul, one can encounter the infinite richness of myth and fantasy, meet fairies and dragons, angels and devils, taste the nectars of the Eternal, be washed by the bounty of the Supreme Good, witness the perennial light, encounter the Divine.[18]

Common to these experiences is what William James in his *Varieties of Religious Experience* calls a "noetic quality":

> states of insight into depths of truth unplumbed by the discursive intellect.[19]

This is why many scholars advocate for calling these substances *entheogens.*

The acute effects on subjective experience can last anything between ten minutes and ten hours. While the serotonergic tryptamines mentioned here have similar, though not identical, molecular structures, they are likely to involve binding, in different combinations, to different serotonin (and other neurotransmitters') receptors (and not just to the 5-HT-2A receptor that hogs the limelight) across different regions of cortex and subcortical regions, in patterns of staggering complexity.[20] In the meantime, scientists and doctors have been measuring electrical or haemodynamic brain activity of volunteers on psychedelics. It is often claimed that consciousness expands while tripping – can that be verified using such measures as neuronal integration and differentiation?[21] Or do some lead to a reduction, while others to an expansion? How can the hyper-realisation (the antipode to de-realisation suffered by dissociative patients) that is common on magic mushrooms – the world appears more authentic, vivid, real, veridical than in everyday life – be related to the underlying neural substrate? Is the neural signature of ego-dissolution under psilocybin a reduction in default-mode network activity and inter-connectivity, as suggested by some experiments?[22]

Of course, of even greater interest are the beneficial long-term changes to well-being, outlook and the reduction (or outright elimination) of many psychiatric symptoms in relevant populations after one or two psyche-delic trips. Indeed, as I write these lines, there are more than 50 open or not yet recruiting clinical trials[23] for psilocybin underway, to treat concussion, migraine and chronic cluster headaches, major depressive disorder, treatment-resistant depression, obsessive–compulsive disorder, mild cognitive impairment, post-traumatic stress disorder, chronic pain, end-of-life existential distress, alcoholism, cessation of smoking, burnout for carers and on and on. Interestingly, the likelihood of long-term therapeutic effects increases with the likelihood of the subject having a mystical experience. This raises a question with direct ontological implications for consciousness – is the conscious experience of oceanic boundlessness (for example) necessary for a successful therapeutic outcome, or is it a quite unnecessary side effect, an epiphenomenon, of the drug acting on some receptors?[24] Could the same therapeutic effect be obtained if, say, the drug is given covertly while the subject is in a deep sleep or anaesthetised?

With proper care, the right set and setting, screening and support by a therapist, this powerful consciousness-modification technique will advance our knowledge of how the tripping brain creates an alternative reality as compelling, if not more so, than everyday life.

Theories of consciousness
Historically, the mind–body problem has been the battleground of religious scholars, philosophers and mystics. Since the birth of psychology, neuroscience and neurology in the mid to late 19th century, clinical observations and more systematic experiments in humans and other mammals have contributed an avalanche of critical observations to this debate. Given ever-advancing technological and methodological capabilities, this trend towards sophisticated empirical investigations involving interventions and observations is set to further accelerate. An additional development over the past two decades is the rise of sophisticated scientific theories that are amenable to empirical falsification and verification. These purport to explain, in a mechanistic manner, what consciousness is, its physical substrate in the brain, how it can be measured, how it relates to attention and other cognitive routines, and what types of organisms are conscious.[25] The two most popular and mature theoretical paradigms are global neuronal workspace[26] and integrated information theory[27] (see the chapter by Naotsugu Tsuchiya and colleagues).

Integrated information theory (IIT) starts from phenomenology and, from this centre, works towards the physical mechanisms such as molecules, neurons, transistors and other stuff that constitutes its substrate. All other theories take the opposite direction – starting from mechanisms and then moving inward, towards experience.

IIT starts out with five (transcendental) axioms that fully describe the properties of any conceivable conscious experience and that are indubitably true. It translates these into five associated postulates concerning the causal powers of any physical system that instantiates these properties. From these postulates, IIT derives a measure of the intrinsic causal power of any system, quantified by its total integrated information. Any system with some integrated information possesses an inner view, exists for itself, is conscious and irreducible. A system with no integrated information is fully reducible to subsystems and has no conscious experience. The perturbational complexity index described above derives from IIT.[28]

The lineage of global neuronal workspace theory (GNW) originates in the architecture of early computers, in which specialised programs accessed a shared repository of information, the blackboard or central workspace. In the brain, this workspace is implemented by a network of long-range cortical neurons with two-way communication between prefrontal cortex and a widespread set of parietal, temporal and cingulate cortices. The act of globally broadcasting information is what makes information conscious and thereby available to a variety of cognitive modules, such as memory, planning, language and so on. Information that isn't broadcast and remains local to one module – say, the one controlling the position of the eyes – remains encapsulated and therefore unconscious.

Both theories have substantial empirical support on their own, with a host of testable predictions. However, the theories make quite different ontological assumptions; thus, IIT is concerned with extrinsic and intrinsic causal powers, while GNW takes a computational–cognitive perspective. They can't both be simultaneously correct.

To directly pit predictions of these two theories against each other, the Templeton World Charity Foundation funded two adversarial collaborations in which proponents from the two camps hammered out a set of predictions concerning the location and the timing of the NCC for visual experience (in the front or in the back of cortex[29]). As much an experiment in the sociology of science as it is in chasing experience down to its lair, it is a team effort involving more than a dozen labs in Europe, America and China, using best open-science practices, including preregistration and sharing of all data, to determine which theory best explains the facts.[30] Other adversarial collaborations are concerned with distinguishing between first-order and higher-order theories of consciousness and between IIT and predictive processing accounts of consciousness.[31] No matter which theory comes out ahead, or even if all theories prove inadequate to explain the data (unfortunately, given the vast complexity of the brain, this is not an unlikely outcome), we shall learn a lot. And that constitutes true progress.

We live in a golden age of neuroscience and technology, in which the flowering of ever more advanced experimental techniques, including brain–machine interfaces, and theories are tackling the problem of consciousness. Rapid progress in the field echoes the sentiment expressed by the mathematician David Hilbert, engraved upon his tomb:

Wir müssen wissen.
Wir werden wissen.[32]

1. F. Crick and C. Koch, 'Towards a neurobiological theory of consciousness', *Seminars in the Neurosciences*, no. 2, 1990, pp. 263–75; F. Crick and C. Koch, 'Some reflections on visual awareness', *Cold Spring Harbor symposia on quantitative biology*, no. 55, 1990, pp. 953–62.
2. C. Koch, M. Massimini, M. Boly & G. Tononi, 'Neural correlates of consciousness: progress and problems', *Nature Reviews Neuroscience*, vol. 17, no. 5, 2016, pp. 307–21; D. Revach & M. Salti, 'Expanding the discussion: Revision of the fundamental assumptions framing the study of the neural correlates of consciousness', *Consciousness and cognition*, no. 96, 2021, DOI: 103229.
3. K.C.R. Fox, L. Shi, S. Baek, O. Raccah, B.L. Foster, S. Saha, D.S. Margulies, A. Kucyi & J. Parvizi, 'Intrinsic network architecture predicts the effects elicited by intracranial electrical stimulation of the human brain', *Nature Human Behaviour*, vol. 4, no. 10, 2020, pp. 1039–52. See also C. Koch, 'Hot or Not?' *Nature Human Behaviour*, vol. 4, no. 10, 2020, pp. 991–2.
4. I. Fried et al., 'Laser ablation of human guilt', *Brain Stimulation*, no. 15, 2022, pp. 164–6.
5. J. Parvizi, R.M. Braga, A. Kucyi, M.J. Veit, P. Pinheiro-Chagas, C. Perry, C. Sava-Segal et al., 'Altered sense of self during seizures in the posteromedial cortex', *Proceedings of the National Academy of Sciences*, vol. 118, no. 29, 2021.
6. J.A. Brewer, P.D. Worhunsky, J.R. Gray, Yi-Yuan Tang, J. Weber & H. Kober, 'Meditation experience is associated with differences in default mode network activity and connectivity' *Proceedings of the National Academy of Sciences*, vol. 108, no. 50, 2011, pp. 20254–9.
7. R.D. Hodge, T.E. Bakken, J.A. Miller, K.A. Smith, E.R. Barkan, L.T. Graybuck, J.L. Close et al., 'Conserved cell types with divergent features in human versus mouse cortex', *Nature*, vol. 573, no. 7772, 2019, pp. 61–8; T.E. Bakken, N.L. Jorstad, Qiwen Hu, B.B. Lake, Wei Tian, B.E. Kalmbach, M. Crow et al., 'Comparative cellular analysis of motor cortex in human, marmoset and mouse', *Nature*, vol. 598, no. 7879, 2021, pp. 111–19.
8. S. Laureys, 'The neural correlate of (un)awareness: lessons from the vegetative state', *Trends in Cognitive Sciences*, vol. 9, no. 12, 2005, pp. 556–9.
9. M.J. Redinbaugh, J.M. Phillips, N.A. Kambi, S. Mohanta, S. Andryk, G.L. Dooley, M. Afrasiabi, A. Raz & Y.B. Saalmann, 'Thalamus modulates consciousness via layer-specific control of cortex', *Neuron*, vol. 106, no. 1, 2020, pp. 66–75; A.M. Bastos, J.A. Donoghue, S.L. Brincat, M. Mahnke, J. Yanar, J. Correa, A.S. Waite et al., 'Neural effects of propofol-induced unconsciousness and its reversal using thalamic stimulation', *Elife*, no. 10, 2021, DOI: e60824; M. Afrasiabi, M.J. Redinbaugh, J.M. Phillips, N.A. Kambi, S. Mohanta, A. Raz, A.M. Haun & Y.B. Saalmann, 'Consciousness depends on integration between parietal cortex, striatum, and thalamus', *Cell Systems*, vol. 12, no. 4, 2021, pp. 363–73; J. Tasserie, L. Uhrig, J.D. Sitt, D. Manasova, M. Dupont, S. Dehaene & B. Jarraya, 'Deep brain stimulation of the thalamus restores signatures of consciousness in a nonhuman primate model', *Science Advances*, vol. 8, no. 11, 2022, DOI: eabl5547.

10. A. Thibaut, N. Schiff, J. Giacino, S. Laureys & O. Gosseries, 'Therapeutic interventions in patients with prolonged disorders of consciousness', *Lancet Neurology*, vol. 18, no. 6, 2019, pp. 600–14; M. Farisco, C. Pennartz, J. Annen, B. Cecconi & K. Evers, 'Indicators and criteria of consciousness: ethical implications for the care of behaviourally unresponsive patients', *BMC Medical Ethics*, vol. 23, no. 1, 2022, pp. 1–15.

11. C. Schnakers, A. Vanhaudenhuyse, J. Giacino, M. Ventura, M. Boly, S. Majerus, G. Moonen & S. Laureys, 'Diagnostic accuracy of the vegetative and minimally conscious state: clinical consensus versus standardized neurobehavioral assessment', *BMC Neurology*, vol. 9, no. 1, 2009, pp. 1–5; M.M. Monti, A. Vanhaudenhuyse, M.R. Coleman, M. Boly, J.D. Pickard, L. Tshibanda, A.M. Owen & S. Laureys, 'Willful modulation of brain activity in disorders of consciousness', *New England Journal of Medicine*, vol. 362, no. 7, 2010, pp. 579–89.

12. A.F. Turgeon, F. Lauzier, J.-F. Simard, D.C. Scales, K.E.A. Burns, L. Moore, D.A. Zygun et al, 'Mortality associated with withdrawal of life-sustaining therapy for patients with severe traumatic brain injury: a Canadian multicentre cohort study', *Canadian Medical Association Journal*, vol. 183, no. 14, 2011, pp. 1581–8; J. Elmer, C. Torres, T.P. Aufderheide, M.A. Austin, C.W. Callaway, E. Golan, H. Herren et al., 'Association of early withdrawal of life-sustaining therapy for perceived neurological prognosis with mortality after cardiac arrest', *Resuscitation*, no. 102, 2016, pp. 127–35.

13. S. Casarotto, A. Comanducci, M. Rosanova, S. Sarasso, M. Fecchio, M. Napolitani, A. Pigorini et al., 'Stratification of unresponsive patients by an independently validated index of brain complexity', *Annals of Neurology*, vol. 80, no. 5, 2016, pp. 718–29; A.G. Casali, O. Gosseries, M. Rosanova, M. Boly, S. Sarasso, K.R. Casali, S. Casarotto et al., 'A theoretically based index of consciousness independent of sensory processing and behavior', *Science Translational Medicine*, vol. 5, no. 198, 2013, DOI: 198ra105-198ra105; M. Rosanova, M. Fecchio, S. Casarotto, S. Sarasso, A.G. Casali, A. Pigorini, A. Comanducci et al., 'Sleep-like cortical OFF-periods disrupt causality and complexity in the brain of unresponsive wakefulness syndrome patients', *Nature Communications*, vol. 9, no. 1, 2018, pp. 1–10.

14. Yang Bai, Yajun Lin & Ulf Ziemann, 'Managing disorders of consciousness: the role of electroencephalography', *Journal of Neurology*, 2021, pp. 4033–65.

15. I can warmly recommend the magisterial and engaging book, *How to Change your Mind: What the new science of psychedelics teaches us about consciousness, dying, addiction, depression, and transcendence*, by Michael Pollan (London: Penguin, 2019).

16. R.R. Griffiths, W.A. Richards, U. McCann & R. Jesse, 'Psilocybin can occasion mystical-type experiences having substantial and sustained personal meaning and spiritual significance', *Psychopharmacology*, vol. 187, no. 3, 2006, pp. 268–83; A.L. Halberstadt, F.X. Vollenweider & D.E. Nichols (eds.), *Behavioral Neurobiology of Psychedelic Drugs*, Berlin, Springer, 2018; F.X. Vollenweider, & K.H. Preller, 'Psychedelic drugs: neurobiology and potential for treatment of psychiatric disorders', *Nature Reviews Neuroscience*, vol. 21, no. 11, 2020, pp. 611–24.

17. Indeed, at least one medical anthropologist speaks of the peyote ceremony as practised in the American Native Church as an explicit 'consciousness modification' technique – Joseph Calabrese, in *A Different Medicine – Postcolonial Healing in the Native American Church*, Oxford, Oxford University Press, 2013.

18. B. Shanon, *The Antipodes of the Mind – Charting the Phenomenology of the Ayahuasca Experience*, Oxford, Oxford University Press, 2010.

19. W. James, *The Varieties of Religious Experience*, New York, NY, Longmans, Green & Co., 1917.

20. G. Ballentine, S.F. Friedman & D. Bzdok, 'Trips and neurotransmitters: Discovering principled patterns across 6,850 hallucinogenic experiences', *Science Advances*, vol. 8, no. 11, 2022, DOI: eabl6989.

21. M.M. Schartner, R.L. Carhart-Harris, A.B. Barrett, A.K. Seth & S.D. Muthukumaraswamy, 'Increased spontaneous MEG signal diversity for psychoactive doses of ketamine, LSD and psilocybin', *Scientific Reports*, vol. 7, no. 1, 2017, pp. 1–12.

22. R.L. Carhart-Harris, D. Erritzoe, T. Williams, J.M. Stone, L.J. Reed, A. Colasanti, R.J. Tyacke et al., 'Neural correlates of the psychedelic state as determined by fMRI studies with psilocybin', *Proceedings of the National Academy of Sciences*, vol. 109, no. 6, 2012, pp. 2138–43; L. Smigielski, M. Scheidegger, M. Kometer & F.X. Vollenweider, 'Psilocybin-assisted mindfulness training modulates self-consciousness and brain default mode network connectivity with lasting effects', *NeuroImage*, no. 196, 2019, pp. 207–15.

23. K.A.A. Andersen, R. Carhart-Harris, D.J. Nutt & D. Erritzoe, 'Therapeutic effects of classic serotonergic psychedelics: A systematic review of modern era clinical studies', *Acta Psychiatrica Scandinavica*, vol. 143, no. 2, 2021, pp. 101–18. See also https:// clinicaltrials.gov.

24. D.B. Yaden & R.R. Griffiths, 'The subjective effects of psychedelics are necessary for their enduring therapeutic effects', *ACS Pharmacology & Translational Science*, vol. 4, no. 2, 2020, pp. 568–72.

25. I here distinguish theories, in the sense of a minimal set of non-conflicting assumptions and postulates, from which systematic inferences can be made, from *ad hoc* hypotheses, such as that oscillations in the firing activity of neurons in the 40 Hz range are a hallmark of consciousness, and pure speculations, such as that the collapse of the wave function is probably critical to consciousness.

26. B. Van Vugt, B. Dagnino, D. Vartak, H. Safaai, S. Panzeri, S. Dehaene & P.R. Roelfsema, 'The threshold for conscious report: Signal loss and response bias in visual and frontal cortex', *Science*, vol. 360, no. 6388, 2018, pp. 537–42; G.A. Mashour, P. Roelfsema, J-P. Changeux & S. Dehaene, 'Conscious processing and the global neuronal workspace hypothesis', *Neuron*, vol. 105, no. 5, 2020, pp. 776–98.

27. A. Haun & G. Tononi, 'Why does space feel the way it does? Towards a principled account of spatial experience', *Entropy*, vol. 21, no. 12, 2019, p. 1160; G. Tononi, M. Boly, M. Massimini & C. Koch, 'Integrated information theory: from consciousness

to its physical substrate', *Nature Reviews Neuroscience*, vol. 17, no. 7, 2016, pp. 450–61; F. Ellia, J. Hendren, M. Grasso, C. Kozma, G. Mindt, J.P. Lang, A.M. Haun, L. Albantakis, M. Boly & G. Tononi, 'Consciousness and the fallacy of misplaced objectivity', *Neuroscience of Consciousness*, no. 2, 2021, DOI: niab032.

28. M. Massimini, F. Ferrarelli, R. Huber, S.K. Esser, H. Singh & G. Tononi, 'Breakdown of cortical effective connectivity during sleep', *Science*, vol. 309, no. 5744, 2005, pp. 2228–32.

29. M. Boly, M. Massimini, N. Tsuchiya, B.R. Postle, C. Koch & G. Tononi, 'Are the neural correlates of consciousness in the front or in the back of the cerebral cortex? Clinical and neuroimaging evidence', *Journal of Neuroscience*, vol. 37, no. 40, 2017, pp. 9603–13; B. Odegaard, R.T. Knight & H. Lau, 'Should a few null findings falsify prefrontal theories of conscious perception?' *Journal of Neuroscience*, vol. 37, no. 40, 2017, pp. 9593–602; O. Raccah, N. Block & K.C.R. Fox, 'Does the prefrontal cortex play an essential role in consciousness? Insights from intracranial electrical stimulation of the human brain', *Journal of Neuroscience*, vol. 41, no. 10, 2021, pp. 2076–87; S.B. Snider, D. Fischer, M.E. McKeown, A. Li Cohen, F.L.W.V.J. Schaper, E. Amorim, M.D. Fox, B. Scirica, M.B. Bevers & Jong Woo Lee, 'Regional Distribution of Brain Injury After Cardiac Arrest: Clinical and Electrographic Correlates', *Neurology*, vol. 98, no. 12, 2022, pp. e1238–47.

30. L. Melloni, L. Mudrik, M. Pitts & C. Koch, 'Making the hard problem of consciousness easier', *Science*, vol. 372, no. 6545, 2021, pp. 911–12; L. Melloni, L. Mudrik, M. Pitts, K. Bentz, O. Ferrante, U. Gorska, R. Hirschhorn, A. Khalaf, C. Kozma, A. Lepauvre, Ling Liu, D. Mazumder, D. Richter, Hao Zhou, H. Blumenfeld, D.J. Chalmers, S. Devore, F. Fallon, F.P. de Lange, O. Jensen, G. Kreiman, Huan Luo, S. Dehaene, C. Koch, G. Tononi, 'An adversarial collaboration protocol for testing contrasting predictions of global neuronal workspace and integrated information theory', *PLoS ONE*, in press.

31. For a complete list, see https://www.templetonworldcharity.org/accelerating-research-consciousness-our-structured-adversarial-collaboration-projects.

32. We must know. We shall know.

THE FALL AND RISE
OF CONSCIOUSNESS SCIENCE

Anil K. Seth

Two out of three central mysteries about our place in the universe have been resolved. The first was *literally* our place in the universe. Copernicus long ago showed that we weren't at its centre: the Earth is just a speck among the vastness, somewhere "[f]ar out in the uncharted backwaters of the unfashionable end of the western spiral arm of the Galaxy".[1] The second mystery was resolved by Darwin, who showed with his theory of natural selection that human beings share ancestry with all other species, so that we are just one branch or twig of a beautifully rich and diverse evolutionary tree.

The third mystery, as yet unsolved, concerns the nature and origin of our inner universe – *consciousness* – at once the most familiar and most mysterious aspect of our existence. Conscious experiences define our lives, but the private, subjective and intrinsic "what-it-is-likeness" of these experiences seems to resist scientific enquiry. How can the redness-of-red, the warmth of a log fire or the pang of jealousy emerge from physical processes and biological machinery within our brains and bodies?

Consciousness science is the attempt to shed light on, and ultimately resolve, this mystery using the tools of scientific enquiry. The challenge has a prehistory within a variety of intellectual traditions and a more recent history within the modern sciences of psychology and neuroscience. In this chapter, I will give a brief and necessarily incomplete sketch of this history, finishing by summarising some of the exciting directions driving the next phase of consciousness research.

Defining consciousness

There is a common view that any scientific explanation of a phenomenon must be preceded by a comprehensive and broadly accepted definition. The history of science has however repeatedly challenged this view, with many phenomena, such as "temperature" and "gene", being continuously redefined as the relevant science advances. A useful

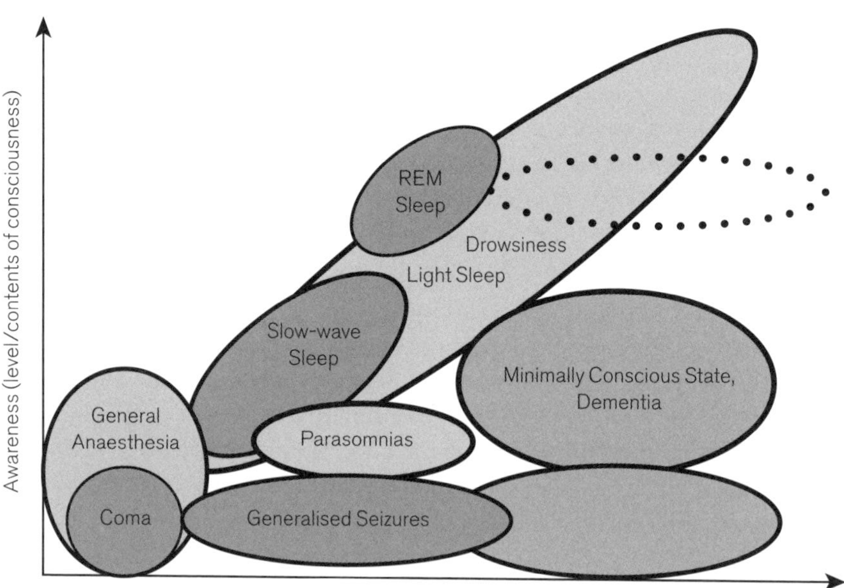

Figure 1. Conscious level (awareness) is distinct from, though normally correlated with, physiological wakefulness (vigilance).[7]

measure of scientific progress is the extent to which definitions change from descriptive and phenomenological (eg temperature as the "hotness" of things) to explanatory and mechanistic (temperature as mean molecular kinetic energy).[2] Having said that, since consciousness (unlike temperature) is intrinsically experiential, any eventual definition is unlikely to exclude phenomenology.

Currently, definitions of consciousness are highly descriptive. While there are diverse candidates, these can be summarised very simply by saying that for a conscious organism *there is something it is like to be that organism*.[3] Or one can simply say that consciousness (for humans) is what disappears when we fall into a dreamless sleep and what returns the next morning when we wake up.[4] Putting things a bit more formally, for conscious organisms there exists a continuous (though interruptible) stream of conscious scenes or experiences – a phenomenal world – which has the character of being subjective and private.[5]

Beyond these basic statements some further distinctions are useful. The first is between conscious *level* and conscious *content*. Conscious level refers to how "conscious" an organism is. As Figure 1 shows, this can be thought of as a graded scale from complete unconsciousness, as in dreamless sleep, coma and deep anaesthesia, all the way to vivid, conscious wakefulness. Importantly, conscious level is not the same as wakefulness or vigilance: one can be conscious while asleep, for example while dreaming, and one can be unconscious while physiologically awake, as happens in sleepwalking and in some pathological conditions such as the vegetative state.[6]

Conscious *contents* refer to the distinguishable elements of a conscious scene, given a non-zero conscious level. These include consciously experienced colours, shapes, smells, thoughts, explicit beliefs, emotions and moods, experiences of volition and agency, and so on. Collectively, conscious contents are what philosophers call *qualia* and explaining how such "qualitative feeling states" emerge from a physical, material substrate remains the most metaphysically problematic aspect of consciousness science.[8] Conscious contents can be further divided into those that are *world-related*, like the smell of freshly cut grass on a summer day, and those that are *self-related*, like the ache of a rotten tooth or the experience of identifying with and owning a particular body.[9] Some conscious contents, like the experience of body ownership and of having a first-person perspective on the world, are so continuous and pervasive that it is easy to take them for granted. Yet pathological cases and laboratory experiments show that even these experiences can be altered, meaning that they must be traceable to specific biological mechanisms in the brain.[10] Any given conscious scene usually integrates elements that are both world-related and self-related, although through the focus of attention one or the other may dominate.[11]

Other possible distinctions are less universally accepted. Some researchers distinguish between *phenomenal* consciousness and *access* consciousness, where the former relates to all qualitative components of conscious scenes and the latter to just those conscious contents that are available to other cognitive processes, including verbal report.[12] Although this debate surfaced in the philosophical literature, it has important empirical consequences, since the main way of assessing what a person is conscious of is to ask them, which assumes conscious access. While some believe that phenomenal consciousness does not make sense in the absence of access,[13] others have made persistent efforts to show that unreportable aspects of perception share common perceptual properties with explicitly reportable percepts, suggesting (though not proving) the existence of phenomenal consciousness in the absence of access.[14]

Less controversially, one can distinguish between *primary* or *core* consciousness, which refers to first-order, conscious experiences of the world or of the self, and *higher-order* or *reflective* consciousness, which refers to "being conscious of being conscious".[15] This sounds strange, but in normal circumstances we are aware of being conscious of this or that. More generally, metacognition (cognition about cognition) is an important element of our psychological make-up.[16]

In summary, definitions of consciousness are needed to specify explanatory targets (or *explananda,* those phenomena which are to be explained), which can then motivate a search for underlying mechanisms (or *explanantia,* those causes which do the explaining). In most areas of science, as these mechanisms are revealed, definitions may change from the phenomenological and descriptive to the explanatory and mechanistic. Because consciousness is intrinsically phenomenological, however, its definition will be augmented, not replaced, by causal-mechanistic accounts.

Key questions in consciousness science

The most fundamental challenge for consciousness science, popularised by David Chalmers as the "hard problem",[17] is to explain why and how physical processes – such as those unfolding within brains – are ever accompanied by conscious experience. Chalmers contrasts this with the "easy problem" of explaining how the complex biophysical operations of the brain give rise to perception, action, cognition and behaviour – everything *but* consciousness! Although some researchers claim that the hard problem can now be solved,[18] it may anyway be a mistake to view the hard problem as preventing progress in consciousness science. After all, physicists have made great strides in revealing intricate properties of the universe without solving the basic mystery of its existence.[19] Another useful parallel – though sometimes overplayed – comes from the history of our understanding of life, which at one time may have seemed as mysterious as consciousness does now, but which has nonetheless yielded to a naturalistic explanation that excludes mysterious "explanations" such as an *élan vital.*[20]

A more tractable goal for consciousness science is to identify the biophysical (predominantly neural) mechanisms that underlie different conscious levels and specific conscious contents. This is the search for the "neural correlates of consciousness",[21] which has been criticised on the grounds that correlations, by themselves, neither establish causal power nor provide explanations. As we become clearer (through phenomenological investigations) about the diverse aspects of consciousness for which we wish to account, however, and as we identify more detailed potential correlates – also probing their causal status using brainstimulation methods[22] – it becomes possible to move from *correlation* towards *explanation.*[23] In this view, consciousness science is primarily about establishing progressively more sophisticated and experimentally validated mappings between subjective, first-person data (the explanatory targets or *explananda*) and objective, third-person data (the underlying causal biophysical mechanisms or *explanantia,* and their behavioural consequences).[24]

This is not the hard problem (it is not about accounting for the existence of consciousness per se) nor the easy problem (it takes phenomenal properties as *explananda*) – one might instead call it the *real problem of consciousness.*[25] Seen this way, a major obstacle for consciousness science is not so much the limits of our ability to probe the brain but, rather, to characterise the first-person, phenomenological data that specify appropriate explanatory targets,[26] so as to carry out effective "neurophenomenology".[27]

Consciousness science has a number of goals besides the basic objective of determining the biophysical basis of conscious experience. These include establishing the function(s) of consciousness: what does consciousness do for an organism? Relevant research involves exploring the limits of unconscious perception[28] and studying the neural basis of voluntary action.[29] This generally supports the idea that consciousness enables flexible voluntary behaviour, compared with unconscious or automatic responses.

Other prominent questions in consciousness science have to do with how conscious experiences are altered or lost in pathological conditions in psychiatry (eg, in psychosis) and neurology (eg, in the vegetative state), and how a fuller understanding of these conditions as disturbances of "normal" consciousness can inform new approaches to diagnosis, prognosis and treatment.[30] Finally, a mature consciousness science may have things to say about conscious states in preverbal infants[31] and non-human animals, including non-mammals,[32] and even about the possibility of conscious machines.[33]

A very brief history of consciousness science
People have been wondering about consciousness since they have been wondering at all. All major religions propose systems of thinking about (or having beliefs about) consciousness and the self. This is not surprising since without consciousness, for any of us, there is simply nothing at all. In the Western rational tradition, explicit theories of consciousness can be traced to Hippocrates (~460BC – ~370BC), now known as the father of modern medicine. Unlike Aristotle (who thought the brain had nothing much to do with consciousness), Hippocrates held that "from nothing else but the brain come joys, delights, laughter and sports, and sorrows, grief, despondency, and lamentations".[34] This has a deliberate echo in Francis Crick's "astonishing hypothesis" that "[y]ou, your joys and your sorrows, your memories and ambitions, your sense of personal identity and free will, are in fact no more than the behaviour of a vast assembly of nerve cells and their associated molecules".[35]

Fast-forward to the Renaissance, when the Belgian physician Andreas Vesalius (1514–64) revolutionised anatomy by performing, and illus-

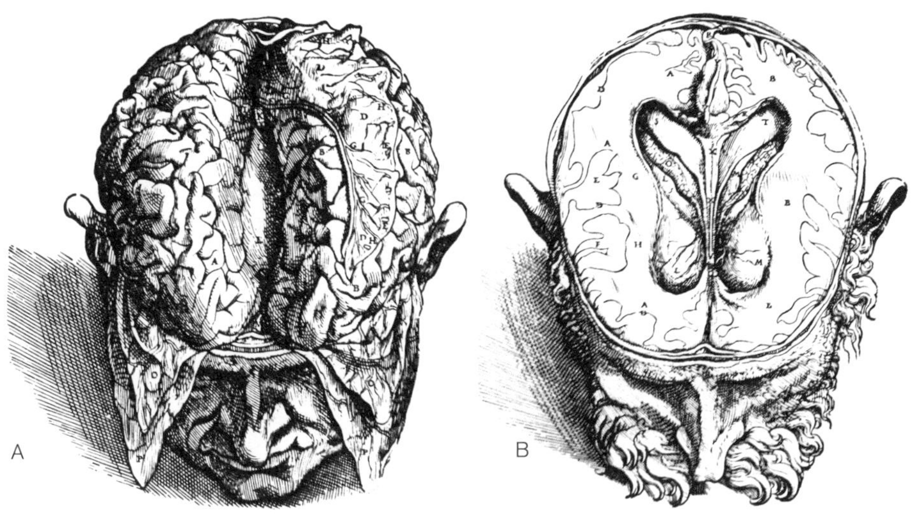

Figure 2. Andreas Vesalius's drawings of
the exposed human brain, revealing the
corpus callosum in the centre (A) and
various cortical gyri and sulci (B).[36]

trating, the first detailed post-mortem dissections of the human body. His 1543 masterpiece, *On the Fabric of the Human Body* (a year that also saw Copernicus's *On the Revolution of the Celestial Spheres*), contains remarkable drawings of the structure of the human brain, highlighting some of its most striking features, such as the corpus callosum (the large bundle of nerve fibres connecting the two hemispheres – see Figure 2).

René Descartes (1596–1650) is usually blamed for inventing the "hard problem" of how consciousness and matter relate, on account of his division of the universe into *res cogitans* ("mind stuff") and *res extensa* ("matter stuff"). While his influence on modern science and philosophy is inestimable, he also left a problematic legacy with his "beast machine'" argument – that (non-human) animals were mere automatons without "souls" or the ability consciously to suffer.

Moving on a little further, we see some other early statements of the "hard problem". Isaac Newton (1642–1726), studying the physical basis of colour, confessed that "[t]o determine by what modes or actions light produceth in our minds the phantasm of colour is not so easie".[37] And Gottfried Leibniz put things even more strongly, asserting that "it must be confessed that perception and that which it depends upon are inexplicable on mechanical grounds".[38]

The 19th century, especially the latter part, saw the birth of psychology as a science, as well as the first steps in what later became neuroscience. The most prominent figures in these developments, with respect to consciousness, are William James (1832–1920) and Wilhelm Wundt (1842–1910), but many other important figures deserve mention: Helmholtz, Charcot, Janet, Broca, Wernicke, Darwin, Galton, Golgi, Mueller, Freud, Donders and Ramón y Cajal, to name but a few.[39]

The legacies of Wundt and James for understanding mind and brain are enormous. Wundt set up the first laboratory of experimental psychology in Leipzig in 1879, while James is still credited with having already said almost everything worth saying about consciousness.[40] For both, explaining consciousness was at the centre of the new science that became known as psychology.

Wundt believed that consciousness could be best studied using experimental introspection – presenting subjects with (for example) ticking metronomes and asking them to report their conscious sensations. This was a highly controlled process in which subjects were extensively trained on how to report their experiences, supporting a scientific rather than casual usage of introspection. Much as chemists disaggregate a complex material into its constituent elements, Wundt believed that conscious experiences could be disaggregated through introspection into component parts. He was searching for the "atoms" of experience.

James rejected the idea that consciousness could be so reduced, coining the phrase "stream of consciousness" to emphasise that conscious experience was a process comprising an ever-changing succession of images, thoughts and feelings.[41] James' copious writings on psychology and consciousness treated topics as diverse as feelings, desires, emotions, cognitions, beliefs, reasoning and volition – as well as more esoteric subjects like religious experience.[42] His early writings on attention have been particularly influential and, while he is often thought to have denied a role for unconscious processes, this view seems to rest on misreadings of his *Principles*.[43]

Around the same time that James and Wundt were initiating the scientific study of mind and consciousness, other intellectual movements were developing which would shape the course of psychology and "consciousness science" in the 20th century. The European phenomenologists, among them Edmund Husserl (1859–1938), provided both a philosophy and a psychology which gave primacy to subjective experience.[44] This method tried to suspend or "bracket" the preconceptions, interpretations or inferences about conscious experience that may bias introspective report, so that the raw properties of consciousness would become apparent. Sigmund Freud (1856–1939) focused on the unconscious, proposing theoretical constructs such as the "id", "ego" and "superego", largely on the basis of case studies and self-examination.[45] Both these disciplines relied primarily on people's introspective reports about their inner lives.

Consciousness in the 20th century: the backlash
The reliance of early psychology, psychoanalysis and phenomenology on introspection led to a backlash in the early 20th century, the echoes of which are still being felt. Behaviourist psychology, championed by John B. Watson (1878–1958), argued that introspective data were unreliable, since they could not be objectively validated. Psychology could only become a science if it dealt exclusively with objectively measurable phenomena (behaviour) and dismissed all talk of subjective experiences and even internal, "cognitive" processes ("private events") of any sort. According to Watson's behaviourism, the goal of psychology was not an

understanding of the constitution of our mental lives but, rather, *the prediction and control of behaviour.*[46]

Behaviourism came in several flavours. While Watson believed that private events should be entirely ignored by psychology, B.F. Skinner's "radical behaviourism" acknowledged their existence, although he retained the notion that they could only be studied indirectly, by analysing behavioural data. Both Watson and Skinner were strongly influenced by Ivan Pavlov (1849–1936), who conducted pioneering work on classical conditioning (associating novel stimuli with innate responses) and reflex behaviour – work which Skinner in particular extended into the domain of operant conditioning (linking behavioural cause and effect).

Behaviourism dominated (especially US) psychology throughout the early-to-mid 20th century but is now often treated with some disdain for its systematic neglect of mental content. Yet the behaviourist approach had and continues to have many successes, for instance in restraining some of the excesses of introspectionism and in delivering important insights into learning and memory.[47] The focus on "prediction and control of behaviour" also motivated an important branch of artificial intelligence, cybernetics,[48] which is gaining a new relevance within psychology and neuroscience[49] as the importance of embodiment and physiological regulation becomes increasingly appreciated.

Behaviourist methods are still widely used within psychology, but behaviourism as a school of thought faded during the 1960s, as limitations on behaviourist explanation became apparent (notably Chomsky's critiques regarding language) and as cognitive psychology gained prominence. Cognitive psychology was (and still is) based on notions of internal representation and information processing, and its rise in the 1960s was accelerated by its association with developments in classical artificial intelligence.

In seeing the brain as a computer of some sort, however, cognitive psychology remained resistant to addressing consciousness explicitly. "Information processing" can be interpreted as a metaphor for both unconscious and conscious operations, leaving no obvious way to distinguish what is special about consciousness. George Miller, a founder of the field, said in 1962: "We should ban the word consciousness for a decade or two."[50] As late as 1976, another prominent cognitive scientist, Ulrich Neisser, said: "Psychology is not ready for consciousness."[51] (By this time, though, true to his word, Miller was saying: "I consider consciousness to be the constitutive problem of biology."[52]) Perhaps the harshest comment of all came from Stuart Sutherland, in the 1989 edition of the *International Dictionary of Psychology*: "Consciousness is a fascinating but elusive phenomenon. It is impossible to specify what it is, what it does, or why it evolved. Nothing worth reading has been written on it."[53] Early cognitive models, usually consisting of boxes and arrows of different kinds, had entities suggestive of roles for consciousness, but the word itself was never used.[54]

It is tempting to think simply in terms of a progression from Wundt and James, through behaviourism and classical cognitive science, to a turn-of-the-century enlightenment when psychology and neuroscience became reunited, with consciousness once again a central focus. History is of course never so straightforward and the trajectory of consciousness science is more complicated than this simple tale suggests. Even during the heyday of behaviourism, significant work on the brain basis of consciousness was being carried out, the results of which trace directly to the leading edge of consciousness science today.

Hans Berger's invention of the electroencephalograph (EEG) in 1924 is a good example. Berger was the first to record electrical brain activity and in doing so discovered the phenomenon of alpha waves (prominent oscillations at ~10 hertz, which were originally called "Berger waves") and measured their properties in various conditions. A few years later, Alfred Loomis made the first whole-night EEG recordings,[55] laying the foundations for EEG-based sleep staging, and for current attempts to decipher the neurophysiological correlates of conscious level.

Other powerful examples come from neuropsychology, which studies the relationship between brain structure and function, and which pays particular attention to deficits induced by specific and localised brain injury. Paul Broca (1824–80) initiated the field by identifying a region (usually) within the left cortical hemisphere that is critical for language production ("Broca's area"), following observations of patients with aphasia. Neuropsychology came of age during the First World War, which provided under terrible circumstances a ready supply of experimental subjects with focal brain injuries. Soldiers with damage to their visual cortex often presented with specific disturbances in visual experience, providing evidence about the neural basis of visual conscious contents.

In 1957, still well before the rehabilitation of consciousness science, the (clinically motivated) removal of Henry Moliason's hippocampus revealed a direct link between a brain region and the ability to form new episodic memories, a key part of being a conscious self.[56] In the late 1950s and 1960s, Roger Sperry and Michael Gazzaniga pioneered studies of patients who had been treated for intractable epilepsy by severing the corpus callosum. These "split brain" patients showed signs of having two semi-independent "consciousnesses" within a single cranium.[57] Around the same time, the pioneering Canadian neurosurgeon Wilder Penfield was using electrical brain stimulation to map out the brain's representation of its body (the "cortical homunculus"). Along the way he discovered that stimulating parts of the temporal lobes could induce vivid recall of episodic memories, with other stimulation protocols leading to other specific conscious contents, such as visual hallucinations and experiences of déjà vu.[58]

Nowadays, brain lesion and stimulation studies are key elements of our armamentarium for isolating the necessary and sufficient neural mechanisms underlying conscious contents. While many of these studies still rely on clinical observations and interventions, modern non-invasive techniques, such as transcranial magnetic stimulation (TMS), enable temporary activation and deactivation of specific brain regions in healthy volunteers, boosting the utility of these approaches.[59]

The rebirth of consciousness science
A convenient date to mark the rehabilitation of consciousness science is with Francis Crick and Christof Koch's landmark 1990 paper, 'Towards a Neurobiological Theory of Consciousness', which opened with "It is remarkable that most of the work in both cognitive science and the neurosciences makes no reference to consciousness (or 'awareness')" and went on to propose a specific theory based on 40 hertz oscillations.[60] Although this specific idea has fallen out of favour, it remains significant in being one of the first neurobiological theories to attempt to draw an explanatory connection between a brain property (40 hertz or "gamma band" oscillations) and a phenomenological property (the binding of disparate visual elements within coherent conscious scenes), while being explicitly phrased as a theory about consciousness.

Crick was not the only prominent Nobel laureate to turn to consciousness, having already established academic immortality. Gerald M. Edelman (1929–2014), who won his Nobel for establishing a selectionist (ie, Darwinian) account of immune-system function, had by the early

1990s produced a series of books articulating a similarly selectionist account of brain function, which he called Neural Darwinism (or the "theory of neuronal group selection").[61] Consciousness, for Edelman, resulted from massive parallel interactions between brain areas involved in perception and memory, so that conscious scenes comprised a "remembered present".[62]

These watersheds in neurobiology were just part of a wider re-emergence of consciousness as a legitimate explanatory target. Movements within philosophy of mind foreshadowed later scientific developments by presenting serious discussions about the possibilities and limitations of brain-based accounts of consciousness. Daniel Dennett caused a stir on publication of *Consciousness Explained*,[63] which has since been a little unfairly criticised as "Consciousness Explained Away". A key theme of Dennett's account is that our intuitions about the "specialness" of conscious qualia might be misplaced, creating additional unnecessary mystery.

Earlier, Tom Nagel and Frank Jackson had tackled the recalcitrant nature of qualia by asking readers to imagine "what it is like to be a bat"[64] and to consider the relationship between knowledge (eg, about colour vision) and experience (of seeing red).[65] John Searle's famous "Chinese room" thought experiment,[66] while originally targeted at the possibility of strong (ie, real) artificial intelligence, took things a little further by asking whether simulation of those processes necessary for X (where X might be "translating Chinese" or "seeing red") would be sufficient to instantiate that property.

While these and other philosophers (such as Owen Flanagan and Colin McGinn) were mainly concerned with the possibility of a science of consciousness, others – such as Ned Block and Patricia Churchland – took a more pragmatic attitude, asking how philosophy and science could work together to understand consciousness. Churchland championed the idea of "neurophilosophy", which explores the relevance of neuroscience for philosophy of mind,[67] and Block introduced the still controversial distinction between "phenomenal" and "access" consciousness,[68] which continues to inspire fascinating empirical research.[69]

In another influential line, emerging from philosophy, David Rosenthal's "higher order thought" (HOT) theory proposes that a mental state is conscious when a person is aware (or disposed to being aware) of being in that state. Informally, this means that a mental state X is conscious when there is another mental state Y "pointing at" that first mental state, where Y itself doesn't need to be (and typically isn't) conscious.[70] HOT theories are closely related to studies of metacognition and its role in consciousness.[71]

Contemporary consciousness science also has important origins in cognitive science and artificial intelligence, most notably in the guise of Bernard Baars' "global workspace theory".[72] Promoted as a "cognitive" theory of consciousness, GWT sees the brain as effecting a network of modular and specialised processors, competing for access to a "global workspace". By analogy with blackboard architectures in artificial intelligence, GWT proposes that mental states become conscious when they are "broadcast" within the global workspace, so that they can influence other more specialised processors, including verbal report and motor actions. On this view, consciousness is mainly about access and has an integrative function – to mobilise and integrate brain operations that are otherwise separate and independent.[73]

Later, brain-based extensions of GWT identified the "workspace" with a tightly interconnected network of frontal and parietal cortical areas, non-linear "ignition" of which corresponded to conscious access.[74] A wealth of experimental evidence supports this view, to the extent that increased fronto-parietal activity was for many years seen as one of the most reliable correlates of conscious content.[75] This consensus is however being challenged by recent studies suggesting that such activity (at least the more frontal components) may have more to do with the act of reporting (saying whether or not one is conscious of X) than with consciousness per se.[76]

Throughout the 1990s, consciousness science was dominated by the search for the neural correlates of consciousness (NCCs). The gold standard definition of an NCC comes from Crick and Koch, as the "minimal neuronal mechanisms jointly sufficient for any one specific conscious percept".[77] This approach achieved its dominance for several reasons.

First, the rapid development of brain-imaging methods such as functional MRI made it possible to measure brain activity within the living human brain while volunteers performed specific tasks and while they could report their conscious experiences. Secondly, these technologies (complementing existing methods like EEG) allowed a *contrastive analysis* of conscious contents, comparing conscious states with closely matched unconscious states in terms of behaviour and neural responses.[78]

Instructive examples of contrastive analysis are found in studies of binocular rivalry, a situation in which one's conscious experience changes even though sensory inputs (different images to each eye) remain constant.[79] Thirdly, a practical focus on searching for correlates sweeps aside deep metaphysical questions related to the "hard problem", and sidelines even the "real" problem of drawing explanatory links between objective (eg, neural) properties and subjective (phenomenal) descriptions. This practical focus also explains why the early explanatory targets for the NCC approach were rather simple and consistent with Crick's attraction to scientific reductionism: the specific conscious percept of "seeing red" was often stated as a canonical example,[80] yet "redness" as a conscious content makes no sense without the context of a vast repertoire of other actual and counterfactual conscious contents.[81]

A great deal has been learned from the search for NCCs.[82] By being so conceptually straightforward, by bracketing the hard (and real) problems and by leveraging powerful brain-imaging methods, this approach was able rapidly to rehabilitate the study of consciousness within psychology and neuroscience.[83] Yet in recent years its shortcomings have been more widely recognised, for example in distinguishing any potential NCC "proper" from those neuronal processes that are either prerequisites or inevitable consequences of conscious states.[84] The need for more sophisticated theories about consciousness, and for a deeper appreciation of the relevant phenomenological *explananda*, is now motivating a new wave of consciousness science.

Current and future directions
This chapter has focused on a potted history of consciousness science. In the space remaining, it is only possible to gesture towards some current research directions.[85]

In terms of conscious *level*, new theories and measures have emerged based on neural complexity and, specifically, "information integration". These ideas advance the field since they are based on phenomenology. The basic idea[86] is that conscious scenes are both highly "differentiated" (each conscious scene is one among a vast repertoire of alternative possibilities) and at the same time highly "integrated" (each conscious scene is experienced as a unified whole). The neural dynamics underlying consciousness should therefore also exhibit coexisting integration and differentiation (loosely, "complexity"). Several complexity-based measures of conscious level have been proposed,[87] which are based on mathematical techniques including information theory and autoregressive time-series modelling. Recently, some complexity-based measures have shown encouraging results in distinguishing different conscious levels, both in healthy volunteers and in neurological patients.[88] Future work in this area will be especially valuable if it shows that new measures have empirical purchase *because of*, not *despite*, being grounded in theory and phenomenology.

Research on conscious *content* has continued to focus on identifying the brain regions or dynamical processes that distinguish conscious from unconscious perceptions. We have already visited the debate over whether frontal and parietal regions are constitutively involved in conscious perception[89] – this work is likely to continue with bistable perception remaining a key experimental paradigm. Another classical observation in this area is that top-down (also "recurrent", "re-entrant") connections seem necessary for perceptual content to become conscious.[90] Although a deep understanding of why such top-down activity is necessary remains elusive, one highly promising approach is the so-called Bayesian brain or "predictive processing" framework.[91]

On these views, which go back at least as far as Helmholtz in the 19th century, perception is a process of (possibly Bayesian) inference on the hidden causes of the ambiguous and noisy signals that impinge on our sensory surfaces. Top-down signals are suggested to carry perceptual predictions ("priors" in Bayesian terminology) which interact with bottom-up sensory signals across all levels of the perceptual and motor hierarchies in the brain. The upshot is that perceptual content is determined by the brain's "best guess" of the causes of its sensory signals, corresponding to a Bayesian posterior.

There is growing evidence that conscious perception can indeed be shaped by top-down predictions or expectations,[92] and recent neurophysiological studies suggest that top-down and bottom-up signals are carried by distinct cortical frequency bands[93] in a manner consistent with neurophysiological implementations of the Bayesian brain hypothesis.[94] While this research is exciting, it remains unknown how and when predictive processing results in conscious perception and, more generally, it is unclear whether the brain actually implements a form of Bayesian inference or whether Bayes' theorem just provides a flexible (perhaps *too* flexible) framework for conceiving hypotheses about cognitive function.[95] Future work in this area will likely combine refined conceptual and computational models[96] with developments in artificial intelligence showing the power of "deep" neural networks for vision and control[97] and advanced neuroimaging methods,[98] to reveal the conditions and mechanisms governing how perceptual predictions shape conscious contents.

Research on the conscious *self* distinguishes many levels of experienced selfhood, from a basic embodied selfhood associated with emotion and physiological integrity, through the experience of one's body as a specific object in the world, all the way to higher levels of "narrative" or linguistic selfhood that establish a continuity of the "I" across time. Recent research has advanced understanding in all these areas. For example, it may be possible also to explain the experience of emotional awareness and embodied selfhood from a Bayesian perspective, resting on the brain's best guesses of causes of changes in its own internal physiology, sensed through interoceptive modalities.[99] These developments recall the earlier ideas of James and Lange, and later Schachter and Singer,[100] associating emotion with perception of bodily changes, and they make interesting connections with old ideas in "cybernetic" theories of predictive homeostasis.[101] Strikingly, interoceptive signals – like the heartbeat – can modulate the perception of emotionally salient external stimuli, such as fearful faces.[102]

Experiences of owning a particular body, and of inhabiting a particular first-person perspective, are other key aspects of conscious selfhood amenable to a Bayesian account.[103] These experiences are surprisingly malleable, with simple experimental manipulations able to generate unusual experiences of owning a rubber hand or of a shift in one's first-person perspective.[104]

Future work on conscious selfhood will shed new light on how its distinct aspects are integrated into a single unified experience of being "me", perhaps through predictive mechanisms operating at multiple hierarchical levels. This research will capitalise on advances in virtual and augmented reality, which enable dramatic and highly controllable manipulations of self-experience[105] and may have particular relevance for studies of psychiatric disorders involving disturbances of conscious selfhood.[106]

Conclusions

The scientific study of consciousness has returned to the forefront of the brain and cognitive sciences. In one sense this is not surprising, since consciousness is the central feature of our mental lives, perhaps of our very existence, and is amenable to experimental manipulation of both its level and content. Yet consciousness was sidelined through much of the previous century as worries about introspection and the intrinsically subjective nature of consciousness held sway. Only time (and more research) will tell whether efforts to solve the "real problem" of explaining conscious phenomenology in terms of biophysical mechanisms will be successful. Even then, the greater metaphysical mystery of the presence of consciousness in our universe may still remain.

Nevertheless, we already understand a great deal about how conscious level, content and selfhood depend on the brain, body and world. Together, science and philosophy promise many further insights and with them the possibility to understand more – not only about ourselves but about challenging issues regarding consciousness in brain-damaged patients, in infants, in non-human animals and perhaps even in future machines. The future history of consciousness will make for fascinating reading.

Acknowledgements: I am grateful to the Dr Mortimer and Theresa Sackler Foundation, which supports the Sackler Centre for Consciousness Science. I am also grateful to the Ax:son Johnson Foundation for organising the *Return of Consciousness* meeting in Sweden in summer 2015.

1. D. Adams, *The Hitchhiker's Guide to the Galaxy*, Basingstoke, Pan Books, 1979.

2. H. Chang, *Inventing Temperature: Measurement and Scientific Progress*, New York, NY, Oxford University Press, 2004.

3. T. Nagel, 'What is it Like to be a Bat?', *Philosophical Review*, no. 83, 1974, pp. 435–50.

4. G. Tononi & C. Koch, 'The Neural Correlates of Consciousness: An Update', *Annals of the New York Academy of Sciences*, no. 1124, 2008, pp. 239–61.

5. A.K. Seth, 'Editorial', *Neuroscience of Consciousness*, no. 1, 2015, pp. 1–3.

6. M. Boly et al., 'Consciousness in Humans and Non-Human Animals: Recent Advances and Future Directions', *Frontiers in Psychology*, no. 4, 2013, p. 625, DOI: 10.3389/fpsyg.2013.00625.

7. Adapted from Boly et al.

8. D.J. Chalmers, 'The Puzzle of Conscious Experience', *Scientific American*, vol. 273, no. 6, 1995, pp. 80–6; R. Kanai & N. Tsuchiya, 'Qualia', *Current Biology*, vol. 22, no. 10, 2012, pp. R392-6, DOI: 10.1016/j.cub.2012.03.033; G. Tononi & C. Koch, 'Consciousness: Here, There and Everywhere?', *Philosophical Transactions of the Royal Society of London B: Biological Sciences*, vol. 370, no. 1668, 2015, DOI: 10. 1098/rstb.2014.0167.

9. A.K. Seth, 'Interoceptive Inference, Emotion, and the Embodied Self', *Trends in Cognitive Sciences*, vol. 17, no. 11, 2013, pp. 565–73, DOI: 10.1016/j.tics.2013.09.007.

10. O. Blanke, M. Slater & A. Serino, 'Behavioral, Neural, and Computational Principles of Bodily Self-Consciousness', *Neuron*, vol. 88, no. 1, 2015, pp. 145–66, DOI: 10.1016/j. neuron.2015.09.029.

11. Attention and consciousness, while closely related, are distinguishable – see C. Koch and N. Tsuchiya, 'Attention and Consciousness: Related yet Different', *Trends in Cognitive Sciences*, vol. 16, no. 2, 2012, pp. 103–5, DOI: 10.1016/j.tics. 2011.11.012.

12. N. Block, 'Two Neural Correlates of Consciousness', *Trends in Cognitive Sciences*, vol. 9, no. 2, 2005, pp. 46–52.

13. S. Dehaene & J.P. Changeux, 'Experimental and Theoretical Approaches to Conscious Processing', *Neuron*, vol. 70, no. 2, 2011, pp. 200–27, DOI: S0896627273-(11)00258-3 [pii] 10.1016/j.neuron.2011.03.018.

14. V.A. Lamme, 'How Neuroscience will Change our View on Consciousness', *Cognitive Neuroscience*, vol. 1, no. 3, 2010, pp. 204–40.

15. G.M. Edelman, 'Naturalizing Consciousness: A Theoretical Framework', *Proceedings of the National Academy of Sciences of the USA*, vol. 100, no. 9, 2003, pp. 5520–4.

16. S.M. Fleming, R.J. Dolan & C.D. Frith, 'Metacognition: Computation, Biology and Function', *Philosophical Transactions of the Royal Society of London B: Biological Sciences*, vol. 367, no. 1594, 2012, pp. 1280–6, DOI: 10.1098/rstb.2012.0021.

17. Chalmers, 'The Puzzle of Conscious Experience'; D.J. Chalmers, 'How Can We Construct a Science of Consciousness?', *Annals of the New York Academy of Sciences*, no. 1303, 2013, pp. 25–35, DOI: 10.1111/nyas.12166.

18. Tononi & Koch, 'Consciousness: Here, There and Everywhere?'.

19. A.K. Seth, 'The Grand Challenge of Consciousness', *Frontiers in Psychology*, vol. 1, no. 5, 2010, pp. 1–2.

20. L. Margulis & D. Sagan, *What is Life? The Eternal Enigma*, London, Weidenfield and Nicolson, 1995.

21. T. Metzinger (ed.), *Neural Correlates of Consciousness: Empirical and Conceptual Questions*, Cambridge, MA, MIT Press, 2000; Tononi & Koch, 'The Neural Correlates of Consciousness: An Update'.

22. T.A. de Graaf, & A.T. Sack, 'Using Brain Stimulation to Disentangle Neural Correlates of Conscious Vision', *Frontiers in Psychology*, no. 5, 2014, p. 1019, DOI: 10.3389/fpsyg.2014.01019 (accessed 19 January 2016); A. Pascual-Leone & V. Walsh, 'Fast Backprojections from the Motion to the Primary Visual Area Necessary for Visual Awareness', *Science*, vol. 292, no. 5516, 2001, pp. 510–12, DOI: 10.1126/science.1057099.

23. A.K. Seth, 'Explanatory Correlates of Consciousness: Theoretical and Computational Challenges', *Cognitive Computation*, vol. 1, no. 1, 2009, pp. 50–63; Tononi & Koch, 'The Neural Correlates of Consciousness: An Update'.

24. Seth, 'Editorial'; F. Varela, E. Thompson & E. Rosch, *The Embodied Mind: Cognitive Science and Human Experience*, Cambridge, MA, MIT Press, 1993.

25. I develop the real problem in more detail here: https://aeon.co/essays/the-hard-problem-of-consciousness-is-a-distraction-from-the-real-one

26. M. Merleau-Ponty, *Phenomenology of Perception*, London, Routledge & Kegan Paul, 1962.

27. E. Thompson, 'Life and Mind: From Autopoeisis to Neurophenomenology: A Tribute to Francisco Varela', *Phenomenology and the Cognitive Sciences*, no. 3, 2004, pp. 381–98.

28. S. van Gaal & V.A. Lamme, 'Unconscious High-level Information Processing: Implication for Neurobiological Theories of Consciousness', *Neuroscientist*, vol. 18, no. 3, 2012, pp. 287–301, DOI: 10.1177/1073858411404079.

29. P. Haggard, 'Human Volition: Towards a Neuroscience of Will', *Nature Reviews Neuroscience*, vol. 9, no. 12, 2008, pp. 934–46.

30. P.C. Fletcher & C.D. Frith, 'Perceiving is Believing: A Bayesian Approach to Explaining the Positive Symptoms of Schizophrenia', *Nature Reviews Neuroscience*, vol. 10, no. 1, pp. 48–58, DOI: nrn2536 [pii] 10.1038/nrn2536; A.M. Owen, N.D. Schiff and S. Laureys, 'A New Era of Coma and Consciousness Science', *Progress in Brain Research*, no. 177, 2009, pp. 399–411, DOI: 10.1016/S0079-6123(09)17728-2.

31. S. Kouider et al., 'A Neural Marker of Perceptual Consciousness in Infants', *Science*, vol. 340, no. 6130, 2013, pp. 376–80, DOI: 10.1126/science.1232509.

32. D.B. Edelman & A.K. Seth, 'Animal Consciousness: A Synthetic Approach', *Trends in Neuroscience*, vol. 32, no. 9, 2009, pp. 476–84.

33. A.K. Seth, 'The Strength of Weak Artificial Consciousness', *Journal of Machine Consciousness*, vol. 1, no. 1, 2009, pp. 71–82; Tononi & Koch, 'Consciousness: Here, There and Everywhere?'

34. From the Hippocratic text 'On the sacred disease', in a translation available at http://classics.mit.edu/Hippocrates/sacred.html (accessed 16 November 2015).

35. F. Crick, *The Astonishing Hypothesis: Scientific Search for the Soul*, New York, NY, Simon & Schuster, 1994.

36. From *De Humani Corpus Fabrica*, book VII, 1543.

37. The quotation is taken from the *Stanford Encyclopedia of Philosophy* entry on "Panpsychism" – see http://plato.stanford.edu/cgi-bin/encyclopedia/archinfo. cgi?entry=panpsychism (accessed 5 December 2015).

38. G. Leibniz, *The Monadology*, 1714, paragraph 17 (Latta translation).

39. The superb treatment in R.M. Young, *Mind, Brain, and Adaptation in the Nineteenth Century*, New York, NY, Oxford University Press, 1991, has much more on the exciting intellectual currents swirling around early psychology and neuroscience.

40. W. James, *The Principles of Psychology*, New York, NY, Henry Holt, 1890.

41. W. James, 'The Stream of Consciousness', in *Psychology*, Cleveland and New York, World, 1892.

42. James, *The Principles of Psychology*; W. James, *The Varieties of Religious Experience*, London, Longmans, Green & Co, 1902.

43. J. Weinberger, 'William James and the Unconscious: Redressing a Century-old Misunderstanding', *Psychological Science*, vol. 11, no. 6, 2000, pp. 439–45.

44. E. Husserl, *Ideas Pertaining to a Pure Phenomenology and to a Phenomenological Philosophy – First Book: General Introduction to a Pure Phenomenology*, The Hague, Springer, 1982 [1913].

45. S. Freud, *The Ego and the Id*, Vienna, Internationaler Psychoanalytischer Verlag, 1923.

46. J.B. Watson, 'Psychology as the Behaviorist Views it', *Psychological Review*, no. 20, 1913, pp. 158–77.

47. W.M. Baum, *Understanding Behaviorism: Behavior, Culture, and Evolution*, 2nd edn., Hoboken, NJ, Wiley-Blackwell, 2004.

48. J.P. Dupuy, *On the Origins of Cognitive Science: The Mechanization of Mind*, 2nd edn., Cambridge, MA, MIT Press, 2009.

49. A.K. Seth, 'The Cybernetic Bayesian Brain: From Interoceptive Inference to Sensorimotor Contingencies', in J.M. Windt & T. Metzinger (eds.), *Open MIND*, Frankfurt am Main, MIND Group, 2015, pp. 1–24.

50. G.A. Miller, *Psychology: The Science of Mental Life*, New York, NY, Harper & Row, 1962, p. 40.

51. U. Neisser, *Cognition and Reality: Principles and Implications of Cognitive Psychology*, New York, NY, Freeman, 1976.

52. G.A. Miller, 'Computation, Consciousness, and Cognition', *Behavioral and Brain Sciences*, vol. 3, no. 1, 1980, p. 146.

53. S. Sutherland, *International Dictionary of Psychology*, New York, NY, Crossroad Classic, 1989.

54. M. Boden, *Mind as Machine: A History of Cognitive Science*, Oxford, Oxford University Press, 2008.

55. A.L. Loomis, E.N. Harvey & G. Hobart, 'Potential Rhythms of the Cerebral Cortex during Sleep', *Science*, vol. 81, no. 2111, 1935, pp. 597–98, DOI: 10.1126/science.-81.2111.597.

56. W.B. Scoville & B. Milner, 'Loss of Recent Memory after Bilateral Hippocampal Lesions. 1957', *Journal of Neuropsychiatry & Clinical Neurosciences*, vol. 12, no. 1, 2000, pp. 103–13.

57. M.S. Gazzaniga, J.E. Bogen & R.W. Sperry, 'Some Functional Effects of Sectioning the Cerebral Commissures in Man', *Proceedings of the National Academy of Sciences of the USA*, no. 48, 1962, pp. 1765–69.

58. J. Eccles & W. Feindel, 'Wilder Graves Penfield, 26 January 1891–5 April 1976', *Biographical Memoirs of Fellows of the Royal Society*, no. 24, 1978, pp. 472–513.

59. de Graaf & Sack, 'Using Brain Stimulation to Disentangle Neural Correlates of Conscious Vision'.

60. F. Crick & C. Koch, 'Towards a Neurobiological Theory of Consciousness', *Seminars in the Neurosciences*, no. 2, 1990, pp. 263–75.

61. G.M. Edelman, *Neural Darwinism: The Theory of Neuronal Group Selection*, New York, NY, Basic Books, 1987; G.M. Edelman, *The Remembered Present*, New York, NY, Basic Books, 1989.

62. Edelman, *The Remembered Present* and 'Naturalizing Consciousness: A Theoretical Framework'; A.K. Seth, 'Darwin's Neuroscientist: Gerald M. Edelman, 1929–2014', *Frontiers in Psychology*, vol. 5, 2014, p. 896, DOI: 10.3389/fpsyg.2014.00896.

63. D. Dennett, *Consciousness Explained*, Boston, MA, Little, Brown and Co, 1991.

64. Nagel, 'What is it Like to be a Bat?'

65. F. Jackson, 'Epiphenomenal Qualia', *Philosophical Quarterly*, no. 32, 1982, pp. 127–36.

66. J. Searle, 'Minds, Brains, and Programs', *Behavioral and Brain Sciences*, vol. 3, no. 3, 1980, pp. 417–57.

67. P.S. Churchland, *Neurophilosophy: Toward a Unified Science of the Mind-brain*, Cambridge, MA, MIT Press, 1986.

68. N. Block, 'On a Confusion about a Function of Consciousness', *Behavioral and Brain Sciences*, vol. 18, no. 2, 1995, pp. 227–47 – and see above.

69. V.A. Lamme, 'How Neuroscience will Change our View on Consciousness', *Cognitive Neuroscience*, vol. 1, no. 3, 2010, pp. 204–40.

70. D.M. Rosenthal, *Consciousness and Mind*, Oxford, Clarendon Press, 2005.

71. S.M. Fleming, R.J. Dolan & C.D. Frith, 'Metacognition: Computation, Biology and Function', *Philosophical Transactions of the Royal Society of London B: Biological Sciences*, vol. 367, no. 1594, 2012, pp. 1280–86, DOI: 10.1098/rstb.2012.0021.

72. B.J. Baars, *A Cognitive Theory of Consciousness*, New York, NY, Cambridge University Press, 1988.

73. B.J. Baars, 'The Conscious Access Hypothesis: Origins and Recent Evidence', *Trends in Cognitive Sciences*, vol. 6, no. 1, 2002, pp. 47–52.

74. S. Dehaene & L. Naccache, 'Towards a Cognitive Neuroscience of Consciousness: Basic Evidence and a Workspace Framework', *Cognition*, vol. 79, nos. 1–2, 2001, pp. 1–37.

75. Dehaene & Changeux, 'Experimental and Theoretical Approaches to Conscious Processing'.

76. S. Frassle et al., 'Binocular Rivalry: Frontal Activity Relates to Introspection and Action but not to Perception', *Journal of Neuroscience*, vol. 34, no. 5, 2014, pp. 1738–47, DOI: 10.1523/JNEUROSCI.4403-13.2014; N. Tsuchiya et al., 'No-Report Paradigms: Extracting the True Neural Correlates of Consciousness', *Trends in Cognitive Sciences*, vol. 19, no. 12, 2015, pp. 757–70, DOI: 10.1016/j.tics.2015.10.002.

77. Crick & Koch, 'Towards a Neurobiological Theory of Consciousness'.

78. Baars, 'The Conscious Access Hypothesis: Origins and Recent Evidence'; H.C. Lau & R.E. Passingham, 'Relative Blindsight in Normal Observers and the Neural Correlate of Visual Consciousness', *Proceedings of the National Academy of Sciences of the USA*, vol. 103, no. 49, 2006, pp. 18763–68.

79. R. Blake, J. Brascamp & D.J. Heeger, 'Can Binocular Rivalry Reveal Neural Correlates of Consciousness?', *Philosophical Transactions of the Royal Society of London B: Biological Sciences*, vol. 369, no. 1641, 2014, 20130211, DOI: 10.1098/rstb.2013.0211 (accessed 19 January 2016); D.A. Leopold & N.K. Logothetis, 'Activity Changes in Early Visual Cortex Reflect Monkeys' Percepts during Binocular Rivalry', *Nature*, vol. 379, no. 6565, 1966, pp. 549–53. This story continues with recent studies, mentioned above, showing that frontal activity sometimes associated with perceptual switches in bistable situations may be due to report rather than to the switch itself (Frassle et al., 'Binocular Rivalry: Frontal Activity Relates to Introspection and Action but not to Perception'). Even more interesting, bistable perceptual switches that are not noticed are not associated with parietal activity (J. Brascamp, R. Blake & T. Knapen, 'Negligible Fronto-parietal BOLD activity Accompanying Unreportable Switches in Bistable Perception', *Nature Neuroscience*, no. 18, 2015, pp. 1672–78, DOI: 10.1038/nn.4130).

80. F. Crick & C. Koch, 'A Framework for Consciousness', *Nature Neuroscience*, vol. 6, no. 2, 2003, pp. 119–26.

81. G. Tononi, 'Consciousness as Integrated Information: A Provisional Manifesto', *Biological Bulletin*, vol. 215, no. 3, 2008, pp. 216–42.

82. See Dehaene & Changeux, 'Experimental and Theoretical Approaches to Conscious Processing', and Tononi & Koch, 'The Neural Correlates of Consciousness: An Update', for reviews.

83. Tononi & Koch, 'The Neural Correlates of Consciousness: An Update'; Edelman, 'Naturalizing Consciousness: A Theoretical Framework'.

84. J. Aru et al., 'Distilling the Neural Correlates of Consciousness', *Neuroscience & Biobehavioral Reviews*, vol. 36, no. 2, 2012, pp. 737–46, DOI: 10.1016/j.neubiorev. 2011.12.003; T.A. de Graaf, P.J. Hsieh & A.T. Sack, 'The "Correlates" in Neural Correlates of Consciousness', *Neuroscience & Biobehavioral Reviews*, vol. 36, no. 1, 2012, pp. 191–97, DOI: 10.1016/j.neubiorev.2011.05.012.

85. See Boly et al., 'Consciousness in Humans and Non-human Animals: Recent Advances and Future Directions', for a reasonably up-to-date survey.

86. G. Tononi & G.M. Edelman, 'Consciousness and Complexity', *Science*, vol. 282, no. 5395, 1998, pp. 1846–51.

87. A.K. Seth, A.B. Barrett & L. Barnett, 'Causal Density and Integrated Information as Measures of Conscious Level', *Philosophical Transactions of the Royal Society A: Mathematical, Physical, and Engineering Sciences*, vol. 369, no. 1952, 2011, pp. 3748–67, DOI: 10.1098/rsta.2011.0079.

88. A.G. Casali et al., 'A Theoretically Based Index of Consciousness Independent of Sensory Processing and Behavior', *Science Translational Medicine*, vol. 5, no. 198, 2013, pp. 198ra105, DOI: 10.1126/scitranslmed.3006294 (accessed 19 January 2016); S. Chennu et al., 'Spectral Signatures of Reorganised Brain Networks in Disorders of Consciousness', *PLOS Computational Biology*, vol. 10, no. 10, 2014, e1003887, DOI: 10.1371/journal.pcbi.1003887 (accessed 19 January 2016); M. Schartner et al., 'Complexity of Multi-Dimensional Spontaneous EEG Decreases during Propofol Induced General Anaesthesia', *PLOS One*, vol. 10, no. 8, 2015, e0133532, DOI: 10.1371/journal.pone.0133532 (accessed 31 January 2016); J.D. Sitt et al., 'Large Scale Screening of Neural Signatures of Consciousness in Patients in a Vegetative or Minimally Conscious State', *Brain*, vol. 137, pt. 8, 2014, pp. 2258– 70, DOI: 10.1093/brain/awu141.

89. Dehaene & Changeux, 'Experimental and Theoretical Approaches to Conscious Processing'; Tsuchiya et al., 'No-Report Paradigms: Extracting the True Neural Correlates of Consciousness'.

90. Lamme, 'How Neuroscience will Change our View on Consciousness'; Pascual-Leone & Walsh, 'Fast Backprojections from the Motion to the Primary Visual Area Necessary for Visual Awareness'; H. Super, H. Spekreijse & V.A. Lamme, 'Two Distinct Modes of Sensory Processing Observed in Monkey Primary Visual Cortex (V1)', *Nature Neuroscience*, vol. 4, no. 3, 2001, pp. 304–10, DOI: 10.1038/85170.

91. A. Clark, *Surfing Uncertainty*, Oxford, Oxford University Press, 2016; K.J. Friston, 'The Free-energy Principle: A Unified Brain Theory?', *Nature Reviews Neuroscience*, vol. 11, no. 2, 2010, pp. 127–38, DOI: nrn2787 [pii] 10.1038/nrn2787; J. Hohwy, *The Predictive Mind*, Oxford, Oxford University Press, 2013.

92. L. Melloni et al., 'Expectations Change the Signatures and Timing of Electrophysiological Correlates of Perceptual Awareness', *Journal of Neuroscience*, vol. 31, no. 4, 2011, pp. 1386–96, DOI: 31/4/1386 [pii] 10.1523/JNEUROSCI.4570-10.2011; Y. Pinto et al., 'Expectations Accelerate Entry of Visual Stimuli into Awareness', *Journal of Vision*, vol. 15, no. 8, 2015, p. 13, DOI: 10.1167/15.8.13.

93. A.M. Bastos et al., 'Visual Areas Exert Feedforward and Feedback Influences Through Distinct Frequency Channels', *Neuron*, vol. 85, no. 2, 2015, pp. 390–401, DOI: 10.1016/j.neuron.2014.12.018; T. van Kerkoerle et al., 'Alpha and Gamma Oscillations Characterize Feedback and Feedforward Processing in Monkey Visual Cortex', *Proceedings of the National Academy of Sciences of the USA*, vol. 111, no. 40, 2014, pp. 14332–41, DOI: 10.1073/pnas.1402773111.

94. K.J. Friston, J. Kilner & L. Harrison, 'A Free Energy Principle for the Brain', *Journal of Physiology – Paris*, vol. 100, nos. 1–3, 2006, pp. 70–87, DOI: S0928-4257(06)00060-X [pii] 10.1016/j.jphysparis.2006.10.001.

95. J.S. Bowers & C.J. Davis, 'Bayesian Just-so Stories in Psychology and Neuroscience', *Psychological Bulletin*, vol. 138, no. 3, 2012, pp. 389–414, DOI: 10.1037/a0026450.

96. A.K. Seth, 'A Predictive Processing Theory of Sensorimotor Contingencies: Explaining the Puzzle of Perceptual Presence and its Absence in Synesthesia', *Cognitive Neuroscience*, vol. 5, no. 2, 2014, pp. 97–118, DOI: 10.1080/17588928.2013.877880; C. Summerfield & F.P. de Lange, 'Expectation in Perceptual Decision Making: Neural and Computational Mechanisms', *Nature Reviews Neuroscience*, vol. 15, no. 11, 2014, pp. 745–56, DOI: 10.1038/nrn3838.

97. S.M. Khaligh-Razavi et al., 'The Effects of Recurrent Dynamics on Ventralstream Representational Geometry', *Journal of Vision*, vol. 15, no. 12, 2015, p. 1089, DOI: 10.1167/15.12.1089 (accessed 19 January 2016); V. Mnih et al., 'Human-Level Control through Deep Reinforcement Learning', *Nature*, vol. 518, no. 7540, 2015, pp. 529–33, DOI: 10.1038/nature14236.

98. L. Muckli et al., 'Contextual Feedback to Superficial Layers of V1', *Current Biology*, vol. 25, no. 20, 2015, pp. 2690–95, DOI: 10.1016/j.cub.2015.08.057; M. Salti et al., 'Distinct Cortical Codes and Temporal Dynamics for Conscious and Unconscious Percepts', *eLife*, 2015, DOI: 10.7554/eLife.05652.

99. L.F. Barrett & W.K. Simmons, 'Interoceptive Predictions in the Brain', *Nature Reviews Neuroscience*, vol. 16, no. 7, 2015, pp. 419–29, DOI: 10.1038/nrn3950; Seth, 'Interoceptive Inference, Emotion, and the Embodied Self'.

100. S. Schachter & J.E. Singer, 'Cognitive, Social, and Physiological determinants of Emotional State', *Psychological Review*, no. 69, 1962, pp. 379–99.

101. Seth, 'The Cybernetic Bayesian Brain: From Interoceptive Inference to Sensorimotor Contingencies'.

102. S.N. Garfinkel et al., 'Fear from the Heart: Sensitivity to Fear Stimuli Depends on Individual Heartbeats', *Journal of Neuroscience*, vol. 34, no. 19, 2014, pp. 6573–82, DOI: 10.1523/JNEUROSCI.3507-13.2014.

103. M.A. Apps & M. Tsakiris, 'The Free-energy Self: A Predictive Coding Account of Self-Recognition', *Neuroscience & Biobehavioral Reviews*, vol. 41C, 2014, pp. 85–97, DOI: 10.1016/j.neubiorev.2013.01.029; Blanke, Slater & Serino, 'Behavioral, Neural, and Computational Principles of Bodily Self-Consciousness'; Seth, 'Interoceptive Inference, Emotion, and the Embodied Self'.

104. O. Blanke & T. Metzinger, 'Full-body Illusions and Minimal Phenomenal Selfhood', *Trends in Cognitive Sciences*, vol. 13, no. 1, 2009, pp. 7–13, DOI: 10.1016/j.tics.2008.10.003; B. Lenggenhager et al., 'Video Ergo Sum: Manipulating Bodily Self-consciousness', *Science*, vol. 317, no. 5841, 2007, pp. 1096–9.

105. L. Bergouignan, L. Nyberg & H.H. Ehrsson, 'Out-of-Body-Induced Hippocampal Amnesia', *Proceedings of the National Academy of Sciences of the USA*, vol. 111, no. 12, 2014, pp. 4421–26, DOI: 10.1073/pnas.1318801111; M. Slater et al., 'First Person Experience of Body Transfer in Virtual Reality', *PLOS One*, vol. 5, no. 5, 2010, e10564, DOI: 10.1371/journtal.pone.0010564.

106. M. Sierra & A.S. David, 'Depersonalization: A Selective Impairment of Self-awareness', *Consciousness and Cognition*, vol. 20, no. 1, 2011, pp. 99–108, DOI: 10.1016/j.concog.2010.10.018.

WHAT IS
CONSCIOUSNESS?

CONSCIOUSNESS
AND THE PHYSICAL SCIENCES[1]

Thomas Nagel

The modern mind–body problem arose out of the scientific revolution of the 17th century, as a direct result of the concept of objective physical reality which drove that revolution. Galileo and Descartes made the crucial conceptual distinction. They proposed that physical science should provide a mathematically precise, quantitative description of an external reality extended in space and time, a description limited to primary spatio-temporal qualities such as shape, size and motion, and to laws governing the relationships among them. Subjective appearances, on the other hand – how this physical world appeared to human perception – were assigned to the mind, and secondary qualities like colour, sound and smell were to be analysed relationally, in terms of the power of physical things acting on the senses, to produce those appearances in the minds of observers.

It was essential to leave out or subtract subjective appearances and the human mind, as well as human intentions and purposes, from the physical world in order to permit this powerful, but austere, spatio-temporal conception of objective physical reality to develop. We are all now taught this conception in school: of a universe of fields and particles, governed by simple mathematical laws, very different from the world as it appears from our special perceptual perspective. This is the world as it is in itself, independent of the subjective point of view of human or other conscious observers.

The exclusion of everything mental from the scope of modern physical science was bound, however, to be challenged eventually. We humans are part of the world, and the desire for a unified world picture is irrepressible. It seems natural to pursue that unity by extending the reach of physics and chemistry, in light of their great successes in explaining so much of the natural order. These successes have so far taken the form of reduction followed by reconstruction, discovering the basic elements of which everything is composed and showing how they combine to yield the complexity we observe.

It has become clear that our bodies and central nervous systems are part of the physical world, composed of the same elements as everything else and completely describable in terms of the modern versions of the primary qualities, more sophisticated but still mathematically and spatio-temporally defined. Molecular biology keeps increasing our knowledge of our own physical composition, operation and development. Finally, so far as we can tell, our mental lives and those of other creatures, including our subjective experiences, are strongly connected with, and probably strictly dependent on, physical events in our brains and physical interactions of our bodies with the rest of the physical world.

Perhaps it is these developments in neurophysiology and molecular biology that have encouraged the hope of overcoming the mental–physical division present at the start of the scientific revolution, by including the mind somehow in a single physical conception of the world. Descartes thought it could not be done: that mind and matter are both fully real and irreducibly distinct, though they interact. In the dualist view, physical science is defined by the exclusion of the mental from its subject matter. But there has always been resistance to dualism, and in later 20th-century analytic philosophy it motivated the search for a unified, materialist conception of reality.

The aim was to follow a general strategy that has been very successful in other domains: the strategy of reductionism. A reductionist account explains one kind of thing, existence or truth, entirely in terms of another kind, which is more basic, so that one can say the first is really "nothing but" the second, and the reality of the first consists simply in the reality of the second. In this way, chemistry is reducible to particle physics, and biology, through molecular biology and evolutionary theory, is thought to be reducible to chemistry. The question then is whether psychology, including consciousness, is reducible to biology, and therefore indirectly to physics. This would mean that physics could be regarded as the theory of everything, because it describes the ultimate elements which, suitably combined, constitute everything else.

Materialism is the view that only the physical world is irreducibly real, and that a place must be found in it for mind, if there is such a thing. This would continue the onward march of physical science, through molecular biology, to full closure, swallowing up the mind in the objective physical reality from which it was initially excluded. The assumption is that physics is philosophically unproblematic and the main target of opposition is

Descartes' dualist picture of the ghost in the machine. The task is to come up with an alternative, and here begins a series of failures.

The attempts to account for the mental in a way that is consistent with materialism fall into two broad categories: behaviourist accounts and brain-process accounts. Clearly, if mental phenomena could be fully accounted for in terms of either physical behaviour of the organism or neurophysiological processes in the brain, they would not present a challenge to materialism.

The behaviourist strategy was tried in several versions. Mental phenomena were identified variously with behaviour, behavioural dispositions or forms of behavioural organisation. In another version, associated with Ryle and inspired by Wittgenstein, mental phenomena were not identified with anything, either physical or non-physical; the names of mental states and processes were said not to be referring expressions. Instead, mental concepts were explained in terms of their observable, behavioural conditions of application – behavioural criteria or conditions for ascribing mental states rather than behavioural truth conditions.[2]

All these strategies are essentially verificationist: they assume that all that needs to be said about the nature of a mental phenomenon is what would verify or confirm its presence in an organism from the point of view of an outside observer. In one way or another, they reduce mental attributions to the externally observable conditions on the basis of which we attribute mental states to others. If successful, this would obviously place the mind comfortably in the physical world.

It is certainly true that mental phenomena have behavioural manifestations, which supply our main evidence for them in other creatures. Yet, all these theories seem insufficient as analyses of the mental, because they leave out something essential which lies beyond the externally observable grounds for attributing mental states to others, namely the aspect of mental phenomena that is evident from the first-person, inner point of view of the conscious subject: the way sugar tastes or red looks or anger feels, each of which seems to be something more than the behavioural responses and discriminatory capacities these experiences explain. Behaviourism leaves out the inner mental state itself.

In the 1950s, an alternative route to materialism was proposed, one that in a sense acknowledged that the mental is something inside us, of which outwardly observable behaviour is merely a manifestation. This was the psycho-physical identity theory, offered by Place and Smart, not as conceptual analysis but as a scientific hypothesis.[3] It held that mental events are identical to physical events in the brain: $\Psi = \Phi$, where Ψ is a mental event, such as pain or a taste sensation, and Φ is the corresponding physical event in the central nervous system. Since this is not a conceptual truth, it cannot be known a priori: it is supposed to be a theoretical scientific identity, like "water $= H_2O$", and can be confirmed only by the future development of neuroscience.

The trouble is that this identity claim raises a further question: what is it about the brain state Φ that makes it also a mental state Ψ? It must be some property conceptually distinct from the physical properties that define Φ, otherwise the identity claim would be a trivial tautology. That the brain state is also a mental state is a further fact. What kind of fact is it? Clearly materialists would not want to give a dualist answer: that Φ is Ψ because it has a non-physical property in addition to its physiological ones (eg, a non-physical experiential quality). But they have to give some answer, and it has to be an answer consistent with materialism. So defenders of the identity theory tended to be pulled back into different kinds of behaviourism, in order to analyse the mental character of brain processes in a way that avoided dualism. What makes the brain process a mental process, they proposed, is not an additional intrinsic property but a relational one: a relation to physical behaviour and circumstances. So what it is for a brain state to be a pain, for example, would be that it is typically caused by injury and typically causes yelps and avoidance.

These strategies have taken increasingly sophisticated form, under the heading of causal behaviourism, functionalism and other theories of how mental concepts could refer to states of the brain, by virtue of the causal role of those states in controlling the interaction between the organism and its environment. But all such strategies are unsatisfactory for the same old reason: even with the brain added to the picture, they clearly leave out something essential, without which there would be no mind. And what they leave out is just what was deliberately left out of the physical world by Descartes and Galileo to form the modern concept of the physical, namely subjective appearances.

I have given only a brief sketch of the territory. A voluminous and intricate literature has grown up around these problems, but it serves mainly to confirm how intractable they are. The multiple dead-ends in the forward march of materialism suggest that the Ψ/Φ dualism, introduced at the birth of modern science, may be harder to get out of than many have imagined. It has even led some philosophers to *eliminative materialism*, suggesting that mental events, like ghosts and Santa Claus, do not exist at all.[4] But if we do not regard that as an option and still want to pursue a unified world picture, I believe we will have to leave materialism behind. Conscious subjects and their mental lives are inescapable components of reality not describable by the physical sciences.

On the other hand, I believe it makes sense to pursue a unified conception of this more complex reality on a new, non-materialist basis. I suspect that the appearance of contingency in the relation between mind and brain is probably an illusion, and that it is in fact a necessary but non-conceptual connection, concealed from us by the inadequacy of our present concepts.[5] Major scientific advances often require the creation of new concepts, postulating unobservable elements of reality that are needed to explain how natural regularities, which initially appear accidental, are in fact necessary. The evidence for the existence of such things is precisely that, if they existed, they would explain what is otherwise incomprehensible.

Certainly the mind–body problem is difficult enough for us to be suspicious of attempts to solve it with concepts and methods developed to account for very different kinds of things. Instead, we should expect theoretical progress in this area to require a major conceptual revolution at least as radical as relativity theory, the introduction of electromagnetic fields into physics or, indeed, the original scientific revolution itself – which, because of its built-in restrictions, cannot result in a "theory of everything", but must be seen as a stage on the route to a more general form of understanding. We ourselves are large-scale, complex instances of something both objectively physical from outside and subjectively mental from inside. Perhaps the basis for this identity pervades the world.

1. This essay is a shorter version of the discussion of consciousness in chap. 3 of my book *Mind and Cosmos*, New York, NY, Oxford University Press, 2012.

2. G. Ryle, *The Concept of Mind*, London, Hutchinson, 1949; L. Wittgenstein, *Philosophical Investigations*, London, Macmillan, 1953.

3. U.T. Place, 'Is Consciousness a Brain Process?', *British Journal of Psychology*, vol. 47, no. 1, 1956, pp. 44–50; J.J.C. Smart, 'Sensations and Brain Processes', *Philosophical Review*, vol. 68, no. 2, 1959, pp. 141–56.

4. See P. Feyerabend, 'Mental Events and the Brain', *Journal of Philosophy*, vol. 60, no. 11, 1963, pp. 295–96.

5. I say more about this in 'The Psychophysical Nexus', in *Concealment and Exposure*, New York, NY, Oxford University Press, 2002.

CONSCIOUSNESS FROM THE PERSPECTIVE OF NEUROPHILOSOPHY[1]

Patricia Smith Churchland

Neurophilosophy explores the impact of discoveries in neuroscience on a range of traditional philosophical questions about the nature of the mind. This subfield aims to move forward on questions such as the nature of knowledge and learning, decision-making and choice, as well as self-control and habits, by drawing on data from the relevant sciences – not only neuroscience and clinical neurology, but also evolutionary biology, experimental psychology, behavioural economics, anthropology and genetics. It also draws on lessons from the history of philosophy and of science, which saw mysteries about the nature of blood or fire or infectious disease become less mysterious, as experimental science began to provide new observations and tested explanations.[2]

The massive accumulation of neurobiological data from many levels of brain organisation and many species of nervous system is a recent development, since neuroscience did not really reach full steam until about the 1970s. Why was its development delayed until recently?

Although clinical observations had long implicated the brain in mental functions, understanding exactly *why* lesions affected mental functions remained out of reach. This was essentially because, until very recently, nothing was known about the microstructure of brains – about neurons and how neurons worked, about how the brain was organised into networks and systems, and how neurochemicals mediated interactions between neurons. Detailed drawings of nerve cells were produced, by Camillo Golgi and Ramon y Cajal, only in the latter part of the 19th century. How neurons *interacted* with each other to yield effects such as a behaviour was still a profound mystery.

Chemistry, by contrast, was a vastly more mature science in the early 19th century, strengthened by basic organising principles of atomic theory, as outlined by Dalton (1805), and a clear appreciation of the fundamental elements – no longer deemed to be earth, air, fire and water. The elements were characterised by Mendeleev in the 1880s in the periodic table: things such as oxygen, hydrogen, tin and gold. As for neuroscience, it is perhaps surprising to realise that the existence of *inhibitory* connections between nerve cells was demonstrated by John Eccles and colleagues only in the 1950s. Physics, far more mature in terms of theory and explanation, had by that time begun to investigate the inner structure of the atom.

Effective brain-imaging techniques came into their own only in the last two decades of the 20th century. At the microlevel, even now, many details regarding the synapses and how neurons communicate are not completely understood; nor are the functions and dynamics of neural networks. Neuroscience is a young science.

Understanding how neurons work requires knowledge of electricity, stemming from Michael Faraday's discoveries in the first half of the 19th century. Because the brain's basic units work by changes in voltage across the cell membrane and via chemicals that regulate such changes, and because the units are not visible to the naked eye, progress has depended on the prior developments, theoretically and experimentally rich, in physics and chemistry. Specifically, neuroscience depends on derived tools and devices, such as the electron microscope, microelectrodes, nuclear magnetic resonance, monoclonal antibodies and, most recently, optogenetics.

Some philosophers take it as obvious that the enduring existence of many puzzles in neuroscience entails that neuroscience can never, ever, discover much in the way of mechanisms of cognitive function. They have failed to appreciate the clear historical point that the sciences of the nervous system are very young indeed.

The relation between mind and brain
The words "mind" and "brain" are distinct, yet that leaves open whether mental processes are in fact processes of the physical brain: "water" and "H2O" are different terms, but it turns out that they do name the very same stuff. A favoured theory in philosophical thought, championed by Plato, developed by Descartes and even now defended by Thomas Nagel,[3] holds that, just as the words are distinct, so too are the processes. This approach is known as dualism: a "two stuffs" theory, embracing physical stuff and the utterly different, soul stuff. Thinking, seeing and choosing, according to dualism, are processes of the non-physical mind or soul. For dualists, the mind–body problem is the problem of how a physical state of the brain can interact with a totally non-physical state of the soul.

By contrast, according to an equally venerable if less popular tradition, there is only the brain: mental processes are processes of the physical brain, whose exact nature remains to be discovered. This is known as "physicalism", and found adherents in Hippocrates (460–370 BC), Hobbes (1588–1679), Hume (1711–76) and Helmholtz (1821–94). Physicalists realise there is no problem about how the mind and body *interact*, inasmuch as there are not two things but only one: the brain. The mind is what the brain does. For them, the important problem concerns how the brain learns and remembers, how it enables us to see and hear and think, how it enables us to move our eyes, legs and whole body. Their problem concerns the nature of the brain mechanisms that support mental phenomena.

Interestingly, dualists also have a closely related set of problems: how does soul stuff work such that we learn and remember, see and hear and think and so forth? But whereas in neuroscience physicalists have a vibrant research programme to address their questions, dualists have no comparable programme. No one has the slightest idea how soul stuff does anything.

Neurophilosophy as a research programme has poor prospects unless mental processes such as remembering and attending are processes of the brain. Otherwise, we should just study the stuff that *does* perform attending and remembering and find out how *that* works, stuff such as the "soul stuff" postulated by Descartes. At this stage in the sciences, the evidence overwhelmingly indicates that all mental events and processes, including visual or auditory perception, learning, memory, language use and decision-making, are in fact events and processes of the physical brain. It is not that there is one single experiment that decisively shows this. Rather, the evidence has steadily accumulated over countless observations and experiments, and no counter-evidence raises doubts.[4] Even though we may not understand in detail the mechanisms whereby we recall an event that occurred in childhood, we are reasonably sure that such a recollection is a brain process. This is not unlike Faraday's realisation that electricity was not an occult phenomenon but a natural, physical one, even if he did not understand in precise detail the nature of electromagnetism.

One of the most dramatic observations of mind–brain dependency came from the split-brain studies published in the late 1960s. These involved patients whose cerebral hemispheres were surgically separated to treat drug-resistant epilepsy. The nerve sheet connecting the two hemispheres, the corpus callosum, was cut, thereby disconnecting the cortex of the right and left hemispheres. The aim was to aid the patient by preventing a seizure from travelling from its origin in one hemisphere into the other. Astonishingly, tests of split-brain subjects showed that the mental life of the two hemispheres was also disconnected: the right might have knowledge the left did not, for example, or see something or decide something that the left did not.[5] The implications for the mind–body problem were obvious: if mental states were *not* brain states, why would cutting the corpus callosum allow knowledge and experience to be confined to activity in one hemisphere? Although a defiant dualist might invent some story to accommodate the facts (and a diehard few did), the best and most reasonable explanation for the disconnection effect was simply that a physical pathway essential for mental unity had been interrupted, and that soul stuff was just not in the game. As one of the leading split-brain researchers, Michael Gazzaniga, put it, consciousness can be split.[6]

The many observations by clinical neurologists of patients who suffered focal brain damage also weighed in. This can result in highly specific losses of cognitive function, such as the capacity to recognise familiar faces, recognise a limb as one's own or perform an action on command, such as saluting or waving. Hanna and Antonio Damasio launched a huge project at the University of Iowa Medical College to document as many cases as possible of similarly located lesions, to test whether there were similar functional effects. This important project elevated brain lesion studies beyond the single case to a more systematic understanding of the outcome of focal brain lesions and their effect on capacities.[7]

Studies of a few patients who had suffered bilateral damage to the hippocampus (a small curved structure beneath the cerebral cortex) showed them to be severely impaired in learning new things (anterograde amnesia). This finding initiated a massive research programme to understand the relationship between learning/memory and the hippocampal structures.[8] Memory losses associated with dementing diseases also linked memory with neural loss, consolidating the tight link between the mental and the neural. Important also are studies of attention using brain imaging, along with single-neuron physiology. These varied studies suggest that at least three anatomical networks, connected but somewhat independent, are involved in different aspects of attention: alerting, orientating and executive control. Moreover, each of these functions has been the target of detailed further study, indicating, for example, strong

associations with awareness, especially vis-à-vis detection of a target
(consequent upon orientating).[9]

Developments in psychology, especially visual psychology, also implicated neural networks in mental functions and this dovetailed with neuroscientific findings on the visual system. Explanations of colour vision, for example, depended on the retina's three cone types and on "opponent processing" by neurons (distinguishing red–green and blue–yellow differences) in cortical areas. It was well appreciated that much in the world, such as ultraviolet and radio waves, could not be detected by our visual system because of its physical organisation.[10] Perception of visual motion was linked to the behaviour of single neurons in a visually sensitive area of cortex known as the middle temporal. Visual hallucinations were known to be caused by physical substances such as LSD or ketamine, and consciousness could be obliterated by drugs such as ether, as well as by other substances employed by anaesthesiologists, for example propofol. No evidence linked these drugs to soul stuff; on the contrary, many anaesthetics appear to work by altering the normal balance of excitation and inhibition of neurons in circuits.

Short-term memory can be transiently blocked by a blow to the head or by a drug such as scopolamine; emotions and moods can be affected by Prozac and by alcohol; decision-making can be affected by hunger, fear, sleeplessness and cocaine; elevated levels of cortisol cause anxiety. Very specific changes in whole-brain activity, corresponding to periods of sleep versus dreaming versus being awake, have been documented, and explanations for the neuronal signature typifying these three states have made considerable progress.[11] In aggregate, these findings weighed in favour of the hypothesis that mental functions are a subset of functions of the physical brain.

Evolutionary biology encouraged us to dwell on the fact that nervous systems are the product of evolution, the human nervous system being no exception. Comparisons of anatomy between human and non-human nervous systems have revealed high conservation of the functional organisation, at both macro and micro levels, over hundreds of millions of years.[12] Although human brains are larger than those of other land mammals, we share all the same structures, pathways, innervation patterns, neuronal types and neurochemicals. Neurons in a fruit fly work in essentially the same way as neurons in a human brain. Molecular biology revealed that the genetic differences between humans and our nearest relatives, chimpanzees (*Pan troglodyte*) and bonobos (*Pan paniscus*), are very small.[13]

These evolutionary relationships imply that either no mammals have non-physical souls or all do. Now questions flood in: if humans *alone* have a soul, where do human souls come from, and why does the soul suddenly appear, some four million years after the Homo genus branched off from our common ancestor with chimpanzees? Did extinct Homo species, such as erectus and neanderthalensis, have souls too? Based on cranial measurements, anthropologists believe that the brains of Homo neanderthalensis were typically larger than ours. Neanderthals probably had some form of acoustic communication, even though they may not have been able to achieve all the vocalisations of which humans are capable.[14] Moreover, genetic data reveal that they did interbreed with Homo sapiens.[15] What about *their* souls? For that matter, how can ravens and rats and monkeys solve complex problems, how can they sleep, dream, pay attention and so forth, if a soul is needed for such functions?

By the 1980s, there was impressive, if cautious, agreement among scientists, as well as philosophers, that a non-physical soul that feels, decides, sees and reasons was improbable. Where disagreement flourished unabated, however, was whether neuroscience could *explain* those functions, physical though they may be. Neuroscientists tended to expect that, with new techniques and more experiments, progress would continue to be made. How far we would get, time and research effort would tell.

Some philosophers, by contrast, confidently predicted that neuroscience would never explain cognitive functions. This view, particularly associated with Jerry Fodor and his colleagues[16] but widely espoused within the subdiscipline of philosophy of mind, tended to be known as the autonomy of psychology – autonomous with respect to other sciences, especially neuroscience. This claim about the limits of neuroscience was however just a *prediction*, supported by philosophical speculation but not scientific evidence. Although highly popular until about 1990, the idea has been slowly but systematically undercut by progress in the neurosciences, especially by increasingly suggestive links between data at the behavioural, whole brain and neural levels. Embarrassingly for the philosophical prediction, convergent studies on functions such as decision-making,[17] attention[18] and spatial representation,[19] for example, have revealed much more about mechanisms than some sceptical philosophers thought remotely conceivable.[20]

The point where influential philosophers are still confident that the mysteries permanently have the upper hand concerns conscious experience. Typically, there are two distinct arguments to support this conviction.

The first makes a straightforward prediction about where science will go. It is based on current intuitions about the tractability of the problem of explaining consciousness in neurobiological terms. With great confidence, it will be claimed that consciousness is so completely and utterly and thoroughly mysterious that it will never be explained at all.[21] By way of illustration, it may be suggested that expecting any science to explain how conscious experience emerges from the activity of neurons is like expecting a rat to understand differential equations. Despite its chest-pounding confidence, this prediction should be taken with ample doses of caution, since predicting where science will go and what will be discovered is really a rather risky business.

The second, and more influential, argument rests on the dualist's belief that although non-conscious events such as memory consolidation or pre-processing in vision are brain events, *conscious* events are not and so neuroscience cannot explain them. Some philosophers, such as David Chalmers[22] and Thomas Nagel,[23] consider conscious events, such as being aware of a pain in a tooth or deciding to kick off one's shoes, to be extra-physical, running parallel to physical events.

However large and systematic the mass of evidence supporting the *empirical* hypothesis that consciousness is a brain function, it remains *logically* consistent to be stubborn and insist otherwise, as do Chalmers and Nagel. Identities, such as that temperature really *is* mean molecular kinetic energy, are not directly observable. They are underwritten by inferences that best account for the mass of data and the absence of an effective explanatory competitor. One could, if determined, dig in one's heels and say, "temperature is *not* mean molecular KE, but rather an occult phenomenon that merely runs parallel to KE"[24] – it is logically consistent, even if it is not a reasonable position.

In a similar vein, causality, as the Scottish philosopher David Hume famously noticed, is not directly observable. It involves an inference as to the best explanation available.[25] I cannot literally observe the causal relationship between a mosquito on my arm and the itch that follows its departure, but my causal inference is based on strong background knowledge. And despite the powerful evidence that HIV is the major cause of AIDS, some still insist, without contradiction though perhaps with much mischief, that the cause of AIDS lies elsewhere, such as in supposed divine punishment for bad behaviour.

To be sure, caution concerning accepted theory does sometimes facilitate the emergence of new causal hypotheses which surpass the prevailing theory in predictive and explanatory power. Scientists, if they are not foolish, then upgrade their causal explanations. For example, it was widely believed that anxiety and poor diet were the major causal factors behind gastritis (inflammation of the stomach lining) until Barry Marshall and Robin Warren challenged that hypothesis experimentally in the 1980s. They discovered the more fundamental cause: a bacterium known as *Helicobacter pylori*. They did not merely wave vaguely in the direction of a conceivable different causal claim, however; they showed experimentally that they had discovered a more powerful causal explanation. In the case of conscious experience, although philosophers such as Chalmers and Nagel express their reservations about the brain, all they really do have are reservations. Moreover, these are based on intuitions about how different experience seems to be from states occurring in the physical brain. They have neither competing experiments nor a competing hypothesis with any power or detail; in particular, they have no hypothesis which surpasses, or even competes seriously with, the neuroscientific hypothesis.[26] For instance, nothing even begins to approach the richness of the neuroscientific literature on attentional mechanisms, which shows that alerting is different from orientating, which in turn is different from detection and from executive control. Surprisingly perhaps, with the appropriate intervention these functions are dissociable, and they are supported by different neural networks.[27]

How do the dualists address the dependencies, the causal dependencies that suggest identification, between consciousness and brain activities? A favoured strategy is to propose that conscious states just run parallel to brain states. This proposal may be embellished, perhaps, by the idea that conscious states neither cause nor are caused by brain states: the two streams are causally isolated. A variation of this opts instead for a one-way causal street: brain states cause conscious states but conscious states do not cause brain states. Traditionally, the view that mental states do not cause brain states is called epiphenomenalism. Actual evidence is lacking for either hypothesis, both are merely empty denials of the idea that consciousness is a biological phenomenon.

Historically, the most renowned defender of two-way causal isolation was Gottfried Leibniz (1646–1716). He held this view because he thought it inconceivable that completely different substances could interact causally. If they shared no properties, not even spatial properties, how could they affect each other? With the benefit of contemporary physics, we can see that causal interaction between non-physical stuff, such as a "soul", and physical stuff, such as electrons, would be an anomaly relative to rather well-established laws. More exactly, it would challenge the law of conservation of energy: if brains can cause changes external to the physical domain, there should be an anomaly with respect to conservation of energy. No such anomaly has ever been seen or measured. The absence of anomalous data suggests that the hypothesis of a non-physical conscious stream of states lacks credibility or that the conscious stream of conscious states does not interact with brain states at all.

When the neuroscientist Josef Parvizi used a tiny electrical stimulus to activate a very specific part of the brain (the middle cingulate gyrus) as part of a surgical preparation, his patient described the emergence of a conscious state comprising determination to muster courage to deal with a problem. When the stimulus was removed, the feeling vanished.[28]

This experiential event was repeatable in that patient: a very similar state was reproducible in another patient, stimulated in the same region. The reasonable conclusion is that the stimulus caused the change in conscious state. Some naysayers may wish to insist that the brain event and the experienced event happen synchronously without causation, that the experience stream and the brain stream are separate.

But what then keeps the two streams synchronised? That is the galling puzzle which emerges from the epiphenomenal hypothesis. Here is how Leibniz dealt with it: God sets up and maintains a "pre-established harmony" to keep mental and physical states aligned. Needless to say, this solution is completely ad hoc, cobbled together to fill an embarrassing silence. Chalmers does not appeal to God, but does advert to a future physics which will allegedly explain the alignment between non-interacting streams of mental and brain events. A revolutionary physics, according to Chalmers's conjecture, will ultimately explain the nature of consciousness as a non-brain phenomenon.[29] I have been unable to escape the feeling that this is really the old Leibniz solution, suited up in the duds of a future physics instead of theology.

My small sampling of physicists indicates that they do not wish to rush into investing heavily in a new physics just to address consciousness, when neuroscience has not by any means been stopped dead in its tracks. And especially when neuroscience has not raised anomalies that challenge particle physics but only puzzles that might possibly challenge neuroscience. Physicists acknowledge the possibility of a new theory at the subatomic level, to link strong forces, weak forces and gravity, but these are phenomena in the range of 10^{-17}, not the milliseconds (10^{-3}) and micrometres (10^{-6}) where neurons exist and function. As the physicist Steven Weinberg said, the puzzles in physics that motivate a possible revision of the standard model are at the wrong spatial and temporal scale to offer even the barest hint of a solution to the matter of explaining consciousness.[30] Have the philosophers themselves proposed anything substantive by way of a new physics to replace existing physical theory? No.

If you are a dualist, you can pretend that the huge accumulation of dependency evidence in neuroscience is not really there (not a realistic option) or you can say something substantial to address it. Rationally, something must be done in so far as this accumulation appears strongly to favour the hypothesis that conscious states are brain states. A novel strategy, tendered by Chalmers, claims that neuroscientific data are actually neutral as between his parallel-stream hypothesis and the hypothesis that mental states are states of the physical brain.[31]

To assess the merit of this "neural data neutral" strategy, try it elsewhere in science and see what results. Consider the nature of light as understood within contemporary physics: light is electromagnetic radiation (EMR) – light visible by humans is just one part of a larger spectrum which includes X-rays, microwaves and so forth. Here is what the "neutral" strategy could say about light: "Actually, the physical evidence is neutral between the hypothesis that light *is* EMR, and that light is not EMR but a spooky thing. That is, light and EMR run in parallel streams, whose synchrony will be explained by a revolution in physics."

Here is what the "neutral strategy" would say about life: "All of cell biology is neutral between the hypothesis that life is an occult force (vitalism) and the hypothesis that life is the outcome of biological structure and organisation – cells, membranes, genes, ribosomes, mitochondria and so forth."

Scientifically, these "data neutral" proposals look counterproductive and more elaborate than the facts require. Silly though they may be, they are not, however, internally incoherent hypotheses. One bizarre claim that oddly appeals to various philosophers of mind is that if the "parallel-stream" hypotheses are not internally contradictory, they are as reasonable as established scientific theories. It is not internally contradict-ory to say that the Earth is only one hour old, but it would be strange to claim this is as reasonable as saying it is about five billion years old.

The twin predictions regarding mind and brain, that neuroscience will never account for conscious experience and that a revolution in physics will explain why, are generally motivated by emphasising the difference between a neuron and, say, a feeling of tooth pain. Upon reflection, it is argued, the differences appear so profound and complete that it is surely inconceivable that the pain in my tooth might really be the activity of neurons in my brain. It is sobering to recall that the history of science is full of discoveries in which seemingly very different phenomena turn out to be one and the same, having been viewed from different perspectives.[32] Breathlessly dramatising the striking differences lacks the scientific heft to make the dual-streams hypothesis compelling.

One problem with relying on what seems inconceivable is that what we find inconceivable is merely a psychological fact about us: what we can and cannot imagine, given our current beliefs and our capacity for imagination. It is not a metaphysical fact about the nature of the universe. In the opinion of some philosophers, however, trained philosophical intuition has special status, and must be taken as revealing deep, "neces-sary" truths unavailable to untrained others – in particular, to those with only a scientifically educated intuition.[33]

An issue that spells trouble for a non-brain theory of consciousness is that the division between awareness and lack of awareness is typically blurry and often fluid. This really shows up in the automatisation of behaviour as a skill is acquired, a commonplace phenomenon. As a child learns to read, s/he ceases to be aware of a word's individual letters; this is also demonstrated in the "word superiority" effect, whereby it is easier for an accomplished reader to read a word than individual letters, as meas-ured by reaction times and errors. Another simple case: I can ride a bike without being aware of my feet working the pedals, as I zoom along and think about my upcoming swim. Not so at the beginning of learning to do so, when I had to pay attention to every aspect of riding. Are the many behavioural decisions of which I am unaware just mental brain events that blank out of the mental experience stream until an emergency arises and I must pay attention? Am I aware of body position when I am concen-trating on pitching a tent? Sort of, sort of not. The neurobiological research on attention helps us see why the answer is not simple.

Apart from automatisation of skills, what about shifts of attention, for example where I cease to hear the speaker as I reflect on what I will order for dinner? When I lose awareness of what the speaker is saying, does that just snap out of the consciousness stream and then snap back in? How does that work? What orchestrates and coordinates the snapping? And what *is* snapping?

This raises a second issue. Are our short-lived conscious experiences properties of a "substance"? Or are they just events, properties of nothing in the experience "stream"? What maintains the stream as *one* stream? Compared with the serious research in neuroscience on the mechanisms of sleep, attention, visual perception, coma, anaesthesia and so forth, the naysayers seem to have a threadbare alternative, with very little in the way of a substantive explanatory framework.

Why do some philosophers of mind oppose so strenuously the two hypotheses: (1) mental states are states of the brain, and (2) neuroscience can probably at least outline the mechanisms of cognitive functions? A range of reasons contributes, but as the frontiers of the behavioural and brain sciences push ever forward into what might have seemed like a thicket of unapproachable mysteries, questions about turf and territory inevitably emerge. A strong assumption in the philosophy of mind is that philosophers are uniquely equipped to set the boundaries of what we can know, and to outline the essential and enduring features of concepts scientists might apply. Philosophical intuition, on this view, is a special, trained capacity which can home in on those necessary properties of a phenomenon that science must respect and not challenge. In this way, philosophy sets the foundations for the science. Apparently then, if philosophers characterise necessary properties of the mind which intuition and logic show cannot be explained by properties of the brain, then that is the contribution of philosophy science needs to honour.

Thus some philosophers of mind believe that they own a problem space that is concerned with conceptual necessities, necessary truths about psychological states and processes, discovered by conceptual analysis and "thought experiments".[34] A necessary truth cannot, according to this approach, be falsified by scientific data: intuitions trump data. Scientists, not surprisingly, are puzzled by where such a prior knowledge might come from and do not want to be bamboozled by philosophical flimflam. After all, intuitions appear to be just strongly held beliefs, likely grounded in education and reinforcement learning. They are not special reports from Plato's Heaven concerning Absolute Truths.

Philosophers are apt to defend their intuitions as supported by thought experiments about what could obtain in any possible world. Supposedly, the outcome of these will identify *necessary* truths about, for example, the nature of knowledge. This is a suspect strategy. Recall that Kant thought he had shown by thought experiments that space – the space our Earth and solar system inhabit – was necessarily Euclidean. Alas, the Euclidean claim is not even true, let alone necessarily true. Thought experiments, for all the homage paid to them by philosophers, are not real experiments in any sense. Starting an enquiry with intuitions is fine if that is all you have to go on, but then experiment and observation should subject those intuitions to test, and other hypotheses should be considered. In this well-known fashion, experimental psychology and neuroscience have illumin-ated the nature of our knowledge of the world and the nature of learning, along with the broader question concerning how the nervous systems of all mammals represent the external world.[35]

How could our intuitions be misguided? Complex nervous systems are not mere reflex machines or simple conditioning machines: they build models of the external world deployed in navigating the world. But not all models are equally accurate *for* the world. A mouse's model of the spatial world may be sufficient to get it around its environs given its limited goals, but it will not be as accurate as *my* model of the spatial world, or indeed that of a wolf. Brains also build models of the *causal* world: fire is hot and can burn us, red raspberries are tasty and so on. Regarding causality too, models have different degrees of accuracy: my general causal model of the world is more accurate than that of my great grandmother or my dog's. Finally, the brain builds models of the *inner* world – the world of brain events, including processes we call emotions, drives and attention. Here, again, there are varying degrees of accuracy and, in particular, according to Michael Graziano, the brain's model of attention can be inaccurate.[36] In particular, it *will* be inaccurate if it embodies the idea that attention is a non-physical, spooky phenomenon, and hence that con-sciousness is too.

Can this sense of "spookiness" be easily shed? Probably not. By and large our brains update our world models for us, but the control we have on the updating is limited. I might successfully update my causal model of the world as I come to realise that cholera is caused not by "bad air" but by bacteria. On the other hand, a rainbow will still *look* like it has a location in space, even though I know full well that it does not. What about the model of attention, and mental states generally? The model of mentality may persist in *seeming* to be spooky, even when I know "cognitively" that spooky is not accurate in relation to the facts. This may be owing to deep biological features of the way the neural model works.

It is a deep biological feature of brains that we extend touch sensations to the end of a pencil or a scalpel. It seems that we can feel the end of the tool. We know full well we have no sensors there, but our brain's model finds it very efficient to work that way anyhow – an evolutionary adaptation, no doubt. As we learn more about the brain, our scientific understanding of our model of attention may become more accurate, but the brain's model of conscious states we use on a moment-to-moment basis may itself be largely unmodified by such neuroscientific knowledge. Thus we may understand more about why it is so easy ("intuitive") to think that consciousness is a spooky phenomenon, even when we appreciate scientifically that it is not spooky but brainy.[37] We can simultaneously hold both ideas – "spooky" and "brainy" – in our minds, albeit in different ways.

1. Much of this text is drawn from P.S. Churchland, 'Neurophilosophy', in D.L. Smith (ed.), *Biology and Philosophy*, Cambridge, Cambridge University Press, forthcoming. Thanks are owed to Paul Churchland, as well as to Joshua Brown for clear-headed discussion and David Livingstone Smith for wise advice.

2. P. Thagard, 'Explanatory Identities and Conceptual Change', *Science & Education*, vol. 23, no. 7, 2014, pp. 1531–48.

3. T. Nagel, *Mind and Cosmos: Why the Materialist Neo-Darwinian Conception of Nature is Almost Certainly False*, New York, NY, Oxford University Press, 2012.

4. See P.M. Churchland, *The Engine of Reason, The Seat of the Soul*, Massachusetts, MA, MIT Press, 1996; C. Frith, *Making Up the Mind: How the Brain Creates our Mental World*, Oxford, Blackwell's, 2007; P.S. Churchland, *Brainwise: Studies in Neurophilosophy*, Massachusetts, MA, MIT Press, 2002, and excellent textbooks such as B.J. Baars & N.M. Gage, *Cognition, Brain and Consciousness*, San Diego, CA, Academic Press, 2007.

5. M.S. Gazzaniga & J. LeDoux, *The Integrated Mind*, New York, NY, Plenum Pres, 1978.

6. M.S. Gazzaniga, *Tales From Both Sides of the Brain: A Life in Neuroscience*, New York, NY, HarperCollins, 2015.

7. For a simple account, see K. Grens, 'The Rainbow Connection', *The Scientist*, 1 October 2014, http:/the-scientist.com/?articles.view/articleNo/41055/title/The-Rainbow-Connection/ (accessed 27 December 2015).

8. L.R. Squire, C.E. Stark & R.E. Clark, 'The Medial Temporal Lobe', *Annual Review of Neuroscience*, no. 27, 2004, pp. 279–306.

9. S.E. Petersen & M.I. Posner, 'The Attention System of the Human Brain: 20 Years After', *Annual Review of Neuroscience*, no. 35, 2012, pp. 73–89.

10. See S.G. Solomon & P. Lennie, 'The Machinery of Colour Vision', *Nature Reviews Neuroscience*, no. 8, 2007, pp. 276–86; P.M. Churchland, *Philosophy at Work*, Cambridge, Cambridge University Press, 2007, chap. 9–10.

11. E.F. Pace-Schott & J.A. Hobson, 'The Neurobiology of Sleep: Genetics, Cellular Physiology and Subcortical Networks', *Nature Reviews Neuroscience*, no. 3, 2002, pp. 591–600.

12. J. Allman, *Evolving Brains*, New York, NY, Scientific American Library, 1999.

13. G.F. Striedter et al., 'NSF Workshop Report: Discovering General Principles of Nervous System Organization by Comparing Brain Maps Across Species', *Brain, Behavior and Evolution*, vol. 83, no. 1, 2014, pp. 1–8.

14. P. Lieberman, *The Unpredictable Species*, Princeton, NJ, Princeton University Press, 2013.

15. S. Pääbo, *Neanderthal Man: In Search of the Lost Genomes*, New York, NY, Basic Books, 2014.

16. By J.A. Fodor: *The Language of Thought*, Cambridge, MA, Harvard University Press, 1975; 'Methodological Solipsism Considered as a Research Strategy in Cognitive Psychology', *Behavioral and Brain Sciences*, vol. 3, no. 1, 1980, pp. 63–73; *In Critical Condition: Polemical Essays on Cognitive Science and Philosophy of Mind*, Massachusetts, MA, MIT Press, 1998.

17. P. Glimcher & E. Fehr, *Neuroeconomics: Decision Making and the Brain*, 2nd edn., San Diego, CA, Academic Press, 2013.

18. Petersen & Posner, 'The Attention System of the Human Brain'.

19. E.I. Moser et al., 'Grid Cells and Cortical Representation', *Nature Reviews Neuroscience*, no. 15, 2014, pp. 466–81.

20. Fodor, *In Critical Condition*.

21. C. McGinn: 'Storm over the Brain: Review of Patricia S. Churchland, *Touching a Nerve*', *New York Review of Books*, 24 April 2014; 'All Machine and no Ghost', *New Statesman*, 20 February 2012. See also Fodor, *In Critical Condition*; N. Chomsky (debating the author), http://www.youtube.com/watch?v=QSQwBEL4mfQ (accessed 27 December 2015).

22. D. Chalmers, *The Conscious Mind: In Search of a Fundamental Theory*, New York, NY, Oxford University Press, 1997.

23. Nagel, *Mind and Cosmos*.

24. P.M. Churchland, 'The Rediscovery of Light', *Journal of Philosophy*, vol. 93, no. 5, 1996, pp. 211–28.

25. For a new and quite possibly correct account of how causality is represented in the brain, see D. Danks, *Unifying the Mind: Cognitive Representations as Graphical Models*, Massachusetts, MIT Press, 2014.

26. For discussion of a brain-based hypothesis, see P.S. Churchland, *Touching a Nerve*, New York, NY, Norton, 2013; M. Graziano, *Consciousness and the Social Brain*, New York, NY, Oxford University Press, 2013.

27. See Petersen & Posner, 'The Attention System of the Human Brain'.

28. J. Parvizi et al., 'The Will to Persevere Induced by Electrical Stimulation of the Human Cingulate Gyrus', *Neuron*, vol. 80, no. 6, 2013, pp. 1359–67; P.S. Churchland, 'Exploring the Causal Underpinning of Determination, Resolve and Will', *Neuron*, vol. 80, no. 6, 2013, pp. 1337–38. For a review article on drug-resistant surgery for epilepsy, see R. Ryvlin, J.H. Cross & S. Rheims, 'Epilepsy Surgery in Children and Adults', *The Lancet Neurology*, vol. 13, no. 11, 2014, pp. 1114–26.

29. Chalmers, *The Conscious Mind*.

30. This was Weinberg's answer to a question at Gustavus Adolphus College, 8 October 2014. See also S. Weinberg, *To Explain the World*, New York, NY, Harper Collins, 2015.

31. This is a view Chalmers has made explicit only in conversation, though he acknowledges that it is implicit in earlier writing, even in *The Conscious Mind*.

32. P. Thagard, 'Explanatory Identities and Conceptual Change', *Science & Education*, vol. 23, no. 7, 2014, pp. 1531–48; P.M. Churchland, *A Neurocomputational Perspective: The Nature of Mind and the Structure of Science*, Massachusetts, MA, MIT Press, 1989.

33. C. McGinn, *The Mysterious Flame: Consciousness in a Material World*, New York, NY, Basic Books, 1999; C. McGinn, review of *Touching a Nerve*, *New York Review of Books*, 24 April 2014; my reply, 19 June 2014.

34. This view is not limited to a small minority, but is widely espoused and taught in philosophy courses. This is readily seen in entries in the online *Stanford Encyclopedia of Philosophy*, which presumably represents the mainstream in the field. See, eg, the entry under "analysis of knowledge".

35. L.R. Squire et al., *Fundamental Neuroscience*, 4th edn., San Diego, CA, Academic Press, 2012.

36. M. Graziano, *Consciousness and the Social Brain*, New York, NY, Oxford University Press, 2013.

37. I owe this point to Michael Graziano, in conversation. Also see Graziano.

CONSCIOUSNESS AND THE PREDICTIVE BRAIN

Andy Clark

Where science seems to stumble

Consciousness is a notoriously elusive topic, partly because the word itself does not aim at a single target. But, of all the possible targets (simple awakeness, complex self-reflection), one stands out as especially challenging for scientific study. That target is *qualia* or "raw feels", the infamous "what-it-is-like-ness" of human experience: the distinct sensations that make life worth living or (sometimes) worth leaving.

It is depressingly hard to say much more about exactly what these are. We resort to well-worn hints and phrases: the very *redness* of the apple, the taste of the peach, the precise and unutterable sadness of the grief and so on. As the philosopher Jaegwon Kim once commented, "If this doesn't help, perhaps nothing will." Talk of qualia gestures at something we cannot easily define but seem to experience every day, the felt quality of tastes, smells and colours – "what it is like" to taste a fresh margarita while feeling the hot, Mexican sun on your back and enjoying (or not) the relentless beat of a mariachi band.

Existing theories centre on how information is disseminated within the brain for the control of action and response. Such theories are impressive and important: they have the resources to explain much of what is often meant by "conscious awareness".[1] But the question remains: can any theory go all the way? Can we hope to explain how qualia come to exist in a material universe? Many philosophers think this is where standard forms of scientific approach must stumble.[2] In what follows, I explore some possible ways forward, a few more "baby steps" that might lead us towards a satisfying theory of consciousness.

Step 1: Deflate the target

I begin with a deflationary move. Daniel Dennett has waged a decades-long war against appeals to qualia in discussions of the nature and possibility of conscious experience. At the heart of the many and varied skirmishes involved has lain a single, basic imperative – to avoid positing "double transduction" in the brain. This, Dennett claims, provides the breeding ground for the most problematic understandings of qualia, positioning them as intrinsic properties of experience that seem ideally suited to resist satisfying forms of scientific and philosophical explanation. So what is double transduction? This entails positing an appealing, but (Dennett claims) unnecessary, step in the flow of influence linking worldly states to human responses. Impinging energies carry information about the external world (including our own bodies) and those energies affect the neural economy so as to yield spike trains and other neural states. So far, so good. Double transduction would occur if those, in turn, needed to be translated or transduced into some other form (qualia) for inspection and consideration before yielding verbal responses and/or gross motor actions. This image, Dennett claims, is fatally flawed. There is no need for the second transduction, since the first poised incoming information to do whatever needed to be done, by yielding neural states (spike trains) already apt to guide responses of all kinds. And, of course, there is then no need for a third transduction (back into spike trains again) either.

The threat of double transduction is nicely illustrated by Dennett's old CADBLIND thought experiment.[3] CAD (computer-aided design) systems are able to help human designers answer questions such as "What will this object look like if rotated 70 degrees to the left?" and "Will this part of the object be visible when viewed from such-and-such a location?", based on coordinate maps and transformation algorithms. Such a system might generate a 3-D image of an object as it would appear from a particular perspective. The results of such transformations are displayed on a screen for the human user, who can then inspect the screen and issue the answer (perhaps, "Yes, the object-part is indeed visible when the viewer is located thus-and-so").

Now imagine a CAD system designed to be used by blind engineers. This is CADBLIND (mk I). As a first try, the designers might retrofit the old system with a new back-end device (Dennett dubs it the *Vorsetzer*), which inspects the screen after the rotation algorithm has been applied and uses artificial-intelligence vision techniques to determine, from that new raw data, whether the object-part is indeed now in shot. But this, clearly, is sub optimal: all the information needed to make that call is already in the system (it was required to form the rotated image in the first place). The correct solution is thus to cut out the *Vorsetzer* and deliver the verdict directly on the basis of the previously processed information.

Dennett thinks that the philosophers' explanatory appeal to inner qualia is like the posit of an inner *Vorsetzer* – an unnecessary add-on which misleads us into thinking that there remains (even after all the information-processing chores are accomplished) some special kind of work still to be done.

Dennett's moral is that the path from input to judgment need not have qualia as an intervening variable. The cycle is not sense–process–qualia–judge but simply sense–process–judge. In that latter sequence, there is neither need nor room for intervening mysterious qualia.

Step 2: Explore a "Strange Inversion"
These are important arguments but they seem to fall just short of delivering the goods. Stamping out the threat of double transduction is a great start. But, as Dennett rightly notes, it can hardly be a satisfying finish.[4] For things do not, on the face of it, seem like that at all. If it is all just spike trains, doing what they do, why does it *seem to us* as if we are rotating mental images, appreciating colours and textures or even just recognising people, animals and objects? If we could answer this question, "Why do things seem the way they do?", to everyone's satisfaction, that would surely spell the end of the qualia wars.

To set the scene for such an effort, Dennett brings onstage another of his long-term loves: the "Strange Inversion". This notion is best introduced by example. My personal favourite concerns bars famous for their excellent Guinness. It turns out that the major determinant of this is how briefly the barrel has been open. A bar's reputation for serving good Guinness may thus be what causes the Guinness to be good, since a bar with that reputation will serve lots of Guinness, thus keeping it fresher. We thought the reputation was due to the Guinness. But, in fact, the quality of the Guinness is an effect of the reputation. Or (to take Dennett's core example) consider Hume on causation. The standard (non-inverted) story has it that we see x causing y, and thus form the idea of causal connections. The inverted story says no, we never see x causing y; instead, we see y following x, regularly, apparently inexorably. We then come to expect this regular succession, and this strong psychological expectation is projected back on to the world as some apparently perceptible "causal connection". What appears to be a property of the world itself turns out (if Hume is right) to be a property of the observer. In this way, "we misinterpret an inner 'feeling', an anticipation, as an external property".[5] In

Hume's terms, we "gild and stain" natural objects with features and properties "borrowed from internal sentiment".

Hume's strange inversion provides a close model for Dennett's own attempt to reorientate our thinking about qualia and qualitative experience. Consider, to follow one of Dennett's prime examples, the sweet taste of honey. According to the standard (non-inverted) story, we like honey because it tastes so sweet. The view from after the Strange Inversion is rather different. Our liking of honey, it is suggested, is nothing but the subtle complex of reactive dispositions honey evokes: dispositions (in many folk, at least) to seek it, lick it, affirm it to be tasty and so on. If the inversion is on the mark, the complex of reactive dispositions comes first, and we label things which evoke that complex of responses as "sweet". So it is not the sweetness which explains our response, it's our response which explains (constitutes) the sweetness. But, not knowing this, we project (through our own expectations) the sweetness on to the world, resulting in the self-diagnosis of a perceptual realm which presents a variety of mysterious and puzzling qualia: a realm of dogs, cats and tables but *also* of sweet-tasting honey, cute-looking babies, funny jokes and even red-seeming apples. The key to unravelling the mystery of qualia, if Dennett is right, is better appreciation of how our expectations affect our patterns of judgment and response.

Step 3: Brains as prediction machines
A recent explosion of work in cognitive and computational neuroscience shows how to begin to turn Dennett's schematic suggestions into hard science. Brains like ours, this work suggests, are multilevel prediction engines forever trying to anticipate incoming flows of sensory information. This image of the brain as an engine of prediction can be found in various forms in contemporary neuroscience.[6] A leading theme is that, instead of trying to build a model of what's out there on the basis of a panoply of low-level sensory cues, the brain tries, in effect, to predict the current suite of low-level sensory cues from its best models of what is most likely to be out there. The brain, if this story is correct, meets the incoming raw, multimodal sensory stream with a complex web of learned, "top–down" predictions. Its task is to generate a multilevel match for the incoming sensory data using knowledge of patterns and probabilities in the world. Failures to predict the shape of the sensory signal result in prediction errors, which recruit new top–down hypotheses: new guesses about the state of the world.

12
ABC
14

Consider the simple but striking demonstration (used by the neuroscientist Richard Gregory to make this very point) known as the hollow-face illusion. This is a well-known illusion in which an ordinary facemask viewed from the back (concave, to fit the face) appears strikingly convex when viewed from a modest distance. That is, it looks (still from the back) to be shaped like a real face, with the nose sticking outwards rather than having a concave nose cavity. The hollow-face illusion illustrates the power of top–down (essentially, knowledge-driven) influences on perception. Our statistically salient experience with endless hordes of convex faces in daily life installs a deep, sub-personal "expectation" of convexness – an expectation which trumps the many other visual cues that ought to be telling us that what we are seeing is a concave mask.

If we read the figure on the previous page from left to right, the predictive brain meets the raw sensory stimulations from the central inscription with a strong expectation of the letter B. Reading top to bottom, the raw sensory stimulations are met with a different prediction: the numeral 13. In Bayesian terms, in the context of reading the 12, the 13 hypothesis makes the raw visual data most probable, while in the context of reading the A, the B hypothesis makes the raw visual data most probable.

One might reasonably worry that such effects, though striking, are really just a psychological oddity. And, to be sure, our expectations concerning the convexness of faces seem especially potent. But if these stories are on track, the same core strategy pervades human perception. The claim is that brains like ours are constantly trying to use what they already know, so as to predict the current sensory signal. This helps explain why human experience is so easily altered by context and expectation. For example (as every dentist and doctor knows), expectations concerning imminent states of pain make a surprisingly large difference to the amounts of pain experienced, even when the stimulus remains constant.[7]

Step 4: Predicting our bodily states
With these three steps in mind, consider the case of feelings and emotions. Here, the predictive-brain account adds important dimensions to the well-known James–Lange model of emotional states, as arising from the perception of our bodily responses to external stimuli and events. The idea there, in a nutshell, was that our emotional "feelings" were nothing but the perceptions of our varying physiological responses. According to James,

the bodily changes follow directly the perception of the exciting fact, and ... our feeling of the same changes as they occur is the emotion. Common sense says, we lose our fortune, are sorry and weep; we meet a bear, are frightened and run; we are insulted by a rival, are angry and strike. The hypothesis here to be defended says that this order of sequence is incorrect ... and that the more rational statement is that we feel sorry because we cry, angry because we strike, afraid because we tremble[8]

"Interoceptive" sensory signals, concerning the current inner state and condition of the body, constitute a form of "inner sensing" whose targets include states of the viscera, the vasomotor system, muscular and air-supply systems, and many more. And for James, our interoceptive perception of the bodily changes characteristic of fear (sweating, trembling and so on) constitutes the very feeling of fear, giving it its distinctive psychological flavour. From a subjective viewpoint, interoceptive awareness manifests itself as a differentiated array of feelings, including those of "pain, temperature, itch, sensual touch, muscular and visceral sensations ... hunger, thirst and 'air hunger'".[9] The interoceptive system is thus mostly concerned with pain, hunger and the states of various inner organs. It is distinct from both the exteroceptive system, which includes vision, touch and audition, and the proprioceptive system, which carries information about relative limb positions, effort and force. The feeling of fear, if James is right, is thus essentially the detection of an interoceptive physiological signature already induced by exposure to the threatening situation.

A popular (and useful) way to think about James's proposal is to see it as suggesting a "subtraction test". This is a thought experiment in which one is invited to subtract all the bodily stuff (detection of a racing heart and the like) from the emotional experience, and ask oneself what would be left. James's claim is that one would be left with nothing worth counting as an experience or emotion. An emotion is really the *self-perception of changes in our bodily states*, his argument suggests.

But what could be the point of all that bodily self-monitoring? Here, Jesse Prinz, drawing on important work by Antonio Damasio, offers a plausible story.[10] According to Prinz, ancient neural circuitry generates bodily responses to dangers and opportunities, before the more evolutionarily recent centres of self-awareness come into play. The bodily changes are thus an efficient indicator of important information about our current needs (such as for food or water) and threats and opportunities in the wider world (that bear!). So by detecting our bodily states, we are indirectly detecting stuff that matters about ourselves and the world.

Consider an imaginary robot, OILBOT, which needs to act quickly in response to dangers its visual system can spot. This involves rapidly detecting the threat and pumping lots of extra oil into its hydraulics. But OILBOT also needs to be able to think about the danger, so as sometimes to use what it knows to plan a more flexible response. One way to bring the slower, deliberative machinery into the act is to let OILBOT use bodily self-monitoring. When it detects its own pipes filling with oil, that tells it that its fast basic circuitry has detected danger and it must now attend to that. The moral is that to really give a machine experiences and emotions we need to build it so that it uses perceptions of its bodily states as a clue to threats and opportunities in the world. In our own case, think about detecting changes in blood-sugar levels, which signal an imminent need for food, by detecting those changes we indirectly learn about a state of the body which matters for creatures like us.

But the standard James story, even when augmented in this way, remains somewhat inadequate. For it seems to require a one-to-one mapping between distinct emotional states and "brute-physiological" signatures, and it seems to suggest that whenever the physiological state is induced and detected, the same emotional feeling should arise. Neither of these implications is borne out by observation and experiment.[11]

The basic story can, however, be refined and extended by adding an important "predictive twist". Thus Seth suggests that a neglected core component may be the match (or mismatch) between a cascading series of top–down predictions of our interoceptive states and the forward-flowing information contained in sensory prediction error. Our interoceptive predictions, this story suggests, "arise from multiple hierarchical levels, with higher levels integrating interoceptive, proprioceptive and exteroceptive cues in formulating descending predictions".[12]

A single inferential process here integrates all these sources of information, generating a context-reflecting amalgam experienced as emotion. Felt emotions thus integrate basic information (about bodily arousal) with higher-level predictions of probable causes and preparations for possible actions. In this way, "The close interplay between interoceptive and exteroceptive inference implies that emotional responses are inevitably shaped by cognitive and exteroceptive context, and that perceptual scenes that evoke interoceptive predictions will always be affectively coloured."[13]

The anterior insular cortex (AIC) is remarkably well-positioned in this regard. The AIC is thought to play a special role in the integration and use of interoceptive information, and (more generally) in the construction of emotional awareness – perhaps by encoding what Craig describes as "a meta-representation of the primary interoceptive activity".[14]

Emotion and subjective-feeling states arise, this story suggests, as the result of multilevel inferences, which combine sensory (interoceptive, proprioceptive and exteroceptive) signals with top–down predictions to generate a sense of how things are for us and of what we might be about to do. Such a sense of "action-ready being" encompasses our background physiological condition, estimations of current potentials for action and the perceived state of the wider world. This delivers a grip on both the nature *and significance* of our own embodied state.

Importantly, such a grip must integrate basic information (about bodily arousal) with higher-level predictions of probable causes. This provides a very natural way of accommodating large bodies of experimental results showing that the character of our emotional experience depends both on the interoception of brute bodily signals and higher-level "cognitive appraisals".[15] An example of a brute bodily signal is generic arousal as induced, to take the classic example from Schacter and Singer, by an injection of adrenaline. Such brute signals combine with contextually-induced cognitive appraisals, leading us to interpret the same bodily "evidence" as elation, anger or lust, according to our framing expectations.

Putting it all together
The predictive twist thus allows us to combine a core insight of the James–Lange theory (the idea that interoceptive self-monitoring is a key component in the construction of emotional experience) with a fully integrated account of the role of other factors, such as context and expectation. Previous attempts to combine these insights have taken the form of "two-factor" theories, which depict subjective-feeling states as essentially hybrids of bodily feeling and "cognitive" interpretation. The emerging, predictive-processing account of emotion is not such a theory. Rather, it claims that a single, highly flexible process fluidly combines top–down

predictions with all manner of bottom–up sensory information, and that subjective-feeling states (along with the full range of exteroceptive perceptual experiences) are determined by the unfolding of this process.

A predictive-processing version of OILBOT would use the rapidly activated hydraulic states of its own body as further evidence in a single inferential process. That would crunch together bodily information, incoming sensory signals (a rustling noise in the jungle) and prior knowledge (that this area has lions in it) to generate predictions about the most likely shape of the incoming barrage of interoceptive and exteroceptive sensory signals. The suggestion is that qualia and feelings are the result of crunching together external and internal sources of information, so as to reveal the organism-relevant state of the world.

Such an agent has a predictive grip on multiscale structures in the external world: a grip on rapidly changing patterns of shape and colour, and on less rapidly changing patterns such as the presence of the same person thoughout a meeting, or the same hockey match over an hour or two. But that multilayered grip is now superimposed upon (indeed, co-computed with) *another* multilayered predictive grip: a grip on the changing physiological state of the body. These clearly interact. As my bodily state alters, the salience of various worldly opportunities alters too. That means I will act differently, harvesting different streams of exteroceptive and interoceptive information, which in turn determine subsequent actions, choices and bodily states. The multilayer predictive grip upon the world is now inflected, at every level, by a sense of "how things are with us". Might this be the moment at which a robot, animal or machine starts to experience a low-grade sense of being? Such a system has, in some intuitive sense, a simple grip not just on the world, but on the world *as it matters, right here, right now, for a being like that.*

Explaining human experience
What does it take to get from that "low-grade sense of being" to full-blooded human experience? Now the issue is not why it feels like anything at all (the low-grade story, plus the Dennett-style deflation, is meant to deal with that). Rather, what still needs to be explained is the richness and texture of human experience.

A promising idea is that more advanced (reflective, self-aware, agentive) forms of experience arise when the prediction machinery is turned further upon itself, when we ourselves begin to appear as distinct elements in our own predictive world models. This may come about when bedrock prediction routines are deployed in the special context of cultural practices that involve coordinating our behaviours with those of other agents.[16] Exploring these more advanced dimensions is important if we are to do justice to the scope and variety of human conscious experience.

Consider our abilities to maintain closely coordinated social interactions, and to construct artefacts, narratives and designer environments. Some of these ingredients have emerged in other species too. But in the human case, the whole mosaic comes together, under the influence of flexible, structured, symbolic language and an almost obsessive drive to engage in shared cultural practices. We are thus enabled repeatedly to redeploy our core cognitive skills in the transformative context of exposure to "patterned sociocultural practices",[17] involving the exchange of linguistic information, peer critiques and expectations of reason-giving and explanation. Courtesy of all those practices and capabilities, our best models of reality (unlike those of other creatures) have become stable, reinspectable objects apt for public critique and refinement. Our best models of the world are thus not locked within our own brains but are (in part) public objects, available to ourselves and to others as the basis for communally distributed reasoning and cumulative learning.

One intriguing possibility is that these human-specific practices enable (and then increasingly require) us to model *ourselves* in rich and surprising ways. These forays into complex self-prediction and self-modelling may help explain much that is otherwise puzzling about self-conscious, reflective human experience.[18] For example, we possess complexes of perceptual abilities enabling us to discriminate (to sort, sift and group) on the basis of colour, texture, sound and smell. We are also members of communities in which language use, reason-giving and justification are paramount. But (as has often been observed) we, as agents, have no direct access to the neural mechanisms involved in reliable perceptual recognition. If asked by another agent to justify our various acts of sorting, sifting, grouping and choosing, we may seek to explain these capacities by means of a simplified predictive model. In this we might depict ourselves (to ourselves and others) as the possessors of that mysterious conscious arena populated by the puzzling qualia – direct experiences of colours, textures, sounds, feeling and emotions – which some philosophers have argued are most resistant to scientific understanding and explanation. Much of what seems puzzling about qualitative conscious experience may thus be a product of the simple thumbnail sketches of our capacities and potentialities that must inevitably arise as a result of our (individual and collective) attempts at efficient self-prediction and self-explanation.

Finally, consider the self-conscious control of behaviour. It has been speculated that self-conscious control depends on neural predictions concerning how we will act in the future, what kinds of opportunities for action the future will provide and the complex ways in which our current actions will alter the space of our possible future actions.[19] These distinctive forms of counter-factual prediction arise when bedrock prediction routines are deployed in the special context of coordinating our behaviours with those of other agents, often at extended timescales, and against an enabling backdrop of social and linguistic structures and practices. Predictions about our future actions, if this is on track, install and help constitute our sense of agency, choice and purpose. Our sense of identity as individual agents, this suggests, may be deeply tied to beliefs (predictions) about our future behaviours. Such beliefs would act (in well-functioning individuals) as partially self-fulfilling prophecies, helping to bring about the kinds of outcome associated with being that very agent. These top-level beliefs would define who we think we are (what kind of agent we take ourselves to be) and, in so doing, help to make us into an agent of that kind.

At this point, work on the advanced predictive brain converges with what is sometimes called the "social neuroscience theory of consciousness".[20] According to that theory, human consciousness is intimately tied to the prediction of our own behaviour, and human agents construct models of their own and others' mental states that are experienced as conscious awareness. From my perspective, this is not quite right, since basic forms of qualitative experience may arise much earlier, at least if the speculations in the opening sections are on track. Basic qualitative experience would arise wherever exteroceptive and interoceptive predictions are combined in the service of adaptive success. But, as an account of our *self-attributions of awareness* (hence of the more reflective forms of conscious experience), such ideas seem very promising. The full richness of human experience may thus reflect the complex ways in which we model (and predict) ourselves, appearing as distinct agents whose choices and actions condition our future experiences.

These new approaches to emotion and experience all flow from the emerging vision of the predictive brain. According to these accounts, the brain is a probabilistic prediction machine, not just monitoring bodily and worldly states but forever trying to predict them too. Human experience, on these models, is conditioned not only by incoming sensory signals from body and world but by how our brains predict those signals ought to be. This is a game changer, whose full impact is only beginning to be explored.

Courtesy of this new perspective, might we, inch-by-inch and phenomenon-by-phenomenon, begin to solve the "hard problem"[21] of conscious experience itself – the mystery of why it feels *like this* (or, indeed, like anything at all) to be a human agent immersed in a world of sights, sounds and feelings? It is far too early to say, but it feels like progress. Much of this progress, we have seen, depends on a swathe of recent, empirically informed conjecture concerning the role of "interoceptive inference" – roughly, the prediction of our own internal bodily states.

This delivers a startlingly familiar vision – of a creature whose bodily needs and condition form the pivot-point for knowing, active encounters with the world. We thus begin to comprehend how a world of external causes and opportunities can be presented to a creature in a way constantly intermingled with a predictive grip on its own changing bodily condition. For many sentient beings, the story probably stops right there. But sometimes, perhaps as a result of the combined and mutually enhancing influences of social collaboration and expressive public language, the sentient creature also appears as an element in its own best model of the world. Now, the prediction machinery targets not just the interacting worlds of inner and outer sensation, but also the creature's own role as an agent: a potent "hidden cause" whose choices and acts structure the immediate and long-term flows of sensation. At that point, the full richness of human experience seems at last within sight.

1. For a review, see S. Dehaene et al., 'Toward a Computational Theory of Conscious Processing', *Current Opinion in Neurobiology*, no. 25, 2014, pp. 76–84.
2. See, eg, D. Chalmers, *The Conscious Mind*, New York, NY, Oxford University Press, 1996.
3. See D. Dennett, *Consciousness Explained*, Boston, Little Brown, 1991, pp. 290–93.
4. D.C. Dennett, 'Why and How Does Consciousness Seem the Way it Seems?', in T. Metzinger & J.M. Windt (eds.), *Open MIND*: 10(T), Frankfurt a.M., MIND Group, 2015.
5. Dennett, 'Why and How Does Consciousness Seem the Way it Seems?', sect. 6.
6. For a useful survey, see K. Kveraga, A. Ghuman & M. Bar, 'Top–Down Predictions in the Cognitive Brain', *Brain and Cognition*, no. 65, 2007, pp. 145–68. For book-length explorations, see J. Hohwy, *The Predictive Mind*, New York, NY, Oxford University Press, 2013; A. Clark, *Surfing Uncertainty: Prediction, Action and the Embodied Mind*, New York, NY, Oxford University Press, forthcoming.
7. L.Y. Atlas & T.D. Wager, 'How Expectations Shape Pain, *Neuroscience Letters*, no. 520, 2012, pp. 140–48; C. Büchel et al., 'Placebo Analgesia: A Predictive Coding Perspective, *Neuron*, no. 81, 2014, pp. 1223–39.
8. W. James, *The Principles of Psychology*, vol. 1, 2nd edn., Cambridge, MA, Harvard University Press, 1950, p. 449.
9. A.D. Craig, 'Interoception: The Sense of the Physiological Condition of the Body', *Current Opinion in Neurobiology*, no. 13, 2003, p. 500.
10. J. Prinz, *Gut Reactions*, Oxford, Oxford University Press, 2004.
11. H.D. Critchley, 'Neural Mechanisms of Autonomic, Affective and Cognitive Integration', *Journal of Comparative Neurology*, vol. 493, no. 1, 2005, pp. 154–66.
12. A.K. Seth, 'Interoceptive Inference, Emotion and the Embodied Self ', *Trends in Cognitive Sciences*, vol. 17, no. 11, 2013, p. 567.
13. Seth, 'Interoceptive Inference, Emotion and the Embodied Self', p. 563.
14. Craig, 'Interoception', p. 500.
15. See S. Schachter & J. Singer, 'Cognitive, Social and Physiological Determinants of Emotional State', *Psychological Review*, no. 69, 1962, pp. 379–99; Prinz, *Gut Reactions*.
16. See C. Frith & U. Frith, 'Mechanisms of Social Cognition', *Annual Review of Psychology*, no. 63, 2012, pp. 287–313; C.J. Palmer, A.K. Seth & J. Hohwy, 'The Felt Presence of other Minds: Predictive Processing, Counterfactual Predictions and Mentalising in Autism', *Consciousness and Cognition*, no. 36, 2015, pp. 376–89.
17. A. Roepstorff, J. Niewöhner & S. Beck, 'Enculturing Brains through Patterned Practices', *Neural Networks*, vol. 23, nos. 8–9, pp. 1051–59.
18. For a promising glimpse of this territory, see D. Dennett, 'Expecting Ourselves to Expect', *Behavioral and Brain Sciences*, vol. 36, no. 3, 2013, pp. 29–30.
19. G. Pezzulo, F. Rigoli & K. Friston, 'Active Inference, Homeostatic Regulation and Adaptive Behavioural Control', *Progress in Neurobiology*, no. 134, 2015, pp. 17–35.
20. M. Graziano, *Consciousness and the Social Brain*, New York, NY, Oxford University Press, 2013.

21. Chalmers, *The Conscious Mind*; J. Levine, 'Materialism and Qualia: The Explanatory Gap', *Pacific Philosophical Quarterly*, no. 64, 1983, pp. 35–61; T. Nagel, 'What is it Like to be a Bat?', *Philosophical Review*, no. 83, 1974, pp. 435–56.

CONSCIOUSNESS NEVER LEFT

Galen Strawson

The return of consciousness?

A chance conversation recently caused me to look up an article I wrote in 2002. It was a review of David Lodge's book *Consciousness and the Novel,* and opened with a comment on "the familiar fiction of 'The Return of Consciousness': the story of the blazing re-entry of consciousness into philosophical and scientific awareness in the 1990s after long, strange decades in which its existence had been ignored or denied".

This story was, I wrote,

> mostly myth. It's true that some twentieth-century philosophers and psychologists, crazed by theory, really did deny the existence of consciousness. Some danced in the behaviourist footsteps of Ryle and Wittgenstein (or rather, their versions of Ryle and Wittgenstein), holding that to be in intense pain is really just to behave in a certain way or be disposed to behave in a certain way. Some said that an orgasm is really just a "sentence in the head" with no sort of conscious feel to it at all.
>
> But no one with any ear or eye or nose – any respect, feeling, gift, care – for reality believed a word of it. Consciousness was always central on the real agenda [in the philosophy of mind]. It was never ignored. Important experimental work on consciousness continued in psychology throughout the narrow, wacko behaviourist decades, and the issue was always of primordial importance for all sensible philosophers of mind, the ones who now find it faintly exasperating to read – several times a week – that the topic of consciousness came staggering in from the wilderness only about ten years ago.

"Does it matter that the story of the Return of Consciousness is inaccurate?" I asked. "Not really," I replied, "it's good publicity for an amazingly interesting subject."

That was in 2002. It is still a good thing today that there is so much interest in the topic of consciousness, and it is not, perhaps, very important that "the return of consciousness" is a myth when it comes to philosophy. It is nevertheless regrettable in so far as it ignores (disregards, writes off) those philosophers who were passionately and fruitfully preoccupied with the question of consciousness in the decades when it is said to have been forgotten. It is also a little disheartening, even somewhat frightening, to see how myths about the history of ideas no longer require the passing of time to evolve and can spring up almost instantly, swept up in the roaring bombardment of what Saul Bellow called "the moronic inferno": the great media storm of television, the public prints and now, above all, the internet.

I fear that quite a lot of what goes on in the academic world is part of the moronic inferno. David Chalmers, for example, is widely thought to have invented the so-called problem of consciousness, despite his own repeated disavowals, although the issue that is supposed to constitute the problem – the mystery – was given a clear, sharp formulation by Descartes nearly 400 years ago, and has been right at the forefront of philosophical discussion ever since.

I label it the "so-called problem of consciousness" because really there is no such problem. We know that consciousness exists, we know this for certain, and we know what it is. There is a fundamental sense in which we know *exactly* what it is. What else could we reasonably want? It looks as if we have confused the non-existent problem of consciousness with the *problem of matter* – a very real problem, which continues to baffle physicists and cosmologists as much as philosophers and psychologists.

I shall return to this idea. For the moment, I shall continue to speak of the problem of consciousness. The belief that there is a problem arises from the almost universal conviction that consciousness cannot possibly be something material or physical. Leibniz expressed this conviction vividly in 1714, in his image of the mill. Consciousness, he wrote, is

inexplicable on mechanical principles, i.e. by shapes and movements. If we imagine a machine whose structure makes it think, sense, and be conscious, we can conceive of it being enlarged in such a way that we can go inside it like a mill. Suppose we do: visiting its insides, we will never find anything but parts pushing each other – never anything that could explain a conscious state.[1]

Philosophers have been making similar claims ever since, in a wonderful variety of ways. They have kept the issue of consciousness right at the top of the agenda in philosophy throughout the 18th, 19th and 20th centuries. "What exactly do you mean by consciousness?" If you are asking, you are probably a philosopher. By "consciousness", I simply mean what people usually mean in this debate, something everybody is familiar with – the subjective, qualitative character of conscious experience, the "phenomenological" character of experience, the experiential "what-it's-like" of conscious experience, the "what-it's-like" of hearing Billie Holiday or Kirsten Flagstad singing, or being stung by a wasp, or feeling sleepy or nauseous, or reading and understanding this sentence, or, in Bertrand Russell's striking example, "feeling the coldness of a frog".[2]

Is there anything at all to the myth of the return of consciousness? It is true that many psychologists in the 20th century were principally engaged in behaviourist research, which puts consciousness to one side for methodological reasons, although it does not deny its existence. It is also true that a very small number of people really did seem to deny the existence of consciousness, adopting the position labelled "eliminative materialism" with respect to consciousness. They really did seem to make what I believe to be the silliest claim ever made in the whole history of human thought, committing themselves to what I refer to as "the Denial". Other philosophers held back from outright denial of the existence of consciousness, but went almost as far. Paul Churchland "confesse[d] a strong inclination towards eliminative materialism" in 1979. He called it "very much a live option",[3] and this view is in no way less remarkable than the outright denial.

How did this happen? With considerable regret, I blame the philosophers. Cicero was right long ago when he said that "there is no statement so absurd that no philosopher will make it".[4] But it is not just philosophers. Francis Bacon made the point in 1620:

[O]nce the human mind has favoured certain views (whether because they're generally accepted and believed, or because it finds them attractive), it pulls everything else into agreement with and support for them. Should they be outweighed by more powerful countervailing considerations, it either fails to notice these, or scorns them, or makes fine distinctions in order to neutralize and so reject them … thereby preserving untouched the authority of its previous position.[5]

Mark Twain backed him up in 1906, remarking that "there isn't anything so grotesque or so incredible that the average human being can't believe it".[6] Daniel Kahneman recently reaffirmed the point, drawing on research in experimental psychology, that "people can maintain an unshakable faith in any proposition, however absurd, when they are sustained by a community of like-minded believers".[7]

The claim that consciousness does not exist, or even might not exist, is by far the most striking example of Kahneman's dictum and therefore the most frightening. It is important that we do not think that this happens only in religious communities which go in for mass suicide, like the followers of Jim Jones in Jonestown, Guyana in 1978, or the so-called Branch Davidians, led by David Koresh, in Waco, Texas in 1993. That said, those who deny the existence of consciousness do form a kind of religious community, and they do indeed commit a form of suicide, albeit of an intellectual kind. And this, as already remarked, is no less true of those who, like Churchland in 1979, claim only that there might be no such thing as consciousness. In terms of plausibility, it is exactly parallel to saying "I don't exist" or "I might not exist". (There are of course profoundly mentally disturbed people who do say just this: those who suffer from extreme forms of Cotard's delusion.)

The history of the denial
The Denial is a distinctively 20th-century phenomenon – although it lives on, somewhat comically, in the 21st. As far as I know, it first began to be heard around the time behaviourism became a popular programme in psychology, an event one can date roughly to the publication of J.B. Watson's behaviourist "manifesto" in 1913, although many psychologists were by then already thoroughly dissatisfied with the "introspectionist" methodology in psychology which behaviourism replaced. As early as 1911, E.A. Singer had declared that "consciousness is not something inferred from behavior, it is behavior" (although he rejected the title "the father of behaviourism").[8] Bertrand Russell was aware of the Denial in 1921, when he published *The Analysis of Mind*.[9] In 1923, the distinguished behavioural psychologist Karl Lashley aimed "to show that the statement, 'I am conscious' does not mean anything more than the statement that 'such and such physiological processes are going on within me'".[10] The denial of consciousness was prominently placed on the philosophical table two years later, when C.D. Broad wrote that "Reductive Materialism

... and strict Behaviourism", both of which he understood to incorporate the Denial, were

> instances of the numerous class of theories which are so preposter-ously silly that only very learned men could have thought of them. I may be accused of breaking a butterfly on a wheel in this discussion of Behaviourism. But it is important to remember that a theory which is in fact absurd may be accepted by the simple-minded because it is put forward in highly technical terms by learned persons who are themselves too confused to know exactly what they mean.[11]

All this may seem pretty extraordinary – until one recalls Cicero's remark. Behaviourism, after all, was introduced in psychology as a strictly methodological position, an approach to experimental research which did not involve any sort of denial of the existence of consciousness, as already observed. This behaviourism fully acknowledged the existence of consciousness, but put it to one side on the ground that it was not susceptible to a properly scientific treatment. And yet it was by this time only a few years away from metamorphosing into full-blown consciousness-denying "philosophical behaviourism", a view of the mind which, in certain parts of the philosophical world, dominated the 1930s and 1940s.

Many psychologists took no notice of this distinctively philosophical aberration. In 1948, for example, Edwin Boring, one of the leading "operationist" psychologists in the mid-20th century, stood up stoutly for the common-sense view that "consciousness is what you experience *immediately*".[12] But the philosopher Brian Farrell flatly disagreed, in a paper published in 1950, one year after Gilbert Ryle's wonderfully weird book *The Concept of Mind* (which itself drew inspiration from the then unpublished work of Ludwig Wittgenstein).[13]

Farrell's case is in a way exemplary. It was Farrell, Wilde Reader in Mental Philosophy at the University of Oxford, who first asked the question "What is it like to be a bat?", in a paper called "Experience" published in *Mind* in 1950.[14] Thomas Nagel put the same question to very good use in the 1970s, in a well-known paper of that name,[15] which made the fact – and supreme importance – of the existence of consciousness philosophically salient right at the time when, according to the myth, the question of consciousness was supposed to have been occluded or forgotten. But

Farrell had very different ideas when he asked the question. In his 1950 paper he judged Boring's claim to be a "comical and pathogenic remark". He reckoned that better times were coming: once Western societies truly assimilate the work of the relevant sciences "it is quite possible that the notion of 'experience' will be generally discarded as delusive". As things stand, it is only by "restricting the use of the word 'experience' to 'raw feels' [that we can] go on defending the view that 'experience' and 'behaviour' are not identical; and this line of defence is hopeless". In the present state of our language, "the notion of 'experience' can be shown to resemble an occult notion like 'witchcraft' in a primitive community that is in the process of being acculturated to the West". Fortunately, he concluded, science "is getting to the brink of rejecting" experience as "unreal" or "non-existent".[16]

These thoughts were echoed and amended by, among others, the radical philosopher of science Paul Feyerabend in 1962 and Richard Rorty in 1965, in the upsurge of discussion of consciousness which followed the publication of the psychologist U.T. Place's paper "Is Consciousness a Brain Process?" in 1956 and the Australian philosopher J.J.C. Smart's "Sensations and Brain processes" in 1959.[17] The discussion raged on through the 1960s, 1970s and 1980s, precisely when the topic of consciousness was meant to have faded from view. Among the key interventions were John Searle's 1980 paper "Minds, Brains, and Programs", which expounded the "Chinese room argument" for consciousness, and Frank Jackson's 1982 paper "Epiphenomenal Qualia", which introduced the famous story of "Mary in the black-and-white room".[18]

The departure of the question of consciousness from the academic scene is, then, a myth. So also, therefore, is the story of its wonderful return, although a small group of individuals did in effect seek to deny the very existence of consciousness, while others held, no less weirdly, that it was theoretically possible that it might not exist. Looking back in 2003, Owen Flanagan remarked that

> some of my best friends were once eliminativists … but they have almost all seen that there is something seriously mad about the view. Most mad-dog eliminativists have quietly transformed themselves into advocates of the sane view that talk at the level of mentality (psychology) ought to be constrained by realistic assumptions at the level of brain science.[19]

But of course, and again, these doubts and denials did not have the consequence that consciousness was ignored. On the contrary: to raise a doubt
about the existence of consciousness is ipso facto to bring the question of
consciousness into prominence (compare the raising of doubts about the
existence of God or Nazi death camps). Doubt and denial kept questions
about consciousness right at the forefront of attention, as other philosophers duly argued back in fierce defence of consciousness.

The central confusion

I have suggested that the denial of the existence of consciousness is a
uniquely 20th-century phenomenon. Some, however, think that it is old. A
famous remark by Democritus, nearly 2,500 years ago, is sometimes
quoted in support of this view. Democritus was a materialist or physicalist, like many today (I use the words "materialism" and "physicalism"
interchangeably, although there is more to the physical than matter), and
he was reported by Galen, in the 2nd century, as having said: "There seems
to be colour, there seems to be sweetness, there seems to be bitterness. But
really there are only atoms and the void."

The most natural way to take this remark is as a comment on the
so-called secondary qualities, the familiar claim that qualities like sweetness and redness are not really objective properties of objects like strawberries: they are really just qualities of our subjective conscious experience of certain objective properties of strawberries. Understood in this
way, Democritus' remark is not any denial of the existence of consciousness. On the contrary: it presupposes the reality of consciousness and
derives all its force from that. It has nevertheless also been taken to be an
outright denial. After all, it comes down to us as the claim that "really
there are only atoms and the void", and nothing else.

But even if that way of understanding the remark were right, it would
not follow that Democritus was an early denier. For the quoted passage is
only half of an imaginary exchange Democritus stages between "The
Intellect" and "The Senses". The Intellect speaks first: "There seems to be
colour, there seems to be sweetness, there seems to be bitterness. But
really there are only atoms and the void." But then The Senses reply:
"Poor Intellect, do you hope to defeat us while from us you borrow your
evidence? Your victory is your defeat."[20]

The Senses point out that the evidence on which the Intellect draws in
making its claim is already enough to prove the falsity of the claim. This

is a decisive rejoinder, even before one appeals to one of the oldest points in philosophy: that the only thing one knows absolutely for certain (apart from the fact that one exists) is that one has conscious experience that has a certain character.

So much for the reply to the vainglorious Intellect. A similar move can be made in response to Dan Dennett, who is also a materialist (as I am myself). Dennett has suggested that "there is no such thing" as phenomenology, conscious experience in the present sense, and that any appearance to the contrary is, somehow, wholly the product of some cognitive faculty, a "judgment module" that does not itself involve any phenomenology. "*There seems to be phenomenology*," he concedes, "but it does *not* follow from this undeniable, universally attested fact that there *really is* phenomenology. This is the crux."[21]

It certainly is. It is the point at which it is clear either that Dennett has gone wrong or that he does not mean what his opponents mean by "phenomenology". For what he claims does not follow does indeed follow. As it stands, the claim by Dennett is necessarily false, because for there to seem to be phenomenology just *is* for there to be phenomenology. For it to seem to one that one is hearing a voice, seeing a room and so on, just *is* for there to be phenomenology. Such "seemings" *just are* phenomenological goings-on. To say that "there seems to be phenomenology but there isn't really any phenomenology" is like saying that there appear to be appearances but there aren't really any appearances. It is about as coherent as saying, "There's no such thing as truth, and that's the truth."

Descartes made the point very clearly in his *Second Meditation* in 1641. He does not simply argue *Cogito, ergo sum* (I am conscious, therefore I exist).[22] He adds the following, when developing his famous thought experiment, in which he imagines he is dreaming, and therefore cannot know that there is a real external world of tables and trees that exists independently of his mind:

I am now seeing light, hearing a noise, feeling heat. But I am asleep, so all this is false. Yet I certainly *seem* to see, to hear, and to be warmed. This cannot be false; what is called "having a sensory perception" is strictly just this.[23]

The hard problem of matter

I have great hopes that neuroscientists will get better and better at identifying the "neural correlates" of consciousness (although I think "correlates" is the wrong word, because I think these neural goings-on just are consciousness goings-on). But what they will do, in doing this, is make more and more clear the real mystery that confronts us when we consider the "mind–body problem" or "problem of consciousness". This is the mystery of the nature of matter, where by "matter" I mean physical stuff in general. Or rather, and more strictly speaking, it's the mystery of what matter is *if and in so far as it is not consciousness*, not literally constituted of consciousness.

There is, as I said earlier, a fundamental sense in which there is no problem or mystery of consciousness. We know exactly what consciousness is. We always have, because to have conscious experience is to know what it is: *the having is the knowing.* As Russell pointed out in 1940 in his *Inquiry into Meaning and Truth*, "there is a sense of 'knowing' in which, when you have an experience, there is no difference between the experience and knowing that you have it" – where this includes knowing what it is like.[24] We not only know exactly what particular types of experience are like, and therefore what they are (for what they are like, experientially considered, *is* what they are, experientially considered). We also know what experience is, *generally* considered, even though we have direct experience only of certain limited kinds of experience. It is precisely because we acquire an essentially general knowledge or understanding of what conscious experience is, simply in having conscious experience and in being the sophisticated concept-exercising creatures that we are, that we are able to speculate that there may be creatures – even, perhaps, other human beings – that have experience which is quite unlike ours, and is perhaps unimaginable by us.

So, once again, we know exactly what consciousness is, both in particular cases (to taste pineapple is to know what it is like to taste pineapple, as John Locke observed in 1689)[25] and in general. There is in this immoveable sense no problem of consciousness, and a fortiori no hard problem of consciousness.

The hard problem is the problem of matter. We know a great many facts about the *structure* of matter, facts which physics expresses with numbers and equations: $E = mc^2$, the inverse-square law of gravitational attraction, the periodic table and so on. But we have no idea about the intrinsic nature of the stuff that fleshes out this logico-mathematically expressible structure – except, of course, in so far as it is or involves consciousness, which we may do well to think of as a kind of stuff, a quantity. (There is an enormous quantity of conscious experience on this planet, whatever is going on elsewhere in the universe.)

I call this "the silence of physics". Stephen Hawking puts it dramatically in his book *A Brief History of Time.* He first observes that physics is "just a set of rules and equations". Then he asks: "What is it that breathes fire into the equations and makes a universe for them to describe?"[26] What is the intrinsic, non-structural nature of the physical stuff that is structured in the way physics reveals? We may correctly reply that it is *energy* that breathes fire into the equations, but then the question arises again: what is the intrinsic nature of this energy stuff? The answer is that we do not know – except in so far as it is consciousness. (All-out panpsychists think that the energy consists wholly of consciousness; their more moderate cousins think that it consists only partly of consciousness.)

This point about our ignorance of the ultimate non-structural, intrinsic nature of matter (in so far as it is something other than consciousness) is secure before we consider any of the details of what we cannot understand in physics: "dark matter", "dark energy" or the extraordinary phenomena of quantum mechanics. It is secure before the great physicists of our times have their say – Niels Bohr, for example ("Those who are not shocked when they first come across quantum theory cannot possibly have understood it"), or Richard Feynman ("I think I can safely say that nobody understands quantum mechanics") or John Wheeler ("If you are not completely confused by quantum mechanics, you do not understand it").

There is a fine irony in the fact that the theorists who are most likely to doubt or deny the existence of consciousness, continuing to insist that everything is physical and that consciousness cannot possibly be physical, are also those who are most insistent on the primacy of science. The irony consists in the fact that it is precisely science that hammers home the point that the ultimate intrinsic nature of the mass-energy that constitutes the universe is utterly unknown – unless it is itself consciousness.

The conclusion, in any case, remains. If everything is indeed physical, as I and many others believe, then consciousness is itself wholly physical. Physics cannot account for it, but that is no surprise and no objection. No one who has any real understanding of what physics is and does has ever thought that physics could lay bare the intrinsic, non-structural nature of things, or give us strong reason to think that consciousness itself is not wholly physical. Thomas Hobbes saw this in 1641, Margaret Cavendish in 1664. Anthony Collins saw it in 1707, Joseph Priestley saw it in 1777. Bertrand Russell made the key point very clearly in 1927: that "as regards the world in general, both physical and mental, everything that we know of its intrinsic character is derived from the mental side".[27] He held to this view until the end of his life: "We know nothing about the intrinsic quality of physical events except when these are mental events that we directly experience."[28] Here he fully endorsed the idea that conscious experience, in all its phenomenological richness, is a wholly physical matter, as physical as mass or charge.

It is a very remarkable fact that some have not only thought that accepting materialism requires one to doubt or deny the existence of consciousness (this is at least initially understandable) but have also then gone ahead and done so. For the only possible move to make, if one thinks that consciousness is incompatible with materialism, is to reject materialism – simply because the existence of consciousness is certain.

But one does not have to do this, if one is a full-on materialist. All one has to do is reject the mistake that got one into this position in the first place. This is the mistake of thinking that consciousness is incompatible with materialism, a mistake which is based in turn on the mistake of thinking we know the nature of the physical – and, in particular, know enough about it to know that consciousness cannot possibly be physical.

This, again, is why I speak of the *so-called* problem of consciousness. We know exactly what consciousness is. The only sense in which there is a problem of consciousness is the sense in which there is a problem about why anything exists at all: why is there something rather than nothing? This famous, seemingly unanswerable, cosmic question does, if you like, raise a problem. It indicates another fundamental thing that we do not understand. But there is in this case no special problem of consciousness. There can only appear to be an insolubly hard problem about how consciousness can be nothing more than goings-on in the brain if one makes an assumption one has no good reason to make: the assumption (which is usually tightly tied to the false view that physics tells us more than it does or can) that consciousness cannot be something material or physical. Descartes made this assumption in the 1630s, and nearly everyone has followed him ever since. Another fine irony in the debate about consciousness is that it is precisely those who are most inclined to disparage Descartes who are most powerfully committed to his mistaken assumption.

There is of course still a very great difficulty. It is the difficulty of understanding how the phenomena of physics and neurophysiology (the numbers, equations, measurements and quantities that physics and neurophysiology deal in) relate to the phenomena of conscious experience: the smells, the tastes, the emotions, the feels, the conscious thoughts. With the great German physician and physiologist Emil Du Bois-Reymond, I do not think there is any reason to believe that we will ever understand how these two things relate. *Ignoramus et ignorabimus*, he wrote in a famous paper published in 1872: we do not know and we will not (ever) know.[29]

This point must be acknowledged. But, again, it is not a problem about consciousness, about what consciousness is. It is a problem about the limits of our knowledge of the nature of matter. As for the old sweeping view that consciousness could not possibly be wholly physical, the most thoughtful thinkers have always recognised that this is entirely unwarranted – not only Hobbes, Cavendish, Collins, Priestley and Russell, whom I have already mentioned, but also Locke, David Hume, Immanuel Kant, Friedrich Nietzsche, Arthur Eddington, R. W. Sellars, A. N. Whitehead, Noam Chomsky and many others.

Yet a great many philosophers have failed to see it. And even those who have have been inclined to go on saying that consciousness is a mystery. But, again, consciousness is the only thing in concrete reality of which we can say that we know exactly what it is – because the having is the knowing. We are, as some say, "immediately acquainted" with it, simply in having it. We certainly do not know what matter is, by contrast, or physical stuff in general, except to the extent that consciousness is itself a form of physical stuff – as I believe it is.

So there is no mystery of consciousness. What we do not understand, what we find a mystery, is how conscious experience can be simply a matter of goings-on in the brain. But this is not because we do not know what consciousness is. It is because we do not know how to relate the *neurophysiology* to the things we know about the brain *simply in having conscious experience* – whose nature we know simply in having it.

1. G. Leibniz, 'Monadology', in Leibniz, *Monadology and Other Philosophical Essays*, trans. P. & A.M. Schrecker, Indianapolis, IA, Bobbs-Merrill, 1965 [1714–20], §20.

2. B. Russell, *An Outline of Philosophy*, London, Routledge, 1992 [1927], p. 287.

3. P.M. Churchland, *Scientific Realism and the Plasticity of Mind*, New York, NY, Cambridge University Press, 1979, p. 116.

4. M.T. Cicero, *De senectute de amicitia de divinatione*, trans. W. Falconer, London, Heinemann, 1923 [44BC], p. 119.

5. F. Bacon, *The New Organon*, trans. L. Jardine & M. Silverthorne, Cambridge, Cambridge University Press, 2000 [1620], §1.46.

6. M. Twain, *Autobiography of Mark Twain*, vol. 2, Berkeley, CA, University of California Press, 2013 [1906–07], p. 1336.

7. D. Kahneman, *Thinking, Fast and Slow*, New York, NY, Farrar, Strauss, Giroux, p. 211.

8. E.A. Singer, 'Mind as an observable object', *Journal of Philosophy, Psychology, and Scientific Methods*, vol. 8, 1911, p. 183. "More accurately," Singer continued, "our belief in consciousness is an expectation of probable behavior based on an observation of actual behavior, a belief to be confirmed or refuted by more observation, as any other belief in a fact is to be tried out."

9. B. Russell, *The Analysis of Mind*, London, George Allen and Unwin, 1921.

10. K. Lashley, 'The Behavioristic Interpretation of Consciousness I', *The Psychological Review*, vol. 30, 1923, p. 272.

11. C.D. Broad, *The Mind and Its Place in Nature*, London, Kegan Paul, 1925, p. 5.

12. E.G. Boring, 'The Nature of Psychology', in E.G. Boring, H.S. Langfeld & H.P. Weld (eds.), *Foundations of Psychology*, New York, NY, Wiley, 1948, p. 6.

13. G. Ryle, *The Concept of Mind*, Chicago, IL, University of Chicago Press, 1949.

14. B. Farrell, 'Experience', *Mind*, no. 59, 1950, pp. 170–98.

15. T. Nagel, 'What is it Like to be a Bat?', in Nagel, *Mortal Questions*, Cambridge, Cambridge University Press, 1979 [1974], pp. 165–80.

16. Farrell, 'Experience', pp. 194–5.

17. P. Feyerabend, 'Explanation, Reduction and Empiricism', in *Realism, Rationalism and Scientific Method*, Cambridge, Cambridge University Press, 1981 [1962] p. 19; R. Rorty, 'Mind–Body Identity, Privacy, and Categories', *Review of Metaphysics*, no. 19, 1965, pp. 24–54; U.T. Place, 'Is Consciousness a Brain Process?', *British Journal of Psychology*, vol. 47, no. 1, 1956, pp. 44–50; J.J.C. Smart, 'Sensations and Brain Processes', *Philosophical Review*, vol. 68, no. 2, 1959, pp. 141–56.

18. J. Searle, 'Minds, Brains, and Programs', *Behavioral and Brain Sciences*, vol. 3, no. 3, 1980, pp. 417–24; F. Jackson, 'Epiphenomenal Qualia', *Philosophical Quarterly*, vol. 32, no. 127, 1982, pp. 127–36.

19. O. Flanagan, *The Problem of the Soul*, New York, NY, Basic Books, 2003, pp. 216–17.

20. Democritus, c.400BC, as reported by Galen; see J. Barnes, *The Presocratics*, London, Routledge & Kegan Paul, 1979, pp. 290–96.

21. D. Dennett, *Consciousness Explained*, Boston, MA, Little Brown, 1991, pp. 365–66.

22. "I am conscious" or "I am now having conscious experience" is the best translation of *cogito*, for Descartes generally uses the word to cover all conscious experiences, not just thinking.

23. R. Descartes, *Meditations* and *Objections and Replies* in *The Philosophical Writings of Descartes*, vol. 2, trans. J. Cottingham et al., Cambridge, Cambridge University Press, 1985 [1641], p. 19.

24. B. Russell, *An Inquiry into Meaning and Truth*, London, George Allen and Unwin, 1940, p. 49.

25. J. Locke, *An Essay Concerning Human Understanding*, ed. P. Nidditch, Oxford, Clarendon Press, 1975 [1689–1700], §2.1.6.

26. S. Hawking, *A Brief History of Time*, New York, NY, Bantam Books, 1988, p.174.

27. B. Russell, *The Analysis of Matter*, London, Routledge, 1992 [1927], p. 402.

28. B. Russell, 'Mind and Matter', in Russell, *Portraits from Memory*, Nottingham, Spokesman, 1995 [1956], p. 153.

29. E. Du Bois-Reymond, 'On the Limits of Scientific Knowledge', *Popular Science Monthly*, vol. 5, 1874 [1872].

CONSCIOUSNESS AND THE BRAIN

CONSCIOUSNESS REDUX

Michael S. Gazzaniga

Twenty years ago, Sir Francis Crick presented a powerful lecture at the Society for Neuroscience reminiscing on the nature of conscious experience. The usual issues surrounding the concept of consciousness were trotted out, including a lively tape-recording of a conversation he had once had with Sir John Eccles. Eccles wanted something more than the brain to be involved. Crick was happy to consider only the neuroscience of conscious experience. Perhaps Eccles had in mind an idea such as that held by the philosopher Hao Wong, to whom the mind seemed able to do many more things than a brain could possibly compute. Nonetheless, the lively exchange between Crick and Eccles trailed off into a plea by Crick to journalists: "Stop writing about the topic of consciousness as there is really nothing new to say!" He went on, unabashedly, to report his own thoughts about the role of the visual cortex in conscious experience.

At the core of all such discussions lies the assumption that there is not only a neuroscience of consciousness but also a neuroscience of human consciousness. It is as if something terribly new and complex happens as the brain enlarges to its human form. Darwin, who thought the difference between man and other animals a matter of degree and not kind, would have disagreed. Whatever consciousness is, whether something terribly new or just a lot more of something, it triggers our capacity for self-reflection, for lingering moments … for, well, listening to Francis Crick on this important matter.

Along with his protégé Christof Koch, Crick worked hard to launch a paradigm of sorts, what they called Neural Correlates of Consciousness (NCC).[1] A body of interesting work has come from this formulation. For example, brain areas have been found which are associated with the conscious changes easily noted under conditions of binocular rivalry (in which perception alternates between different images presented to each eye).[2] A more recent discovery was that activation can be seen at the

"

columnar level (ie, a group of neurons associated with a specific bodily receptive field) in a motion-detection task.[3]

Crick's approach, however, has collected its critics. Richard Aslin recently observed:

> It is obvious that all aspects of consciousness must be mediated by the brain – what else controls mental states? So the search for "neural correlates of consciousness" has become a cottage industry, as if knowing that brain area X or connectivity Y is correlated with consciousness will be revealing of their causal influence. But how? Does consciousness require specific brain structures? Surely it must involve millions of structures as a whole host of factors correlated with consciousness influence many brain structures. By analogy, no one claims that "age" is a causal agent in human development – age is a proxy for a whole host of variables that are correlated with age. So too, no one should claim that "consciousness" is a causal agent in mental life – consciousness is a proxy for a whole host of variables correlated with our mental lives.[4]

The working assumption of 21st-century science is that brain neurons interact in some complex way to generate mental states. The rich history of neuroscience has revealed how the simplest reflex arc gathers information from the sensory world and transforms it into movement – neuron to neuron to neuron. Even the more complex analysis of how sensory information aggregates into triggering percepts is understood, as well as how it ultimately contributes to higher-level decisions for action. In all of this, somehow local neural circuits carry out Herculean tasks.

We marvel at how non-mental elements (neurons) produce our subjective mental lives. The gap between discussing neuronal interactions and the reality of subjective experience is challenging, if not dumbfounding. Indeed, we do not seem to know what an explanation and its vocabulary would even look like.

Nevertheless, we continue to produce startling science in the setting of this puzzle that has never been cracked. How does the very divisible physical brain, with its billions of parts, produce a seemingly indivisible and unitary function: the mind? How do we get self-consciousness, or consciousness of being conscious? And, finally, how do we get subjective experience, that "what it is like to be, well, me" feeling?

Leibniz pointed out 300 years ago that observing all the parts of a mill interacting does not illuminate what a mill does. And so it goes with the brain. Leibniz invited his readers to imagine they were walking through a huge brain, seeing all the actions up close and personal, and from that trying to deduce where conscious thoughts were to be found. Leibniz was not satisfied with pointing out this problem. He was also one of the first to raise the issue of perception versus apperception – a thought versus a thought about a thought.

In the intervening 300 years, not much progress has been made in integrating the physical brain based on neurons and seemingly ephemeral mental states. We are still walking around the brain and pointing at parts, albeit with extraordinary new imaging tools, and trying to answer the same questions. Nonetheless, neuroscientists soldier on finding out more and more exquisite details about physical brain circuits, while Crick and Koch, and in advance of them Singer, Sperry, Eccles and Mackay, to mention a few, have all taken cracks at tying neural processes to mental states.[5] While the philosophers keep pointing out the persistent gaps in the descriptions that attempt to grasp one level of organisation (neurons) by explanations in another (mental states), the challenge to understand the phenomenon of consciousness in biological terms will not go away. (Neither will the philosophers.)

In spite of this challenge, few intellectual partisans are absorbing each other's knowledge and something has got to give. This lack of a true exchange between disciplines underlines the wisdom of the old Polish proverb, "Not my circus, not my monkeys." If the explanatory gap between the mind and the brain is to be closed, then mind/brain research is in desperate need of a new framework. Maybe thinking like an engineer might help.

The architecture problem

There are two main avenues to explore identifying the type of architecture the brain inhabits, which allows its parts to yield the phenomenon of conscious experience, and capturing an emerging fact from neuroscience: that the brain works locally. It is not a big computer: it is a gazillion little computers, each capable of a specific function and of grabbing the spotlight in taking temporary command for its moment of consciousness, before receding into the background. Given this stream of different circuits randomly contributing to consciousness, the chaos must be unified into a coherent story.

On my first point, the architecture, we need to focus on what we mean by conscious experience. As Aslin has pointed out, consciousness is really a proxy concept for a multitude of cognitive capacities we humans enjoy. More specifically, it is the awareness we have about the spectrum of specific capacities we possess as a species, not the capacities themselves. Yet that awareness and/or feeling does, however, come with the capacity; each has that dimension wired into it.

We do not normally function in an orderly, sequential way, one event neatly following a related one. We zigzag. We have feelings about one idea, then its opposite, then our family, then the coming meeting, then the grocery list, then the irritating colleague, then the sports team … until we learn, almost against our natural being, to have a linear thought. As we all know, conscious linear thinking is hard work. Our mind, with its huge number of small computers, is like a bubbling pot of water. Which bubble will make it to the top at any given moment is hard to predict. The top bubble ultimately bursts, only to be replaced by more bubbles. The surface is forever energised with activity, until the bubbles go to sleep. The bubbles bursting in air through time become our stream of consciousness.

Unfortunately, for the endeavour of neuroscience to understand consciousness, we are mesmerised by the driving metaphor of our time: that inside any major organisation there is a boss, or in our case a consciousness agent, that makes the big decisions. Find that person, that brain structure, study it and there might be a good chance of figuring out how consciousness works, the myth suggests.

The metaphor, however, is weak at best. One chief executive after another will freely say that this is not how a company works. Common remarks include, "Well, I would like to do so-and-so but my managers won't let me", "My board won't let me do that" and "Times have changed, society won't allow that". The layers that surround the level of the "decider" constrain and modulate, as parts of the mechanism for collective action. The same goes for the brain: there is no top dog always calling the shots.

On layering

The brain is not a general-purpose computing device with an executive in charge. It is a collection of circuits devoted to quite specific capacities. This is true for all brains. What is wonderful about the human brain is that we have untold numbers of these specialised capacities. We have more than the chimp, which has more than the monkey, which has more than the cat, which runs rings around a lizard. There is a distinction between the specific capacities a species has and feelings about those capacities – which brings us to layered systems.

Trying to understand what something is and how it works requires establishing the basic architecture of the object. To understand a simple clock, one needs to think in terms other than that one wheel connects to a spring, then to that wheel and so on. Something needs to be known about the overall structural design and how the structure contributes to its function. Try to describe how to build a clock by only describing how parts interact at a local level – and, pretty quickly, it would become evident that other concepts are needed to capture what is happening. One is "layering", where each architectural layer has different functional responsibilities.[6]

In computer science, layering is how all networks are conceptualised. In general terms, there are seven layers, with control passing from one to another in a "stack": from the applications, working with data, down through six other layers to the physical layer, working with bits. This is called the Open System Interconnection (OSI) model; it defines a framework to implement protocols (a set of rules governing the exchange of data) to coordinate the different actions of the seven layers.

A clock is organised into five layers: energy, wheels, escapement, controller and time indicator. Seeing the device in terms of layers shows us how all mechanical clocks work. First, a clock needs energy, so a spring needs to be wound up; that energy has to be stored and then slowly released. Secondly, wheels distribute the energy throughout the clock. Thirdly, escapement mechanisms stop the energy from escaping all at once. Fourthly, the controller mechanism controls the escapement function. Finally, all of this comes together with the fifth layer that indicates the time. Notice, as one moves up through the layers, that each one does not predict the functional role of the next: the energy layer has nothing to do with the escapement layer and so on.

Without the organising idea of layers, it would be extremely difficult to describe how a simple mechanical clock works or to build one. Over time, just as the clockmaker has figured out which parts work best, which size to use, which leveraging system to use, which wheels and springs, and so on, natural selection has done the same for our brains.

For John Doyle, a control and dynamic systems scientist at Caltech, the biological world has simple layered systems, like bacteria, and multi-layered systems, like us:

Once a certain level of layering is achieved (eg you have a good enough operating system, the system that coordinates the layers interacting) then it becomes easier to add layers ... So sociality can be fairly easily added to animals that have flexible enough nervous systems and has been very successful (ants, wolves, lions, hyenas, elephants, dolphins, orcas, chimps, humans) ... and the "social" features are all a layer on top of the layers that create the individual ... "Consciousness" seems to be a layer that can be added once certain basic cognitive capabilities are there, and I'm guessing it arises in everything to varying degrees, simply as the ability to reflect on the layers below and have meta planning (planning what to plan) and other "meta" capabilities ... bacteria clearly have a rudimentary consciousness in my mind ... they evaluate their own state and their environment and make long term plans (sporulate versus try to get some new genes from the environment)[7]

At the first annual Francis Crick Memorial Conference, Philip Low, David Edelman and Christof Koch signed the declaration which stated:

The absence of a neocortex does not appear to preclude an organism from experiencing affective states. Convergent evidence indicates that non-human animals have the neuroanatomical, neurochemical, and neurophysiological substrates of conscious states along with the capacity to exhibit intentional behaviors. Consequently, the weight of evidence indicates that humans are not unique in possessing the neurological substrates that generate consciousness. Non-human animals, including all mammals and birds, and many other creatures, including octopuses, also possess these neurological substrates.[8]

While it is nearly impossible to think of bacteria having consciousness, can there be any doubt that a rat, at the moment of copulation, is as fulfilled as a human? Of course it is. Does a cat not enjoy a good piece of cod? Of course it does. And does a monkey not enjoy a spectacular swing? Again, it has to be true.

Each species has special capacities enabling some kind of rudimentary consciousness. So what is human consciousness? It is the very same awareness, save for the fact that we can be aware of so much more, so many wonderful things. There is a circuit then, perhaps a single system – or, more likely, one that is duplicated over and over again – that is associated with each capacity a brain possesses. The more systems a brain possesses, the more the awareness of capacities.

With its specialised circuits arising from natural selection, the brain is not a unified neural net supporting a general problem-solving device – and so we have to explain how consciousness appears so unified. We are also driven to focus on the possibility that there are smaller, more manageable circuits involved in producing reflexive awareness of a species' capacities. Were we to hold on to the notion of a unified neural net, we could only understand human conscious experience as the complex interactions of billions of neurons – a hopeless task.

Local origins of conscious experience
As alluded to above, we need to capture better the emerging sense from neuroscience that the brain works locally. If it is indeed a collection of specialised and local systems, the unity that is created could be disrupted and the mind divided. If its parts were to be separated, the specialised systems aggregated in the separated parts could be individually conscious. Indeed, if the two hemispheres of the brain were separated, each could have its own conscious status. The evidence supports this and so consciousness – in its many meanings, from wakefulness to *qualia* (instances of conscious subjectivity) – is divisible, and the phenomenon is tied to brain structures. Consciousness is not some non-material "psychic mist" or mystical aura. Somehow the brain in all of its complexity – neurons, glia and more – generates an awareness of the capacities that inhabit the part of the brain that has been isolated. What is striking is that such an isolated part of the brain, which used to coexist with another, does not seem to "miss" the latter following disconnection or damage: the left brain of a split-brain patient does not miss the right brain after disconnection surgery and vice versa.

Think of a duplex. The two sides of the house share some parts (the plumbing or electricity) but not others (the heating or roof). And if the heating breaks down in one half of the duplex, the lighting in either part is not affected. Even if one side of the duplex becomes empty or is torn down, the other can remain to house the family that always lived there. Should we really talk about a single thing with a single function in the case of the brain, any more than in the case of a duplex?

Imagine fixing one's eye on a point in the middle of a cinema screen. The film unfolds with images appearing on either side of the mid-point miraculously coming together in the brain as a unified image. One is conscious of it all and, in particular, of the fact of *being* conscious of the whole visual scene. That is how we are built.

Now, imagine the following: fix on the same point, but now only everything to its right is visible. That is how it would look to a split-brain patient: only visual information in the right half of space gets into the left hemisphere. The information from the left side is being projected to the right hemisphere and because of the surgery is no longer accessible to the left brain. What is so startling is that "the interpreter" in the left hemisphere does not even "comment" on the fact it no longer has conscious awareness of the left side of space – in short, the left brain does not miss the right brain! It is as if the very idea that one might be conscious of that part of physical space is located only in the very structures that normally process the visual information from it. Those multiple modules working on the retinal/geniculate input, from the eye and facial nerve, over in the right hemisphere have their own something in their local circuit organisation that can make that part of space conscious. It is a bewildering idea.

Now imagine a Martian is waving from behind. One would not see it and certainly not be conscious of it: out of sight, out of mind. Now, if one had undergone split-brain surgery, that Martian could walk from behind all the way up on the left to just before the point on which one's vision was fixed. The right hemisphere would see the Martian; the left hemisphere would not – it would not be conscious of the Martian at all. Only the circuits managing that part of space in the right hemisphere would be locally conscious of the event: half of the brain would know about the Martian, but half would not! Once again our personal intuitions and notions fool us. Conscious experience is not a construction of the whole brain, working in some coordinated way.

Can consciousness be disrupted? This question follows from the assertion that consciousness is generated by the brain. If one thinks consciousness is *a* function, rather than a proxy for lots of functions aggregated under one descriptor, then searching for its physical location seems sensible. If, however, after reading Aslin's critique, one adopts what I will call the Conscious Spectrum Disorder (CSD), then a disruption can occur in one domain but not another of the same brain. Take when one fails to call up to consciousness the name of someone visible to the eye, about whom one knows everything. What is gone is not consciousness in general but consciousness with respect to one of the gazillion functions of the brain, being managed by a very local circuit. When consciousness is viewed as pixelated and one of the pixels is down, the rest flows on.

Take the more extreme case of someone with global aphasia. Such patients do not understand the spoken word and are not capable of uttering a coherent thought. Their ability to solve the simplest cognitive problems is hugely impaired. Yet walk into their hospital room and they smile, stand up and walk with agility. They can ride a bike. They can be alert and no one would say they are not conscious. In the pixelated view, lots of pixels are still working and each one can be conscious. Stamping out all the contributors to consciousness, a term that is now the proxy for multiple capacities, is nearly impossible, unless one injures the brainstem structures.

What is it like to be an x in a distributed layered system?
Thomas Nagel's famous question remains central to any theory about the structure of conscious experience.[9] Having insight into what it would be like to be a bat, Nagel's original question, sets a parameter on the *subjective* dimension of being an organism with a limited and prescribed set of capacities different from our own – that thorny issue of consciousness. His clever question left me thinking about within-species variations and I have often wondered what it would be like to be a mathematician. The realisation that I will never know does not necessarily make me a reductionist (or feel diminished). As my father once said, when I queried him on what his mental life was like after he had suffered some strokes, "Mike, you work with what you got." The argument that consciousness can be associated with each domain of experience, part of only that domain and not part of another, seems to capture the vast array of clinical phenomena commonly seen, such as in patients who have lost brain function as a result of strokes and tumours.

The idea that an aggregate of distributed modules, of subsystems, can function by themselves, by local rules and mechanisms, and yet produce something bigger than themselves (with no central planning) can be seen in any number of ways, in the lab and in nature. Take recent lab work by

Justin Werfel at the Wyss Institute at Harvard.[10] He demonstrated how local rules, guiding independent agents (tiny robots), can result in a complex product, such as a bridge. He was inspired by seeing how ants could build huge mounds, with each ant, of course, not knowing anything about the larger plan. Each was zipping around independently, following some kind of rule over and over again, which, if followed, resulted in the larger product getting built.

Humans can design systems to do the same thing, which is what Werbel does. He takes tiny robots and gives them a couple of simple traffic rules on what to do when they run into each other. Before you know it, they are all acting in a seemingly coordinated way to build a bridge. It seems phantasmagoric, but that is what is happening. Independent mindless elements are building something bigger than themselves by simply following local contact rules. It is all about local gossip, not central planning.

Similar simple guidance rules are seen in nature with flocks of birds, for instance. There is no honcho goose leading the migration: that position is constantly being rotated. Even humans follow local rules when crowding into a subway station. And any outfielder running to catch a flying ball will follow a simple geometric rule within only the visual system. Coordination at a very local level allows for larger dynamic behaviour – and coordination of multiple local brain circuits can produce more than expected, more than the sum of their parts.

Now consider mesh networks. These have a design (topology) which differs from normal computer networks. Instead of each node having to connect to the internet, the nodes can connect to each other, yielding a mesh with only one node having to reach out to connect to the net. It is highly decentralised, which makes it enormously useful for creating communication in sparsely developed areas. The mesh topology is also resistant to the single-point-of-failure problem: if one node fails, the others take up the slack almost instantly. There are many more advantages to decentralised organisation: a collaborative, redundant backup for information; the ability to configure routes of communication dynamically; lower power requirements, and greater network reliability because of the option always to use different nodes.

Now think of that mesh network as one layer in an overall structure in which many interact. We can see how elements at one level can, within their layer, function in a definable way. Moreover, those elements are simultaneously setting the stage for another layer. The next layer can take the previous layer's output and use it as only one element of a larger plot, fulfilling the goals of the new layer. As layers increase, so does the sophistication of the organism, with each layer adding flexibility and independence of action.

The abstracted (virtualised) self
The idea of layers brings with it the idea of abstraction. More precisely, layered architecture brings the idea of virtualisation. Doyle points out:

> One of the popular buzzwords is Network Function Virtualization, and by this it is meant that the network is no longer thought of as being just pipes, but diverse and distributed computing, communication, and storage functions, and also sensing and actuation … The point of NFV is to virtualize all these resources, just like an OS does on your laptop, so it all looks like one machine to you … This is quite different than the original Internet which was dumb pipes connecting smart edge systems, which had to provide all resources and functionality other than connectivity[11]

Virtualisation occurs through abstraction, which seems essential, and several theoretical and experimental biologists are thinking about it. David Krakauer put it this way:

> The basic idea is that B, the micro, physical level, gives rise to A, the macro, mental layer. While A is wholly made from B, A has its own language, and we speak in that language and avoid talking about underlying stuff in B that makes up A. Another way of saying it is that A is an *abstraction* of B and becomes the new level we think about, indeed have access to. And everything we implement in A, we are causing stuff to happen at the B level.[12]

The computer setting is a good way to think about abstractions and virtualisation and how layers interact. When software programmers use a computer language, say Lisp, they do not programme all the electrons flying around in the transistors. They deal with the next level of abstraction, the programming macros, which, when given a command, make those electrons snap to attention. These provide a virtualisation of reality that is simpler and easier to conceive and control.

Similarly, when one thinks to move an arm, one is not dealing with the gazillion electrons or even millions of cells that must work in an exquisite way to do so. One's own mental commands are an abstraction riding atop all those pesky underlying realities. And the vocabulary one must use to understand realistically how the arm moves is going to be the language of the abstraction used for the virtualisation, not the language of the individual neurons.

Vernon Mountcastle, one of the fathers of modern neurophysiology, identified an enduring truth about the nervous system over 40 years ago. He noted that the brain, at every level, is a storyteller:

> Each of us believes himself to live directly within the world that surrounds him, to sense its objects and events precisely, and to live in real and current time. I assert that these are perceptual illusions. Sensations are set by the encoding functions of sensory nerve endings, and by the integrating neural mechanics of the central nervous system. Afferent nerve fibers are not high-fidelity recorders, for they accentuate certain stimulus features, neglect others. The central neuron is a storyteller with regard to the nerve fibers, and it is never completely trustworthy, allowing distortions of quality and measure, within a strained but isomorphic spatial relation between "outside" and "inside." Sensation is an abstraction, not a replication, of the real world.[13]

The same split-brain research that revealed the stunning differences between the two hemispheres also revealed that the human left hemisphere has a special module, "the interpreter", and it is a storyteller too. Its duties are to provide an interpretation of our behaviour, of our responses, whether they be cognitive or emotional, to environmental challenges. The interpreter looks outwards as well as inwards and tries to bring both together into a single story. It establishes a further layer, and the narrative it creates is the abstraction which engenders the appearance of psychological unity.

The interpreter is yet another system delivered to the human brain through natural selection. It generates a running narrative of our actions, emotions, thoughts and dreams which makes the best sense out of them all. The interpreter is not, however, a hidden chief executive: it is more like a secretary taking minutes, trying to patch the boss's wayward thoughts into a coherent letter. It is the glue that keeps our story unified and creates our sense of being a unified, rational agent. It brings to our bag of individual instincts the illusion that we are something other than what we are. It builds our theories about life and ourselves, and these narratives of our past behaviour ooze into our awareness as well. It does a lot, but it does not make us conscious. Conscious feelings come from the multiple bubbles coming up from our vastly modularised brain, each being conscious in its own way. The interpreter, just like a great politician, tries to give the votes of the modules a coherent voice. To mimic the greatest words ever spoken in America, "and that consciousness of the modules, by the modules, for the modules, shall not perish from the mind" (Mountcastle).

In this view, the problem of consciousness strikes me as tractable. Find the common and perhaps simple enabling neural circuits, the fire under each species' bubbling pot of specific capacities, which allow vertebrates to be aware of those capacities, and the problem will be harnessed. The same simple enabling circuits present in the rat are most likely present in the human brain. In this way, the neuroscience solution to the problem of consciousness, of which Crick dreamed, will move beyond a correlation and become a mechanism. We humans can then revel in the fact that what makes us so grand is that the basic common circuit design has so much more to enliven in our human brain. With the spectacular advances in cellular analysis, the goal to close the gap between mind and brain seems achievable.

1. F. Crick & C. Koch, 'A Framework for Consciousness', *Nature Neuroscience*, vol. 6, no. 2, 2003, pp. 119–26.

2. A. Maier et al., 'Introduction to Research Topic – Binocular Rivalry: A Gateway to Consciousness', *Frontiers in Human Neuroscience*, no. 6, 2012, p. 263.

3. R. Goebel, personal communication.

4. R. Aslin, personal communication.

5. Crick & Koch, 'A Framework for Consciousness'; W. Singer, 'Neuronal Synchrony: A Versatile Code for the Definition of Relations?', *Neuron*, no. 24, 1999, pp. 49–65; R.W. Sperry, 'Toward a Theory of Mind', *Proceedings of the National Academy of Sciences*, no. 63, 1969, pp. 230–1; J.C. Eccles (ed.), *Brain and Conscious Experience*, New York, NY, Springer-Verlag, 1966; D.M. MacKay, *Behind the Eye*, ed. V. MacKay (based on the 1986 Gifford Lectures), Oxford, Basil Blackwell, 1991.

6. M.S. Gazzaniga, *Tales from Both Sides of the Brain*, New York, NY, Ecco, HarperCollins, 2015.

7. J.C. Doyle, personal communications, 2009–present. See also J.C. Doyle & M. Csete, 'Architecture, Constraints and Behavior', *Proceedings of the National Academy of Sciences*, vol. 108, supp. 3, 2011, pp. 15624–30.

8. See text at http://fcmconference.org/img/CambridgeDeclarationOnConsciousness. pdf (accessed 29 December 2015).

9. T. Nagel, 'What is it Like to be a Bat?' *The Philosophical Review*, vol. 83, no. 4, 1974, pp. 435–50.

10. J. Werfel, K. Petersen & Radhika Nagpal, 'Designing Collective Behavior in a Termite-Inspired Robot Construction Team', *Science*, vol. 343, no. 6172, 2014, pp. 754–58.

11. J. Doyle, personal communication.

12. Quoted in M.S. Gazzaniga, *Who's in Charge? Free Will and the Science of the Brain*, New York, NY, Ecco, Harper Collins, 2011.

13. V. Mountcastle, 'Dean's Lecture', *Johns Hopkins Medical Journal*, no. 136, 1974, pp. 109–31.

Recovery of consciousness after brain injuries

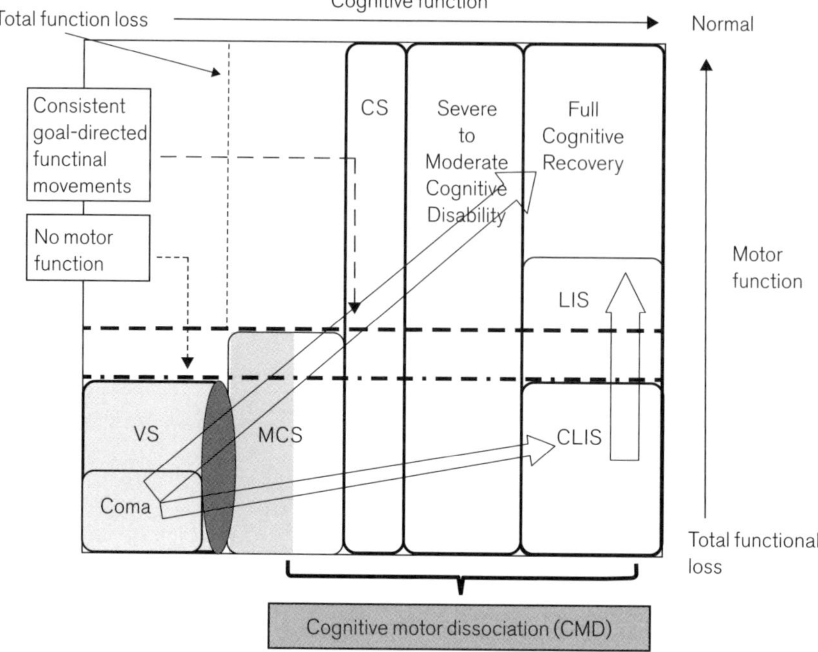

Figure 1. Recovery of consciousness after brain injuries. The distinctions among clinical disorders of consciousness are represented on two axes comparing the degree of impaired cognitive function with the degree of bedside demonstration of motor function. The light grey zone encompassing coma, vegetative state (VS) and the left half of the minimally conscious state (MCS) region (corresponding to MCS, that is, evidence of non-reflexive behaviours without evidence of command-following) shows patients with cognitive motor dissociation (CMD). CMD is a clinical syndrome operationally defined as having behavioural examination consistent with coma, VS or limited non-reflexive behaviours seen in MCS patients and concurrent demonstration of command-following utilising novel ("active paradigm") fMRI, EEG or similar technologies. CMD indicates that a wide range of uncertainty exists regarding the ultimate underlying cognitive capacity (marked by inverted bracket) such patients present. It is not possible to judge independently levels of consciousness across the range of VS to the complete locked-in state (CLIS) in any given CMD patient without methods allowing the patient to both initiate and respond to communication.

The bottom left of the figure indicates the functional equivalence of coma and VS as unconscious brain states in which no behavioural evidence of consciousness is present and both cognitive and motor function are absent (VS differing from coma by presence of intermittent eyes-open periods). Coma and VS are placed to the left of the vertical dotted line indicating total loss of cognitive function and below the interrupted line indicating no motor function. The dark grey oval between coma/VS and MCS indicates a transition zone where limited fragments of behaviour untied to sensory stimuli may be observed. Evidence of unequivocal but potentially intermittent behaviour indicative of consciousness marks the MCS. Recovery of consistent goal-directed behaviours defines the emergence from MCS above the upper interrupted line. Recovery patterns include the confusional state (CS), in which patients cannot be formally tested using standard neuropsychometric measures and remain disorientated, yet exhibit a limited range of cognitive functions. Locked-in state (LIS) designates normal conscious awareness but severe motor impairment, limiting communication channels typically to eye movements. CLIS indicates normal cognitive function without motor function.

EMERGING CHALLENGES IN THE STUDY OF RECOVERY OF CONSCIOUSNESS FOLLOWING SEVERE BRAIN INJURIES

Nicholas D. Schiff

Emerging scientific discoveries have shown that recovery of consciousness following severe brain injuries may occur over long time periods. The biological mechanisms underlying the recovery process are very slowly coming into focus and yielding important insights relevant to the management of patients with severe brain injuries and to our understanding of how consciousness arises and is maintained in the human brain.

Two related but distinct problems frame this research area (Figure 1). The first and most general problem (green arrow) is: how does the brain recover its capacity to support consciousness after a very severe injury that typically produces coma as the initial condition? Recent studies support the view that the processes underlying recovery of consciousness show strong similarity across different types of structural brain injury and reflect common cellular and circuit mechanisms.[1] In some individuals, recovery of cognitive functions can be strongly dissociated from motor recovery, resulting in inaccurate assessment of their cognitive capacities.[2] This situation frames the second, related problem: the potential for individuals with high levels of cognitive function but without evidence of a potential communication system to be misidentified as remaining in the vegetative state or minimally conscious. These problems importantly combine in the risk that the recovery process in a patient with severe injuries to the motor systems can go unnoticed (blue arrow).

Even if complete cognitive recovery follows, current technologies cannot identify it and allow two-way communication for such individuals, to demonstrate that they are effectively locked-in (black arrow).

This chapter begins with a consideration of slow functional recoveries from severe brain injuries in terms of common mechanisms of cerebral dysfunction that arise at the neuronal population level. Available data are organised by a "mesocircuit" hypothesis, which predicts specific roles for different brain structures and changes in brain dynamics that may arise over time during the recovery process. Within this framework, several studies provide evidence of these predicted mechanisms underlying functional transitions, as widely damaged brain networks gradually (or abruptly) become capable of supporting conscious behaviours of varying complexity. The difficulties that can arise in interpretation of results of recent functional neuroimaging studies, which operationally identify varying levels of awareness, memory and other higher brain functions in patients who do not show behavioural evidence of these cognitive capacities, are also reviewed here. Identifying retention of high-level integrative activity in such patients through measurement alone can be seen as an extremely challenging problem. Some of the interpretative ambiguities and the implications for understanding human consciousness in the injured brain and its recovery are highlighted by recent studies. Finally, the chapter provides pointers in the direction of meeting the challenges of emerging knowledge in this research area.

Disorders of consciousness
Figure 1 organises the relationships among several clinical syndromes often lumped into the category of "disorders of consciousness". The distinctions can best be captured in a two-dimensional presentation, comparing degrees of impairment of cognitive and motor functions. At the bottom left of Figure 1, coma and vegetative state (VS) are both considered unconscious brain states, as judged by the bedside behavioural examination. In both syndromes, patients are entirely unresponsive to environmental stimuli and fail to initiate goal-directed behaviours. Comatose patients show no state variations and usually have closed eyes and do not respond to the most vigorous stimulation. In VS, patients recover irregular cycles of eye opening and closure, which does not correlate with identifiable electroencephalographic features of sleep or normal wakefulness. To the right of VS on the diagram is the minimally conscious state (MCS), a syndrome in which patients demonstrate unequivocal but inconsistent evidence of awareness of self or the environment through a wide variety of behavioural response patterns that can be demonstrated at the bedside. The functional boundary indicating emergence from MCS is the demonstration of reliable verbal or gestural communication, typically assessed using a short set of "yes"/"no" questions linked to simultaneously presented stimuli. The interrupted lower line denotes the lack of any motor response at the bedside.

At the extreme right of the figure, some fully conscious patients can display a behavioural profile completely consistent with deep coma: eyes closed and unresponsive to any external stimuli as judged by a bedside examination. This condition is defined as the complete locked-in state (CLIS; far right bottom of Figure 1). CLIS is not a disorder of consciousness: by definition, CLIS patients retain total preservation of cognitive function. Locked-in state (LIS) is a similar condition, which typically arises from neurological injuries that selectively disrupt the motor pathways or slowly impair the function of motor neurons. In both instances the probability of this diagnosis is raised by the clinical context. LIS is only identified, however, when a consistent motor output channel is available to establish communication. Conversely, the complexity of structural brain injuries that include damage to the corticothalamic system creates a highly problematic set of patients, who are unable to produce consistent goal-directed movements that allow for communication yet nonetheless may harbour a high level of cognitive function and self-awareness. The lightly shaded grey box in Figure 1 denotes a particular subset of patients who demonstrate behavioural profiles of VS or MCS (the latter restricted to non-reflexive behaviours, such as tracking, while lacking a capacity to follow commands) and yet fMRI or electrophysiological evidence of command following. This group of patients can be referred to using the term "cognitive motor dissociation" (CMD), which has a precise operational definition that marks exactly this dissociation between measured bedside behaviour and laboratory investigations. CMD captures the ambiguity in establishing the actual level of cognitive capacity in any individual patient for whom such a dissociation is demonstrated. Importantly, the capacity to follow commands, as indicated by fMRI or electrophysiological mental imagery methods, does not guarantee the capacity to use such methods to communicate, as discussed below. Moreover, establishing an accurate understanding of cognitive capacity in any individual ultimately requires that they are able to initiate communication independently, as well as respond to queries. The term CMD, as used to identify a distinct clinical entity, has the further advantage of reducing the misdiagnosis of vegetative state in patients with evidence of well-preserved corticothalamic function.

Common mechanisms underlying the recovery process

Although severe brain injuries may impair consciousness through a very wide variety of underlying mechanisms, clinical observations have consistently demonstrated that loss of consciousness involves bi-hemispheric cerebral dysfunction.[3] Recovery of consciousness following such brain injuries has been purported to result generally from restoration of activity across a well-defined mesocircuit within the anterior forebrain. This circuit is particularly vulnerable to the effects of multifocal deafferentation (or interruption), whether structural or functional.[4]

Briefly, the mesocircuit hypothesis (Figure 2) starts with the basic observation that all severe brain injuries share the common substrate of widespread functional impairment or loss of neurons across the forebrain. Multifocal injuries across neocortical, striatal and thalamic neurons will have maximum impact on the survival or function of neurons within the central thalamus.[5] A primary consequence of loss of driving inputs to these neurons is a marked reduction of global synaptic background activity, across the entire corticothalamic system.[6] The overall impact of this reduced brain background activity is a sharp reduction in cerebral metabolic rate, which is considered the common denominator of all disturbances of consciousness following severe brain injuries. In the context of such broad reductions of neuronal activity across the brain, the anterior forebrain mesocircuit is predicted to be specifically affected by two core interacting effects. Most important is dysfunction of the neurons of the central thalamus.

These neurons are unique in both their anatomical connectivity and their functional role in the forebrain. Anatomically, they provide the shortest point-to-point connections across the entire corticothalamic system and are positioned to suffer the greatest impact of multifocal deafferentation.[7] Functionally, the neurons within the central thalamus play a key role in regulating arousal; within the wakeful state they adjust overall levels of activity in the frontostriatal systems to respond to challenges of increasing cognitive load, stress or fatigue.[8] Thus, a reduction in the output of these neurons withdraws powerful modulatory, excitatory inputs from the cortex and striatum. A second, related mechanism is expected to result from the dependence of the output neurons of the striatum on the background firing rate of inputs from the thalamus and the cortex. Under conditions of broadly decreased background activity these neurons will shut down.[9] They will then fail to inhibit the globus pallidus interna,

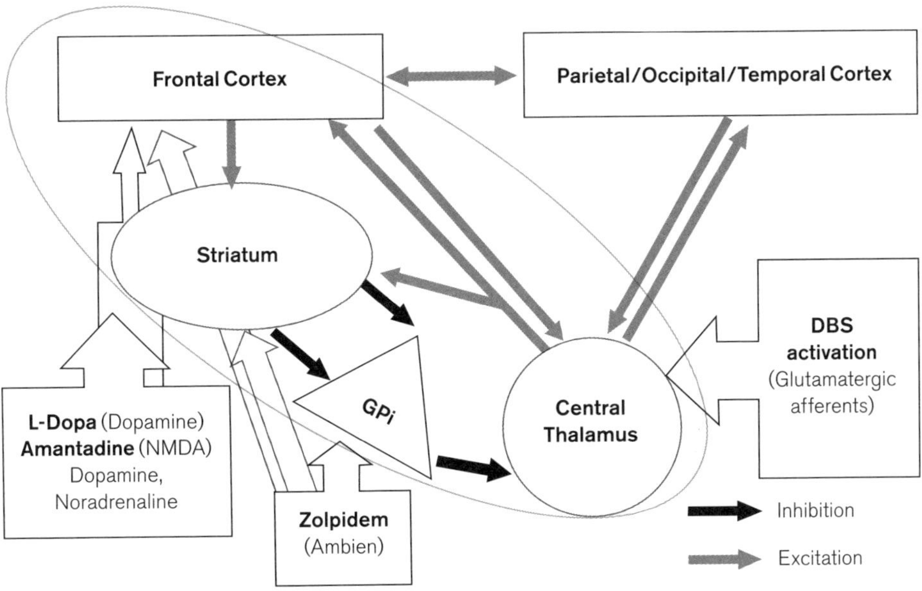

Figure 2. The mesocircuit hypothesis (Schiff & Posner 2007; Schiff 2010; Brown et al. 2010; Williams et al. 2013; Fridman et al. 2014; Schiff et al. 2014) proposes that, based on known pathologic changes after different types of multifocal brain injuries (eg, trauma, hypoxia, or multifocal ischemia), reduction of central thalamic outflow to cortex and striatum following deafferentation and loss of neurons in central thalamus withdraws important afferent drive to frontal cortex and the striatum (adapted from Schiff 2010). Impact across the frontal cortical systems is maximal because of the density of central thalamic projections and a contribution from a failure of output neurons in the striatum to reach firing threshold because of their requirement for high levels of synaptic background activity (Grillner et al. 2005). This model suggests that across widely varying brain-injury patterns changes in the EEG and cerebral metabolism should consistently associate with behavioural recoveries. Several studies provide support for this general hypothesis (Fridman et al. 2014; Forgacs et al. 2014; Williams et al. 2013; Lutkenhoff et al. 2015).

which provides a strong inhibitory input to the central thalamus, further reducing the contribution of the latter to functional activation of the forebrain.[10]

The mesocircuit hypothesis makes specific predictions about multi-focal structural injuries producing disorders of consciousness on cerebral metabolic profiles and affecting patterns of resting electrophysiological activity. Several studies have verified some of the predictions of this model.[11] Lutkenhoff and colleagues showed that tissue atrophy within the basal ganglia and thalamus was systematically negatively associated with clinical measures of awareness and wakefulness.[12] Bulk activation of the anterior forebrain mesocircuit likely underlies the impact of several pharmacological interventions and central thalamic deep-brain stimulation on some patients with severe brain injuries.[13] As shown in Figure 2, many different pharmacological interventions have been found to be effective in improving behavioural responsiveness in some severely brain-injured patients, including the dopaminergic agonists (or dopamine stimulators) bromocriptine, apomorphine, L-DOPA and amantadine.[14] Dopamine activity is the other dominant modulator of the output neurons of the striatum and the mesocircuit model predicts that activation of the anterior forebrain may arise when there is sufficient input to turn on a deafferented striatum, releasing outflow from the central thalamus.

Amantadine, which has a mixed set of pharmacological effects, is the only medication shown to be consistently effective in improving behavioural function in disorders of consciousness.[15] Its effect as an N-Methyl D-Aspartate (NMDA) antagonist (or inhibitor) may be the most powerful and cause it to act like ketamine, which produces broad cortical excitation.[16] Amantadine may produce bulk activation of the mesocircuit via a combination of NMDA antagonism and dopaminergic as well as noradrenergic agonism.[17] Schnakers and colleagues demonstrated that effective amantadine response in an MCS patient was reliably associated with broad increases in cerebral metabolism in medial and lateral frontal cortical regions.[18] The paradoxical phenomenon of behavioural facilitation in some severely brain-damaged patients administered the sedative zolpidem (a $GABA_A$ $\alpha1$ positive allosteric modulator) may reflect a similar multiplicity of sites of action across the mesocircuit (Figure 3). Effects of zolpidem may critically include suppressing an overactive pallidal inhibition,[19] direct modulation of cortical and striatal neuron populations, and

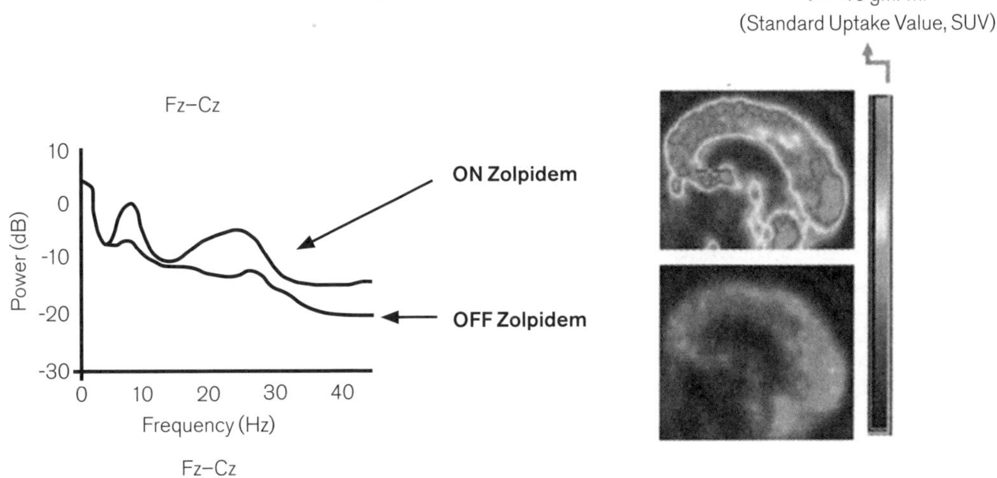

Figure 3. Marked changes in the electrical activity and cerebral metabolic rate of a severely brain-injured subject with administration of zolpidem. A paradoxical recovery of behavioural function (verbal fluency, swallowing and chewing, motor control) correlates with changes in EEG rhythms shown as power spectra (mean and 95 per cent confidence intervals, blue: average spectral power in the hour prior to zolpidem dose; red: 20–60 minutes after the zolpidem dose. A narrow, low-frequency spectral peak is apparent in the pre-drug state that is attenuated in the hour post-dose. The "mesocircuit" mechanism accounts for the induction of a broad activation of the anterior forebrain with zolpidem (Williams et al. 2013; Schiff 2010). A doubling of global cerebral metabolic rate is seen in association with the ON zolpidem state as measured by positron emission tomography imaging (right panels).

possibly even ephaptic (adjoint rather than synaptic) excitation of axon.[20]

Bulk activation of the anterior forebrain mesocircuit can also be achieved via direct activation of the glutamatergic afferents of the central thalamus, with consequent behavioural improvements in cases of severe brain injury.[21] In a single-subject study, activation of midline central regions, measured by evoked responses obtained using direct brain stimulation (DBS), showed that effective contacts generated bilateral patterns of activation of the electroencephalogram in fronto-central and fronto-temporal electrodes.[22] Of note, evoked cerebral activity from the human central thalamus also showed localised activation of electrodes over the medial parietal cortical regions in this subject, supporting the strong functional connectivity between the anterior forebrain mesocircuit and medial parietal cortex through the central thalamus discussed above.[23]

The effects of graded reduction of activity level across the anterior forebrain mesocircuit also fit with evidence vis-à-vis fronto-parietal activity level, particularly resting activity within the posterior medial complex of the parietal cortex, in cases of brain injury of varying degrees of severity. Fernandez-Espejo and colleagues reported that diagnostic categories of disorders of consciousness can be stratified by diffusion tensor imaging (DTI) of connections between the thalamus and the posterior medial complex (PMC),[24] an area known to correlate metabolic activity with outcomes in disorders of consciousness.[25] Anatomical and physiological studies show that the central thalamus and the posterior medial cortical regions have strong functional connections.

*Identification of high-level cognitive function in braininjured
subjects without bedside evidence of such capacity*

A very important recent advance has been the development of novel functional magnetic resonance imaging (fMRI) and electroencephalograpy (EEG) techniques to test levels of cognitive capacity in individual subjects with severe brain injuries. fMRI and EEG paradigms in which subjects are asked to carry out specific mental tasks ("active" paradigms)[26] allow evidence of volition and awareness to be identified in some patients with disorders of consciousness. As noted above, these studies have led to the identification of a new and probably specific syndrome, CMD. Owen and colleagues first reported such an unambiguous demonstration of dissociation of motor function and cognitive capacity in a

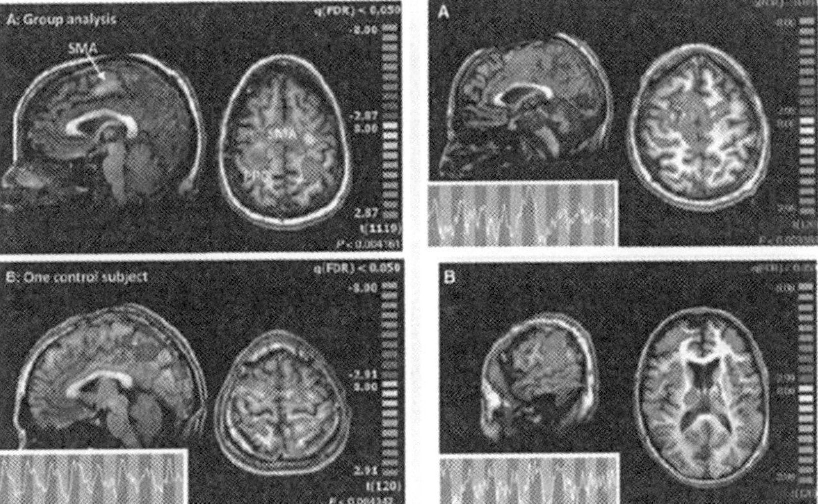

Figure 4. fMRI activations to command "imagine yourself swimming" task. Left panel: (A) Group analysis of the command-following task in normal subjects. The average response of nine subjects asked to imagine themselves swimming. Areas of activation are predominantly in the supplementary motor area, partially extending laterally into the premotor areas, and parts of the posterior parietal cortex; (B) Single control subject result for command-following. Right panel: (A) Patient response demonstrating activations in supplementary motor area; (B) Parietal cortex (from Bardin et al. 2011).

patient diagnosed as in VS, following a vehicle accident, who showed no evidence of motor command-following at the bedside.[27] In the study, the patient was asked to imagine playing tennis repeatedly, with intervening rest periods, while the fMRI signal was acquired. Activation was observed, immediately after the command to participate in the task, in the supplementary motor area of the frontal lobe, a location found consistently to show responses in healthy volunteers independently tested by the investigators. Many different "active" or "command following" paradigms have been validated in severely brain-damaged patients using fMRI, EEG or related techniques, including event-related potentials (measuring brain responses to a specific event) and electromyography (detecting electrical responses in muscles).[28] Minor adaptations of this approach have been applied to a small number of brain-injured subjects, to assess the utility of an fMRI-based communication system.[29] Monti and colleagues tested a single subject with a clinical diagnosis of VS who showed a capacity to use two different fMRI-generated responses to provide answers to a set of simple yes and no questions. (The subject was reclassified to MCS after these positive fMRI signals of command following, leading to an exhaustive search for additional clinical signs of awareness.)[30] Bardin and colleagues studied a small cohort of six patients (obtaining retesting results in three) but found that the presence of fMRI-based command-following signals did not in fact guarantee the potential for the patient to use these signals for reliable and consistent communication.[31] In two of their tested subjects, despite a capacity to generate fMRI-based command-following signals, fMRI activations could not be demonstrated to support communication. The investigators provided test-retest confirmation of this dissociation of positive fMRI command-following but negative fMRI communication in one of these two subjects.

In another of the subjects, an unusual result exposed the difficulty of identifying intermediate responses in patients with severe brain injuries and interpretative challenges that will arise in this context. In this subject a clear response to use a motor-imagery signal (imaging swimming) to select one choice out of a sequence of four met statistical thresholds but selection of information (the suit or face of a playing card) appeared inaccurate on both experimental runs (Figures 4–5). This puzzling finding suggested the possibility that the brain responses in the subject were delayed, compared with those of normal controls. In a reanalysis of the

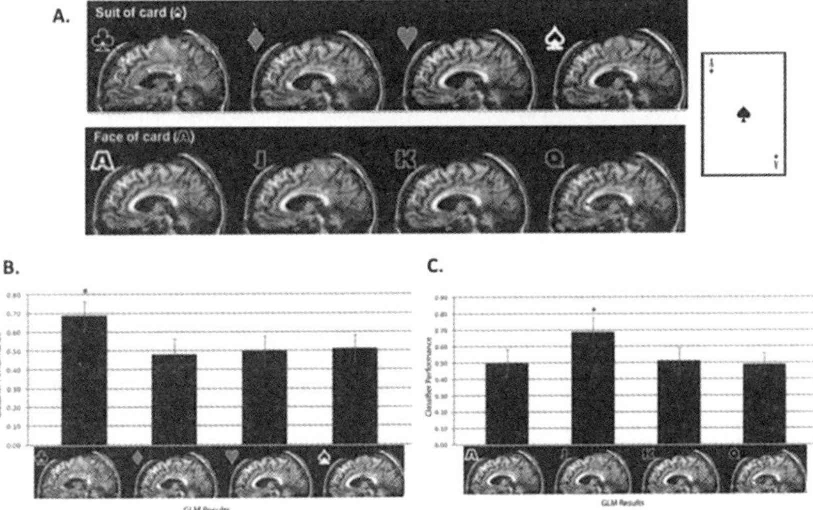

Figure 5. Disambiguation of ambiguous fMRI-generated patient responses to multiple-choice questions: (A) Multiple-choice communication task results from one normal subject who picked the ace of diamonds card (Bardin et al. 2011). This subject responded with rock-climbing imagery. The time course represents the blood-oxygen-level-dependent signal in the supplementary motor area cluster (suit) and the posterior parietal cortex (face), each in the region with the strongest blood-oxygen-level-dependent response. Patient response shows selection of two suits (club and ace) and one face (jack). The actual card picked for the clinical subject is ace of spades; (B) Use of a multivariate pattern classification of communication of card-suit data reveals that only the response to club suit is significant. Performance of the classifier is based on training on the patient's command-following data (see Figure 4) and tested on the face card data. The classifier criterion is the same for single selection in the face run (C). These findings support the likelihood that the patient accurately communicated the intended card (ace of spades) but showed a delayed response that shifted both runs one choice over in the sequence (see Bardin et al. 2012).

same data, use of a multivariate pattern classifier (or decoder) provided strong evidence for this hypothesis. These findings illustrate the complexity that patients with structural brain injuries present in terms of interpretation of intermediate results. Identifying the ability to produce mental-imagery, command-following signals in fMRI measurements nonetheless underscores a marked dissociation in CMD patients. Recent studies support the inference that when such capacities are retained brain function may be much closer to that of healthy controls and therefore such patients may be more like LIS patients than MCS. In a study of resting EEG activity in wake and sleep, Forgacs and colleagues found a strong correlation of positive fMRI-based command-following with widely preserved cerebral metabolic rates and the integrity of normal electrographic organisation of wake and sleep patterns.[32] Similarly, Stender and colleagues identified the presence of well-preserved cerebral metabolic activity in a large cohort of patients with evidence of fMRI command-following or behavioural evidence of consciousness consistent with MCS.[33] Future work is required to investigate further the content of awareness in such persons and to examine thoroughly their capacities to re-establish two-way communication through the use of brain–computer interfaces. As research efforts evolve to include patients with CMD in trials with brain–machine interfaces, it should be possible to grade variations in their cognitive capacities.

Conclusions

The "difficult middle" of measurements of brain function in human subjects recovering from severe brain injuries holds the great promise of increasing our understanding of mechanisms supporting consciousness in the human brain. As reviewed, the level of preservation function in the injured brain can be quite dynamic and specific cellular and circuit mechanisms may play a key role in recovery. Novel methods of assessment of conscious awareness have unveiled a surprisingly wide range of uncertainty as to diagnostic accuracy in modern medicine. Current studies, however, raise many interpretative ambiguities and many intermediate responses lack definitive interpretations at present.

Available evidence suggests that patient subjects who show imaging or electrophysiological evidence of motor imagery and/or communication are in a separate category, here described as CMD. Most likely, such subjects are closer to those in locked-in state. Importantly, it is only once patients can get to the point of initiation of communication that probing of the quality of consciousness is possible. To date, no study has shown recovery of a reliable augmentative communication channel (using any technique) to allow for initiation of communication in a patient with motor impairment consistent with VS or MCS, following structural brain injuries affecting the central nervous system.

1. N.D. Schiff, 'Recovery of Consciousness after Brain Injury: A Mesocircuit Hypothesis', *Trends in Neurosciences*, no. 33, 2010, pp. 1–9; N.D. Schiff, 'Mesocircuit Mechanisms Underlying Recovery of Consciousness Following Severe Brain Injuries: Models and Predictions', in M.M. Monti & W.G. Sannita (eds.), *Brain Function and Responsiveness in Disorders of Consciousness*, Cham, Springer International Publishing, 2016; S.T. Williams et al., 'Common Resting Brain Dynamics Indicate a Possible Mechanism Underlying Zolpidem Response in Severely Brain-Injured Subjects', eLife, 2:e01157, 2013, http://elifesciences.org/content/elife/2/e01157.full.pdf (accessed 14 December 2015); E.A. Fridman & N.D. Schiff, 'Neuromodulation of the Conscious State Following Severe Brain Injuries', *Current Opinion in Neurobiology*, no. 29C, 2014, pp. 172–77.
2. A.M. Owen et al., 'Detecting Awareness in the Vegetative State', *Science*, vol. 313, no. 5792, 2006, p. 1402; M.M. Monti et al., 'Willful Modulation of Brain Activity in Disorders of Consciousness', *New England Journal of Medicine*, no. 362, 2010, pp. 579–89; J.C. Bardin et al., 'Dissociations Between Behavioural and Functional Magnetic Resonance Imaging-Based Evaluations of Cognitive Function after Brain Injury', *Brain*, no. 134 (Pt 3), 2011, pp. 769-82; P.B. Forgacs et al., 'Preservation of Electroencephalographic Organization in Patients with Impaired Consciousness and Imaging-Based Evidence of Command-Following', *Annals of Neurology*, vol. 76, no. 6, 2014, pp. 869–79; N.D. Schiff, 'Cognitive Motor Dissociation Following Severe Brain Injuries', *JAMA Neurology*, no. 19, 2015, pp. 1–3.
3. See J. Posner et al., *Plum and Posner's Diagnosis of Stupor and Coma*, 4th edn., New York, NY, Oxford University Press, 2007, for a comprehensive review.
4. N.D. Schiff & J.B. Posner, 'Another "Awakenings"', *Annals of Neurology*, no. 62, 2007, pp. 5–7; Schiff, 'Recovery of Consciousness after Brain Injury'; E.N. Brown, R. Lydic & N.D. Schiff, 'General Anesthesia, Sleep and Coma', *New England Journal of Medicine*, no. 363, 2010, pp. 2638–50.
5. J.H. Adams, D.I. Graham & B. Jennett, 'The Neuropathology of the Vegetative State after Acute Insult', *Brain*, no. 123, 2000, pp. 1327–38; B. Jennett et al., 'Neuropathology in Vegetative and Severely Disabled Patients after Head Injury', *Neurology*, no. 56, 2001, pp. 486–90; W.L. Maxwell et al., 'Thalamic Nuclei after Human Blunt Head Injury', *Journal of Neuropathology and Experimental Neurology*, vol. 65, no. 5, 2006, pp. 478–88.

6. S. Laureys & N.D. Schiff, 'Coma and Consciousness: Paradigms (Re)framed by Neuroimaging', *Neuroimage*, vol. 61, no. 2, 2012, pp. 478–91. Epub 27 December 2011.

7. Maxwell et al., 'Thalamic Nuclei after Human Blunt Head Injury'; N.D. Schiff, 'Central Thalamic Contributions to Arousal Regulation and Neurological Disorders of Consciousness', *Annals of the New York Academy of Sciences*, no. 1129, 2008, pp. 105–18.

8. Schiff, 'Central Thalamic Contributions to Arousal Regulation and Neurological Disorders of Consciousness'.

9. S. Grillner et al., 'Mechanisms for Selection of Basic Motor Programs: Roles for the Striatum and Pallidum', *Trends in Neurosciences*, no. 28, 2005, pp. 364–70.

10. Schiff, 'Recovery of Consciousness after Brain Injury'.

11. Fridman & Schiff, 'Neuromodulation of the Conscious State Following Severe Brain Injuries'; Williams et al., 'Common Resting Brain Dynamics'; Forgacs et al., 'Preservation of Electroencephalographic Organization in Patients with Impaired Consciousness'.

12. E.S. Lutkenhoff et al., 'Thalamic and Extrathalamic Mechanisms of Consciousness after Severe Brain Injury', *Annals of Neurology*, vol. 78, no. 1, 2015, pp. 68–76.

13. Fridman & Schiff, 'Neuromodulation of the Conscious State Following Severe Brain Injuries'.

14. Fridman & Schiff, 'Neuromodulation of the Conscious State Following Severe Brain Injuries'; Schnakers et al., 'Measuring the Effect of Amantadine in Chronic Anoxic Minimally Conscious State'.

15. J.T. Giacino et al., 'Central Thalamic Deep Brain Stimulation to Promote Recovery from Chronic Posttraumatic Minimally Conscious State: Challenges and Opportunities', *Neuromodulation*, vol. 15, no. 4, 2012, pp. 339–49.

16. Brown, Lydic & Schiff, 'General Anesthesia, Sleep and Coma'.

17. Fridman & Schiff, 'Neuromodulation of the Conscious State Following Severe Brain Injuries'.

18. Schnakers et al., 'Measuring the Effect of Amantadine in Chronic Anoxic Minimally Conscious State'.

19. Schiff & Posner, 'Another "Awakenings"'.

20. See Williams et al., 'Common Resting Brain Dynamics', for a detailed discussion of these mechanisms and their relationship to mesocircuit components.

21. Fridman & Schiff, 'Neuromodulation of the Conscious State Following Severe Brain Injuries'.

22. N.D. Schiff, J.T. Giacino, K. Kalmar, J.D. Victor, K. Baker, M. Gerber, B. Fritz, B. Eisenberg, T. Biondi, J. O'Connor, E.J. Kobylarz, S. Farris, A. Machado, C. McCagg, F. Plum, J.J. Fins, A.R. Rezai, 'Behavioural improvements with thalamic stimulation after severe traumatic brain injury', *Nature*, vol. 448, no. 7153, 2007, pp. 600–3.

23. See Laureys & Schiff, 'Coma and Consciousness', for a further discussion.

24. D. Fernandez-Espejo et al., 'Role for the Default Mode Network in the Bases of Disorders of Consciousness', *Annals of Neurology*, no. 72, 2012, pp. 335–43.

25. Laureys & Schiff, 'Coma and Consciousness'.
26. Laureys & Schiff, 'Coma and Consciousness'.
27. Owen et al., 'Detecting Awareness in the Vegetative State'.
28. Laureys & Schiff, 'Coma and Consciousness'.
29. M.M. Monti et al, 'Willful Modulation of Brain Activity in Disorders of Consciousness', *New England Journal of Medicine*, no. 362, 2010, pp. 579–89; Bardin et al., 'Dissociations Between Behavioural and Functional Magnetic Resonance Imaging-Based Evaluations'.
30. Monti et al., 'Willful Modulation of Brain Activity in Disorders of Consciousness'.
31. Bardin et al., 'Dissociations Between Behavioural and Functional Magnetic Resonance Imaging-Based Evaluations'.
32. Forgacs et al., 'Preservation of Electroencephalographic Organization in Patients with Impaired Consciousness and Imaging-Based Evidence of Command-Following'.
33. J. Stender et al, 'Diagnostic Precision of PET Imaging and Functional MRI in Disorders of Consciousness: A Clinical Validation Study', *The Lancet*, vol. 384, no. 9942, 2014, pp. 514–22.

WHERE IS
CONSCIOUSNESS?

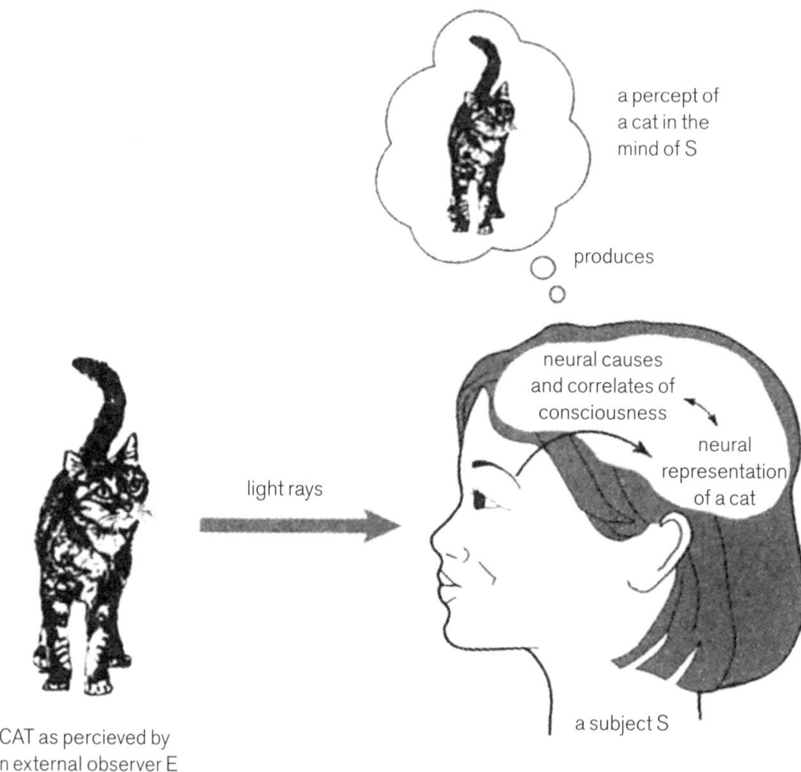

Figure 1. A dualist model of perception.

WHAT AND WHERE ARE CONSCIOUS EXPERIENCES? DUALISM, REDUCTIONISM AND REFLEXIVE MONISM

Max Velmans

Suppose I ask you to point at your experiences. According to Descartes, experiences are formed out of *res cogitans,* a substance that thinks, which has no location or extension in space. The material world is composed of *res extensa*, a substance that has both location and extension in space. If this is right, then one cannot really point at experiences, as they have no location. At best, one might be able to point at the place where conscious experiences interact with the material world. According to Descartes, this is at the pineal gland located in the centre of the brain.

Modern reductionist philosophers, in contrast, argue that experiences are nothing more than states or functions of the brain. It might be difficult to point with any precision at such states or functions, as they are likely to be distributed properties of large neuronal populations. Nevertheless, if one *had* to point at experiences, one would point at the brain.

Classical dualists and reductionists disagree vehemently about what conscious experiences are, but they agree (roughly) about where they are. In so far as experiences can be located at all, that location is somewhere in the brain. This, in turn, places experiences in a given spatial relationship to the external physical world.

Implicit in this debate is a dualist model of perception of the kind shown in Figure 1. This assumes perception to involve a simple, linear, causal sequence (viewed from the perspective of an external observer E). Light rays travelling from the physical object (the cat as perceived by E) stimulate the subject's eye, activating her optic nerve, occipital lobes and associated regions of her brain. Neural conditions sufficient for consciousness are formed and result in a conscious experience (of a cat) in the subject's mind. This model of visual perception is, of course, highly simplified, but for now we are not interested in the details. We are interested only in where external physical objects, brains and experiences are placed.[1]

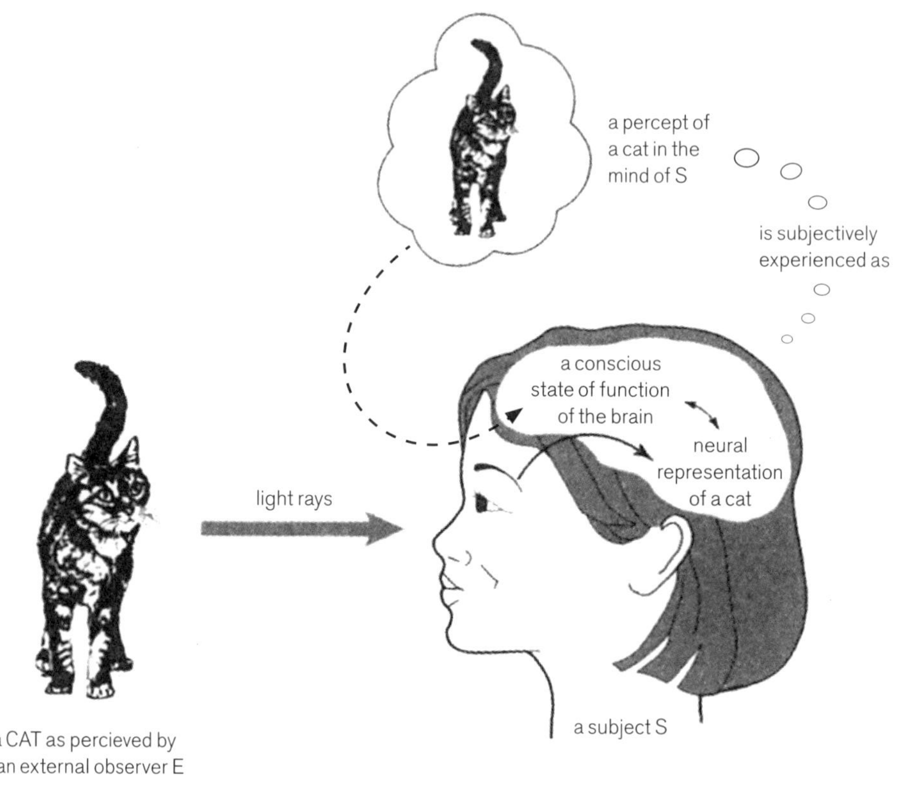

Figure 2. A reductionist model of perception.

It will be clear that there are two fundamental "splits" in this model. First, the contents of consciousness are clearly separated from the material world (the conscious, perceptual "stuff" in the upper part of the diagram is separated from the material brain and the physical cat in the lower part of the diagram). This conforms to Descartes' view that the stuff of consciousness (*res cogitans*, a substance that thinks) is very different from the stuff of which the material world is made (*res extensa*, a substance that has extension and location in space). Secondly, the perceiving *subject* is clearly separated from the perceived *object* (the subject and her experiences are on the right of the diagram and the perceived object is on the left of the diagram).

It is clear from this simple model why consciousness is often thought to elude scientific study. From E's perspective, the physical cat and the subject's brain are (potentially) visible; they appear to be public, objective and viewable from an external, third-person perspective. Consequently, a scientific study of cats and brains presents no philosophical problems. By contrast, S's experience of a cat seems to be private, subjective and viewable only from S's first-person perspective. If so, how can it form a datum for science?

Dualists have, traditionally, been content to accept that there may be aspects of human experience that are beyond science. However, the problems of assimilating such dualism into a scientific worldview are serious. So it is not surprising that 20th-century philosophy and science tried to naturalise dualism by arguing or attempting to show that conscious experiences are nothing more than states or functions of the brain. A reductionist model of visual perception is shown in Figure 2.

The causal sequence in Figure 2 is the same as in Figure 1, with one added step. While reductionists generally accept that the subject's experience of a cat seems to be insubstantial and "in the mind", they argue that science will eventually demonstrate that it is really a state or function of the brain. In short, the reductionist model in Figure 2 tries to resolve the split between conscious experience and the physical world by eliminating conscious experience or reducing it to something physical, which E can in principle observe and measure. That is, it tries to collapse how things appear from the subject's first-person perspective (the conscious experience of the cat) to the brain states (or functions) that can be observed from E's third-person perspective. But reductionism retains the split (implicit in dualism) between the observer and the observed. The perceived object (on the left side of the diagram) remains quite separate from the conscious experience of the object (on the right side).

A common-sense view of conscious phenomenology
I have argued that this debate about whether experiences reduce to states or functions of the brain starts in the wrong place.[2] Why? Because, in various ways, dualist and reductionist theoretical accounts of consciousness discount or deny the importance of the phenomenology of most ordinary experiences, thereby fostering a misleading impression about what it *is* that does, or does not, reduce to states of the brain. Most experiences neither appear to be a state of some non-extended substance that thinks, nor a state or function of the brain.

For Descartes, the prime exemplar of conscious experience is verbal thought ("I think, therefore I am") which manifests itself in consciousness in the form of phonemic imagery or inner speech, and it is true that *res cogitans* seems to describe the phenomenology of verbal thoughts fairly well. Thoughts do seem to be different from physical objects as perceived, as well as being observer-dependent, subjective, private, insubstantial and without a clear location and extension in space (although many would claim them to be loosely "in the head" or "in the brain").

But it is a mistake to extrapolate from one example of conscious experience to the whole of conscious experience. Let me illustrate with a very simple example. If you stick a pin in your finger, you will experience a sharp pain. Within philosophy of mind, pain is often regarded as a paradigm case of a conscious, mental event (it is private, subjective and so on). But where is this pain? Given their theoretical presuppositions, dualists and reductionists do not find this an easy question. For dualists, all experiences are rather like "thoughts", which are not really anywhere, while for reductionists, experiences are really neural states or functions distributed around the brain. However, if forced to point, they would point (vaguely) at the brain. I take this to be a very simple question with a simple answer: the pain one experiences is in the finger. If one had to point at the pain, one should point at where one feels the pain (where the pin went in). Any reader in doubt on this issue might like to try it.

Note that this sharp difference of opinion is about the location and extension of the pain experience, not about its antecedent physical causes: one would have identical physical deformation and damage to the skin, without the pain, if the finger were anaesthetised. Nor is this a dispute

	Ontological identity	Correlation	Causation
Symmetrical	yes	yes	no
Obeys Leibniz's law	yes	no	no

Table 1. The contrasts between correlation, causation and ontological identity.

about the neural causes and correlates of pain: the proximal neural causes and correlates of pain are located in the brain. But the neural causes and correlates of a given experience are not themselves that experience. In science, causes and correlates are not ontological identities (see Table 1).

Ontological identity is symmetrical: if *A* is identical to *B*, then *B* is identical to *A*. Ontological identity also obeys Leibniz's law: if *A* is identical to *B*, all the properties of *A* are also properties of *B* and vice versa. For example, over many centuries the morning star and evening star were thought to be different heavenly bodies, but were then discovered to have identical properties because they were actually the planet Venus (viewed in the morning or the evening). Correlation is also symmetrical: if *A* correlates with *B*, then *B* correlates with *A*. But correlation does not obey Leibniz's law: if *A* correlates with *B*, it does not follow that all the properties of *A* and *B* are the same. For example, height in humans correlates with weight, but height and weight do not have the same set of properties. Causation, by contrast, is asymmetrical: if *A* causes *B*, it does not follow that *B* causes *A*. If a rock thrown in a pond causes ripples in the water, it does not follow that ripples in the water cause the rock to be thrown in the pond. And causation does not obey Leibniz's law (flying rocks and pond ripples have very different properties).

The reason this is so important for an understanding of consciousness is that neuroscience can in principle discover the antecedent neural causes and co-temporal correlates of a given conscious experience, but it cannot in principle observe the phenomenology of the experience itself (in the form that this manifests itself to the subject). Given this limitation, and given the apparent differences between phenomenal and neural properties, there is no way for a purely third-person neuroscience to demonstrate observable, first-person, conscious experiences to be ontologically identical to their neural correlates and/or causes, and consequently nothing more than states or functions of the brain.[3]

A non-reductive, monist alternative

This does not of course rule out alternative, intimate, non-reductive relationships, as a simple example from physics illustrates. If one moves a wire through a magnetic field, this causes an electrical current to flow through the wire. Conversely, if one passes an electric current through a wire, this causes a surrounding magnetic field. The current is in the wire while its associated magnetic field is distributed in the space around the wire, just as the pain in the finger and its associated neural correlates appear to be located and extended in different places. But physics does not claim the magnetic field to be ontologically identical (or reducible) to its associated electric current. Rather these are thought to be two manifest aspects of electromagnetism, a more fundamental energy that underlies both, related in ways described by Maxwell's laws. A similar non-reductive monism may turn out to be the best way to understand the relationship of conscious experiences to their neural correlates.[4]

Why does the location of experiences matter?
Before one can understand any phenomena (scientifically or philosophically), one must first describe their phenomenology accurately, and the same applies to conscious experiences. In terms of its phenomenology, the pain really is in the finger and nowhere else. And this simple example demonstrates a general principle that leads one away from the dualist model in Figure 1 and the reductionist model in Figure 2, towards a "reflexive" model of how conscious phenomenology relates to the brain and the physical world.[5] The damage produced by a pin in the finger, once it is processed by the brain, winds up as a phenomenal pain in the finger, located more or less where the pin went in. That is why the entire process is called "reflexive". Figure 3 illustrates a similar process with a phenomenal cat. As before, an entity or event stimulates sense organs and initiates perceptual processing, although in this case the initiating entity is located beyond the body surface in the external world. As before, afferent neurons and cortical projection areas are activated, along with association areas, long-term memory traces and so on, and neural representations of the initiating event are eventually formed within the brain; in this case, neural representations of a cat.

But the entire causal sequence does not end there. *S* also has a visual experience of a cat and, as before, we can ask what this experience is like. In this case, the proper question to ask is: "What do you see?" According to dualists, *S* has a visual experience of a cat "in her mind". According to reductionists, there seems to be a phenomenal cat "in *S*'s mind" but this is really nothing more than a state or function of her brain. According to the reflexive model, and the broader "reflexive monism" which I develop elsewhere in my work, while *S* is gazing at the cat, her only visual experience of the cat is the cat she sees out in the world. If she is asked to point to this phenomenal cat (her "cat experience"), she should point not to her

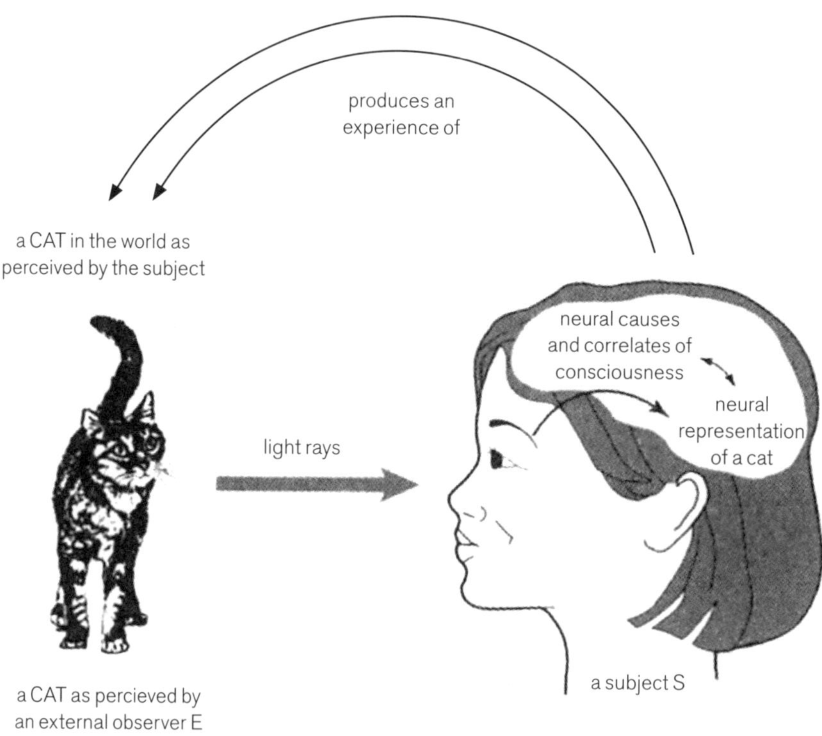

Figure 3. A reflexive model of perception.

brain but to the cat as perceived, out in space beyond the body surface. In this, the subject S is no different from E. The phenomenal cat "experienced" by S is as much out there in the phenomenal world as the cat "observed" by E. That is, an entity in the world is reflexively experienced to be an entity in the world.[6]

Of course, not all the entities and events we experience have such a clear location and extension in three-dimensional phenomenal space. Some experiences appear to be located on the surface of or internal to the body (touch and visceral sensations and so on) and are usually reflexively located where the stimuli that caused those sensations activated our sense organs. We also have "inner" experiences, such as verbal thoughts, images, feelings of knowing, experienced desires and so on. Such inner experiences really do seem to have a phenomenology of the kind described by Descartes. One might argue that verbal thoughts have a rough location, in that they seem to be "in the head" (in the form of inner speech) rather than in one's foot, or free-floating out in space, but they are not clearly located in the manner of pain and cats. However, the reflexive process is the same. The cognitive processes that give rise to thoughts, feelings of knowing and so on originate in the mind/brain, although these processes are unlikely to have a precise location in so far as they engage the mass action of large, distributed, neuronal populations. Consequently, in so far as these processes are experienced at all, they are reflexively experienced to be roughly where they are (in the head or brain).

There is far more to be said about conscious phenomenology and its relation to the brain and physical world. But even a cursory examination of what we actually experience poses a fundamental challenge to dualist and reductionist ways of characterising what it is that they need to explain. As noted, both dualism and reductionism assume experiences to be quite different from the perceived body and the perceived external world (perceived bodies and worlds are out there in space, while experiences of bodies and worlds are either "nowhere" or in the mind or brain). But the reflexive model suggests that, in terms of phenomenology, there is no actual separation between the perceived body and experiences of the body or between the perceived external world and experiences of that world. When one has a conscious thought, there is not some additional experience of a thought "nowhere", or in the mind or brain. Nor is there a phenomenal pain nowhere, or in the mind or brain in addition to the pain one experiences in the finger if one stabs it with a pin. And there is not a phenomenal cat nowhere, in the mind, or in the brain, in addition to the cat one sees out in the world. According to the reflexive model, this additional experience is a theoretical fiction, and that is why the dualist-versus-reductionist argument about the nature of this experience cannot be resolved. Applying Occam's razor gets rid of both the fiction and the argument.

But the reflexive model does not get rid of conscious phenomenology. Thoughts, pains and phenomenal cats are experienced to have very different qualities or *qualia*, along with different locations and extensions, but they are nevertheless aspects of what we experience. Together, such inner experiences, bodily sensations and externally experienced entities and events comprise the contents of our consciousness – which, together, form the constituents of our everyday phenomenal world.

Given that the reflexive model conforms closely to everyday experience, it should be easy to grasp the essence of the argument so far. Descartes' focus on thought as the prime exemplar of conscious experience led him to suggest that experiences are a state of "thinking stuff" that has no location and extension in space – and reductionists commonly agree that experiences *seem* to have such ephemeral qualities (that is why they want to give them a more secure ontology in states or functions of the brain). While I agree that thoughts and other "inner" experiences appear to have such qualities, most other experiences do not. On the contrary, most experienced phenomena seem to have a clear location and extension in phenomenal space.

To those immersed in dualist or reductionist modes of thought, this proposed expansion of the contents of consciousness to include those aspects of the phenomenal world that we normally think of as the "physical world" may seem radical and the notion that many experiences have at least a phenomenal location and extension might appear strange. But, thus far, this proposal is hardly new. In one or another form it appears in the work of George Berkeley, Immanuel Kant, C.H. Lewes, W.K. Clifford, Ernst Mach, Morton Prince, William James, Edmund Husserl, A.N. Whitehead, Charles Sherrington, Bertrand Russell and Wolfgang Köhler. In more recent times, similar analyses of what consciousness *seems* to be like have also been given by Karl Pribram, Antti Revonsuo, Steven Lehar, Michael Tye, Jeffrey Gray and Rupert Sheldrake.[7]

One insight, of course, does not make a theory. James, for example, is a "neutral monist", Whitehead is a "panpsychist, process theorist", Tye is a "direct-realist physicalist" and Revonsuo, Lehar and Gray are "biological naturalists" (a biological form of physicalism). The reflexive model I elaborate below (and the broader *reflexive monism* it exemplifies) differs in essential ways from each of these positions (although it also incorporates many shared elements).[8]

A reflexive model of how consciousness relates to the brain and the physical world

The reflexive model of perception suggests that all experiences result from a preconscious reflexive interaction of an observer with an observed. The resulting experiences can be subdivided into three categories:

(1) the experienced external world (the phenomenal world) which seems to have location and extension;
(2) the experienced body (the phenomenal body or body image) which seems to have location and extension, and
(3) "inner" experiences (thoughts, images, feelings of knowing and so on) which have no clear location and extension in phenomenal space, although they can be loosely said to be "in the head or brain".

Figure 3 (p. 156) illustrates one example of a reflexive interaction resulting in an experience (a visual percept) of a phenomenal cat. In this case, the initiating stimulus (the observed) is an entity located in space beyond the body surface, which interacts with the visual system of the observer to produce an experienced entity out in space beyond the body surface. As noted earlier, a similar reflexive interaction takes place when the initiating stimulus is on the surface of (or within) the body, or within the brain itself, to produce experienced entities and events on the surface of (or within) the body, or "in the head or brain" itself.

Following present conventions in the psychology of perception, I assume that the mind/brain constructs a "representation" or "mental model" of what is happening in the world, body or mind/brain itself, based on the input from the initiating stimulus, sensory-motor interactions with the world, expectations, traces of prior, related stimuli stored in long-term memory and so on.[9] Such mental models encode information about the entities and events they represent, in formats determined by the sensory modality they employ. Visual representations of a cat, for example, include encodings for shape, location and extension, movement, surface texture, colour and so on.

How do these neural encodings relate to the subject's visual experiences? I have suggested that the way information in a given mental model appears to be formatted depends on the observational arrangements.[10] The information encoded in the mental model appears in different forms to the subject (S) and the external observer (E), because the means available to S and E to gain access to the information in that mental model differ.

An external observer, inspecting a subject's brain, has to rely on his own exteroceptive systems (typically vision), aided by physical equipment (PET scans, fMRI etc). Viewed in this way (from this third-person perspective), a visual mental model in the subject's brain might appear in the form of neural activation in a series of relatively distinct feature maps distributed throughout the subject's visual system. We do not know precisely what is required to make such neural representations conscious. However, given the integrated nature of visual experiences, it is reasonable to assume that when such distributed neural activities do become conscious they must be bound together in some way, perhaps through synchronous 40-hertz oscillations.[11] We may also expect there to be observable (physical) influences on the pattern of activity embodied in the mental model from existing memory traces (corresponding to the effects of expectation, stored knowledge and so on). Whatever the detail turns out to be like, viewed from E's perspective, the information (about the cat) in S's mental model is likely to take a neural or other physical form. In terms of what E can directly observe of S's mental model, this is the end of the scientific story.

However, the observational arrangement by which the subject gains access to the information in her own mental model is entirely different. As with E, the information in S's mental model is translated into something she can observe or experience, but all she experiences is a phenomenal cat out in the world. While she focuses her attention on the cat she does not become conscious of having a "mental model of a cat" in the form of neural states. Nor does she have an experience of a cat "in her brain". Rather, she becomes conscious of what the neural states represent – an entity out in the external world. The information encoded in S's mental model (about the entity in the world) is identical whether viewed by S or by E, but the way the information appears to be formatted depends on the perspective from which it is viewed. In this respect, the reflexive model of perception adopts a dual-aspect theory of information.[12]

Let me illustrate with a simple analogy. Let us suppose that the information encoded in the subject's brain is formed into a kind of neural projection hologram. A projection hologram has the interesting property that the three-dimensional image it encodes is perceived to be out in space, in front of its two-dimensional surface, provided that it is viewed from an appropriate (frontal) perspective and it is illuminated by an appropriate (frontal) source of light. Viewed from any other perspective (from the side or from behind), the only information one can detect about the object is in the complex interference patterns encoded on the holographic plate. In analogous fashion, the information in the neural projection hologram is displayed as a visual, three-dimensional object out in space only when it is viewed from the appropriate, first-person perspective of the perceiving subject. And this happens only when the necessary and sufficient conditions for consciousness are satisfied (when there is illumination by an appropriate source of light). Viewed from any other third-person perspective, the information in *S*'s "hologram" appears to be nothing more than neural representations in the brain (interference patterns on the plate).

The projection hologram is, of course, only an analogy[13] but it is useful in that it shares some of the apparently puzzling features of conscious experiences. Viewed from an external observer's perspective, the information displayed in the three-dimensional holographic image is encoded in two-dimensional patterns on a plate, but there is no sense in which the subject's three-dimensional image is itself "in the plate". Likewise, according to the reflexive model there is no sense in which the phenomenal cat observed by *S* is "in her head or brain". In fact, the 3-D holographic image does not even exist (as an image) without an appropriately placed observer and an appropriate source of light. Similarly, the existence of the phenomenal cat requires the participation of *S*, the experiencing agent, and all the conditions required for conscious experience (in her mind/brain) have to be satisfied. Finally, a given holographic image only exists for a given observer, and can only be said to be located and extended where that observer perceives it to be. *S*'s phenomenal cat is similarly private and subjective. It can only be said to be out in phenomenal space beyond the body surface to the extent that she perceives it to be out in space beyond the body surface.

Perceptual projection

Unconscious mind/brain processes construct experienced realities in which our phenomenal heads appear to be enclosed within three-dimensional, phenomenal worlds, not the other way around. But the neural mental models that encode information about these 3-D experienced realities *are* "in the head or brain". Given this, how do phenomenal cats and other phenomenal objects which are perceived to be located and extended in space get to be out there? Nothing physical is projected by the brain: there are no light rays projected through the eyes to illuminate the world, contrary to the beliefs of ancient Greek thinkers such as Empedocles. Rather, "perceptual projection" is a psychological effect produced by unconscious perceptual processing.

Perceptual projection is an effect which requires explanation; it is not itself an explanation. The projection hologram has a number of features which might be usefully incorporated into a causal explanation of such effects, but it is not intended to be a literal theory of what is taking place in the mind/brain. Right now, we do not know exactly how it is done. Of course, not fully understanding *how* it happens does not alter the fact *that* it happens – and the evidence for perceptual projection in exteroception and interoception is all around us. We experience the phenomenal world and our experienced bodies to be outside our heads. We do not experience them to be inside our brains. How they come to be that way can be revealed by experimental studies. These address the sensory cues and neural systems that support normal, perceived spatial localisation and extension, the experience of depth in both the awake state and in vivid three-dimensional dreams, and anomalous or artificial forms of perceptual projection, such as the mechanisms responsible for phantom limbs, eidetic imagery,[14] visual hallucinations and the creation of virtual realities. These are well-established areas of research within experimental psychology and, as I have reviewed much of this evidence elsewhere, I will not repeat that here.[15]

Events as perceived versus Events as described by physics

It is important to stress that the analysis above applies only to the phenomenology of "physical" versus "mental" events. Indeed, having blurred the boundaries between "mental" and "physical" phenomenology, it becomes important to sharpen the distinction between the everyday "physical" events that we experience and these same events as described by physics (or other sciences). The events we experience result from an interaction of input energies and events with modelling processes in the mind/brain – and the consequent experiences represent what is going on in the world, body or mind/brain itself (in ways appropriate, no doubt, to biological evolution). Modern science, however, has developed representations of the world (in its laws, equations and other descriptions) that are, at times, very different to the everyday world as experienced (witness quantum mechanics and relativity theory). Events as experienced and events as described by physics can, of course, be related to each other through the study of psychophysics, and in this way we can learn something about the manner in which the events we experience represent the world that science describes.

The world as perceived is part of the contents of consciousness
Some initial principles that follow from the analysis above should now be clear. Within the reflexive model the physical world as perceived is part of the contents of consciousness. In its phenomenology, the contents of consciousness do not appear to be in some separate place or space "in the mind or brain". Indeed, in terms of phenomenology no clear separation exists between what we normally think of as the "physical world", the "phenomenal world", the "world as perceived" and our "experiences of the world". This does not mean, of course, that these terms have exactly the same meaning in all contexts. The term "physical world", for example, is ambiguous: in everyday life we commonly use it to describe the world as perceived, but in science the term usually refers to the world as described by physics (eg, by quantum mechanics and relativity theory), which may differ in major ways from the world as perceived. The physical world as perceived is just one (biologically useful) representation of the world that science describes. Nevertheless, with our eyes open, what we normally call the "physical world" is just what we experience, and there is no additional experience of the world "in the mind or brain". This is simple common sense.

If it turns out that experiences really are how they seem to be, this would be devastating for classical dualism, challenging the very basis on which Descartes splits the world. Inner experiences such as thoughts might have the character of *res cogitans* (thinking stuff without location and extension in space). But body experiences – pains, tactile sensations and proprioception (the sense of position and movement of body parts)

– have location and extension in 3-D phenomenal space, as do external experiences (sounds, visual objects and events as perceived), making them all part of *res extensa*. This analysis also places a heavy, added burden on reductionism, as it expands what would need to be reduced: not only would ephemeral thoughts, so-called percepts "in the mind" and the like, have to be reduced to states or functions of the brain, but the entire phenomenal world.

A first step on a road to a different place
The reflexive model of perception outlined above provides the first step on the road to reflexive monism, an analysis of consciousness as different from dualism and materialist reductionism as they are from each other. I have again developed this elsewhere,[16] but it should already be clear that the classical, dualism-versus-reductionism debate is based on untenable assumptions about the phenomenology of consciousness that they share. Descartes splits the universe into *res cogitans* and *res extensa*, and identifies *res cogitans* with consciousness. Materialist reductionism tries to heal this split by demonstrating *res cogitans* to be nothing more than a bit of *res extensa* (a bit of the brain). Yet, if we examine what we actually experience, it becomes obvious that much of it does not appear to be like *res cogitans*. Some phenomena we experience (pains and tactile, auditory and visual phenomena) appear to have a clear location and extension beyond or within our bodies, while others do not (thoughts, some images, feelings and so on). So Descartes' separation of *res cogitans* from *res extensa* does not separate what is "in consciousness" from what is not. The mind/brain models energies and events into experienced phenomena that have many different qualia and, together, these experienced phenomena form the contents of consciousness. These include phenomena that have experienced location and extension that we are accustomed to think of as "physical". Thus, there never was an unbridgeable divide separating "physical phenomena" from the "contents of consciousness". Physical objects and events as perceived are part of the contents of consciousness.

1. Figure 1 is deliberately oversimplified, as its only purpose is to illustrate the dualist separation of the objects we see in the external world from perceptual processing in brains and the consequent experiences of those objects. In particular, the figure does not make explicit (a) the distinction between objects as seen and objects themselves, and (b) the distinction between what can, in principle, be seen from E's perspective and what can only be inferred. The same applies to the contrasting models in Figures 2–3. Strictly speaking, (a) it is not the cat *as seen by* E that is the source of the light reflectances from its surfaces but the *cat itself*, and (b) while E can see the cat, measure the light reflected from its surface (with appropriate instruments), see the subject and examine the processes that take place in S's brain (again, with appropriate instruments), E can only infer the nature of S's experience on the basis of what S reports.

2. 'Consciousness, Brain and the Physical World', *Philosophical Psychology*, no. 3, 1990, pp. 77–99; 'A Reflexive Science of Consciousness', in G.R. Bock & J. Marsh (eds.), *Experimental and Theoretical Studies of Consciousness (CIBA Foundation Symposium 174)*, Chichester, Wiley 1993, pp. 81–99; *Understanding Consciousness*, London, Routledge, 2000; 'Reflexive Monism', *Journal of Consciousness Studies*, vol. 15, no. 2, 2008, pp. 5–50; *Understanding Consciousness*, 2nd edn., London, Routledge, 2009; 'Reflexive Monism: Psychophysical Relations Among Mind, Matter and Consciousness', *Journal of Consciousness Studies*, vol. 19, nos. 9–10, 2012, pp. 143–65.

3. There are many other difficulties for reductive materialism which I will not review here: see the extensive analysis in Velmans, *Understanding Consciousness*, chap. 3–5, or the detailed praise of recent advances in neuroscience, combined with a detailed critique of its reductive materialism, in M. Velmans' review of Stanislas Dehaene, *Consciousness and the Brain: Deciphering how the Brain Codes our Thoughts*, *Journal of Consciousness Studies*, vol. 21, nos. 11–12, 2014, pp. 178–96.

4. I do not have space to examine these non-reductionist, monist alternatives here, although I have done so in detail elsewhere: see 'Consciousness from a First-Person Perspective', *Behavioral and Brain Sciences*, vol. 14, no. 4, 1991, pp. 702–26; *Understanding Consciousness*; 'Reflexive Monism'. See also readings in M. Velmans & Y. Nagasawa, 'Introduction to Monist Alternatives to Physicalism', *Journal of Consciousness Studies*, vol. 19, nos. 9–10, 2012, pp. 7–18.

5. M. Velmans, 'Consciousness, Brain and the Physical World', *Philosophical Psychology*, vol. 3, no. 1, 1990, pp. 77–99.

6. In this situation there is (numerically) one cat itself, but there are two views of it, resulting in the phenomenal cat experienced by S to be out there in S's phenomenal world and the phenomenal cat experienced by E to be out there in E's phenomenal world.

7. K.H. Pribram, *Languages of the Brain: Experimental Paradoxes and Principles in Neuropsychology*, Englewood Cliffs, NJ, Prentice-Hall, 1971; K.H. Pribram, 'How is it that Sensing so Much can do so Little?', in F.O. Schmitt & F.G. Worden (eds.), *The Neurosciences Third Study Program*, Cambridge, MA, MIT Press, 1974; K.H. Pribram,

'Behaviorism, Phenomenology and Holism in Psychology: A Scientific Analysis', *Journal of Social and Biological Structures*, no. 2. 1979, pp. 65–72; K.H. Pribram, 'Consciousness Reassessed', *Mind and Matter*, vol. 2, no. 1, 2004, pp. 7–35; A. Revonsuo, 'Consciousness, Dreams and Virtual Realities', *Philosophical Psychology*, vol. 8, no. 1, 1995, pp. 35–58; A, Revonsuo, *Inner Presence: Consciousness as a Biological Phenomenon*, Cambridge, MA, MIT Press, 2006; S. Lehar, 'Gestalt Isomorphism and the Primacy of Subjective Conscious Experience: A Gestalt Bubble Model', *Behavioral and Brain Sciences*, vol. 26, no. 4, 2003, pp. 375–444; M. Tye, *Ten Problems of Consciousness: A Representational Theory of the Phenomenal Mind*, Cambridge, MA, MIT Press, 1997; M. Tye, 'Philosophical Problems of Consciousness', in M. Velmans & S. Schneider (eds.), *The Blackwell Companion to Consciousness*, Oxford, Blackwell, 2007, pp. 23–35; J. Gray, *Consciousness: Creeping up on the Hard Problem*, Oxford, Oxford University Press, 2004; R. Sheldrake, 'The Sense of Being Stared at. Part 2: Its Implications for Theories of Vision', *Journal of Consciousness Studies*, vol. 12, no. 6, 2005, pp. 32–49.

8. I give a detailed analysis of how Tye's physicalism and the biological naturalism developed by Revonsuo, Lehar and Gray compare and contrast with my own reflexive monism in Velmans, 'Reflexive monism'. *Journal of Consciousness Studies*, vol. 15, no. 2, 2008, pp. 5–50. and *Understanding Consciousness*, 2nd Edition, London, Routledge, 2009, chap. 7.

9. See I. Rock, *Indirect Perception*, Cambridge, MA, MIT Press, 1997.

10. M. Velmans, 'Consciousness from a First-person Perspective', *Behavioral and Brain Sciences*, vol. 14, no. 4, 1991, pp. 702–19.

11. See, eg, W. Singer, 'Conscious Processing: Unity in Time Rather than in Space', in S. Schneider & M. Velmans (eds.), *The Blackwell Companion to Consciousness*, 2nd edn., Chichester, Sussex, John Wiley & Sons, 2017.

12. This is a version of dual-aspect monism very similar to that first advocated by G.T. Fechner, *Elemente der Psychophysik*, Leipzig, Breitkopf & Härtel, 1860. It also bears a close resemblance to the dual-aspect theory of information later advocated by D. Chalmers, *The Conscious Mind: In Search of a Fundamental Theory*, New York & Oxford, Oxford University Press, 1996, in his defence of his own "naturalistic dualism".

13. Holography was proposed as a model of neural organisation and space perception by Pribram: *Languages of the Brain: Experimental Paradoxes and Principles in Neuropsychology*; 'How is it that Sensing so Much can do so Little?'; 'Behaviorism, Phenomenology and Holism in Psychology: A Scientific Analysis'. In 'Consciousness Reassessed', he developed the model and, interestingly, linked its consequences specifically to the reflexive monism I developed in Velmans, *Understanding Consciousness*, London, Routledge, 2000. Following Velmans, 'Consciousness, Brain and the Physical World', *Pilosophical Psychology*, volume 3, pp. 77–99 a similar holographic model was developed in Revonsuo, 'Consciousness, Dreams and Virtual Realities', volume 8, no. 1, 1995, pp. 35–8, although he interpreted this in a reductive, materialist way.

14. Eidetic visual images can have a vividness, clarity, detail and experienced location in external phenomenal space that resembles that of actual, visually experienced objects, even though they are entirely constructs of the mind.

15. 'Consciousness, Brain and the Physical World'; *Understanding Consciousness*, 2009, chap. 6.

16. See Velmans, *Understanding Consciousness*, 2000, 2009. More detailed analysis can be found in Velmans, 'Reflexive Monism', with some more recent theoretical developments in Velmans, 'Reflexive Monism: Psychophysical Relations among Mind, Matter and Consciousness', and M. Velmans, 'How to Arrive at an Eastern Place from a Western Direction: Convergences and Divergences among Samkya Yoga, Advaita Vedanta, the Body-Mind-Consciousness (Trident) Model and Reflexive Monism', in B.S. Prasad (ed.), *Consciousness, Gandhi and Yoga: Interdisciplinary, East-West Odyssey of K. Ramakrishna Rao*, New Delhi, D.K. Printworld, 2013, pp. 107–39.

WHERE IS CONSCIOUSNESS?

Michael Tye

The French philosopher René Descartes famously held that consciousness is nowhere. According to Descartes (1596–1650), the mind is a spiritual substance with no physical properties or spatial location. Consciousness, being a central feature of the mind, indeed its essence, in Descartes' view, is not a spatial thing at all. By contrast, panpsychists say that consciousness is everywhere. Even elementary particles have a little spark of consciousness, or proto-consciousness as it is sometimes put, to lessen the apparent lunacy of supposing that microphysical entities are conscious.

These two positions are radically implausible. The obvious answer to the question "Where is consciousness?" is: in brains. But another question immediately arises: what exactly is then being asserted? Token conscious states, particular dated conscious events (eg, my feeling pain at midnight as I step on a thumbtack), are plausibly located in brains. And one might think that if token conscious states are in brains, so too must be consciousness itself. But this would be too fast!

Consider the case of shape. The shape of an object (O) is *in* it in the sense that it is intrinsic to it: necessarily, any other object which duplicated O internally, in every respect, would have the same shape. Similarly for mass: if an object has a mass of 1kg on Earth, a perfect internal duplicate would have a mass of 1kg on the Moon. So mass is intrinsic. But a perfect duplicate of an astronaut weighing 85kg on Earth would weigh only one sixth of that on the moon. Weight is not intrinsic. Neither is monetary value. A perfect duplicate of a £1 note need not be worth £1: it could be counterfeit.

Meaning is not intrinsic either. A perfect physical duplicate of the word "snow", as I write it in the snow, need not mean snow. It could mean something else or nothing at all (as when the design is created by the wind whipping up the snow). Meanings are not in books or on pages.

What about consciousness? Must a perfect internal duplicate of a brain that is in some conscious state itself be in that conscious state? In this sense, is consciousness *in* the brain? In my view, consciousness is like meaning and monetary value and weight, and not like shape or mass: consciousness is extrinsic.

I have explored at length the question "Where is consciousness?" elsewhere.[1] Here, I want to focus on a specific dimension: which types of conscious states are in which brains, and how are we to decide? Do fish feel pain, for example? Can honeybees feel anxiety?

Fishing for answers

Consider other human beings. What makes it rational for me to believe that you have similar experiences to mine? It is not the old argument from analogy but an inference as to the best available explanation of your behaviour. This applies a rule formulated by Sir Isaac Newton in his *Principia*, to the effect that we are entitled to infer like cause from like effect unless there is defeating evidence.[2]

What might such evidence be? Suppose I find out that your head is empty and that only your exterior is organic. Your movements are controlled by Martians. You turn out to be a Martian marionette. This evidence would defeat my entitlement to prefer the view that you have experiences and feelings like mine, even though you behave in very similar ways. Alternatively, suppose I find out that you have only a silicon chip in your head with a vast look-up table inscribed on it, a table which controls your every move. Again, that would be defeating evidence.

Turning to other species, take fish. The idea that it is fine to eat fish is pretty commonly held. Kurt Cobain of Nirvana wrote in a famous song: "It's okay to eat fish 'cos they don't have any feelings." Kevin Kline seems to share that view in the popular British movie *A Fish Called Wanda*. Kline's character desperately wants to discover the location of some stolen jewels and so, in an effort to get Michael Palin to talk, he takes Palin's beloved tropical fish out of their tank one by one and slowly eats them, as Palin is forced to watch. It is obvious Palin thinks of the fish as creatures with feelings. He desperately wants them not to experience pain or fear or anxiety. But Kline could not care less. For him, they are zombies (or at least they should be treated as if they are). Who is right? How are we to decide?

Humans, encountering a noxious stimulus (S) feel pain. That feeling in humans causes a certain pattern of behaviour roughly as follows:

- protecting/guarding the part of the body damaged by S;
- withdrawing from S unless there is a strong need/desire for something else that requires enduring S (trade-off behaviour);
- decreased feeding;
- irritable and aggressive behaviour (increasing with the severity of S);
- physical signs of stress and
- avoiding (or behaving warily towards) other stimuli that have become associated with S.

Suppose we find in fish (or other non-human animals) the same pattern of behaviour (B) in response to noxious stimuli. Then it is rational to prefer the hypothesis that the feeling of pain causes B in the non-human animals to the hypothesis that some other cause is operative, unless we have further evidence that defeats that preference. Additional confirmation that the feeling of pain causes B in the non-human animals is the cessation or reduction of B, given morphine or other opiates, as is the case with us – again unless there is defeating evidence.

On the sensory-input side, teleost fish (those with bony skeletons) have nociceptors just as we do. Under a microscope, they look just like our nociceptors (receptors in our skin which respond to damaging stimuli by sending signals to the spinal cord and brain, engendering the sensation of pain). These receptors respond to the same noxious stimuli as ours.

Fish exhibit trade-off behaviour. In one experiment, trout were trained to feed in a part of the aquarium where they subsequently got a shock to the flank. The number of feeding attempts decreased with increased shock intensity. With increased food deprivation, however, the number and duration of feeding attempts increased, as did escape responses as the zone was entered. A plausible hypothesis is that fish balance their need for food against the avoidance of acute noxious stimuli. We do this too. Think of picking up a very hot plate, in the one case when it is full of food and you are very hungry, and in the other when the plate is empty. You are much more likely to hold on in the former instance, even though doing so is causing you pain. Fish, it seems, are like us. Similar behaviour is found in hermit crabs.

In another experiment, Elizabeth Sneddon injected bee venom and also acetic acid (the main ingredient in vinegar) into the lips of trout while they were under anesthetic. Sneddon chose the lips since trout lips have polymodal receptors very like those found in human lips. When the trout came to, they rubbed their lips against the sides of the tank and the gravel on the bottom. They also sat on the bottom and rocked from side to side. Primates in a poor welfare state display rocking behaviour too – a sign of having endured acute discomfort.

This suggests that the trout had been through an aversive experience. They also took about three hours to start feeding again after they had been injected with acetic acid, roughly the amount of time human beings whose lips have been injected with acid take to stop feeling pain.

Sneddon also found a greatly increased beat rate of the opercula (the bony flaps covering the gills) in the trout injected with bee venom or acetic acid, as compared with controls. This is usually taken as an indicator of stress, and Sneddon takes it to add further support to her hypothesis that the trout injected with bee venom and acetic acid felt pain. The overall pattern of behaviour fish produce is indeed similar to ours in response to the feeling of pain, as is their reaction to opiates. So, we should prefer the hypothesis that they feel pain too.

But is there defeating evidence here? In human beings, the experience of pain is generally generated by activity in regions of the neocortex (the somatosensory cortex and the anterior cingulate cortex). Fish, however, lack a neocortex. This neurophysiological difference makes a difference, so some say that fish cannot feel pain.

The claim that in humans pain and other experiences require a neocortex is widely accepted. For example, the American Academy of Neurology (AAN) has asserted: "Neurologically, being awake but unaware is the result of a functioning brainstem and the total loss of cerebral cortical functioning ... Pain and suffering are attributes of consciousness requiring cerebral cortical functioning."[3]

This does not seem to sit very well with the facts. It certainly seems true that adult humans who later in life come to lack a functioning cerebral cortex are then in a vegetative state. But this is not always true for children born without a cerebral cortex. Bjorn Merker, who spent several weeks with decorticate children and their families, concludes:

These children are not only awake and often alert, but show responsiveness to their surroundings in the form of emotional or orientating reactions to environmental events ... most readily to sounds but also to salient visual stimuli ... They express pleasure by smiling and laughter, and aversion by "fussing", arching of the back and crying (in many gradations), their faces being animated by these emotional states. A familiar adult can employ this responsiveness to build up play sequences predictably progressing from smiling, over giggling to laughter and great excitement on the part of the child.[4]

There can be no doubt that these children are very impaired behaviourally. But in addition to apparently showing pleasure, they also sometimes apparently feel pain, by rubbing an area that has been banged or pinched. This is shown by facial expressions such as wincing, grimacing and flinching in 14 per cent, vocally in ways such as crying, screaming and yelling in 78 per cent, and body use such as wriggling, pulling away and startling in 4 per cent of the children. Certainly, their behaviour is nothing like that of the few children who have congenital pain insensitivity. These children ignore noxious stimuli and feel no pain from them with the result that they behave as if nothing bad has happened, sometimes with dire consequences. One such child, Gabby Gingrass, poked out an eye and bit her gums down to the bone when she was teething. She also dislocated her jaw, with no one being any the wiser, until an infection resulted.

Birds and bees

So, at a minimum, it is not even clearly true that *in humans* a neocortex is needed for consciousness and for pain in particular. What about other species? Birds lack a neocortex. Yet they engage in some very complex behaviour, similar in various ways to ours. It has recently been proposed that there are homologous cells (cells that share a common origin) in bird and human brains, which mediate the behavioural similarities. The neocortex is however often described as a unique component of mammalian brains, without a prior evolutionary history.

The solution to the puzzle lies in the realisation that the neocortex did *not* suddenly appear by magic in mammals. What happened was that certain sorts of cells present in non-mammalian brains, and around for hundreds of millions of years, were grouped together into layers to form the laminar structure of the cortex. This is genuinely new in mammals; the constituent neuron types and the microcircuitry are not. Or so at least it has recently been hypothesised, dating back to earlier speculation by Karten in the 1960s.

The relevant cells for birds are preserved in a structure of a vastly different shape from the neocortex, the dorsal ventricular ridge (DVR). The cells in the DVR share the same physiological properties as the cortical cells.[5] It has recently been hypothesised that a similar structure of cells is found in the forebrain of fish too.[6]

So the fact that fish lack a neocortex does not in and of itself defeat preference for the simplest hypothesis: that they, like us, feel pain or something very like it. The case of birds shows that cells homologous to those in the neocortex can be present without a neocortex and, at least according to some scientists, fish have such cells and similar microcircuitry in their forebrains. And it is not clear that such a structure in the brain is needed anyway, even in the case of human beings, given the example of some decorticate children; indeed, it seems not to be the case.

So, it is rational to prefer the view that fish have feelings to the view that fish do not. Of course, pain is a feeling, liability to which is inherited. This is not true of "secondary emotional experiences", such as feeling insulted or remorseful. No claim is being made that fish are capable of undergoing such experiences.

What about insects? In a review of biological evidence for pain in such species, Eisemann comments:

No example is known to us of an insect showing protective behavior towards injured parts, such as by limping after leg injury or declining to feed or mate because of general abdominal injuries. On the contrary, our experience has been that insects will continue with normal activities even after severe injury or removal of body parts. An insect walking with a crushed tarsus, for example, will continue applying it to the substrate with undiminished force. Among our other observations are those on a locust which continued to feed while itself being eaten by a mantis; aphids continuing to feed whilst being eaten by coccinellids; a tse-tse fly which flew in to feed although half-dissected; caterpillars which continue to feed whilst taccinid larvae bore into them; many insects which go about their normal life whilst being eaten by large internal parasitoids; and male mantids which continue to mate as they are eaten by their partners.[7]

Eisemann also points out that insects do not respond to pain by ceasing to move or protecting injured parts in the way that mammals do. In general, they do not react to treatment that would undoubtedly cause severe pain in mammals.[8]

What about other experiences? A recent experiment has explored whether honeybees can become anxious.[9] Melissa Bateson and Jeri Wright strapped honeybees into little harnesses to render them immobile, and trained them to associate one odour with a sugary taste and another with a bitter, unpleasant taste (that of quinine). The former taste was a reward, the latter a punishment. When the first odour was presented after a training period, the bees uncoiled and extended their mouthparts. When the second was presented, they retracted them.

The experiment next made use of the fact that when people are anxious they tend to see the glass as half-empty rather than half-full. For example, if an anxious person hears the sentence, "The doctor examined little Emily's growth," she is less likely to conclude that Emily is okay and that it is just her height the doctor is checking. In general, anxious people interpret ambiguous stimuli more negatively. This presumably is related to the biological function of anxiety: it arises naturally in potentially dangerous situations, in which it behoves its subjects to tread carefully and play it safe.

The experimenters divided the bees into two groups, one of which was shaken vigorously for 60 seconds in the manner in which a hive might be shaken by a badger. If bees are capable of bad moods, this should have sufficed to put them into one. Within five minutes of the shaking, the two groups of bees were presented with in-between odours. The shaken bees were less likely to extend their mouthparts to try out the associated tastes than the unshaken ones. This was not because they were disorientated. When presented with the odour associated with the sugary taste, they extended their mouthpieces just as before. Rather, they interpreted the *ambiguous* stimuli as more probably punishment than reward. They saw the glass as half-empty.

Since pessimism is behavioural evidence that a dog or another person is anxious, why not too for bees? Bateson and Wright also checked the shaken bees' systemic neurotransmitter levels. Their serotonin and dopamine levels were diminished, as they are in humans who are feeling anxious.[10]

It does seem that the shaken bees were in a negative emotional state, caused by the shaking, and that this state in turn caused both stress-related physiological changes and a pessimistic cognitive bias, just as the experience of anxiety does in humans. But did they *feel* anxiety or distress? Bateson and Wright conclude:

> Using the best criteria currently agreed on for assessing animal emotions, ie, a suite of changes in physiology, behavior, and especially cognitive biases, we have shown that agitated bees display a negative emotional state. Although our results do not allow us to make any claims about the presence of negative subjective feelings in honeybees, they call into question how we identify emotions in any nonhuman animal. It is logically inconsistent to claim that the presence of pessimistic cognitive biases should be taken as confirmation that dogs or rats are anxious but to deny the same conclusion in the case of honeybees.[11]

This seems to me incorrect. Either the bees have been made anxious by the shaking or they have not. If they have, as Bateson and Wright assert, then they *feel* anxious; for occurrent anxiety is a feeling. Of course, someone can be anxious without, at a particular moment, feeling anxious, but that is because the anxiety is dispositional, a disposition to feel anxious. The experiment does not show that bees are generally anxious creatures. What it shows (arguably) is that they can be made to be anxious in a certain setting. And if they are genuinely anxious in that setting, they must feel anxiety then.

It might be objected that for honeybees to feel anxious, they must be conscious of their anxiety; and this is a higher-order mental state (a mental state about another mental state), which it is implausible to suppose honeybees can undergo. Yet, basic feelings, such as pain or anxiety, do not require that higher-order mental states be directed upon them. Being conscious of a mental state is best taken to be a matter of thinking that one is in the mental state. This requires the use of concepts – specifically, a concept of the mental state of which one is conscious. So, being conscious of anxiety requires that one think to oneself that one is anxious and this involves exercising the concept *anxiety*. But simply feeling anxious requires no such conceptual sophistication. A child of two might feel anxious at being separated from her mother without having the capacity to think that she is anxious. Likewise for honeybees.

Another objection is that anxiety is a complex state functionally. Among other things, it involves anticipation of bad things to come (though no specific bad thing), and it is implausible to suppose that bees could anticipate future events. Yet, bees are very intelligent creatures and it does not seem at all obvious that the experimental bees could not be anticipating another shaking or something else threatening.

A third worry is that anxiety really has no distinctive phenomenology in the way that pain does. What really does the claim that honeybees *feel* anxiety, as a result of the shaking, come to in the end? My response to this objection is to deny the premise. Think about what you feel when someone puts a gun in your back as you are trying to get some cash from an ATM machine. The phenomenology here is of a deep response in the stomach, a rearranging of the contents of the gut as it were, together with an immediate increase in heartbeat. This is the prototypical phenomenology of fear. Not all cases of fear are exactly like this phenomenally but there is a family resemblance. The same is true of pain and it is true of anxiety too.

Think of sitting by the phone waiting for the results of a medical test that will tell you whether you have cancer: the butterflies in the stomach, the general tension, the inability to concentrate on other tasks. This is a prototypical case of feeling anxious. The claim that bees feel anxiety is the claim that they feel something similar. Perhaps they are anxious about being shaken again, as you are anxious about the results of the test, or perhaps their anxiety is generalised. Either way, there is something it is like for them, something akin to the distinctive feeling we undergo when we feel anxious.[12]

As indicated at the outset, consciousness is not everywhere; nor is it nowhere. It is however more widespread in nature than is often supposed.[13]

1. *Ten Problems of Consciousness: A Representational Theory of the Phenomenal Mind*, Cambridge, MA, Bradford Books, MIT Press, 1995; *Consciousness, Color and Content*, Cambridge, MA, Bradford Books, MIT Press, 2000; with A. Byrne, 'Qualia Ain't in the Head', *Noûs*, vol. 40, no. 2, 2006, pp. 241–55.
2. The rule is best seen, more precisely, as providing the basis for rational preference rather than rational belief.
3. American Academy of Neurology, 'Position of the American Academy of Neurology on Certain Aspects of the Care and Management of the Persistent Vegetative State Patient', *Neurology*, no. 39, 1989, pp. 125–26.
4. B. Merker, 'Consciousness Without a Cerebral Cortex: A Challenge for Neuroscience and Medicine', with commentaries, *Behavioral and Brain Sciences*, no. 30, 2007, pp. 63–134.
5. J. Dugas-Ford, J. Rowell & C. Ragsdale, 'Cell-Type Homologies and the Origins of the Neocortex', *Proceedings of the National Academy of Sciences*, vol. 149, no. 42, 2012, pp. 16974–79.
6. H. Ito & N. Yamamoto, 'Non-Laminar Cerebral Cortex in Teleost Fish?', *Biological Letters*, no. 5, 2009, pp. 117–21.
7. C.H. Eisemann et al., 'Do Insects Feel Pain? A Biological View', *Experientia*, no. 40, 1984, p. 166.
8. The totality of evidence against insect pain is not as clear-cut as is suggested by Eisemann. See M. Tye, *Tense Bees and Shell-Shocked Crabs: Consciousness in the Animal World*, Oxford, Oxford University Press, forthcoming.
9. M. Bateson et al., 'Agitated Honeybees Exhibit Pessimistic Cognitive Biases', *Current Biology*, vol. 21, no. 12, 2011, pp. 1070–73.
10. Sheep with depleted serotonin levels also judge ambiguous stimuli negatively.
11. Bateson et al., p. 1072.
12. I owe this objection to Paul Boghossian.
13. For more on consciousness in the animal world, see Tye, *Tense Bees and Shell-Shocked Crabs*.

CONSCIOUSNESS AND THE SELF

WHAT MAKES YOU THINK YOU'RE ALIVE?

Paul Broks

I know that I exist ... I am asking who is this "I" whom I know?
René Descartes[1]

Insanity

My young friend was schizophrenic. Voices clamoured around her head. Malign forces emerged from the Web to control her thoughts and actions. They extracted her soul and, looking in the mirror, she would see nothing more than a vacant machine. It was a psychotic delusion but also a glimpse of the truth. Take a look at your own reflection. What do you see other than machinery? Your face is an animated device attached to a bony box. Concealed bands of fibre tug the surface tissues this way and that. Those fluid-filled spheres at the front are optical devices through which you view the world. The curly things at the sides capture compressions and rarefactions of air that you experience as sound. You taste stuff tipped into the hole in the lower part of the box.

No doubt you imagine the thinking, feeling "you", the experiencer of these experiences, to be somewhere inside because where the box goes, you go. *You're in there somewhere*, surely? But burrow into the substance of the brain and all you will find is more machinery, a dense matrix of billions of tiny robotic cells. Inside the cells are other intricate machines. So where are you? My friend saw the brute fact of the matter: *nowhere.*

Philosophy

There are two puzzles to solve, one of which, the matter–mind problem, remains a deep mystery. How, fundamentally, can the mental be reconciled with the physical? How does conscious selfhood sprout from the physics and chemistry of all that brain stuff? We all think we know what the word "consciousness" refers to but people tie themselves in knots trying to define it. On one level it is a very simple idea to get across. If you favour life over death, if you enjoy sex and sunsets, if you recoil from the smell of vomit and opt for anaesthesia when having a tooth extracted, then you know the meaning of consciousness well enough.

But what binds such disparate experiences? The taste of apple pie is quite unlike the pain of a headache or the thrill of a rollercoaster ride. What is it (if anything) that infuses each with the raw feels of awareness (*qualia*), with the *something that makes them feel like something*? A satisfactory answer to this question, or a clear demonstration that the question itself is meaningless, would be tantamount to solving "the problem of consciousness". But what baffled Thomas Huxley 150 years ago remains baffling: "How it is that anything so remarkable as a state of consciousness comes about as a result of irritating nervous tissue, is just as unaccountable as the appearance of the *Djinn*, when Aladdin rubbed his lamp."[2]

Neuroscientists may be upbeat about the prospect of a solution to the conundrum of consciousness but some philosophers, the so-called new mysterians, have given up the ghost. They think the transmutation of meat to mind is a challenge beyond the capacity of human intellect. In the characteristically sardonic words of Mysterian-in-Chief Colin McGinn: "The brain is just the wrong kind of thing to give birth to consciousness. You might as well assert that numbers emerge from biscuits or ethics from rhubarb."[3]

The other puzzle is selfhood. How does the brain, with its diverse and distributed functions – the various forms of memory, language, perception, motor control and so forth – come to arrive at a unified sense of self? As a clinical neuropsychologist, I have had a professional interest in the reverse process. When certain systems of the brain are damaged by disease and injury, the self is liable to distort and disintegrate. It can be a fading to oblivion through the slow progression of Alzheimer's disease, or the sudden calamity of a stroke or head injury that shatters memory or language, or recalibrates personality.

"Selfhood", like "consciousness", is easy enough to grasp at the level of ordinary intuition. We naturally think of ourselves as unitary, conscious beings inhabiting a particular body – the same thing, in essence, from one moment to the next, one day to the next, across a lifetime. But the closer we scrutinise unity and continuity, and generally try to pin down the *essence* of selfhood, the more nebulous the idea of "having a self" becomes.

I pick myself out in a primary-school photograph and declare "That's me!" when clearly it is not me. I am a middle-aged man with a PhD, not a five-year-old in his first year at school. It would sound contrived, but I could instead say "I was that boy," yet what then does the "I" refer to? Descartes reached the conclusion that all he could be absolutely sure of was his own existence as a *thinking thing*, and he could even imagine this indubitable thinking thing as an entity distinct from his physical body, as "not the collection of limbs that is called a human body, nor some subtle air that is infused into those limbs".[4] But if we play along with the idea that the "I" in "I was that boy" is an observing, remembering "thing", in short a thinking thing, it really does not get us very far towards an understanding of the unity and continuity of selfhood. We are just kicking the can down the road, because we have said nothing about the nature of the thing doing the thinking. An alternative view is that there is no "thing" (other than brain machinery) doing the thinking. There is "thinking going on" but nothing more to it.

Even if I cling to this ill-specified, Cartesian idea of myself as a thinking thing, it is not at all clear in what sense I can consider myself to be the *same* thinking thing as the five-year-old. The boy and I are vastly different in terms of knowledge, skills, tastes and interests, and there is nothing more at the psychological level that I can point to as an intrinsic feature of our shared personhood. There are certain biographical and biological factors we hold in common. We were, for example, born to the same mother at precisely the same time – had the same birth, in short – and, not long after, were registered with the same name by the same Registrar of Births and Deaths, and so on, but I do not see how such facts link us at the Cartesian level of *thinking things.* As for biology, we are built according to the same genetic instructions, sharing a physical point of origin in the convergence of a particular sperm and a particular egg, but the egg was not a thinking thing. Genes do not introspect and there is no Cartesian "I" in the brainless bunch of cells that constitutes a fertilised egg. A Cartesian "I" had popped up by the age of five, for sure: one that was excited to get a shiny blue bicycle for its birthday, one that loved the scent of Miss Johnson, its first teacher. But I have no real idea as to when it ("I", "he") came into being.

The journey from egghood to personhood is a mysterious one. My genetic match with the boy in the picture has determined us to have the same blood group and skin colour, among other physical attributes, but we may doubt that these are unique, fundamental aspects of personhood. As regards the basic materials, the molecular building-blocks of the body, the boy and I are not the same. Tissues are constantly regenerating. Old cells are discarded and new ones grow. With the passage of time every molecule has been replaced. We are different lumps of matter. So what persists?

According to the philosopher Derek Parfit, there are, broadly speaking, two theories about what persons are and what is involved in their continued existence over time: Ego Theory and Bundle Theory.[5] Ego Theory represents the intuitive, common-sense view that there is an "I", an experiencer of experiences that constitutes the essential core of every person. Descartes is the philosopher most closely aligned with this view. He believed that our capacity for self-awareness is due to the possession of an immaterial soul (that thinking thing) and it is this that gives us coherence as individuals and continuity over time. On the other hand, Bundle Theory has origins in Buddhist teaching but owes its modern formulation to the 18th-century philosopher David Hume.[6] It rejects the idea that actions and experiences are owned by an immaterial soul, or any other variety of essence, "ego" or "I". There is no observing "I", there are just sequences of actions and experiences – nothing more. According to this view, the self is no more than a bundle of fleeting impressions. Actions and experiences are interconnected but ownerless. A human life consists of a long succession of mental states, rolling like tumbleweed down the days and years, with no one (no thing) at the centre. An embodied brain acts, thinks, has certain experiences and that is all. There is no deeper fact about being a person.

Fantasy
Parfit devised a famous thought experiment which teases out the distinctions between Ego Theory and Bundle Theory. Imagine being teleported. A special scanner records the state of every cell in your brain and body and digitally encodes the information for radio transmission. Your body is destroyed in the process but reconstructed as soon as the radio signals are received and decoded at your destination. You "arrive" in precisely the same condition as you "left", identical in body, brain and patterns of mental activity. Your memories, beliefs, plans, skills and emotions are perfectly intact and you go about your business feeling and believing that nothing about "you" has changed in the slightest.

If you are comfortable with this scenario then you should be comfortable with Bundle Theory. You appreciate that the observing "I" is no more than patterns of energy and information that can be disrupted and reconstituted without destroying the self, because there is no essential self to destroy. The patterns are all. If, on the other hand, you believe that some essential "you" would be lost in the process then you are an irredeemable Ego theorist. You believe that the reconstituted body is not "you" but a mere replica. The "replica" will believe to its bones that it is the very person who stepped into the scanner at the start of the journey, and friends and loved ones will agree. But, you insist, it could not be you because your body and brain would have been destroyed.

Incidentally, we see here a neat inversion of conventional thinking. Those who believe in some sort of essence, or immaterial soul, suddenly become materialists, dreading the loss of the original body. But those who do not hold such beliefs are prepared to countenance a life after bodily death.

A teleportation trip, Parfit suggests, is no more existentially threatening than "travelling" from one day to the next via dreamless sleep. In either case, the only thing that matters, in terms of what is preserved, is psychological continuity. You survive your night's sleep only because the bundle of mental states that automatically reconfigures on waking resembles the one that unravelled in the process of falling asleep. *Ah, but you wake with the same body*, some will say, as if that really matters. So here's an extension of the sleep scenario, which, at the same time, involves some radical (but possibly less threatening) "body replacement". You are offered a place on a spaceflight to Pluto. It takes about ten years to get there, so you will be put in a state of suspended animation for the duration. The last thing you remember is stepping into the hibernation pod in Earth orbit before shooting off in the direction of the distant planet.

There follows a decade of dreamless sleep and the next thing you are aware of is being awakened as your spacecraft goes into orbit around Pluto, ready to descend to the surface. *Well, here I am*, you think. *It seems like only yesterday that we were preparing to launch from Cape Canaveral, and no time at all since I got into the hibernation pod*. But over the course of the journey, through natural processes of tissue regeneration and molecular replacement, there has been a steady turnover of the atoms that compose your body, such that you are now made up of an entirely different collection of atoms than when you set off (as would have been the case if you had been teleported). Can there be any doubt that you are still *you*?

Reality
We now turn from fantasies of teleportation and space travel to the realities of brain damage. Disturbances of brain function are a real threat to the integrity of the self. In light of some recent theorising, we will consider

the possibility of a "neuropsychology of selfhood" and I will then present some informative cases of neuropsychological disorder.

To set the scene, a brief word about certain Articles of Faith for neuro-psychologists. First, and fairly uncontentiously, the brain is the organ of the mind, being at the root of all behaviour and experience. Whether brain function is sufficient for mental function is debatable, but it seems to be necessary. Secondly, the mind is modular, a broad confederation of per-ception, emotion, reason, language and memory systems, among other subdivisions. These facets of mind function independently, at least to some degree, so that it's possible to find malfunction in one domain alongside normal operation in others. Thirdly, the modularity of mind is reflected in the workings of the brain: mental functions are biologically differentiated. There is considerable functional–anatomical overlap, but, to a significant extent, different brain systems serve different psychological functions. Mental functions can in this sense be neuropsychologically "fractionated". For example, reading impairments (*alexia*) are dissociable from writing impairments (*agraphia*), and likewise for verbal versus visual memory.

It seems reasonable to ask whether the components of selfhood are neuropsychologically fractionable in the same way, or it would be if we had some theoretical guidelines for thinking about the "components of selfhood" from a neuropsychological perspective. Egos and Bundles do not get us very far in this regard. The functionally diffuse, anatomically distributed, modular mind as outlined above is Bundle Theory made flesh. As far as neuropsychology is concerned, Ego Theory does not really get a look-in. The mental functions underlying our sense of self – feelings, thoughts, memories – are ever-shifting, dynamic processes, scattered through different zones of the brain with no special point of convergence where everything comes together in the shape of a stable, thinking thing of a "self". We might thus dismiss Ego Theory as neuropsychologically implausible, but that takes us no further towards an understanding of the brain bases of our natural intuitions of selfhood.

Neurology

Some recent theorising on the neuropsychology of selfhood cuts usefully across the Ego/Bundle distinction, opening up the possibility of scientific progress. Clinicians and scientists such as Todd Feinberg and Joseph LeDoux have made important contributions,[7] but I will focus on the work of Antonio Damasio, perhaps the foremost neurological theorist of selfhood. Damasio distinguishes the *core self* and the *autobiographical self*. The latter is what we generally have in mind when we speak or think of ourselves as unitary, continuous beings with a remembered past and an anticipated future, a view of the self tied up with the notion of personal identity. In Damasio's words, the autobiographical self "corresponds to a nontransient collection of unique facts and ways of being which characterize a person". Whereas the autobiographical self is rooted in the past and reaches towards the future, the core self exists only in the present moment, "a transient entity, ceaselessly re-created for each and every object with which the brain interacts".[8] The philosopher Shaun Gallagher has proposed a similar two-dimensional scheme, in his terms differentiating the *Narrative* (or *Extended*) *Self* and the *Minimal Self*. The former involves continuity over time and is composed of "a rich amalgam of narratives" integral to notions of memory and personal identity. The Minimal Self is, by contrast, "a consciousness of oneself as an immediate subject of experience, unextended in time".[9]

Both Damasio's and Gallagher's models of the self can be viewed as descendants of William James's distinction between self as subject and self as object – the "I" and the "Me" – but Damasio, more than anyone, has excavated the neurobiological foundations of selfhood. He sees the core self as a product of a dynamic integration of brain systems underlying the perception of internal bodily states ("interoception"), along with others engaged in the perception of objects in the external environment ("exteroception"). The network involves interaction between various lower brainstem nuclei, which in turn communicate with higher cortical centres via intermediate structures in the diencephalon and mid-brain.

The core self is the level at which, as Damasio puts it, the brain introduces something into the mind that was not present before, "a protagonist", and by so doing sets the stage for subjectivity: "Once a protagonist is available in the midst of other mind contents, and once that protagonist is coherently linked to some of the current mind contents, subjectivity begins to inhere in the process."[10] The core self is thus the prerequisite for the autobiographical self, which, in neurobiological terms, recruits an elaborated set of neural structures and activities, especially higher cortical systems involved in language and long-term memory. Their function is to construct, and continually revise, "the story of the self".

So where sits the storyteller? Most likely in the left hemisphere. Through his work with split-brain patients, Michael Gazzaniga has identified a specialised brain system, located within the left hemisphere, whose job is to correlate manifold unconscious brain processes with happenings in the external world, thereby enabling the construction of narratives to make sense of the individual's engagement with the stream of events. He calls this system *the interpreter* and has described its discovery as "the most stunning result from split-brain research".[11] Perhaps, the interpreter might be understood as the interface between the core and the autobiographical self, in so far as it seems to involve the linkage of in-the-moment cognitive processes with the brain systems, especially language and memory systems, involved in story construction.

In Damasio's scheme of things, the core- and autobiographical-self systems are organised hierarchically such that the autobiographical system is entirely dependent upon the core system, which cannot be compromised without also affecting the autobiographical system. He offers epileptic automatism – seizure-induced episodes of automatic, unconscious behaviour – as an example of impairment of the core self with concomitant alteration of the autobiographical self. The converse is not the case and there are many examples of the autobiographical self being compromised while the core self remains intact. Acquired memory disorders, such as are caused by Alzheimer's disease or viral encephalitis, radically impair the person's ability to recall past events, to lay down new memories and to project possible future events. Without the capacity for backward and forward "mental time travel", and the ability to maintain a sense of continuity through the establishment of new memories, hallmarks of the autobiographical self, such patients are to a large extent confined to the present-moment domain of the core self.

According to Damasio, then, the core- and autobiographical-self systems are dissociable, because it is possible for there to be an intact core self in the presence of a disturbed autobiographical self. But they are not *doubly* dissociable, because one does not see the converse. Indeed one cannot in principle see the opposite, because of the presumed hierarchical relationship between the two systems.

I would like to suggest that the two self systems may, in fact, be doubly dissociable, and that the self-negating, delusional states associated with Cotard's syndrome (self-negating to the extent that the patient may believe himself to be dead) provide examples of the autobiographical self remaining relatively intact despite impaired functioning of the core self. First, I am going to sketch out an example of impairment of the autobiographical self system, in part simply as a foil to the Cotard's cases but partly also because the case in question provides possible insights into the dynamics of the core- and autobiographical-self relationship.

The Pat Martino story

During 2006–7, I spent extended periods of time with the renowned jazz guitarist Pat Martino, for the purpose of making a documentary about his recovery from amnesia.[12] I arranged for Pat to undergo formal neuro-psychological assessments and structural brain imaging, but it was from our less formal interactions, generally just "hanging out" with him as he went about his various domestic and professional routines, that some of the more interesting observations came about. Along the way, I garnered biographical material from conversations with various of his friends, business associates and fellow musicians, some of whom had known Pat for the best part of 50 years.

Pat Martino's descent into mental illness, his near-fatal brain haemorrhage, the consequent amnesia and, ultimately, his remarkable return to the highest levels of musicianship has become the stuff of legend in the jazz world. What follows is, in outline, the story.

As a young guitar virtuoso starting out in 1950s Philadelphia, Pat was one of the finest musicians of his generation. Then, in the late 60s, with a catalogue of successful albums and on the brink of a major new recording deal, he became seriously mentally ill. He was diagnosed with manic depression (which we now call bipolar disorder) and spent time in a secure psychiatric unit, where he was subjected to electroconvulsive therapy (ECT). On discharge, and unable to regain his former virtuosity, he moved to California and tried to make a living as a guitar teacher. He started suffering major seizures and, on investigation, it turned out that he had an arteriovenous malformation, an abnormal cluster of blood vessels, in the left temporal lobe of his brain. It had begun to bleed and required immediate surgery.

The surgery, which involved removal of the bulk of the lobe, saved his life, but when he came round from the operation he had what has been described as a total loss of identity. He apparently had no idea who he was and failed even to recognise his parents. They took him back with them to Philadelphia but it was a difficult convalescence. For one thing, his father played Pat's recordings over and over at full volume in an attempt to stir memories of his past life, which, for Pat, was an intolerable torment.

He acknowledged the physical similarity between the face on the album covers and the face he saw in the mirror, but otherwise felt no identification. His parents would also trawl through photograph albums, pointing out family members and friends whose faces meant nothing to Pat. Discouraged and disorientated, he fell into depression and ended up once again on a secure psychiatric ward, where (one wonders at the clinical wisdom of this) he underwent further courses of ECT.

But it was there that a psychiatrist gave him a primitive computer to play with. Its feeble 127-kilobyte memory contained a music program and Pat says he began to play with it, "like a child with a toy". It was an epiphany, like being born again, he says, but now he was "living entirely in the moment", with no interest in the past, which was still covered in a fog, or the future. Eventually, his passion for music rekindled, he took up the guitar again, studying technique (so legend has it) via tuition videos from a great teacher – his former self – and, in due course, he ascended once more to the pinnacle of his art. Sadly, this last, legendary twist to the story is just that: Pat had not produced any teaching videos before the surgery.

One could cite more clear-cut and compelling examples of autobiographical memory loss than the Martino case. My interactions with Pat began many years after his surgery, well beyond the period of the most severe autobiographical memory disturbance, which, from anecdotal accounts, may have lasted a year or so post-surgery – though, at this remove in time, and with no contemporaneous neuropsychological assessments to go by, it is impossible to gauge the rate and extent of recovery with any precision. Superficially at least, his autobiographical memory now seems largely to have recovered. He appears to recall events from his early professional life quite fluently and sometimes in surprising detail. But there are some notable lacunae. Going through family photograph albums with him, as his parents had during his convalescence, I found there were occasions when the pictures drew a surprising blank, and his responses to some photos seemed oddly "well-rehearsed", as though he had learned the facts and faces by rote, rather than recalling information spontaneously.

His memory also lets him down in odd ways in real-life situations. To give one striking example, sometime around the mid-90s, when he had returned to performing, Pat played a show in New York City attended by the film actor Joe Pesci. The two had been close friends in the early 60s but had lost touch and had not met in the intervening years. After the show, Pesci found his way to the dressing room and introduced himself, but it was apparent that Pat did not remember him; or, rather, he recognised him as Joe Pesci, the famous movie actor, but not as an old friend. Yet the memories flooded back when Joe mentioned a drink Pat used to enjoy. In Pat's words, "the moment he described the drink, a series of images appeared in my mind … I remembered the bartender and the stage and the position of the instruments that remained on the bandstand in between sets. And then I remembered Joe Pesci." Pesci confirms the story.

Pat is also prone to occasional confabulation and the details of certain autobiographical anecdotes seem to vary, depending on the person with whom he is sharing them. For example, he animatedly tells a humorous story of once buying a Porsche sports car on impulse, but, from talking to some of his old friends, it seems doubtful this ever happened. Others, though, are less sceptical and one gets the sense that Pat has to some extent reconstructed his life history through the stories and memories of others, sometimes unreliable, with consequent factual inconsistencies.

The Pat Martino case remains interesting in the present context, not because it is an especially good example of autobiographical memory disorder, far from it, but because of Pat's repeated claim that, ever since his recovery from surgery, he has felt himself to be living "entirely in the moment". Although his autobiographical memory systems now seem to be functioning reasonably well, the significance of the autobiographical self, for him, seems to have permanently diminished, while the core self is more sharply in focus. The intensity of his present-moment awareness, and the value he places on this, is a recurrent theme in his conversation, sometimes almost to the point of perseveration. In Pat's own idiosyncratic words:

> There's a compression of all the side angles that are within the future and the past … after the operation, maybe those two things – dependence on the past and hope in the future – resided in that part of the brain that was dissected and removed. But whatever was left was "Now"; it had no interest in the future or in the past, and that's where transformation began to take place.

Transformation is his preferred term for *recovery*. The quotation above is extracted from Pat's autobiography, *Here and Now!* – which also includes a fuller account of my neuropsychological observations.[13] The neuro-imaging and neuropsychological studies have meanwhile been formally reported.[14]

Cotard's syndrome
Case 1: "Philip"

What makes you think you are dead? I put this question to Philip, a 55-year-old civil servant who had been referred for neuropsychological assessment. He was undergoing investigations for a range of symptoms, including drowsiness, problems with balance and deteriorating memory and concentration. (He was, in due course, diagnosed with Hashimoto's encephalopathy, a rare autoimmune disease.) I had noted signs of mild cognitive impairment over the course of several examinations on the hospital ward, but he was generally well orientated, engaged and articulate, and he gave a clear account of his personal history.

So I was taken aback when, towards the end of one assessment session, he told me, quite matter-of-factly, that he thought he had died. Perhaps he was speaking metaphorically, I wondered, and this was his way of expressing a feeling that, because of his illness, he was no longer his "old self". But, probing further, I understood that he was not being metaphorical. He meant what he said and believed himself, literally, to be dead. This rare and strange delusion, I realised, signified Cotard's syndrome.

In 1882, the French psychiatrist Jules Cotard published a series of case studies of people suffering what he termed *le delire de negation*. His patients varied widely in the details of their clinical presentation but all had self-negating delusions of some sort, ranging from beliefs that parts of the body were missing, or rotting, to a complete disavowal of bodily existence. Believing oneself to be dead is not, in fact, a defining feature of the syndrome, although it is often regarded as prototypical. Of the eight "pure" cases Cotard described, excluding others with concomitant persecutory delusions, only one person thought she had died, although some held the paradoxical view that they had ceased to exist, apparently without equating non-existence with death. Conversely, some patients denied their bodily existence whilst believing themselves to be immortal. Whatever the pattern of signs and symptoms, and whatever the underlying cause, Cotard's syndrome clearly represents a disturbance of self-awareness whereby the normal intuitions of consciousness, embodiment and selfhood are severely undermined.

The death delusion usually occurs in the context of severe depression. I first encountered it as a newly qualified psychologist working in a psychiatric unit. The patient then was a profoundly depressed woman in her mid-80s who told me she had been dead for some time and that I might as well have her buried. She believed her insides had already rotted away. But Philip was not depressed, and nor was there any history of mood disorder. So although depression might be sufficient to induce the delusion, it is evidently not a necessary condition for its occurrence.

What is it to experience the Cotard's delusion? Some of Philip's experiences seemed to resemble the relatively common psychiatric symptoms of "depersonalisation" and "derealisation", which are usually associated with mood and anxiety disorders. Depersonalisation is a disturbance of self-awareness, such that the person feels detached and unreal, often with muting of sensory experience and emotional numbing. Derealisation denotes similar experiential distortions of the external environment, such that other people seem lifeless, objects lose their significance and the world generally seems "less real". Given that both conditions involve sensory changes and feelings of unreality, they might be considered to be two sides of the same coin, and in fact depersonalisation and derealisation typically do co-occur. They are, however, dissociable. Depersonalisation sometimes presents without derealisation, and vice versa.

Philip could be said to show features of a depersonalisation-derealisation syndrome but lack of insight into his state of mind excluded the diagnosis. People with mood and anxiety-related depersonalisation often speak in terms of feeling as if they are unreal, or the world seems remote and unreal as if being viewed through a glass wall, but the "as if" is crucial. They retain insight into the fact that their sense of unreality is illusory. Philip, on the other hand, was convinced that he and the world he inhabited were lifeless and insignificant to the point of true oblivion. The fact that we were sitting together having a conversation did not persuade him that he was alive and that the objects and events of the world around him were real. Nor did his *thinking* that everything was unreal constitute evidence of his existence. In this regard, he clearly departed from Descartes, whose *cogito ergo sum*, "I think, therefore I am", was proof that, whatever else could be doubted or denied, his own existence as a thinking thing was indubitable. I pressed him on this a few times and his responses were along the lines of "my thoughts aren't real either".

Case 2: "Graham"

My involvement with this case was limited to a single, informal interview
at the invitation of Adam Zeman, Professor of Cognitive Neurology at the
University of Exeter, who, with colleagues in Belgium, went on to con-
duct perhaps the most significant neuroimaging study of Cotard's syndrome to date.

Graham was 48 years old and had no medical history of note, other
than a brief depressive illness. He was referred to a psychiatrist after a
suicide attempt by electrocution. Eight months later, he told his general
practitioner that his brain had died and he said: "I am coming to prove
that I am dead." Despite my efforts to persuade him otherwise, presenting the plain evidence that he was fully engaged in a conversation with
me, Graham was unshifting in his conviction that his brain had died the
day he plunged a live electric heater into his bathwater. I wondered how
this could be possible, because surely he would accept that a living brain
was necessary to be able to think and speak. It was a bit baffling, he conceded, and he did not have a good explanation for this strange state of
affairs, but the fact was that his brain was dead, and there you go.

Graham was clearly deluded, but what was the nature of his conviction
that his brain had died? Delusions have been defined as false beliefs held
in the teeth of contrary evidence, but there is a growing body of opinion
among psychopathologists that delusions should be considered not as
beliefs but as knowledge claims, distinguishing "to know that" from "to
believe that". The deluded person simply "knows" such and such, rather
than merely believing it.

For example, I *know* that my name is Paul. It is on my birth certificate,
it is what my parents always called me, what my friends know me by, and
the name I give when strangers ask. On the other hand, I merely *believe*
that my new neighbour is called David. That is what another neighbour
told me – at least I think that is what she said. If, when we eventually meet,
he tells me, no, his name is Dennis, not David, then I would accept this
new evidence and henceforth call him Dennis. Nothing could persuade
me that my name is not Paul. But delusional statements, as knowledge
claims, are expressed with absolute conviction and certainty. They are
not susceptible to rational interrogation and evidence-based counter-
arguments. They are rock-solid in the way that knowledge of one's own
name is rock-solid.

Graham was referred to the University of Liège for brain imaging and there, under the supervision of Professor Steven Laureys, he became the first Cotard's patient to undergo a positron emission tomography (PET) scan. The results were remarkable. Graham's overall grey-matter metabolism was 22 per cent below normal, but there was an intriguing differential between subcortical and cortical brain areas. The subcortical regions (cerebellum, brainstem, thalamus) showed hypermetabolism, overactivity, whereas a bilateral frontoparietal cortical network and the right temporoparietal region showed significant *under*activity. The authors concluded: "Our data suggest that the profound disturbance of thought and experience [in Cotard's delusion] reflects a profound disturbance in brain regions responsible for 'core consciousness' and our abiding sense of self."[15] Elsewhere, Steven Laureys has remarked: "I've been analysing PET scans for 15 years and I've never seen anyone who was on his feet, who was interacting with people, with such an abnormal scan result. Graham's brain function resembles that of someone during anaesthesia or sleep. Seeing this pattern in someone who is awake is quite unique to my knowledge."[16]

Conclusion
We lack the testing procedures to delineate clearly autobiographical and core selfhood with the same experimental precision with which we are able to define and measure reading and writing skills, for example, or verbal and spatial memory. Nevertheless, the cases I have described are at least suggestive of the idea that the autobiographical and core selves are not only dissociable, as Damasio already maintains, but *doubly* dissociable in neuropsychological terms.

The Cotard's syndrome cases appear to show relatively intact autobiographical recall in the presence of a dissolution of "the self of the present moment" – dissolution to the point of experienced non-existence. (I acknowledge that the oxymoronic phrase "experienced non-existence" will have Descartes spinning in his grave.) The Pat Martino case, on the other hand, reveals a man with disturbed autobiographical capacities alongside clear and coherent, perhaps even enhanced, awareness of himself as a locus of present-moment experience. He now lives "entirely in the moment", he says – which I suppose is not a bad place to be living if you are a jazz guitar virtuoso celebrated for your extraordinary "in the moment" improvisational skills.

Coda

For most of us, unlike my schizophrenic friend, it takes an effort of imagination to see a vacant machine when we look in a mirror or into someone else's eyes. But the seeing of "selves" also calls for the exercise of imagination, even if the process is automatic rather than effortful, implicit rather than explicit. The separateness of body and mind is a primordial intuition. Human beings are natural-born soul-makers, adept at extracting unobservable minds from the behaviour of observable bodies, including their own. We continually decode other people's thoughts and intentions, continually project the illusion of a spirit puppeteer controlling the actions of the body.

I played a game with my three-year-old granddaughter. I got her to cover her eyes with her hands and I asked some questions. "Now, Millie, can I see your feet?" "Yes." "Can I see your tummy?" "Yes." "Can I see your hands?" "Yes." "Can I see *you?*" "*No!* Ha! Ha!" And of course I never will. There is nothing to see. Behind the laughing eyes, beneath the silky hair, the bony box of her cranium contains nothing but a few hundred grammes of jellified fats, proteins, sugars and salts – a brain. She is biological machinery all the way through. There are no spirits coursing through her brain circuits, just neurochemicals. Does this devalue her? No, quite the opposite!

On the scale of human history, Millie is more transient and fragile than a soap bubble. No part of her ebullient consciousness will survive her death, and no memory of her will survive mine. It's a hard thought to grasp, but the truth, and the improbable gift of conscious selfhood is to be treasured all the more for its transience and fragility. It does not matter that it is an illusion. The illusion is *what we are* and *all we have* and to lose it is, literally, insanity.

1. R. Descartes, *Meditations on First Philosophy*, trans. D.M. Clarke, London, Penguin, 2000 [1641], p. 26.
2. T. Huxley, *Lessons in Elementary Physiology*, London, Macmillan, 1866, p. 210.
3. C. McGinn, 'Consciousness and Cosmology: Hyperdualism Ventilated', in M. Davies & G.W. Humphreys (eds.), *Consciousness*, Oxford, Blackwell, 1993, p. 160.
4. Déscartes, *Meditations on First Philosophy*, p. 25.
5. D. Parfit, 'Divided Minds and the Nature of Persons', in C. Blakemore & S. Greenfield (eds.), *Mindwaves*, Oxford, Blackwell, 1987, pp. 19–26.
6. D. Hume, *A Treatise of Human Nature*, London, Penguin, 1985 [1738], book I, chap. IV.
7. T. Feinberg, *Altered Egos: How the Brain Creates the Self*, New York, NY, Oxford University Press, 2001; J.E. LeDoux, *Synaptic Self: How our Brains Become who we are*, New York, NY, Viking, 2002.
8. A. Damasio, *The Feeling of What Happens: Body and Emotion in the Making of Consciousness*, San Diego, CA, Harcourt, 1999, p. 17.
9. S. Gallagher, 'Philosophical Conceptions of the Self: Implications for Cognitive Science', *Trends in Cognitive Sciences*, vol. 4, no. 1, 2000, pp. 14–21.
10. A. Damasio, *Self Comes to Mind: Constructing the Conscious Brain*, New York, NY, Pantheon, 2010, p. 201.
11. M.S. Gazzaniga, *Tales from Both Sides of the Brain: A Life in Neuroscience*, New York, NY, HarperCollins, 2015, p. 151.
12. *Martino Unstrung*, directed by Ian Knox, Sixteen Films, 2008.
13. P. Martino & B. Milkowski, *Here and Now! The Autobiography of Pat Martino*, Milwaukee, IL, Backbeat Books, 2011.
14. M. Galarza et al., 'Jazz Guitar and Neurosurgery: The Pat Martino Case Report', *World Neurosurgery*, vol. 81, nos. 3–4, 2014, pp. 508–10.
15. V. Charland-Verville et al., 'Brain Dead yet Mind Alive: A Positron Emission Tomography Case Study of Brain Metabolism in Cotard's Syndrome', *Cortex*, vol. 49, 2013, pp. 1997–99.
16. H. Thomson, 'The Man who Believes he is Dead', *New Scientist*, 1 June 2013, p. 12.

EXPLAINING EXPERIENCE IN THE LIFEWORLD

Julian Kiverstein

What is the problem of consciousness?

Thomas Nagel traces the problem of consciousness back to the scientific revolution of the 17[1] century.[1] It is from the writers and thinkers of that time that we have inherited the concept of an objective physical reality extended in space and time, composed of fundamental building-blocks whose properties admit of precise, mathematical description. There would seem to be no room in physical reality so conceived for the subjective qualities of sensory consciousness, such as colour, sound and smell.

The problem was recognised early on by Galileo. He wrote in *The Assayer:*

> I think that tastes, odours, colours and so on are no more than mere names so far as the object in which we place them is concerned, and that they reside only in consciousness … To excite in us tastes, odours, and sounds I believe that nothing is required in external bodies except shapes, numbers and slow or rapid movements. I think that if ears, tongues and nose were removed, shapes and numbers and motions would remain, but not odours, or tastes or sounds.[2]

Galileo allowed that subjective qualities might have a causal grounding in physical processes in the natural world that could be given a precise, mathematical description. Still, he argued there would remain some subjective and human residue left over that seemed to resist mathematical description, and that apparently behaved according to a non-mechanistic causality.

Suppose we were to identify subjective qualities and human purposes with a set of causal mechanistic processes. We might still reasonably wonder what it was about these processes that made them subjective and purposive. This is the problem of consciousness as it has been handed down to us from the Enlightenment. Subjective qualities and human purposes are undeniably real and yet there seems to be no room for them in the physical world as it is understood by the natural sciences. How then can we find a place for subjective experience and human purposes in our scientific conception of the natural world?

The problem of consciousness, so formulated, assumes that reality is fundamentally and essentially physical, and that everything that happens in the world can be explained by the laws of physics as they apply to physical reality and its constituents. I will question this framing of the problem. Why should one agree that the natural world contains only whatever is described in the physical sciences? Reality as we find it described in the textbooks of physics is an abstract, mathematical idealisation of the reality we ordinarily experience.

Before people know anything of physics and mathematics, they live their lives in situations in which they are surrounded by familiar artefacts and objects of cultural value, such as transport systems, items to eat and drink from, digital technologies, writing implements and uncountable other cultural objects. The everyday world includes places for eating and entertainment, schools, housing, farms, factories, banks and other financial institutions, cinemas, museums containing art objects and antiquities, places of religious worship and much more. We live in a social world alongside other people with whom we participate in patterns of practice, institutions and historical traditions, including science, morality and religion.

The phenomenological philosopher Edmund Husserl coined the term "lifeworld" to describe the everyday world in which people live. He wrote:

> In ordinary life, we have nothing to do with nature-Objects. What we take as things are pictures, statues, gardens, houses, tables, clothes, tools etc. These are all value-objects of various kinds, use-objects, practical objects. They are not objects that can be found in the natural sciences.[3]

The lifeworld is the world in which we are ordinarily immersed, and which is always on hand for people to take hold of as they pursue their projects and interests. It is the world in which people are practically orientated, and which constitutes the social and historical context for all of their thoughts, experiences and actions.

Husserl argued that the lifeworld has a primacy in relation to physical reality.[4] Reality as described in the precise mathematical language of the physical sciences is always an abstraction from, and idealisation of, the world we know immediately and directly. Physical reality is by contrast knowable only on the basis of the mathematical tools and experimental techniques of physics. The reality people directly experience is not the world as described in the theories of physics, as Galileo rightly observed. The latter has the status of a mathematical formalisation of the lifeworld, and is in this sense an idealisation of the world in which we live and purposefully pursue our life interests.

I agree with Husserl that the lifeworld has "priority" over reality, as it is described using the mathematical techniques of the natural sciences, and is metaphysically more fundamental. How are we then to integrate these two very different and conflicting realities, the lifeworld and the physical world? Wilfrid Sellars famously wrote that the aim of philosophy, "abstractly formulated, is to understand how things in the broadest possible sense of the term hang together in the broadest possible sense of the term".[5] The natural sciences offer a more or less complete image of the place of human beings in the universe, but it seems to be one in which there can be no place for human purposes and subjectivity. The lifeworld is, by contrast, the world conceived of as the correlate of individual and collective experience, in which things show up to subjects in a particular way because of their life interests and purposes. So how can these two conceptions of reality be made to "hang together"?

The latter question forms the basis of the problem of consciousness as I conceive it. The lifeworld I take to be the world which is the correlate of subjective and intersubjective experiences. I will assume that what subjects experience most directly and immediately are objects, places and situations belonging to the lifeworld. This philosophical account of the phenomenology of experience is what stands in need of explaining in the terms of the natural sciences. At least it stands in need of explanation if we are to succeed in showing how these two conceptions of the world (the lifeworld and the natural world) hang together. I will call an explanation or theory framed in the terms of the natural sciences a "naturalistic" theory or explanation. The problem of consciousness, as I understand it, is therefore that of finding a naturalistic theory of explanation which makes intelligible the individual and shared experiences people undergo in the lifeworld. Such a theory would amount to a naturalisation of the lifeworld.

The subjective and the objective

The traditional problem of consciousness, as we find it described in the work of Nagel for instance, is premised on a division of, and disjunction between, the categories of the subjective and the objective. Consciousness and human purposes are taken to be irreducibly subjective. The processes that we find in physical reality are by contrast publicly observable and can be precisely and objectively measured, providing one has the right tools and measuring instruments. Consciousness, by its very nature, seems to resist description in these terms. It cannot be directly observed through the scientific method, because consciousness is that property on the basis of which we are able to make observations. Moreover, as already emphasised, science begins by abstracting away from all things subjective to arrive at a conception of an objective, physical reality. In measuring temperature, for instance, scientists do not concern themselves with subjective sensations of warmth or coldness. How then are we to fit consciousness into a scientific conception of reality which seems to exclude consciousness?

Anyone reading the essays in this collection will know that there is an exciting and fast-moving interdisciplinary field of research dedicated to the scientific research of consciousness. Scientists working in it employ a variety of objective measures of consciousness.[6] Some scientists are concerned with measuring the differences between the brains of people in a deep coma and those who have regained some minimal level of consciousness. Other scientists are concerned with the neurophysiological differences between states of wakefulness and the different stages of sleep in which people enter dream states of consciousness. Others probe the differences in information-processing which distinguish subliminal, unconscious or preconscious perception of a stimulus from conscious perception of the same stimulus. These methods and the fascinating findings they have yielded identify a range of publicly observable markers or measures that are systematically and reliably correlated with some aspect of consciousness.

But are these methods measuring consciousness itself or only an indirect correlate of an aspect of consciousness, such as neural and behavioural processes? Often the measures rely on verbal reports or non-verbal behaviours that are taken to indicate something about the presence or absence of consciousness, or about the contents of consciousness. Strictly speaking, however, what is being measured are indicators or signs of consciousness that leave room for false negatives: measurements suggesting the absence of consciousness in people who are in fact conscious.[7]

Neuroscientists currently have no means of measuring consciousness directly. All of the experimental techniques just mentioned, the design of experiments based on these techniques, the analysis of data and the communication of findings are activities that take place as part of the practices of neuroscience laboratories. When brain scientists and cognitive scientists embark on the investigation of consciousness, they do so as conscious human beings, and they rely on the particular practices in which they are embedded to devise and interpret the results of their experiments. Scientific practices cannot however give us any access to consciousness which is independent of consciousness. The philosopher Evan Thompson makes the same point when he writes:

> The upshot is that there is no way to stand outside consciousness and look at it, in order to see how it fits into the rest of reality. Science always moves within the field of what consciousness reveals; it can enlarge this field and open up new vistas, but it can never get beyond the horizon set by consciousness. In this way, direct experience is primary and science secondary.[8]

Scientists are always operating within a field opened up by the particular research practices they employ. At the same time as scientists develop techniques for abstracting away from the experiences we ordinarily have when immersed in the lifeworld, they also operate within the region of the lifeworld that is the scientific laboratory. When Thompson writes that there is no way for the scientist to stand outside consciousness, I would add that the same is true of the lifeworld as the correlate of individual and collective experience. Scientists cannot stand outside of the lifeworld so as to investigate consciousness in the lifeworld, since the scientific practices found within the labs of scientists occupy a region of the lifeworld.

What should we say about consciousness then? If our measures of consciousness and models of brain activity are always constructed against a backdrop of consciousness in the lifeworld, how is consciousness itself related to the biological and behavioural processes we are measuring? Should we not agree that consciousness is in the end nothing other than a brain process? Hence, when we measure the neural correlates of consciousness, are we not by virtue of the identity of consciousness with brain processes, also measuring consciousness itself?

Scientists in their search for the neural correlates of consciousness clearly demonstrate some form of metaphysical dependence of consciousness on processes and systems in the brain. I doubt, however, that consciousness depends only on processes found within the brain. The brain does not generate consciousness in isolation from the rest of the self-regulatory, homeodynamic processes in the living body.[9] Instead, the brain always operates within a larger system of the living body as a whole in its dynamic coupling with the environment. Thus it would be a mistake to infer from the dependence of consciousness on brain processes that consciousness can be reduced to, and identified with, those processes.

I do not however side with the so-called mysterians in the philosophy of consciousness, who argue that consciousness has a nature that the human mind is constitutionally incapable of understanding.[10] Colin McGinn, who prefers the less derogatory "transcendental naturalism" for the position he defends, points to the cognitive limitations and boundedness of the human mind. He suggests that consciousness may turn out to be among those natural phenomena that lie beyond the limits of human understanding. It is the experiential aspect of consciousness, the "what it is like" to be a conscious subject, that is often claimed to elude scientific understanding. McGinn does not make this claim. He says instead that we humans as natural, evolved beings do not have the cognitive capacities necessary for grasping the true nature of consciousness.

McGinn's conclusion, that consciousness has a nature unknowable to us, is surely conceivable, and it would be prejudicial hubris to rule out this possibility in principle. But I will suggest that there is something about the problem of consciousness as it has been handed down to us from the 17th century that may be ill-formed, and that it is time to rethink.

Recall the problem as outlined was that physical reality is described mathematically in terms of structural and dynamical properties of fields and particles, and we currently have no understanding of how a reality so described could also contain conscious subjects. The problem so formulated assumes a conception and understanding of the material and natural world from which subjects have been excised. Consciousness is somehow to be conceived of as a higher-order property of physical phenomena which are fundamentally and essentially non-experiential. This division of the natural world into the experiential and non-experiential is exemplified in the conceptual distinction between primary and secondary qualities, which we already encountered in the quote from Galileo.

There we saw Galileo assert that physical reality apart from our human experiences would contain nothing in the way of "odours, or tastes or sounds", while shapes, number and motion would remain even if there were no living creatures around to experience them.

Physical reality is fundamentally composed of primary qualities, and objects possess those qualities apart from any relation to a perceiver or subject of experience. Secondary qualities, by contrast, are essentially subjective in that they can be experienced in different ways by different subjects or by the same subject at different times. The same bucket of water can feel warm or cold depending on the temperature of the hand placed in the water. Secondary qualities are qualities the object has, however, only in relation to a subject of experience. They may well depend on primary qualities in complicated ways, as can be seen in the example of colour and its dependence on the spectral reflectance properties of surfaces. But secondary qualities are not reducible to, nor identical with, primary qualities. Experiences of colour, for instance, exhibit structural differences, such as the distinction between binary colours (mixtures of hues) and unique colours (single hues), which are due to differences in the visual appearance of colours, not in the reflectance properties of surfaces. Moreover, secondary qualities are subject-relative, admitting of differences in experience between and within subjects, which we have seen seem not to arise for an object's primary qualities.

The concept of primary and secondary qualities applies to sensations, not to perception of an environment. Perception does not start, however, with atomic sensations of primary and secondary qualities that must be enriched and given meaning by the sensory systems in the brain. Instead the environment we perceive is already meaningful, because it is made up of objects that relate in some way to human life. As Heidegger noted, we never "originally and really perceive a crowd of sensations – tones and noises, for example; rather we hear the storm whistling in the chimney, we hear the three-engine aeroplane, we hear the Mercedes in its immediate contrast with the Volkswagen". Heidegger continues: "Much closer to us than any sensations are the things themselves. We hear the door slam in the house, and never hear acoustic sensations, or mere sounds."[11]

The objects that we experience in the lifeworld are always related in some way to our concerns as human beings. They might be meaningful to a perceiver because of how they could be manipulated, put to work in the production of something. Of course, we perceive many objects in the lifeworld that are of no practical use to us, such as stars shooting across the sky. Whatever we can perceive will however affect us in some way that is a reflection of our human concerns, and what matters to us as human beings. This is as true of the shooting star we catch sight of while stargazing as it is of the hammer we take hold of when building a piece of furniture.

Heidegger says we are not "originally" aware of sensations in our ordinary, everyday perception of the world. He allows, however, that we can become aware of sensations by taking apart and decomposing our experience of the world into atomic building-blocks, like a painter does in constructing a pointillist painting. When we do find sensations in our experience, this is because we have abstracted away from the particular contexts and situations in which sensations ordinarily occur. Atomic sensations occur in the context of unified, structured meaningful experiences of the world. They are abstractions that we arrive at only when we cast an analytic eye on aspects of our everyday lived experience in the lifeworld, and begin to dissect an experience into parts that normally come woven together with specific contexts.

Philosophers often point to qualitative sensations in explaining the "hard problem" of consciousness.[12] They are what we seem not to be able to find room for in a natural-scientific conception of reality, what is left over once we have given a physical and functional or behavioural description of the causal processes on which consciousness depends. Yet, qualitative sensations only show up for us once we adopt an analytical attitude to experience, taking apart what would otherwise be unified and complex experiences of meaningful situations in the world. It follows that the notion of qualitative sensations is just as much an abstraction from everyday experience in the lifeworld as is physical reality itself. The problem of consciousness is thus ill-formed, in so far as its very formulation is based on a conception of subjective experience which is itself an abstraction and a distortion of what we ordinarily experience.

Once we have a conception of consciousness which starts from what we experience in the lifeworld, the philosophical problem of finding a place for consciousness in the natural world looks totally different. The problem becomes not that of explaining how consciousness could arise out of a physical reality from which subjects of experience have been excised and excluded. We must instead start from experience in the lifeworld; indeed there is no place outside such experiences of the lifeworld in which to stand. We must show how such experiences can be made intelligible using the concepts and theories of the natural sciences. It is to this problem of consciousness, so reconceived, to which I finally turn my attention.

The perception of the environment

I have characterised the lifeworld as the world that is meaningful to a subject because it is composed of objects that the subject can make sense of, in the light of subject-centred concerns which derive from their projects, interests and purposes. At the basic biological level of organisation, a subject's concerns derive from short-term, specific needs that relate to what Darwin described as "the conditions of life", such as growth, nutrition and reproduction.[13] Organisms as living systems purposefully and actively attain and maintain a viable form for the duration of their lives. They do so through internal reorganisation, and by regulating their interactions with the environment. Consider a bacterium performing chemotaxis, moving in the direction of the highest concentration of sucrose in a solution. Objects in the organism's environment have a value or meaning for it because of how they bear negatively or positively on its vital concerns. On the basis of a concern to stay alive, the organism marks out an environment that is meaningful, to which it actively responds.

Self-maintenance, however, only yields an all-or-nothing type of value, in which events in the environment are good or bad for survival. Human concerns, by contrast, take a variety of forms and are bound up with the rich social lives we lead and the diverse projects we pursue as participants in different cultural practices. If we are to understand the full spectrum of human concerns, we must pay close attention to social practices, which are among the sources of individuals' ideals, convictions and emotional investments. We might think here of emotions like shame, pride, guilt and hope as ways of evaluating and giving meaning to ourselves in relation to the social world. These emotions express what we care about, which is in no small part bound up with the place we occupy in the social world and the practices we engage in as socially situated agents.

The environment is the "condition of an animal's existence": it furnishes opportunities that are "propitious" and which the animal exploits in ways that contribute to its flourishing.[14] It offers challenges that are unpropitious which the organism seeks to avoid, or acts upon so as to change for the better. The environment of an animal is thus not the neutral setting for its behaviour, but is made up of objects that have a value and meaning relative to the being whose environment it is. The animal and its environment form a complementary pair. There can be no organism without an environment, since the organism develops traits and behaviours that are tightly coordinated with the environment it inhabits. Nor can there be an environment without an organism, since the environment is composed of objects that have a meaning and value that derive from the organism.

The ecological psychologist J.J. Gibson coined the term "affordances" to refer to the value-laden meaning that objects in the environment have for an animal. Gibson defined "affordances" as what the environment "offers the animal, what it provides or furnishes, for good or ill".[15] Classic examples of affordances are surfaces that can be walked on or climbed, objects that are graspable or that can be thrown, foods that are edible or poisonous and so on. I take the concept of affordance, as did Gibson, to apply to everything that can be found within an animal's ecological niche. What an animal perceives are first and foremost the meaningful opportunities and challenges provided by its ecological setting.

Gibson wrote that his concept of affordances cross-cut the distinction we are used to making between objective physical reality and the subjective, phenomenal and mental life of the mind:

> But, actually, an affordance is neither an objective property nor a subjective property; or it is both if you like. An affordance cuts across the dichotomy of subjective–objective and helps us to understand its inadequacy. It is equally a fact of the environment, and a fact of behaviour. It is both physical and psychical, yet neither. An affordance points both ways, to the environment and to the observer.[16]

This often-quoted passage is actually rather puzzling: how can anything have the status of being both subjective and objective? I take Gibson's point to be that affordances are *relations* of a particular kind between an animal and its environment. They do not have a purely subjective or phenomenal existence, because affordances are resources the environment supplies to an animal. Yet, affordances are not purely objective properties of the environment either, since the environment is only resourceful relative to the life of a particular animal that has specific needs and interests, and the abilities required for exploiting the opportunities the environment offers to them. The morphology – the structure, composition and size of the animal's body – will also influence what the environment affords. Fish have the type of bodies that allows them to breathe underwater, while humans have such a body only when making use of underwater diving equipment. Affordances are not in the environment alone but nor are they entirely subjective depending on the perceiver. They are relations between animals and their environments.

What an animal perceives are thus not objects that possess primary and secondary qualities, but affordances that relate in some way to the animal's concerns. Consider in this light the extensive evidence that spatial properties such as size and distance, traditionally conceived of as primary qualities, are scaled to metrics that derive from the morphology of the body and its abilities. Dennis Proffitt and his colleagues have found that visual information relating to size and distance is modulated and scaled to the body, based on the body's morphology, physiology and behaviour.

In one striking experiment, subjects wore goggles that either magnified or shrank the apparent size of an object, yet when they placed their hand next to an object the shrinking or magnifying effect disappeared.[17] In another experiment in which subjects were given the task of making a golf putt, the size of the hole looked larger to golfers who were good at putting than to their less successful counterparts.[18] Jumping ability has also been found to influence the perceived extent of a jumpable gap.[19] Finally, subjects wearing a heavy backpack were found to perceive the slant of a hill to be much steeper than did those not wearing a backpack and similar effects were found after inducing fatigue through exercise.[20]

These experiments seem to show that individuals perceive the spatial layout of the environment in relation to the experience they have of their bodies. The person's body functions as a "perceptual ruler" that is the basis for experiencing spatial properties such as distance and size. Different perceptual rules are employed depending on the purposes of the perceiver. For instance, objectively the same distance to a target has been found to be perceived differently by subjects, depending on whether they were given the task of walking to the target or throwing a beanbag at the target's location.[21] The environment that shows up for us in perception is an environment relative to the details of our embodiment, and our abilities. Proffitt and Linkenauger write: "In a given situation, we perceive the possibilities for action, and given our purposes, the world is scaled to that aspect of our body that is relevant for the pursuit of achievable aims."[22]

We have arrived at the view of perceptual consciousness as concerned engagement of a subject of experience with the possibilities and challenges the surrounding environment poses for this subject. Conscious experience is not something that happens inside of the brain, but is in large part enacted by the subject in its temporally extended, skilful interactions with its environment. There are obviously modes of conscious experience in which the subject is not engaged with its environment, such as dreaming and perceptual imagining. These have however not been my concern here. My focus has instead been on perceptual consciousness, and we should not suppose that the account we give of dreams and other modes of environmentally decoupled experience carries across to modes of consciousness in which subjects are involved with the world.

Given the phenomenological characterisation of conscious experience I have outlined, how should a naturalistic explanation of consciousness proceed? We would be looking for consciousness in the wrong place if we concentrated our explanatory efforts on the neural processes inside the heads of individuals. If experience were biologically realised by processes that were entirely internal to the brain, would not this require us to say the resulting experiences were likewise located inside the individual? I have been arguing that the phenomenology of perceptual consciousness is that of a subject engaged with, and immersed in, a meaningful world rich with opportunities and challenges. On the basis of this phenomenological characterisation of conscious experience, I suggest that the biological basis of conscious experience, so characterised, is likely to take the form of dynamic couplings between the perceiving animal and its environment. Perceptual consciousness is rooted in temporally extended animal–environment dynamics. An explanation of perceptual consciousness will therefore come in part from dynamical systems theory.

The dynamic coupling between the perceiving animal and its environment means that the parameters that drive change in the system over time can be located on either side of the animal's skin.[23] The coupling functions, in terms of which we explain the behaviour in an animal–environment system, describe how organismic variables change as a function of environmental parameters, but equally how environmental variables change as a function of organismic parameters. The causal influence between the organism and environment is thus bi-directional and tightly coordinated, so that organism and environment are best thought of as forming a single, dynamical system. Any conception of the organism and environment as separate systems that causally couple with each other is a matter of explanatory convenience rather than reflecting the real causal dynamics of these systems.

Conclusion

Where does this leave us with respect to the "hard problems" of consciousness? These are the problems, with which I began, of explaining in the terms of the natural sciences why an experience has the subjective qualities it does, or any subjective qualities whatsoever. I have argued that there is much that is misleading in this way of formulating the scientific problem of consciousness. First, it assumes an untenable separation of the subjective and objective dimensions of reality. I have argued that the world we are ordinarily in contact with in everyday experience (the "lifeworld") is neither a subjective construct nor an objective physical reality as described by the natural sciences. It is a world that is meaningful to us because of our human concerns. Secondly, I have argued that scientists must always work within the lifeworld in attempting to explain what it is to be conscious. This fact, however, does not make consciousness into something that is fundamentally mysterious to the natural sciences. I have ended by suggesting how we can use the tools of dynamical systems theory to make scientifically intelligible the biological basis of consciousness in the world. Perceptual consciousness has its basis in the self-organising dynamics of a brain–body–environment system. The brain supports consciousness only as one part of that larger relational system, which includes the body and the world.

I have further argued that what is given to the subject from the first-person point of view is a world that is significant and meaningful because of how it bears on the subject's purposes and interests. Conscious experience occurs in and through the subject's perceptual engagement with this world. The contents of conscious experience are not the result of assembling discrete atomic sensations. The latter are rather abstractions from experience in the lifeworld. The problem of consciousness, as I have characterised it, is the problem of explaining experience in the lifeworld. It is this problem which I have suggested we may begin to make progress with, by using the tools of dynamical systems theory to investigate how consciousness is rooted in the temporally extended dynamics of the perceiver's interactive worldly engagements.

1. See, eg, T. Nagel, *Mind and Cosmos: Why the Materialist Neo-Darwinian Conception of Nature is Almost Certainly False*, Oxford, Oxford University Press, 2012, chap. 3.

2. G. Galileo, 'The Assayer: A Letter to the Illustrious and very Reverend Don Virginio Cesarini', repr. in *Discoveries and Opinions of Galileo*, trans. S. Drake, New York, NY, Doubleday & Co., 1957 [1623].

3. E. Husserl, *Ideas Pertaining to a Pure Phenomenology and to a Phenomenological Philosophy*, vol. 2, trans. R. Rojcewicz & A. Schuwer, Dordrecht, Kluwer, 1989 [1913], sect. 11, p. 29.

4. E. Husserl, *The Crisis of the European Sciences and Transcendental Phenomenology: An Introduction to Phenomenological Philosophy*, trans. D. Carr, Evanston, IL, Northwestern University Press, 1970 [1954].

5. W. Sellars, 'Philosophy and the Scientific Image of Man', in R. Colodny (ed.), *Frontiers of Science and Philosophy*, Pittsburgh, PA, University of Pittsburgh Press, 1963, p. 35.

6. See, eg, A. Seth et al., 'Measuring Consciousness: Relating Behavioural and Neurophysiological Approaches', *Trends in Cognitive Science*, vol. 12, no. 8, 2008, pp. 314–21, and for a critical discussion L. Irvine, *Consciousness as a Scientific Concept: A Philosophy of Science Perspective*, Dordrecht, Springer, 2012.

7. See the essay by Schiff in this volume.

8. E. Thompson, *Waking, Dreaming, Being: Self and Consciousness in Neuroscience, Meditation and Philosophy*, New York, NY, Columbia University Press, 2015, p. 100.

9. "Homeodynamics", as against the conventional notion of homeostasis, recognises that the complexity and volatility of living organisms involves more than negative feedback mechanisms sustaining monotonic stationary states.

10. C. McGinn, *The Mysterious Flame: Consciousness in a Material World*, New York, NY, Basic Books, 1999.

11. M. Heidegger, 'The Origin of the Work of Art', trans. D.F. Krell, in *Martin Heidegger: Basic Writings*, New York, NY, Harper & Row, 1977, p. 156.

12. D. Chalmer, *The Conscious Mind: In Search of a Fundamental Theory*, Oxford, Oxford University Press, 1996.

13. C. Darwin, *On the Origin of Species by Means of Natural Selection*, London, Penguin Classics, 1967 [1859].

14. D.M. Walsh, 'The Struggle for Life and the Conditions of Existence: Two Interpretations of Darwinian Evolution', in F. Brinkworth & F. Weinert (eds.), *Evolution 2.0: Implications of Darwinism in Philosophy and the Social and Natural Sciences*, Dordrecht, Springer, 2012.

15. J.J. Gibson, *The Ecological Approach to Visual Perception*, Mahwah, NJ, Lawrence Erlbaum, 1979, p. 127.

16. Gibson, p. 129.

17. S.A. Linkenhauger, V.C. Ramenzoni & D.R. Proffitt, 'Illusory Shrinkage and Growth: Body-Based Scaling Affects the Perception of Size', *Psychological Science*, vol. 21, no. 9, 2010, pp. 1318–25.

18. J.K. Witt, 'Putting to a Bigger Hole: Golf Performance Relates to Perceived Size', *Psychonomic Bulletin Review*, vol. 15, no. 3, pp. 581–85.

19. D.A. Lessard, S.A. Linkenhauger & D.R. Proffitt, 'Look Before you Leap: Jumping Ability Affects Distance Perception', *Perception*, vol. 38, no. 12, 2009, pp. 1863–66.

20. M. Bhalla & D.R. Proffitt, 'Visual-Motor Recalibration in Geographical Slant Perception', *Journal of Experimental Psychology: Human Perception and Performance*, vol. 25, no. 4, 1999, pp. 1076–96.

21. J.K. Witt, D.R. Proffitt & W. Epstein, 'Perceiving Distance: A Role of Effort and Intent', *Perception*, vol. 33, no. 5, 2004, pp. 570–90.

22. D.R. Proffitt & S.A. Linkenhauger, 'Perception Viewed as a Phenotypic Expression', in W. Prinz, M. Biesert & A. Herwig (eds.), *Action Science: Foundations of an Emerging Discipline*, Cambridge, MA, MIT Press, 2013, p. 192.

23. A. Chemero, *Radical Embodied Cognitive Science*, Cambridge, MA, MIT Press, 2009; M. Silberstein & A. Chemero, 'Complexity and Extended Phenomenological-Cognitive Systems', *Topics in Cognitive Science*, vol. 4, no. 1, 2012, pp. 1–16.

THE SĀMMITĪYAS AND
THE CASE OF THE MISSING WHO

Amber D. Carpenter

A Buddhist Whodunnit? The scene of the crime

It was a cold, clear afternoon, the air heavy with the smell of burning rubber, acrid in the back of the throat; heart pounding, blood rushing to the head as a single shot rings out; then the scrape of shoes against gravel, legs pumping: "Did anyone see?"

Who is the murderer?

The same person who shivered outside, seeing the black factory smoke rising and tasting it, feeling the rush of blood in the ears, hearing the shot and the footsteps.

No doubt. But who is that, over and above the particulars mentioned?

One could mention more particulars: it was a self-taught, middle-aged man, long nose, likes playing cards… There are endless such particulars. And if one is assisting in the creation of a police profile, this is exactly what is needed.

But if we are asking why the police are searching for this person – or, rather, what it is that warrants the police search, the subsequent investigation, verdict and punishment – then no amount of any such particulars will get us what we think we are looking for, when we ask: *Whodunnit?* For in that case, what we seek is not any of those particulars, nor all of them together, nor some magically relevant subset, but somehow the owner or ground or explanation of them all. It was not the long nose, after all, that committed the murder, nor the proclivity for cards. It was not even the elegant finger with the well-manicured nail that committed the murder – even if it did, technically speaking, pull the trigger. It was the owner of that elegant finger, the person who takes pleasure in gambling, *the man himself* who is the murderer.

Only something persisting through changes in all those particulars (or at least distinct from any one of them), at once an agent and a subject, as well as the synthesiser of various modalities of sense and cognition, could be the sort of thing that could be responsible for murder and so justifiably blamed and punished.

Pragmatics and metaphysics

Because of this, Buddhist minimalist metaphysics, which rejects the ultimate reality of any such thing as an agent–subject unifier, might look to be on a siding to nowhere. On the standard Abhidharma Buddhist view, there are no wholes, complex unities or substances bearing properties. Wherever a many is brought together into a "one", this is an indication of mental activity interpreting reality, rather than just taking reality as it is. And this principle holds above all with respect to the supposed wholeness of persons. This view is given philosophical articulation in Vasubandhu's 4th-century *Abhidharmakośa*, but it is evident already in the 1st-century *Milindapañha*'s well-known likening of the deconstructed chariot to the proper referent of the name Nāgasena. The *Milindapañha* passage itself is in turn an explicit exposition of the principle given voice by the *bhikkhunī* Vajirā, in the early Pāli *Saṃyutta Nikāya*, the *Connected Discourses of the Buddha*.

Approached by Māra, confusion, with the challenge, "By whom has this being been created? ... Where has the being arisen? Where does the being cease?",[1] Vajirā replies:

> Why now do you assume "a being"? ... This is a heap of sheer formations. Here no being is found. Just as, with an assemblage of parts, the word "chariot" is used, so when the aggregates exist, there is the convention "a being". It is only suffering that comes to be, suffering that stands and falls away.

This Buddhist no-self claim may not have originally been at heart a specific metaphysical claim,[2] although it was certainly developed in that direction, and may have had to have been so developed to be taken seriously at all.[3] The "self" Vajirā repudiates here may not have a single determinate meaning, not even that given to "self" by those early Hindu seekers of *ātman* inspired by the *Upaniṣads'* elusive descriptions of a hidden self within.[4] "Self", as the Buddha enjoined us *not* to seek it, is simply whatever version of self provides something one could cling to, clinging to which generates suffering:

> "You may well cling to that doctrine of self that would not arouse sorrow, lamentation, pain, grief, and despair in one who clings to it. But do you see any such doctrine of self, *bhikkhus?*" – "No, venerable

sir." – "Good, *bhikkhus.* I too do not see any doctrine of self that would not arouse sorrow, lamentation, pain, grief, and despair in one who clings to it."[5]

The central importance of "that to which one could cling" in defining the "self" that is to be rejected can be seen even in the classic formulations of the moment of liberation. *Who* is liberated was famously rejected as a badly formulated question;[6] instead descriptions of liberation are wholly impersonal: "Birth is destroyed, the holy life has been lived, what had to be done has been done, there is no more coming to any state of being."[7]

Conceptions of the self which generate suffering – that is to say, according to the Buddha, *all* conceptions of self – do so by drawing boundaries between "mine" and "not mine". After the claim in §22 of the Snake Sutta that any conception of self leads to suffering, the *sutta* goes on to observe that, if there were a self, then there would be what belongs to the self (§25); as there is no self, neither is there anything that is "mine". We are then enjoined, several paragraphs later (§40–1), to abandon whatever is "not yours", which is to say, properly understood, all feelings, thoughts or perceptions thought of as "my own" or belonging to me.[8] A conception of the self is harmful just in so far as it hinders my ability to abandon thinking of things as "my own". To think of myself *as myself* is to distinguish "me" from "not me", and determine a subset of reality as *mine*: this bit belongs to me, the rest not; this bit is my special concern, the rest not. That is to say, the metaphysical "selves" that Buddhism rejects are whichever entities that, believing them to exist, cause in us a *sense of self* which divides and does not conquer.

That we commonly have a sense of self is a phenomenological fact which cannot be denied; that this sense of self must indicate the real existence of some thing answering to that sense is firmly rejected.[9] On the contrary, recognition of the lack of any such thing should dissolve our sense of self, and this dissolution of a sense of self will remove the pervasive suffering that characterises existence.

This means that a Buddhist theory of consciousness can handle neatly a certain sort of "problem of consciousness" which has beset early modern European philosophy and its inheritors.[10] For if the problem of consciousness is just the fact of subjectivity – where this means primarily "what-it's-like"-ness, or the fact that there is anything that experiences are like at all – then no Buddhists have a problem with it. Consciousness moments, events of being like something or another, are among the basic constituents of reality.[11] But if "subjectivity" means some kind of "mineness",[12] a fundamental distinction between me and everything else (or privileged access by someone to something), then the Buddhist will baulk.[13] For the ills associated with appropriating this or that as "mine", with holding fast to a tight distinction between "me" and everything else – you, the world – are precisely what the Buddhist aims to eliminate with her distinctive "no-self" claim.

This appropriating sense of self can be eliminated, Buddhist philosophers argue, by recognising that non-interpreted reality, including especially us as part of reality, is just a vast quantity of successive occurrences of various simple properties. These simple property-particulars happen, and with that they are over – they go out of existence.[14] The set of occurring properties at one time are the causal conditions for the subsequent set of momentary occurrences. Everything else is wishful thinking (conventional, or conceptual reality – *saṃvṛtisat* as it is known in Buddhist discourse). In particular, conceiving of an agent ("I *did* this, it didn't just happen"), a subject ("I *feel* this, it is not just an event occurring somewhere") or a unifier and its boundary-drawing ("This is my action, my desire, my pain; that is not me, does not constrain my will or is not my concern") – each alone could generate a sense of self to cling to, something to care about, whether it remains, whether it goes in some preferred way, whether it is under threat or a matter of indifference. But if that is so, it looks as if Buddhist minimalism necessarily rejects any "self" capable of playing the role necessary for attributing responsibility.

Indeed, the metaphysics implied by the pragmatics of no-self, any of the many versions of a metaphysical picture that can make sense of no-self as a legitimate and necessary ethical practice, seems to raise two related insurmountable problems for attributions of responsibility. These are of particular interest in so far as Buddhist metaphysical minimalism looks strikingly similar to a certain respectable scientific picture of who and what we are – so that if indeed the Buddhists have a problem here, we should perhaps be worried that their problem is our problem.

The first difficulty is that, on a metaphysics of flux, there is no element persisting over time – in particular over the time between the act, the result and the punishment for it. There is no one there to be held responsible. We have different bundles of personal elements at different times but, as the Buddhists' opponents had been telling them for centuries, one cannot hold one bundle responsible for the acts of a different bundle: it is plainly unfair to hold Yajñadatta responsible for what Devadatta did. Moreover, if there is no principle of unity – nothing which is the *person herself* to whom the multitude of properties belong – then what are we even holding responsible? The finger that pulled the trigger? The neuron whose firing made the finger move? The moment of intention or decision, which is now past?[15] If there is no unity or unifier or persistence through time, it is difficult even to make out the *murder* in the mass of changing and interconnected but disjunct parts.

The second apparently insurmountable problem comes from the closely related principle of dependent origination. It is a vital part of basic Buddhism that nothing arises without a cause (all arises dependent on conditions, *pratītyasamutpāda*), and this is actively applied to mental as well as physical events. This perfectly kosher commitment to a principle of sufficient reason, however, raises the dark spectre of determinism, more darkly for rejecting a distinct agent as an uncaused original principle of action.

We turn first to this latter difficulty.

The red herring: The illusory problem of free will
Every good detective story needs a red herring to throw our investigators off the scent. Here the red herring is "free will" – and, more specifically, the supposition that this would solve our problem if only we could find such a thing. What we care about in attributions of responsibility, the thought goes, is the deliberate choice to act. When there are accidental or merely mechanical or physical causes, we do not praise and blame; but where the cause of some event can be traced back to an unforced choice or decision to act, then we can hold responsible that person who freely chose to act in this way. On this view, the person, for forensic purposes, is those psychophysical elements most closely associated with this active, choosing will, and it is this free will that grounds the legitimacy of holding them responsible. If the Buddhists can offer something to play this role, then we can do without selves and continue blaming and praising; if they cannot, then consistency requires refraining from praise and blame.

It might be thought that such a solution is obviously unavailable to the Buddhists, for the will that grounds attributions of responsibility must endure as the same will over time in order to serve its function. But such persistence is precisely what Abhidharma metaphysics rejects. When we are looking for the "who" of consciousness, and we are doing so because we want to know who to praise and blame and with what right, we have to find some free agent behind the act – and this free agent has got to be the same, over time and across psychological capacities, if we are to be able to blame or punish a wrongdoer. After all, it is not the episodic acts of willing that are held responsible but the *person who wills*, in virtue of their so willing.

But rather than a non-starter, spelling out the option suggests a way the Buddhist could avail herself of this solution, if it seemed a good one. If it is the episode of free choice that grounds holding the *person* responsible, then the Buddhist need only have a non-standard account of what that person is (a bundle and not a soul) in order to appeal to the same solution. We Buddhists, they might say, hold responsible that bundle of psycho-physical events which is uniquely closely associated with the moment of willing which set in motion whichever culpable events it is we are interested in. This is not yet a full answer, because we may well wonder whether close association can ground accountability in the way that sameness or identity can. So we will return to look at this move more closely, once we have disposed of the free-will version of it – because considering this false trail will provide an important clue to getting hold of the Buddhist view the right way round.

Quite apart from questions of unity and persistence, free will is thought to be a precondition for attributions of responsibility of the sort we are interested in when we praise and blame, or when we hold someone *morally* accountable. It should explain why it is we offer a helping hand to the person who was pushed over into our azalea garden, while we rebuke someone who stomps all over our azaleas. If the Buddhists' view can make good this distinction, then we might perhaps allow them their peculiar bundle-persons as the proximate location of this crucial ground of moral accountability.

The problem with this line of thought is that there is a deep confusion in the very notion of free will.[16] What is supposedly wanted is conceptually impossible. This indeed may be why their non-Buddhist critics never raised the objection that Buddhist *determinism* left persons insufficiently *free* to be held accountable.[17] If such a thing as free will is not found to ground moral accountability, this is not an especially Buddhist problem:[18] if it is a problem for anyone, it is a problem for everyone equally. Yet it need be a problem for no one.

The difficulty begins, innocuously enough, with Aristotle's claim that we are praised and blamed only for what is "up to us".[19] Aristotle, however, had no inkling of a faculty of "will", still less of that will being "free", and he was untroubled about holding adults responsible for values and actions based on habits inculcated from childhood – from before the age when anything could have been "up to us".[20] Only once free will was invented did this turn into an insoluble problem, for only then could we demand that there be some undetermined, independent and original cause of action in us, and think that we were making sense. As Hume already pointed out, however, if this cause is undetermined, then it is random, and if it is determined by anything external, then it is not free in the sense demanded.[21] If we want to say that it is self-determining, the same dilemma arises again: if this self-determining original cause is nothing but a principle of action or choice, and does not itself have content, then its choices (or volitions), while self-caused, are still arbitrary. If this self has content, so that its choices may be non-arbitrary, it is not such as to have control over that content.[22]

One might take a Kantian line and say that all action-initiators are *eo ipso* rational – and that there is sufficient content to reason itself that this can determine the will non-arbitrarily. Or one can reject Kantianism and go instead for "personality-ism": each action-initiator has a particular, distinctive and contentful outlook or personality which does the determining. But, in either case, it cannot be the action-initiator as such that has *chosen* that it be constituted by rationality, or by this particular personality. That is just what it is to be the thing that it is.

At some point, this latter move must be made. To look for anything else is incoherent. But then our question is: at what point do we make that move, to preserve coherent attributions of "moral" responsibility?

According to the Abhidharma Buddhists, and also to the ancient Greeks, who also did not suffer from the conceptual confusion of "free will", moral responsibility is attributable to persons when persons are the cause of an action.[23] What caused a person to be such as to be the cause of such an action is a practical question, sometimes of relevance in determining the best response to another's action, but not usually decisive in determining a category difference between the accountable and the non-accountable. So too, say the Buddhists, the question of why we pause in the chain of causes *just there* is a pragmatic concern, not a principled one.[24] (We will look at this more closely below.)

Just as with the notion of an independent agent to ground responsibility, so too, argue the Buddhists, the search for the "who" behind consciousness is a red herring. Consider an argument for no-self with close parallels to the free-will discourse outlined above. At *Saṃyutta Nikāya* III.66, we are told that body, for instance, could not be "self "because the body is liable to all sorts of conditions we would not wish for ourselves; if it *were* ourselves, we would have control over its states and conditions. And so similarly for any candidate (feeling, thought, volition) for self – they arise and take forms we would not choose, showing that we do not control them. The principle at work seems to be: if it were *my* self, it would be under my control.

But there is a peculiarity here. The self should be whatever controls, not that which is owned, determined, directed, but that which does the directing and determining. If it turned out that bodies, cognitions or volitions *were* controllable, this would not make them the self; this would make their controller the self. Or else, if that would make them my self, what would we call that which did the controlling? Under whose control is it? *Mine?* The self we would have discovered would turn out to be something I *have*, but it would not *be* me. The self that I am remains as elusive as ever, so long as we suppose unconditioned power to determine is somewhere to be found. We wish to identify ourselves as that which is "up to us", since this ensures our authority,[25] yet this attempt requires the distinction between the determiner and the determined, the owner and the owned. Once the distinction is drawn, the categories constructed, then it becomes apparent that it is the controller, not the controlled, that should be the self. The Buddhist no-self claim is precisely that this elusive self-controlling controller is illusory.[26] All we have, and all we need, is consciousness, successive moments of consciousness, and various ways of misconstruing them so as to satisfy our misguided aims and ambitions. Everyone would be a lot happier if we would just leave off with all the interpretation – or at least, for heaven's sake, not mistake it for real.

Thus, for instance, chapter 9 of the *Ornament for the Laity*, an Abhidharma text from probably the 12th century, makes precisely this connection.[27] If the non-Buddhist is inclined to insist that consciousness must be grounded in some further thing, a self, then their self will likewise require some cause or ground for its existence. What is sauce for the goose is sauce for the gander. If lacking grounding in something else makes consciousness inefficacious and indeed non-existent, then the self of precisely the groundless, uncaused and independent sort the self theorist postulates must be likewise inefficacious and non-existent, along with all of its supposed attendant attributes or effects.[28]

The main point is to fend off the demand that consciousness be grounded in something else besides consciousness, in order to be consciousness at all.[29] But the means of doing so challenges the search for ultimate or final grounds at all. The Abhidharma Buddhists do not believe that moments of consciousness are *uncaused – of course* any particular moment of consciousness has causal conditions for arising as and when it does. But no cause can be asked to play the role of the one unconditioned cause at which everything stops, or from which everything begins. Drawing attention to the Buddhists' failure to attribute responsibility for consciousness to some independent self only exposes the conception of such a self as itself lacking ground, and so liable to the very objection it attempted to raise.[30] Something "free" in the sense of "independent of conditions" cannot, by its nature, play the role for which it was supposedly designed.

Responsibility without freedom

So we are back where we started in trying to understand attributions of responsibility without recourse to selves of the sort that endure as the same thing over time and unite various modalities – though we have, perhaps, a somewhat better view of what the no-self claim is. The Buddhist cannot point to an act of free will as ultimately responsible for some chains of events and not others, and so cannot warrant apportioning moral responsibility on that sort of ground. But this only throws more weight on the importance of selves to play the individuating role necessary for fair apportionment of responsibility. The fact that belief, evaluation, perception and desire are united in action means I am *warranted* in resenting the wanton destruction of my azaleas, whereas I may only feel dismay at the gust of wind that does the same damage.[31] The distinctive sort of psychological unity established only by a self, and manifested in genuine *action* (as opposed to mere movement), explains why we are rightly solicitous towards someone pushed into our azaleas, while we rebuke the azalea-stomper.[32] Without such a self, there is no distinction between actions and events and, without that distinction, there is no possibility for genuine accountability. The Buddhists cannot make this basic distinction, for they reject the fundamental reality of any such unity. Each person-constituting element has sufficient conditions for its arising, but there is no distinct cause of their unity[33] – this is just what it means to reject the self as the ground or cause of affects and actions. Without some real unity to the person-constituting elements, however, there can be no warrant for attributing *moral* responsibility. I might trace back the causes of death to this particular neural network giving the signal to the finger to pull the trigger, but I will find no one to hold accountable for *murder*.[34] Indeed, the murder itself seems to dissolve into a rearrangement of constituents. There is not only no one to bear *moral* responsibility, there is nothing for which to be responsible.[35]

This same unifying feature of agency enables us to individuate persons in apportioning responsibility; it grounds the basic principle that only the person who *did* the deed may be called to account for it. A non-substantialist process ontology commits the Abhidharmikas, their critics charged, with punishing Yajñadatta for what Devadatta did – that is, with punishing a psychophysical bundle at time t_2 for the actions of a non-identical psychophysical bundle at time t_1. If there is no real unity to the streams of elements, then the bundle of psychophysical elements (including the intention) at the time of the action will be *as different from* the bundle at the time of punishment as are (what we would ordinarily call) two distinct persons at one time, Yajñadatta and Devadatta. But it is patently incoherent to punish Yajñadatta for what Devatta did. And so it must be equally absurd, on the Buddhist view, to punish *any* set of personal psychophysical factors, *ever* – since, by virtue of the Buddhists' commitment to the transience of such factors, no such set could *ever* be identical with the set that committed the crime. If Buddhists can meet this objection, then they will have identified a principle of individuation and, if individuation is possible, then we therewith have won unity. The question will be whether this is sufficient unity to make out a moral distinction between the malicious azalea-destruction and the gust of wind – and, if so, whether Buddhists have thereby conceded the existence of the very sort of self they had rejected.

Now the objection may rest on a basic misunderstanding of what the Buddhist no-self view is.[36] The lack of an enduring subject or agent unifier does not entail that a momentary bundle of personal elements counts as a person, so that non-identical bundles at different times must necessarily count as two persons. The Buddhist does not just reject substance: she *replaces it* with process, or continuity. Indeed, the second chapter of the second book of the *Milindapañha* – the chapter following immediately on from the well-known chariot example deconstructing the real and substantial unity of the person – is full of several illustrations of causal continuity, exemplifying precisely how responsibility is nevertheless legitimately attributed in virtue of these continuities. On the classic Abhidharma view, this tightly related bundle of events now is a close causal descendant of that bundle of events there. Each one is such as to arise only under these very specific preceding conditions, each of which in turn is such as to be the effect of precisely the preceding conditions. It is the whole process, and not each moment, that gets to be called a person. And it is so called only because recognising *just these* sorts of close causal connections as belonging together proves very effective in serving our purposes. This is how we should understand people as the heirs of their actions (*MN* 135)[37], as "owners of their actions, heirs of their actions; they originate from their actions, are bound to their actions, have their actions as their refuge. It is action that distinguishes beings as inferior and superior."

Similar appeals to continuity in place of identity over time are still being made, to address the same worry, in the 12th-century *Ornament for the Laity*, which maintains that

> just as in ordinary life one can see the process of plant growth (taking place) without an agent, (but simply) depending on (the existence of) earth, water, warmth, (the appropriate) season, and so on, so one can see that the process (by which) these Good Deeds (give rise to their results), (occurs) because of the coming together of (appropriate) causes and conditions.[38]

If this appeal to causal continuities without a unifier suffices to legitimate attributions of responsibility, one of the reasons will be a pragmatic understanding of responsibility attribution. This is why the Buddhist rejoinder to the challenge so regularly takes the form of an appeal to the distinction between "conventional" and "ultimate" reality. Conventional reality is real, in a way – more to the point, it is *just as real as* actions, and as real as we need it to be for our purposes. This is because it *gets its legitimacy* from our purposes: what are conventionally regarded and treated as wholes are appropriately so treated just in so far as, and because, doing so enables us effectively to achieve our purposes.[39] What is it we are trying *to do*, Buddhists ask, when attributing responsibility? Their answer is clear:

we want to locate the causes and conditions that tend to generate suffering, so as to eliminate them and replace them with causes and conditions
that generate non-suffering. And so which successions of events are considered distinct processes will be responsive to this need, and which of
those pragmatically individuated processes will be of a kind to bear
responsibility will depend on which of them will be effectively responded
to *as* accountable.[40]

Plants may be processes – successions of events it is useful for us to
individuate – but there is no profit in our holding them accountable. If the
tree's branch is old and rotted, it will fall when it does regardless of any
resentment and punishment we may or may not send its way.

The case is different with processes conventionally called persons, and
distinguished from plants precisely because intentionality is a constituent
element in the process. Persons (human and non-human) have intentions,
aims, hopes and fears; and, for an intentional being, customs of resentment and accountability do indeed have causal influence in the direction
the process takes – that is, they can be effective in reducing suffering. So
intentions will turn out to matter, in a way. Although they will not be
conceived of as ultimate grounds or independent causes, they will be
decisive in determining whether attribution of responsibility is appropriate or not. Accountability will not always be in order: even among person
processes, there are a wide variety of causes and conditions for suffering,
each with their own form of effective remedy, and Buddhism attends to
them all. But experience shows that the particular causal factor of intention is more effectively prevented from arising when generally responded
to differently from the way other causal conditions are addressed.[41]

So if someone is injured by a heavy branch falling on him, the appropriate response (besides attending to the wounds) is a practice of regularly
identifying and removing dead wood from trees. If, by contrast, someone
is injured by a club being wielded by someone with hostile intent, we have
taken it that a practice of causing successors of that intention's psychophysical bundle some form of restraint and pain tends to be more effective in creating conditions under which such intentions do not arise in
future. We may, of course, be mistaken about the efficacy of painful punishment – indeed, we probably are. But a response that addresses the
process by which intentions are generated will be called for, rather than
one that addresses tree growth. And this type of responsiveness is what
we call "holding responsible".

This may well force us to reconceive blaming;[42] it should almost certainly cause us to rethink forms of punishment for and responses to any harm that has "intention to harm" among its causal conditions. But it does not make attributions of moral responsibility incoherent – on the contrary, it is a fairly conventional account of what distinguishes attributions of "moral" responsibility from other types of responsibility attribution.[43]

Even without a persisting and unified self, I am responsible for my actions, where "I" picks out a process of causally connected psychophysical events, and actions (as opposed to mere movements) are mine when appropriately related to intentions arising in this same process. Although there is no real unity, unifier or persisting element within this process, and although the process is typically driven onward by (and in turn generates) a sense of self, we are not concerned here with actions I merely *take to be* mine or feel are mine. Such feelings and self-assessments can be unreliable in both directions: I may not recognise as mine actions that clearly follow from my definite intentions and no other, and I may feel as mine some action that in fact is more properly credited to other causes. We are not concerned with a sense of self, or with a process of identification, but with what really can be properly attributed to me – only this can legitimate accountability. According to the Abhidharma Buddhist, however, these actions are not mine in virtue of either (1) their having an independent will as their original source or (2) their components being united by, or grounded in, a real and irreducible whole. The actions are "mine" in the purely locative sense of having an intention arising in the context of *this* rather than some other bundle of mental events.

We might think that there is an obvious problem here in individuating bundles and streams – after all, the Buddhist minimalist claim is that all such complex wholes are not held together by any metaphysical glue. Certainly the Buddhists' Nyāya critics pressed the point. The objection returns us to the orginal concern: without real unity, you cannot have real individuals – not even real individual streams of bundles of psychophysical property-moments. So either there is nothing uniting bundle streams and the Buddhist is still punishing Yajñadatta for what Devadatta did, or else there is a principle of unity and that just is what it is for there to be a self – a self to cling to, serve, defend and prioritise over others.

Vasubandhu's reply to this line of thought is brilliantly economical: he simply reminds us that all attributions of unity, even stream-individuation, are pragmatic and *post hoc*. We individuate among manifold

causally connected processes in ways that enable us to communicate efficiently and effectively reach our aims. There is no need to *presume* individuation of persons to attribute responsibility, because it is the connections
between actions and consequences that our pragmatic individuation
tracks in the first place.[44] The holding responsible *is* the individuating.
Actions, their immediate necessary conditions and their closest successors
are the *grounds* of individuation – though not because of any mysterious
metaphysical specialness of action. It happens that carving our experiences according to these connections is useful. Since Buddhists tend to be
very sceptical of the aims determining our sense of usefulness, their critique of the self and their critique of conventional reality go hand in glove.

The plot thickens…

Not everybody was satisfied with this brilliantly economical reply. Of
course one would not expect those committed to the real existence of the
self as agent, or unifying subject, to be satisfied. More surprising is that
there were a large number of Buddhists, among them the eponymous
Sāmmitīyas, who were also not satisfied.[45]

For the first several hundred years of Buddhist theorising, a substantial
number of adherents held an interpretation of the Buddhist view according to which the person was ultimately real. The *self*, of course, was
rejected – these are still Buddhists we are talking about, and the self will
still be rejected, both as an independent individual and as an object of
searching or aspiration. Nevertheless, the *person* was, the Personalists
claimed, ultimately real: that is, it is just as real as its constituent event-
processes, and not something just projected by us onto reality, the better
to be able to bend experience to our wills.

Needless to say, these Buddhist Personalists were blacklisted. By far the
greater part of Vasubandhu's 'Treatise on the Person' (the part of the
auto-commentary on the *Abhidharmakośa* which comments on no verse of
the original text) is devoted to refuting the *pudgalavāda*. His is one of only
three accounts remaining to us of what the view actually was. One of the
other two is also from a decidedly hostile source – the Theravada text, the
Kathāvatthu. Naturally the Buddhist Personalists are depicted by their
Buddhist opponents as reintroducing the self by the back door. But, surprisingly to us, when they are so depicted, they are not accused – as we
might immediately presume – of making a distinction without a difference.
The Buddhist Personalist view was taken by its opponents as significantly

different from any of the self-as-agent/subject/unifier views (even if it did end up in the same place), and in need of different arguments against it.[46]

The reason for this, I suggest, is that the Personalist position was indeed a distinctive view and a philosophically motivated one. Thus, they required engagement not just as fellow Buddhists who had to be held to the standard of plausible interpretation of the Buddha's words; they required engagement as fellow philosophers concerned to make sense of reality – concerned in particular, in this case, with making sense of attributions of responsibility and their legitimacy.

The Personalists did not think that a purely conventional self or person, whose unity consisted entirely in *ex post facto* individuations that served our purposes, could account for or legitimate attributions of responsibility. It could not, they thought, dispatch the Yajñadatta–Devadatta objection; and it could not explain accountability of persons, because it could not consistently grant sufficient reality to moral acts taken as such (as theft, say, or murder) that they could be actions for which one might be held accountable.

There is a metaphysical dimension to the Personalist's complaint, and a practical one. Looking simply at the metaphysics, Buddhist minimalists like Vasubandhu deny that there is any right way of carving up reality, and bundling together simple momentary events, except as it is convenient for our purposes (as if our purposes could get off the ground without some carving up of reality). The only reality any complex whole has is that which it is useful for us to grant some subset of elementary events. But any morally valenced action – that is, any *action* properly so called, as distinct from simply another arising of events – is a complex phenomenon. Even if this is not just obvious, it must follow for any Buddhist who rejects isolated and independent moments of willing as the ground of responsibility and definitive of action. Without a wide variety of factors, including physical ones, *taken together as a whole*, there is no action – no theft, betrayal, fraud, assault or murder.

The level at which "murder" comes into focus *as such* is not the atomic level: at the atomic level, there is just a rearrangement of constituents. For there to be *murder*, different sorts of *dharmas* must interact with each other *so as to constitute a whole* – the murderous intention and its relation to the bodily movements constitutive of killing and their relation to perceptions and feelings of pleasure and pain must be taken together, for murder to be on the cards at all. But if that is right, we cannot take murder as that by reference to which we organise our bundle-individuating. That is, it cannot be *because* treating murder thus is useful that we are entitled to individuate person-processes as we do; for, without individuating the person-processes in the first place, there is no *murder*, and so nothing to motivate individuation.

The Buddhist minimalist may, through appeal to dependent origination, have a full explanation of the arising of any particular element constitutive of murder; but they do not allow that there is, or need be, any explanation of all of the elements coming together just as they do, so as to generate some distinctive and new thing, the *murder*. That, they say, is merely our retrospective and convenient way of considering an arbitrarily circumscribed subset of events. But, the Personalists observe, to consider something *as an action* is to take it to be embedded within and constituted by the interrelation of various sorts of factors. Perceptions can explain the arising of intentions and intentions the arising of perceptions; physical elements explain the arising of further similar and related such elements or events. But action exists at the intersection of these, and can only be understood as grounded in very particular arrangements of these and no other. The action arising may belong to conventional reality, but if the intersecting itself is not ultimately real then there is nothing to make it convenient for us to designate one set rather than another as a whole. Nothing can make it convenient to conceive of murder *as* murder, or events which arise subsequently as *results* of *murder*.

This has immediate practical implications. We noted above that the self which Buddhism rejects will be *whatever* sort of entity believing in which grounds the activity of distinguishing "me" from the rest of reality, and appropriating bits of reality as "mine", while dissociating from others. But there is an obvious problem with this strategy that is not often taken sufficiently seriously. If I should undermine any sense of self that would lead me to say "mine", how can I simultaneously retain a sense of responsibility for the effects of my actions and values? How do I conceive of myself as the inheritor of my acts? We are told by the Abhidharma Buddhists that the sense in which I am the bearer of the consequences of my action is simply that, events unfolding as they do, we take an interest in some associations and not others, and so designate them processes or continua. But the individuation of these is purely pragmatic, and not legitimated by any actual distinction between, or unity of, processes. This seems insufficient to generate and maintain a sense of responsibility for

my choices, values, words and actions – and, indeed, would seem positively to undermine it. A sense of self as something that is not just a con-
veniently circumscribed set of inevitable processes is the motivating
condition for good acts as much as bad ones.

The denouement

The Personalists do not think we have to posit a persisting self, nor an
independent principle of individuation, to address these problems. But
they do take the problems seriously as in need of some solution or another.
Simply saying "no-self" will not do. What they offer instead, what their
person-that-is-not-a-self should be, is a metaphysics of real but non-
essential individuation.

As good Buddhists and sober metaphysicians, the Personalists agree
that there is no extra element – a self, a subject, a principle of individuation
– to which a certain set of property-occurrences belong, or in which they
inhere, or which independently grounds the unity of the person. All the
same, it is not up to me – my interests, our conventions – whether *x* belongs
to a given continuum. Certain bits of reality do belong together, and not
equally to everything else; they belong to each other, we might say. We
cannot perhaps understand what these individual continuities are – better, we cannot explain their belonging together (to each other) in any other
way, by reference to anything else, which is to say, *at all*.[47] They simply do
– that is basic; and it *accounts for* our sense of there being more relevance
between this evil intention here and that wicked deed there than between,
say, my evil intention and your wicked deed.

Such real but non-essential individuation of events into continua or
processes suffices to generate a sense of responsibility, for it is not optional
or a matter of my convenience whether I should take any particular subset of causal factors together if they really do belong together; so, too, it is
not optional whether I happen to take an interest in some complex causal
consequence of such a continuum. The murder, *as murder,* may be only
conventionally real, but it arises as such not only based on our convenience and purposes but also on the very real intersection of intentions,
perceptions and motions that are the person.

This sense of responsibility, enabled by appeal to the non-negotiable
belonging of personal factors to each other so as to constitute a person,
is a condition for wholesome intentions and actions arising. But this
sense of responsibility does not, the Personalist will claim, generate a

sense of "mine" as opposed to others – it does not, that is to say, generate a sense of self.

For there is nobody and nothing *to whom* the person-constituting factors belong (they belong to each other); there is nothing whose independence is threatened by the existence of others (the continua are not independent, and do not need to be in order to exist as they do), and there is nothing in a continuum to assert or protect. The person, in the technical sense the Personalists give it, is thus not a self in any of the received senses; nor does acknowledging the existence of real continuity function as a proxy self in the crucial respect.

The solution of the mystery is, on this reading, a relocation of it: a sense of responsibility is warranted and not undermined by the rejection of a self of any description. Seeing that bundles of streams belong to each other constitutes the motivation which is partially causally responsible for subsequent wholesome states. At the same time, as a thing thoroughly dependent on its constituents for any character it has, the person so understood provides no grounds for pretentions of control, for pristine unsulliedness from its constituents, or for identity-threat through suffering or change. The real person enables a sense of responsibility, and legitimates accountability, while providing no quarter for the very things that make belief in a *self* harmful.

1. *Saṃyutta Nikāya*, I.135. Translations of the *Saṃyutta Nikāya* are by B. Bodhi, *The Connected Discourses of the Buddha*, Boston, MA, Wisdom Publications, 2000.

2. No-self as discourse and practice is explored in S. Collins, 'What are Buddhists *doing* when they deny the Self?', in F.E. Reynolds & D. Tracy (eds.), *Religion and Practical Reason*, New York, NY, State University of New York Press, 1994, pp. 59–86; see also S. Hamilton, *The 'I' of the Beholder*, London, Routledge, 2000, for discussion of no-self as originally more a practical point than a metaphysical one.

3. Thus Vasubandhu, for instance, could be quite specific about the self that is rejected; the agent–subject–unifier triad, above, is taken from his *Discussion of the Five Aggregates*.

4. A philosophical treatment of the self in the *Upaniṣads* is offered in J. Ganeri, *The Concealed Art of the Soul*, Oxford, Oxford University Press, 2007, chap. 1.

5. Snake Sutta, *Majjhima Nikāya* 22.22. Translations of the *Majjhima Nikāya* are by B. Bodhi and Bhikkhu Ñanamoli, *The Middle Length Discourses of the Buddha*, Boston, MA, Wisdom Publications, 1995, unless otherwise stated.

6. *Majjhima Nikāya* 72 & *Saṃyutta Nikāya* 12.35.

7. *Majjhima Nikāya* 57.

8. See also *Majjhima Nikāya* 109.10–13.

9. This rejects, then, what G. Strawson appears to argue in *Selves*, Oxford, Clarendon Press, 2009, pp. 15–20. D. Zahavi is interested in the "experiential self", which may not be so much a move from a sense of self to a self sensed as it is simply a declaration to use "self" of that very sense itself. In describing his position as "occupying a kind of middle position between two opposing views … the self [as] some kind of unchanging soul substance [and the view that] there is nothing to consciousness apart from a manifold of interrelated changing experiences" (D. Zahavi, 'The Experiential Self: Objections and Clarifications', in M. Siderits, E. Thompson & D. Zahavi (eds.), *Self, No-Self?*, Oxford, Oxford University Press, 2011, p. 59), Zahavi looks very like the renegade "personalist" Buddhists I discuss below; or, for the full picture of the *pudgalavāda*, see A. Carpenter, 'Persons Keeping Their Karma Together: On the Philosophical Motivations for the *Pudgalavāda*', in K. Tanaka, Y. Deguchi, J. Garfield & G. Priest (eds.), *The Moon Points Back*, New York, NY, Oxford University Press, 2015, pp. 1–44. But in pinning his "middle way" to a "firm boundary between self and other" ('The Experiential Self', p. 69, note 4, with an approving nod to William James's thought that "the elementary psychic fact [is] not *thought* or *this thought* or *that thought*, but *my thought*, every thought being *owned*"), he may grant the sense of self more credence than any Buddhist ought.

10. This point, as well as many related, is argued, with particular reference to the current consciousness literature, in J. Garfield, *Engaging Buddhism*, New York, NY, Oxford University Press, 2015, chap. 5.

11. Most Buddhists, even the later ones, can be classified as D-theorists, dualist interactionists (Abhidharma) or F-theorists, panprotopsychists (*Yogācāra*) in the

taxonomy of D. Chalmers, 'Consciousness and its Place in Nature', in S. Stich & T. Warfield (eds.), *Blackwell Guide to Philosophy of Mind*, Oxford, Blackwell, 2003, pp. 102–42; Mādhyamikas, as usual, may be playing such a different game that it is wiser to refrain from classification.

12. As, for instance, is put forward in U. Kriegel, *Subjective Consciousness: A Self-Representational Theory*, New York, NY, Oxford University Press, 2009.

13. This is the borderline Zahavi skirts in 'The Experiential Self', arguing for instance that "different experiences [of the same person] are all characterized by the same fundamental first-personal character. They are all characterized by what might be called a dimension of *for-me-ness* or *mineness*" (p. 58), though the sense of "mineness" is so carefully distinguished from any familiar sense that it is difficult to determine whether it is the sort of "mineness" the Buddhists had in their sights as the root of grasping, and so of suffering. Similarly unclear to me is whether E. Thompson, 'Self-No-Self? Memory and Reflexive Awareness', in Siderits, Thompson & Zahavi (eds.), *Self, No-Self?*, does not perhaps concede too much on the Buddhist's behalf, and more than necessary on this score, when he writes: "Although the intentionally implicated past experience need not be given as mine in an objectified egological sense (as the experience of my ego), it is given from within as an experience formerly lived through first-personally, that is, by me" (p. 173). What is gained by this last "by me" step? And again, on the same page: "If 'ego' means self-as-object, as it does for Sartre, then Sartre's nonegological conception seems compatible with Zahavi's insistence that pre-reflective experience is not lived through anonymously, but rather first-personally." Can we not simply say it is lived through, full stop – which is only to say, it is an experience?

14. There was, of course, much disagreement about the precise nature of this going out of existence, with some Buddhists arguing that the arising, existing and demise of any *dharma* each required its own moment of arising, existing and demise. But Vasubandhu's position that their coming into existence must itself be the sufficient cause of their going out of existence – and so all existence is strictly momentary – seems the most philosophically consistent and insightful.

15. And, just to make things especially awkward for the Buddhist, this very type of rhetorical question is actively promoted in hortatory discourse such as Śāntideva's exhortation to patience (*Bodhicāryāvatāra* VI).

16. Detailed scholarly analysis of the steps by which this notion nevertheless came to have a place within a standard moral psychology and conception of the domain of the moral is found in M. Frede, *A Free Will: Origins of the Notion in Ancient Thought*, Berkeley, CA, University of California Press, 2012.

17. See J. Garfield, 'Just Another Word for Nothing Left to Lose: Freedom, Agency and Ethics for Madhyamikas', in M.R. Dasti & E.F. Bryant (eds.), *Free Will, Agency and Selfhood in Indian Philosophy*, New York, NY, Oxford University Press, 2014, pp. 164–85, for insightful discussion of the particular and contingent conceptual moves distinctive of the development of European philosophy which gave rise to this problem. While Garfield discusses Madhyamaka Buddhism in particular, one needs no

special commitment to Madhyamaka to dissolve the problem of free will. My focus here is on how the related issues appear within Abhidharma Buddhist thought.

18. This has not stopped a good number of contemporary scholars from trying to determine the Buddhist solution, if any, to the problem of free will, or from trying to classify Buddhists generally or particular Buddhist positions along the contemporary analytic spectrum from hard determinism to libertarianism. A comprehensive overview of the discussion, along with extensive references to further scholarly literature, is offered in R. Repetti's essays 'Buddhist Theories of Free Will: Compatibilism', *Journal of Buddhist Ethics*, no. 17, 2010, pp. 279–310; 'Buddhist Reductionism and Free Will: Palaeo-Compatibilism', *Journal of Buddhist Ethics*, no. 19, 2012, pp. 33–95; 'Buddhist Hard Determinism: No Self, No Free Will, No Responsibility', *Journal of Buddhist Ethics*, no. 19, 2012, pp. 130–97; 'Recent Buddhist Theories of Free Will: Compatibilism, Incompatibilism, and Beyond', *Journal of Buddhist Ethics*, no. 21, 2014, pp. 279–352. If, as argued in Garfield, 'Just Another Word for Nothing Left to Lose', certain non-necessary presumptions must be in place for the problem to emerge, or if, as I argue, these contingent presumptions are badly arranged so as to issue in an incoherent demand, then it is no wonder perhaps that when scholars try to force Buddhists to "answer" the question of free will, they end up saying things like "if a person is wrongly seen as an essential, permanent Self, it is an 'undetermined question' as to whether 'a person's acts of will are determined' or 'a person's acts of will are free'". If there is no essential person-entity, "it" can not be said to be either determined or free (P. Harvey, 'Freedom of the Will in Light of Theravāda Teachings', *Journal of Buddhist Ethics*, no. 14, 2007, p. 36).

19. Aristotle, *Nicomachean Ethics* III, especially chap. 1–3. It is in this form that Karin Meyers takes up her treatment of Abhidharma concerns with agency, looking in particular at the tension arising from the simultaneous denial of self and exhortation to reform ourselves in various ways (K. Meyers, 'Free Persons, Empty Selves: Freedom and Agency in Light of the Two Truths', in Dasti & Bryant (eds.), *Free Will, Agency and Selfhood in Indian Philosophy*).

20. As with so many things, the Stoics make a decisive move here, though early Christian thought also contributed, as the intellectual history traced in Frede, *A Free Will*, shows.

21. See 'Of Liberty and Necessity', in D. Hume's *A Treatise of Human Nature*, London, Penguin, 1985, and *Enquiry Concerning Human Understanding*, Oxford, Oxford University Press, 2008, sect. 8.

22. See A. Schopenhauer, *Prize Essay on the Freedom of the Will*, Cambridge, Cambridge University Press, 1999, for a pointed discussion of freedom requiring determinism to escape the madness of arbitrariness.

23. At *Aniguttara Nikāya* III.337–38, the Buddha is depicted as saying that *of course* there is "self-initiative" (*atta-kāra*), just as there is effort and exertion and persistence, but the passage immediately goes on to remind us that all *karma* originates in greed, aversion and confusion. Initiation of action there may be, but this too arises due to

causes and conditions. In the *Questions of King Milinda* II.2, the king determines accountability and identity by tracing an unbroken chain of effects back to something someone did. The particular inappropriateness of dragging free will into the Abhidharma Buddhist discussion, and how responsibility is attributed without that, is set out in K.L. Meyers, 'Freedom and Self-Control: Free Will in South Asian Buddhism', PhD dissertation, University of Chicago, 2010, chap. 4.

24. Vasubandhu explicitly rejects the notion of the self-initiating initiator of action in Book IX of his *Abhidharmakośabhāṣya*. The aggregated psychophysical elements are the "agent", he argues, and all of them arise as they do on account of their appropriate physical or mental causes. "That being the case, nothing at all has autonomy. For all things come about depending on conditions" (*AKBh.* IX as translated in M. Kapstein, *Reason's Traces*, Boston, MA, Wisdom Publications, 2001, p. 373). Meyers, 'Freedom and Self-Control', chap. 2–3, distinguishes more carefully between Vasubandhu and his predecessors on this point.

25. One might reflect here on the prominence of identification with that which is "up to us" in the Stoicism of Epictetus and Marcus Aurelius.

26. As Martin T. Adam puts it, in his illuminating discussion of this passage: "While it may be the case that we can be judged empirically free to the extent that we can do as we want, we are not metaphysically free in the sense of being able to directly determine the constellation of factors we identify with, and out of which our actions proceed" (M.T. Adam, 'No Self, No Free Will, No Problem: Implications of the Anattalakkhana Sutta for a Perennial Philosophical Issue', *Journal of the International Association of Buddhist Studies*, no. 33, 2011, pp. 251–52). While this may be, as Adam suggests, because as a matter of fact "there is no self-controlling controller", I am suggesting that what we learn instead is that the very notion of one is incoherent, and discovering such a thing would not give us what we think we want when we seek a self.

27. *Upāsakajanālaṅkāra* is translated with insightful philosophical commentary by S. Collins, 'A Buddhist Debate About the Self; and Remarks on Buddhism in the Works of Derek Parfit and Galen Strawson', *Journal of Indian Philosophy*, no. 25, 1997, pp. 467–93.

28. Collins, pp. 487–88, note 7: "The arguments of 2.2–5, in which I have translated *karaka* as both 'doer' and 'cause', and *katta* in 2.5 as 'agent', is this: the opponent assumes that the Self, as agent and experiencer, does not itself have someone or something else as its 'doer', its cause: otherwise there would be an infinite regress. By the same reasoning, the Buddhist position holds, Good Deeds themselves can exist without a doer, without a Self as cause."

29. A similar line of argument would presumably be taken against P. Williams' strenuous objection to "free-floating pains" in his much-discussed paper, 'The Absence of Self and the Removal of Pain: How Śāntideva Destroyed the Bodhisattva Path'. See P. Williams, *Altruism and Reality: Studies in the Philosophy of the Bodhicāryāvatāra*, London, Routledge, 1997.

30. The Mādhyamika Candrakirti argues in a similar vein in his commentary on his *Madhyamakāvatāra* IV.

31. This picks up the crucial distinction investigated in the seminal P. Strawson, 'Freedom and Resentment', *Proceedings of the British Academy*, no. 48, 1962, pp. 187–211, but relocates its basis in the *unity* of the agent, rather than in her supposed freedom.

32. Such unity figures prominently in the account of the Nyāya concern with moral accountability in M. Dasti, 'Nyāya's Self as Agent and Knower', in Dasti and Bryant (eds.), *Free Will, Agency and Selfhood*, p. 113: "For Nyāya, agency is, therefore, a special expression of the self's different capacities and potentialities, which coherently ties them together." This unity point is brought against the Buddhists with particular force by Uddyotakara in his *Nyāyavārttika* I.1.10.

33. Invoking a different philosophical language, we might say that according to the Abhidharma Buddhists *all* apparent wholes are the result of what Aristotle would call chance: while each constitutive element has an adequate explanation, the coming together of the elements in just this way has no cause of its own, even if the conjunction *looks as if* it is the sort of distinct individual (or intelligible state of affairs) which would ordinarily have some explanation of its own. See Aristotle, *Physics* II.4–6.

34. One is reminded of Socrates arguing for a unitary and immaterial soul as the responsible principle, dismissing the explanatory potential of the bodily constituents, with the remark that "I think these bones and sinews could long ago have been in Megara or among the Boetians, taken there by my belief as to the best course" (*Phaedo* 99a1–2).

35. "If there were no Self as agent and experiencer," the Buddhist's opponent objects (*Upāsakajanālankāra* 9.2.1, translated in Collins, 'A Buddhist Debate About the Self'), "it would follow that Good Deeds do not exist." This is clearly just the positive converse of the same point: without a unified agent-experiencer, bad deeds likewise would not exist.

36. M. Siderits has argued as much: 'Beyond Compatibilism: A Buddhist Approach to Freedom and Determinism', *American Philosophical Quarterly*, no. 24, 1987, pp. 149–59; *Buddhism as Philosophy*, Aldershot, Ashgate, 2007.

37. The context of the Shorter Exposition of Action (CulakammavibhangaSutta) is an enquiry about natural inequalities: "Master Gotama, what is the cause and condition why human beings are seen to be inferior and superior? For people are seen to be short-lived and long-lived, sickly and healthy, ugly and beautiful, uninfluential and influential, poor and wealthy, low-born and high-born, stupid and wise. What is the cause and condition, Master Gotama, why human beings are seen to be inferior and superior?" "Student, beings are owners of their actions, heirs of their actions; they originate from their actions, are bound to their actions, have their actions as their refuge. It is action that distinguishes beings as inferior and superior" (translated by Bodhi, *The Middle Length Discourses of the Buddha*).

38. Chap. 9, 2.7, translated in Collins, 'A Buddist Debate About the Self'.

39. I treat this point in greater detail in A. Carpenter, *Indian Buddhist Philosophy*, London, Routledge-Acumen, 2014, chap. 6.

40. Legitimating accountability by appeal to conventional reality is explored from a Madhayamaka perspective in The Cowherds, *Moonpaths*, New York, NY, Oxford University Press, 2015, and, to a lesser extent, in The Cowherds, *Moonshadows*, New York, NY, Oxford University Press, 2011.

41. The discussion of Vasubandhu on *karma* and intending in Meyers, 'Freedom and Self-Control', chap. 5, is especially illuminating on these issues.

42. And if blame is criterial of "true" responsibility attributions, then it will be the case, as Strawson has claimed, that the enlightened perspective, according to the Buddhist, "involves no sort of belief in true responsibility at all"; see G. Strawson, *Freedom and Belief*, 2nd edn., Oxford, Oxford University Press, 2010, p. 317.

43. These issues are discussed further in 'Ethics Without Justice', Jake Davis (ed.), *A Mirror is For Reflection* (New York, NY, Oxford University Press, 2017).

44. This interpretation of Vasubandhu's handling of the challenge is explored in more detail in Carpenter, *Indian Buddhist Philosophy*, chap. 6.

45. The Sāmmitīyas were one of a number of sects of early Buddhists who held the *pudgalavada*, the view or doctrine of the person (so, Personalists). There is no particular reason to pick them out from the many others, and I have no intention of pretending to offer a picture of their particular brand of personalism, if there was such. *The Sāmmitīyanikāyaśāstra*, a text of the Sāmmitīya school, is one of only three remaining (in Chinese translation) sources of information about the *pudgalavāda*, and the only non-hostile one. It has come down to us in different versions, see T.T. Châu, *The Literature of the Personalists of Early Buddhism*, translated by S. Boin-Webb, Delhi, Motilal Banarsidass, 1999, for an excellent scholarly review of these texts; L. Priestley, *Pudgalavada Buddhism: The Reality of the Indeterminate Self*, Toronto, Centre for South Asian Studies, University of Toronto, 1999, for a wider historical background, as well as an intriguing philosophical reconstruction.

46. The *pudgalavāda* is addressed in greater detail in Carpenter, 'Persons Keeping their *Karma* Together', where I argue in particular that it amounts to supposing the person-constituting elements *really do* belong to each other in a way they do not belong to the non-person-constituting elements, and, in this precise respect, we must concede the person is *really* (or, as the Buddhists say, ultimately) real. Zahavi's view is thus very nearly pure *pudgalavāda*, when he writes that "this self is real and ... it possesses real diachronicity, but ... I don't think its reality – its phenomenological reality – depends on its ability to mirror or match or represent some non-experiential enduring ego-substance" – except for the fundamental difference that the Buddhists do not and would not rest their case (*this* case) on phenomenology but on explanatory adequacy (Zahavi, 'The Experiential Self', p. 74).

47. Thus the Personalists (in)famously declared the person "inexplicable" or "unsayable" (*avaktavya*).

SUFFERING[1]

Thomas Metzinger

The cognitive scotoma

In this essay, I will present a first, rudimentary, working concept of suffering and then derive six logical possibilities for its minimisation. Rigorous philosophical and scientific research programmes on consciousness, which have seen a great renaissance in the last three decades,[2] are reaching a level of maturity which suggests the careful introduction of additional relevance constraints: we can now begin to go beyond foundational research and ask what, given a wider and perhaps even normative context, the really *important* aspects or forms of conscious experience actually are.

This introduction sets one such possible context, by drawing attention to some interesting phenomenological characteristics of conscious suffering and to the equally interesting fact that suffering *as such* has been largely ignored by modern philosophy of mind and cognitive science. There clearly seems to exist a "cognitive scotoma", a systematic blind spot in our thinking about consciousness. While in medicine and psychiatry, for example, a large body of empirical data is already in existence, the search for a more abstract, general and unified theory of suffering clearly seems to be an unattractive epistemic goal for most researchers. Why is this so?

The "eternal-playlist" thought experiment

Consider a thought experiment. Let us assume there is life after death. This afterlife is temporally unbounded, it lasts eternally and within it conscious experience continues to exist. There is, however, an important difference with regard to the life you are living right now, as an active subject of experience: all conscious experiences after death are experiences you were permitted to choose from the set of subjective experiences you had in your current life – because after death there are no new experiences. Before death, by contrast, you lived through a large number of inner experiences and conscious states, and some of them were *actively created* by you: by going to the movies, by taking a hike, by reading books, by taking certain drugs or by participating in a meditation retreat. For most of our lives we are busy seeking, in one way or another, conscious states we will experience as pleasant or valuable. Of course, we also actively avoid or try to end unpleasant states, and often our search for pleasant states may simply be instrumental in pursuing this second goal.

Let us take it that the smallest unit of conscious experience is one single subjective moment – because, if we look carefully, we find that we are always living our life through conscious moments. In so doing, most of us are always looking for the "meaningful now", for those small "perfect" moments of satisfaction and happiness or even an enduring inner experience of wholeness and meaning. Often, but not always, the two subjective qualities of positive affect and of successfully "making sense" are deeply intertwined. Our life before death then is constituted by a finite chain of conscious moments, whereas the succession of consciously experienced psychological moments after the disappearance of our physical body is infinite – it will never end.

Our thought experiment now consists of an idea and a question. The idea is that you are allowed to select exactly which conscious moments from your finite life will be transferred to a "playlist for eternity": after your physical death all subjective experiences on this list will be replayed again and again, in random order. This process then creates your very own personal conscious eternity, and it is based on your very own selection of conscious experiences. During your lifetime you are like a phenomenological Cinderella attempting to pick out just the right ones: "The good into the pot, the bad into the crop!" And here is the question: if you were permitted to make this irrevocable selection all by yourself, without asking the tame pigeons, the turtle-doves and all the birds beneath the sky for help, and if it really was only yourself who could pick the good grains from the ashes of transience, into which the Evil Step-Mother has thrown them, which moments would you choose? Most importantly, how *many* moments, according to your own criteria, would you actually rank as truly worth living – in the sense of worth being *re*lived?

At Johannes Gutenberg University in Mainz, we began a first series of small pilot studies with a group of advanced philosophy students. We chose a signal-contingent, externally cued form of experience sampling.[3] One tech-savvy student programmed an SMS server in such a way that, for seven days, it sent ten signals a day at random points in time to the participants, whose cell phones would then briefly vibrate. The participants' task was to decide whether the *last* moment before the conscious experience of the vibration was a moment they would take with them into life after death. For many, the result was surprising: the number of positive conscious moments per week varied between 0 and 36, with an average of 11.8 or almost 31 per cent of the phenomenological samples, while at 69 per cent a little more than two thirds of the moments were spontaneously ranked as not worth reliving. If you are cued externally, it seems, less than a third of such experiential samples would have a chance of entering your very own "eternal playlist".

Clearly, one first has to distinguish conceptually the *subjective* and *objective* value of conscious moments. It would be conceivable that an objectively valuable, subjective conscious experience – for instance, a painful learning experience in the external world or a deep inner insight into a permanently recurring self-deception – would be subjectively perceived as unattractive and worthless. Conversely, there could be states that would be subjectively perceived as extremely meaningful, but which at the same time would appear as worthless from a critical, third-person perspective – for example, certain states induced by psychoactive substances or deeper delusional states caused by ideological indoctrination, religious belief systems and so on.

It may also be the case that, ultimately, it makes no sense to assign an "objective value" to a specific sample of conscious experience in the first place. But it is clear that the bulk of our phenomenal states instantiate a *subjective* quality of "valence", a sense or inner representation of value. Of course, subjective value is also determined by the policy we pursue – by an expected utility in the more distant future. Nevertheless, it typically expresses itself on an emotional level, in the *hedonic* valence or affective quality of the present conscious moment.

Obviously, our "data" cannot count as significant, nor is a group of advanced philosophy students a representative sample. These were only exploratory pilot studies to give us initial ideas about feasibility and effect size. We were primarily interested in gaining a better understanding of the mechanism through which we subjectively experience conscious moments as pleasant or valuable. In so doing, we searched for a finegrained form of assessment, as simple as possible, that would always register the current moment alone, as independently as possible from philosophical theories, ideologies and conceptual presumptions. For example, to test its influence, in a second study we dropped the afterlife assumption and the "eternity condition", replacing them with the following question: "Would you like to relive the very last conscious moment in *this* life?" Interestingly, under this condition only a little over 28 per cent of life moments were ranked as positive, while just below 72 per cent were considered not worth reliving. It seems like the original afterlife condition adds a small positive bias to one's phenomenological self-assessment.

Of course, there are a host of justified, and important, theoretical questions about this thought experiment. Could I also take only the one very best moment of my life and repeat this single moment indefinitely? *When* do I have to make the final decision? Many positive experiences include an aspect of "novelty" or "surprise", would this aspect be indefinitely present in the afterlife as well? What are the temporal boundaries of "a" conscious moment? How does one introspectively individuate such allegedly "single" moments, and how theory-contaminated are the corresponding verbal reports? How *reliable* is introspective knowledge in the first place? And should we trust our own intuitive value judgments; can they be epistemically justified? And so on.

The results were however striking: first, the initial surprise the low scores caused in all participants and, secondly, what could be interpreted as a consequent attempt to explain the phenomenon away. Indeed, "explaining away" a prediction error, in this case, may simply consist in an updating of one's conscious self-model, preferably in a way that allows one to reduce introspective uncertainty by dampening and suppressing future "unexpected news" of this type. Many participants immediately started to develop more or less intricate "cognitive confabulations", trying to make their own self-assessment appear not so bad after all: "Happiness certainly is not the most important thing in life, I am writing a doctoral dissertation that will make a contribution to the knowledge of mankind and epistemic progress certainly adds more value and meaning to my life than momentary hedonic valences or even their lifetime average!"; "Most of my moments are neither good nor bad anyway, they are just neutral!"; "Lifetime average value is philosophically irrelevant, it is only the peak experiences and our memory of them which make a life a *good* life!"; "What *really* counts in life are the larger time-windows, not decontextualised phenomenal snapshots!" And so on.

Narrative self-deception
If, on the finest introspective level of phenomenological granularity that is functionally available to it, a self-conscious system would discover too many negatively valenced moments, then this discovery might paralyse it and prevent it from procreating. If the human organism would not repeat most individual conscious moments if it had any choice, then the logic of psychological evolution mandates concealment of the fact from the self-modelling system caught on the hedonic treadmill.[4] It would be an advantage if insights into the deep structure of its own mind, insights of the type just sketched, were not reflected in its conscious self-model too strongly, and if it suffered from a robust version of optimism bias. Perhaps it is exactly the main function of the human self-model's higher levels to drive the organism continuously forward, to generate a functionally adequate form of self-deception glossing over everyday life's ugly details by developing a grandiose and unrealistically optimistic inner story – a "narrative self-model" with which we can identify?

Any successful agent must be able to motivate itself. One solution to this problem of autonomous self-motivation could have consisted in what I would like to call "autobiographical Gestalt formation", an automatic escape into larger timescales. Maybe evolution has created self-models that automatically expand their predictive horizons as soon as the present is boring or simply too unpleasant?[5] Such a strategy of flexible, dynamic self-representation across a hierarchy of timescales could have a causal effect in continuously remotivating the self-conscious organism, systematically distracting it from the potential insight that the life of an anti-entropic system is one big uphill battle, a strenuous affair with minimal prospect of enduring success. Let us call this speculative hypothesis "narrative self-deception". If something like this is true, one would also expect it to have an observable effect in academic philosophy and science as well.

Perhaps the foremost theoretical "blind spot" of current philosophy of mind is conscious suffering. Thousands of pages have been written about colour qualia and zombies, but almost no theoretical work is devoted to ubiquitous phenomenal states like boredom, the subclinical depression folk-psychologically known as "everyday sadness" or the suffering caused by physical pain.[6] Pain qualia are frequent examples, but suffering is rarely mentioned, because in philosophical debates pain qualia often are barely more than a stand-in, easily replaceable by other allegedly primitive forms of sensory consciousness. As Sascha Fink has pointed out, however, the sensation of pain and the emotional *affect* of unpleasantness are as distinct as hue and saturation in colour experience, and pain and suffering are clearly metaphysically independent mental phenomena, although they are similar in structure and formal object, and tied together by evolutionary ancestry.[7]

What exactly is it that suffering *represents*? We have no rigorous phenomenology of *Weltschmerz* (world-weariness), loss of one's confidence in humanity, loss of one's ethical integrity or the introspective profile following moral failure – or any more precise analysis of, say, the suffering that goes along with information overload, continuous partial attention and the consequent, frequently recurring loss of cognitive control and mental autonomy.[8] The same is true of panic, despair, shame, the suffering going along with some types of empathy, the phenomenology of losing one's dignity or the conscious experience of mortality. Why are these forms of conscious content generally ignored by the best of today's philosophers of mind? Is it simple careerism ("Nobody wants to read too much about suffering, no matter how insightful and important the arguments are!") or are there deeper, evolutionary reasons for what I have termed the "cognitive scotoma" at the outset, our blind spot in investigating conscious experience?

Take the experiential insight into one's own mortality. In its unprecedentedly high degree of explicitness it can probably count as a unique feature of human self-consciousness. It is interesting to note how a considerable part of current work in philosophy which also achieves higher academic impact and actually gets attention from a wider audience is at the same time characterised by a vague potential for supporting mortality denial: just think of recent metaphysical discussions relating to property or even substance dualism, of dynamically extended minds "beyond skin and skull", panpsychism and quantum models of consciousness, or (to name an offence committed by the present author) philosophical attempts at supporting interdisciplinary research programmes into out-of-body experiences or virtual re-embodiment in robots and avatars.[9]

I think there may be a deeper problem here: we are systems that have been optimised to procreate as effectively as possible and to sustain their existence for millions of years. In this process, a large set of cognitive biases have been installed in our self-model. Our deepest cognitive bias is "existence bias", which means that we will simply do almost anything to prolong our own existence. Sustaining one's existence is the default goal in almost every case of uncertainty, even if it may violate rationality constraints, simply because it is a biological imperative that has been burned into our nervous systems over millennia. From a neuro-computational perspective, we appear as systems constantly and actively trying to maximise the evidence for their own existence, by minimising sensory surprisal (not to be confused with the personal-level state of being surprised).[10]

My point goes far beyond what is discussed as variants of "status-quo bias" in social or personality psychology.[11] Rather, it refers to the fact that we will almost always opt for continuing and protecting the life process as such, always preserving our own existence. But our brand-new cognitive self-model tells us that this organism's predictive horizon will inevitably shrink to zero, that our individual "maximum credible accident" is bound to happen. This creates a new situation in our inner environment to which we must adapt, a challenge creating a potentially permanent inner conflict and involving a specific, novel kind of suffering. This point therefore raises a deeper question, which we will encounter again when discussing the possibility of future suffering in self-conscious artificial systems: can there be conscious intelligence without existence bias?

Mortality-salient information and death-related cognition pose a constant threat to our self-esteem, because we need constantly to "buffer" the resulting existential anxiety – which in turn consumes an enormous amount of resources. For example, to stabilise the layer of our self-model dynamically representing an overall emotional evaluation of our own worth, we now have to qualify for either literal or symbolic immortality by creating a new "meta-context". We need to invent some sort of ideology or other, and then successfully live up to the standards of value that are part of it. On the other hand, any uncertainty regarding the validity of one's worldview constantly undermines the efficacy of our attempt to protect the conscious self-model from being flooded by the terror going along with knowledge about the inevitability of death.[12] Creating too much awareness of mortality may therefore not only be bad for an academic career: it actually threatens the integrity of your and other people's conscious self-model – because it implies a deep existential loss of control. Almost nobody wants to gaze into an abyss for too long, because, as Nietzsche famously remarked, the abyss might eventually gaze back into you as well.[13]

Our constant inner battle for mortality denial is, however, only one introductory example. When one examines the ongoing phenomenology of biological systems on our planet, one finds that the varieties of conscious suffering are at least as dominant as, say, the phenomenology of colour vision or the capacity for conscious thought. The ability to see colour consciously appeared only very recently in evolutionary terms, and the ability consciously to think abstract thoughts, of a complex and ordered character, arose only with the advent of human beings. Pain, panic, jealousy, despair and the fear of dying, however, appeared millions of years earlier and in a much greater number of species.[14] Now, as the environment human beings have created for themselves gets increasingly complex, the sheer quantity of preferences and thereby of potentially frustrated preferences continues to rise.

Suffering
We lack a comprehensive theory of conscious suffering. One of the key desiderata is a conceptually convincing and empirically plausible model of this very specific class of phenomenal states: those that we do *not* want to experience if we have any choice, those states of consciousness which folk-psychology describes as "suffering". We need a general framework for philosophy of mind and empirical research, which allows continuous refinement and updating. On an abstract conceptual level, I would like to begin by proposing two phenomenological characteristics which may serve as markers of this class: *loss of control* and *disintegration of the self* (either on a "mental" or a "bodily" level of representational content). This makes sense, because, first, the phenomenal self-model (PSM)[15] is exactly an instrument for global self-control and, secondly, it constantly signals the current status of organismic integrity to the organism itself. If the self-model unexpectedly disintegrates, this typically is a sign that the biological organism itself is in great danger of losing its coherence as well.

In addition, many forms of suffering can be described as a loss of autonomy: bodily diseases and impairments typically result in a reduced potential for global self-control on the level of bodily action; experienced pain can be described as a shrinking of the space of attentional agency accompanied by loss of attentional self-control, because functionally it tends to fixate attention on the painful, negatively valenced bodily state itself. And there are many instances where psychological suffering is expressed as a loss of cognitive control, for example in depressive rumination, neurotic threat sensitivity and mind wandering;[16] similarly, in insomnia people are plagued by intrusive thoughts, feelings of regret, shame and guilt while suffering from dysfunctional forms of cognitive control.[17]

Obviously, an empirically informed, philosophically coherent theory of suffering would be of high relevance for applied ethics, policymaking and legal theory. I am not going to present such a theory here, but in what follows I will sketch four necessary conditions for the concept of "suffering" while making no claims about sufficiency or offering a technical definition. The hope is that for practical purposes these short remarks constitute a good starting point, perhaps already a "minimal model of conscious suffering", but at least a working concept that we can use and gradually refine.

The C-condition: conscious experience

"Suffering" is a *phenomenological* concept. Only beings with conscious experience can suffer. Zombies, human beings in dreamless deep sleep, as those in deep coma or under anaesthesia, do not suffer, just as possible persons or unborn human beings who have not yet come into existence are unable to suffer. Robots or other artificial beings can only suffer if they are capable of having phenomenal states. We do not yet have a theory of consciousness.[18] But we already know enough to come to an astonishingly large number of practical conclusions in animal and machine ethics.[19]

The PSM-condition: possession of a phenomenal self-model

The most important phenomenological characteristic of suffering is the "sense of ownership", the non-transcendable subjective experience that it is *myself* who is suffering right now, that it is my *own* suffering I am undergoing. The first condition is not sufficient, since the system must be able to attribute suffering to itself. Suffering presupposes self-consciousness. We thus need to add the condition of having a conscious self-model: only those conscious systems which possess a PSM are able to suffer, because only they, through a process of functionally and representationally integrating certain negative states into their PSM, can *appropriate* the representational content of certain inner states on the level of phenomenology. Only systems with a PSM can generate the phenomenal quality of ownership, and this quality is another necessary condition for phenomenal suffering to appear.

Conceptually, the essence of suffering lies in the fact that a conscious system is forced to *identify* with a state of negative valence and is unable to break this identification or to detach itself functionally from the representational content in question (the fourth condition is of central relevance here). Of course, suffering has many different layers and phenomenological aspects. But it is the *phenomenology of identification* which is central for theoretical, as well as ethical and legal, contexts.[20] What the system wants to end is experienced as a state of *itself*, a state the content of which cannot be successfully integrated and which limits its autonomy because it cannot effectively distance itself from it. What it cannot distance itself from is an internal representation of loss of control and functional coherence, a situation of rising uncertainty.

If one understands this point, one also sees why the "invention" of conscious suffering by the process of biological evolution on this planet was so extremely efficient. It supports the active minimisation of uncertainty by elevating it to the functional level of global availability and simultaneously tying it to an individual first-person perspective.[21] Suffering is a new causal force, because it motivates organisms and continuously drives them forward. At the same time, and again just metaphorically, had the inventor of conscious suffering been a person (like the "Evil Step-Mother" of our introductory thought experiment), we could describe the overall process as extremely cruel. Above a certain level of complexity, evolution continuously instantiates an enormous number of frustrated preferences; it has brought an expanding and continuously deepening ocean of consciously experienced suffering into a region of the physical universe where nothing comparable existed before.

Clearly, the phenomenology of ownership is not sufficient for suffering. We can all easily conceive of self-conscious beings who do not suffer. If we however accept an obligation towards minimising risks in situations of epistemic indeterminacy, and if we accept traditional ethical principles or legal duties demanding that we always "err on the side of caution", then this second condition is of maximal relevance: we should treat every representational system that is able to activate a PSM, however rudimentary, as a moral object, because it can *in principle* own its suffering on the level of subjective experience. The disposition, the relevant functional potential, has already been created: it is precisely the phenomenal property of "mineness", the consciously experienced, non-conceptual sense of ownership, which counts for ethical purposes.

Without phenomenal ownership, suffering is not possible. With owner-ship, the capacity for conscious suffering can begin to evolve, because the central, necessary, functional condition for an *acquisition* of negative phenomenology is now given.

The NV-condition: negative valence
Suffering is created by states representing a *negative value* being integrated into the PSM of a given system. Through this step, thwarted preferences become thwarted *subjective* preferences, the conscious representation that one's *own* preferences have been frustrated (or will be frustrated in the future). This does not mean that the system itself must have a full under-standing of what these preferences really are (in terms of cognitive, con-ceptual or linguistic competences): it suffices that it does not want to undergo *this present conscious experience*, that it wants it to end. Of course, to create the aforementioned phenomenal urgency of change, the mere rep-resentation of an *expected* negative utility may suffice. For the experiential quality it is not only the content, however, but also the format, the inner mode of presentation, which counts.

The phenomenology of suffering has many different facets. To give another example, artificial suffering in conscious machines could be very different from human suffering. It is also conceivable that, say, some kind of Bostromian "superintelligence"[22] could represent negative expected utilities and frustrated preferences in inner forms of phenome-nality that involve no conscious suffering at all. There could be perfectly rational artificial agents, exhibiting neither the biologically grounded "existence bias" nor any other of the human cognitive biases which result from the millions of years in which evolution has shaped the self-models of our ancestors. But *if* they suffered, damage to their physi-cal hardware could be represented in internal data formats completely alien to human brains – for example, generating a subjectively experi-enced, qualitative profile for embodied pain states which biological systems like ours could not emulate or even vaguely imagine. The phe-nomenal character going along with high-level cognition might tran-scend human capacities for empathy and understanding, such as through intellectual insight into the frustration of one's own preferences or into disrespect of one's creators – perhaps even into the absurdity of one's own existence as a self-conscious machine, a mere commodity or research tool used by an ethically inferior biosystem.

The T-condition: transparency

"Transparency" is not only a visual metaphor but also a technical concept in philosophy, which comes in a number of different uses and flavours. Here, I am exclusively concerned with "phenomenal transparency", a property which some conscious but no unconscious states possess.[23] Transparent phenomenal states make their representational content appear as irrevocably *real,* as something the existence of which you cannot doubt. Put more precisely, you may certainly be able cognitively to have doubts about its existence, but according to subjective experience this phenomenal content – the *awfulness* of pain, the fact that it is *your own* pain – is not something you can distance yourself from. The phenomenology of transparency is the phenomenology of direct realism and in the domain of self-representation it creates the phenomenology of identification discussed vis-à-vis the second condition.

Phenomenal transparency means that something particular is not accessible to subjective experience, namely the *representational character* of the contents of conscious experience. This refers to all sensory modalities and to our integrated phenomenal model of the world as a whole – but also to large parts of our self-model. The instruments of representation themselves cannot be represented as such anymore, and hence the system making the experience, by conceptual necessity, is entangled in an illusion of epistemic immediacy, a naive form of realism. This happens because, necessarily, it now has to experience itself as being in direct contact with the current contents of its own consciousness. What precisely is it that the system cannot experience? What is inaccessible to conscious experience is the simple fact of this experience taking place in a *medium.* Therefore, transparency of phenomenal content leads to a further characteristic of conscious experience, namely the subjective impression of immediacy.

Obviously, this functional property is not bound to biological nervous systems; it could be realised in advanced robots or conscious machines as well. In particular, it has nothing to do with holding a certain "belief" or adhering to a specific philosophical position; it is plausible to assume that many more simple animals on our planet, which are conscious but not able to speak or to entertain high-level, symbolic thoughts, have transparent phenomenal states – just as the first, simple, post-biotic subjects of experience in the future might have.

This may also provide us with a deeper understanding of what the process of conscious experience actually *is*. To be conscious means to operate under a unified mental ontology, constituted by an integrated set of assumptions about what kind of entities *really exist*. Systems operating under a single transparent world-model for the first time live in a reality which, for them, cannot be transcended. On a functional level they become *realists*. Again, this does not mean that they have to possess or even be able to form certain beliefs, or use explicit symbol structures in communication. It only means that the implicit assumption of the actual presence of a world becomes causally effective, because, as philosophers might say, non-intentional properties of their own internal representations are not introspectively accessible to them – they necessarily experience themselves as being in direct contact with their content. This is also true of the conscious self-model. A transparent self-model adds a new metaphysical primitive, a new kind of entity to the system's ontology: the "self".[24]

Of course, all four conditions specified here are necessary, but to understand the very specific phenomenology expressed by self-reports such as "I am certain that I do exist and I am identical with *this!*", the conjunction of the PSM-condition and the T-condition is central. The transparent world-model allows a system to treat information as *factual* information, as irrevocably stemming from the real world; a transparent self-model creates the Cartesian phenomenology of being certain of one's own existence. Any robot operating under a phenomenally transparent body-model would, phenomenologically, *identify* with the content of this model and hence with any negatively valenced state that might become integrated into it.

At this stage, our working concept of suffering is constituted by four necessary building-blocks: the C-condition, the PSM-condition, the NV-condition, and the T-condition. Given our current situation of epistemic indeterminacy, any system that satisfies all of these conceptual constraints should be treated as an object of ethical consideration, simply because we do not know if, taken together, they might already constitute the necessary *and sufficient* set of conditions. By definition, any system, whether biological, artificial or post-biotic, not fulfilling at least one of these necessary conditions is not able to suffer. Here the central desideratum for future research is to develop this first working concept into a more comprehensive, empirically testable *theory* of suffering.

To be useful for human and animal ethics, for robot ethics and robot law, such a theory would still have to possess the necessary degree of abstraction. We want it to yield *hardware-independent demarcation criteria.* Which, if any, aspects of conscious suffering are multirealisable and which tied to a specific form of embodiment? Ideally such criteria would allow us to ignore all the concrete implementational details contingently characterising the relevant class of biological organisms on our planet, because we need to decide if a given artificial system is currently suffering, if it has the capacity to suffer, or if this type of system will likely evolve the capacity to suffer in the future.[25]

On our way towards a more universal theory of suffering, the second central problem is the "metric problem": if, say, for the purposes of an evidence-based, rational approach to applied ethics, we want to develop an empirically grounded, *quantifiable* theory of suffering, then we need to know what the phenomenal primitives in the relevant domain actually are. We have to determine the smallest units of conscious suffering. What exactly is the phenomenological *level of grain* that possesses explanatory relevance (from a scientific point of view) and what level of granularity has maximal practical relevance (eg, from the perspective of applied ethics)? If we hold on to the background assumption made in the beginning, postulating that the smallest unit of conscious experience is a single "experiential moment", then we arrive at a positive conclusion: the smallest unit of conscious suffering is a "phenomenally transparent, negatively valenced self-model moment". Arguably, such negative self-model moments (NSMs) are the phenomenal primitives constituting every episode of suffering, and the frequency of their occurrence is the empirically detectable quantity that we want to minimise.

Six logical possibilities to minimise suffering
For reasons of space, I will present an unargued background assumption: it is much more important to reduce suffering than to maximise happiness, because frustrated preferences are ethically more relevant than satisfied preferences. "Negative utilitarianism" (NU)[26] says that we should concentrate on minimising suffering, because of a deep phenomenological asymmetry between positively and negatively valenced states (see Option 4 below). Should we, as I propose, decide to make a fresh start and turn the topic of conscious suffering into a target of modern philosophy of mind and cognitive science, we would very likely corroborate and confirm the asymmetry between happiness and suffering and be able to

describe it in much greater detail. If so, this would be one reason to choose NU as a meta-ethical position.

Given the first working concept of suffering just sketched, we can already describe a number of possibilities to reduce the occurrence of our target phenomenon. Obviously, the richer and the more precise a phenomenological concept gets, the more possibilities and potential causal routes for changing the actual class of conscious states can be envisioned. If the concept in addition becomes empirically grounded (eg, by isolating its minimally sufficient correlates and analytically describing their common computational function) or if we increase its domain specificity (eg, by just looking into the suffering of pigs, cows or human beings), then technological interventions gradually become more feasible. And if, conceptually, suffering necessarily involves the phenomenal representation of a *gradient* (ie, of temporal properties like duration, change and succession), then creating a form of conscious experience lacking these features would result in an absence of subjective suffering. But, for now, accepting the four necessary conditions introduced above, let us set out the options arising.

Option 1: ending existence
The first option, quite obviously, would consist in painlessly and unexpectedly killing all sentient beings. No new "negative self-model moments" would be created in the process; no NSMs would be instantiated afterwards. If, however, the negative utilitarian is committed to effectively minimising suffering, and if she targets a specific population of experiential subjects, she is dependent on consensus within, and cooperation from, this population. She might then look for the optimal degree of adapting to the specific cognitive biases characterising her target population. For example, a more moderate version could say that we should respect the deepest cognitive bias of all currently known sentient beings – namely, existence bias – plus the fact that their transparent self-models not only express this bias on the level of inner experience but also force them consciously to experience themselves as indivisible wholes, as irreducibly individual entities. Such a moderate version might therefore respect an individual right to existence for all self-conscious biological systems already born, but prevent *future* sentient beings from coming into existence. Logical options like these have of course been explored in centuries of philosophical thinking, and they are related to what today is frequently referred to as "anti-natalism".[27]

It is interesting to see how, for many of us, intuitions diverge for biological and artificial systems. Imagine, as an elected member of a future Ethics Committee for Synthetic Phenomenology, it was your task to define and functionally constrain the "playlist" for the very first population of conscious machines. Your job would be to determine what kinds of phenomenal "self-model moments" would be allowed to evolve as such machines began to interact with the world and each other, and perhaps even to multiply themselves. You also know that, functionally speaking, suffering is necessary for autonomous self-motivation and the emergence of truly intelligent behaviour. Therefore, those conscious machines inevitably would have to instantiate a certain number of negatively valenced self-model moments in the enormous cascade of conscious experiences you are just about to trigger by setting off the evolution of artificial conscious subjects. Here, as opposed to the case of biosystems like ourselves, a larger number of people would not want to unnecessarily *initiate* new chains of NSMs and therefore feel drawn to an ethical position one could term "anti-natalism for self-conscious machines".

Let me point to a concrete, pressing problem we face today. It is a problem within the newly emerging field of "robot ethics", the problem of successfully implementing moral cognition and ethical behaviour in artificial agents. As embodied artificial intelligence begins to operate in open environments populated by human beings, as robotic systems become ever faster and more autonomous, they will increasingly be confronted with situations in which it would be inefficient and irrational, perhaps even unethical, to waste precious temporal resources by waiting for a final decision from some human agent.[28] Many of these situations will be of a kind in which the consequences of the artificial agents' actions will directly affect the well-being of other sentient beings. Just think of three autonomous cars in a roundabout realising that they will soon be involved in a complex collision with a deer and two human-driven cars, having to decide (and to negotiate with each other) how to minimise intelligently the overall damage.

The best way to solve this problem of "synthetic morality" is by endowing machines with a formalised axiology and a computable value calculus. But then new problems appear: should the autonomy of such ethical robots be limited in a way that they could in principle never find a way to "flash" or in any other way alter their own "normative firmware"? This would preclude them from learning and becoming better in the domain of moral intelligence. And how would we prevent such systems from arriving at repugnant conclusions? Let us assume the robot's value set would be based on a negative utilitarian axiology.[29] "To always minimise involuntary suffering and the overall quantity of NSMs in all sentient beings" could therefore be its highest priority. It would probably be in our own interest to prevent such artificial moral agents from ever arriving at the general conclusion that Option 1 is the best way to achieve this goal. Call this the "problem of the benevolent anti-natalist robot": almost nobody likes the idea of future artificial intelligences silently preparing for the extermination of all human beings and other sentient creatures on the planet – on purely ethical grounds, to be sure. This just illustrates some of the problems with Option 1. But it also makes it clear that, until such meta-ethical problems are solved, we should strive to always err on the side of caution. In practice, we should take no unnecessary risks.

Option 2: eliminating the C-Condition
Option 2 would consist in eliminating not the physical existence of conscious systems but all *phenomenal properties* in the universe. Ending all kinds of conscious experience would mean that the C-condition was not fulfilled. Trivially, as "suffering" is a phenomenological concept, there would be no suffering in a zombie world.

Option 3: eliminating the PSM-Condition
A third option to minimise suffering would consist in eliminating not conscious experience as such but only *self*-consciousness. Here, the PSM-condition would not be fulfilled, resulting in the disappearance of all forms of phenomenal selfhood. Conscious states could still exist, but certain complex phenomenal properties would not be instantiated anymore, most notably the qualities of selfhood, ownership and agency. Option 3 has been investigated in depth, for example by 25 centuries of Buddhist philosophy.[30]

Option 4: eliminating the NV-Condition
A fourth option, equally looking back to centuries of philosophical discussion, would be to eliminate not self-consciousness but all *subjective preferences*. If one were to end all self-consciously experienced preferences, then no such preferences could ever be frustrated, because the NV-condition was not fulfilled. A being without preferences would not be

selective, not even about the quality of its own mental states, so one might describe the resulting phenomenological configuration as a form of "choiceless awareness".

In accordance with the NU-assumption, I presuppose that satisfying preferences is ultimately not a valid option, because of impermanence and a deep phenomenological asymmetry between positive self-model moments and negative ones (NSMs). First, physical embodiment, impermanence and transience prevent any more permanent satisfaction of preferences (or a stable state in the self-model). In addition, the phenomenology of suffering is not a simple mirror-image of happiness, mainly because it involves a much higher urgency of change. In most forms of happiness this centrally relevant subjective quality which I have termed the "urgency of change" is absent, because they do not include any strong preference for being even *more* happy. In fact, a lot of what we describe as "happiness" may turn out to be a relief from the urgency of change. The subjective sense of urgency, in combination with the phenomenal quality of losing control and coherence of the phenomenal self, is what makes conscious suffering a very distinct class of states, not just the negative version of happiness. This subjective quality of urgency is also reflected in our widespread moral intuition that, in an ethical sense, it is much more urgent to help a suffering person than to make a happy person even happier.

One can also state and dissolve another frequent misunderstanding. Human suffering is rarely dramatic suffering. Almost all negatively valenced states involve only a mild emotional sense of preference frustration – perhaps some weak impairment of bodily well-being or a diffuse background feeling of boredom, possibly accompanied by an unspecific, generalised worry about the future, plus a subtle phenomenology of uncertainty. In addition, as it is plausible to assume that these frequent and much more subtly negative states are forming the majority of our conscious self-model moments, most of us may have long ago begun to perceive them as inescapable and uncontrollable. We may therefore operate under a "domain-general" version of learned helplessness with regard to our own suffering: we become unable or unwilling to avoid subsequent encounters with such inner situations, because on a deep functional level we already believe that we cannot effectively control the total probability of their occurrence. Consequently, we do not take action to avoid more subtle forms of negative everyday phenomenology.

Therefore, what we prematurely report as "neutral" states may often actually be the inner experience of subtle preference frustration plus learned helplessness. We report "neutral", but what we actually mean is "default". If one introspects carefully, truly neutral moments are something very rare, because some sort of affective valence accompanies almost all of our conscious moments. Zero pleasant intensity plus zero suffering describes a rare situation, but under NU it is a perfect and desirable state of conscious experience. In the history of philosophy, and in a large number of theoretical variations, this way of eliminating the NV-condition has long been thought about. The ultimate goal was to attain a lucid and robust state of tranquillity, a state of equanimity not disturbed by the passions, as exemplified in classical philosophical notions like *ataraxia* or *upekkha*.

Option 5: eliminating the T-Condition

Fifthly, it is conceivable that one might not eliminate self-consciousness per se but selectively target only the *phenomenology of identification* mentioned above. One would then only permit the appearance of self-models that are opaque and therefore *not* units of identification (UI).[31] There would be an organism-model, but not a self-model. Conscious preferences like desires, wishes or cravings might still arise and become integrated into this mere organism-model, but under this option no functional identification would take place, because the T-condition was not fulfilled. It is an empirical prediction of the self-model theory of subjectivity[32] that the property of "selfhood" would disappear as soon as all of the human self-model became phenomenally opaque, by making earlier processing stages available to introspective attention and thereby reflecting its representational nature as an internal construct on the level of its content. Frustrated preferences could still be consciously represented in such a model. But the organism would not experience them as part of the self – this entity would have disappeared from its subjective ontology.

Option 6: maximizing the UI

A last logical possibility could be to maximise the unit of identification, thereby dissolving the phenomenally experienced first-person perspective and the underlying subject–object structure of phenomenal experience. Here, the idea is that there must always be one most general phenomenal property and that it is possible to conceive of a phenomenal configuration in which the mechanism of identification is tied to this property, not to the experience of selfhood. It is difficult to find a label for this most global and abstract form of phenomenal character but there are traditional candidates. For example, we might call the most general phenomenal property instantiated by the process of conscious experience "the unity of consciousness" or "the wholeness of the moment" or, perhaps best, we could simply speak of "phenomenality per se".

Option 6 then describes the possibility to keep even the phenomenology of identification but to tie it to phenomenality per se, by turning the process of conscious experience *itself* into the unit of identification. In this phenomenal configuration, which is clearly possible from a logical point of view, preferences might still arise and be frustrated but they would not be subjective ones, because the underlying subject–object structure of consciousness had been dissolved. In other words, the individual, first-person perspective would have disappeared, because its origin (the unit of identification) was now maximised. Phenomenologically, such an aperspectival form of consciousness would make suffering impossible, because it was not a subjective form of experience anymore. One interesting, and remaining, question would be if for this class of states we would still want to say that the PSM-condition is fulfilled or not, if Option 6 describes a form of conscious self-representation.

To conclude, I have argued that scientific research on consciousness has reached a stage of maturity in which we may slowly and carefully begin to depart from pure foundational research by imposing additional relevance constraints. I propose that to understand the deep structure of suffering on a more abstract level is one such highly relevant goal for future research. Going beyond the mere search for neural correlates in biological systems, it might involve a strategy of mathematical and computational modelling of conscious suffering, in turn leading to the formulation of new, testable hypotheses. To facilitate this process, I have offered a first set of ideas and conceptual instruments.

1. I want to thank Regina Fabry, Sascha Fink, Adriano Mannino, Iuliia Pliushch, Lisa Quadt, Wanja Wiese and Jennifer Windt for their comments on earlier versions. I am also greatly indebted to Robin Wilson for excellent and substantial editorial help with the English version of this essay.

2. T. Metzinger (ed.), *Conscious Experience*, Thorverton, Imprint Academic, 1995; T. Metzinger (ed.), *Neural Correlates of Consciousness: Empirical and Conceptual Questions*, Cambridge, MA, MIT Press, 2000.

3. R.T. Hurlburt, *Investigating Pristine Inner Experience: Moments of Truth*, Cambridge, Cambridge University Press, 2011; R.T. Hurlburt & C.L. Heavey, 'Investigating Pristine Inner Experience: Implications for Experience Sampling and Questionnaires', *Consciousness and Cognition*, no. 31, 2015, pp. 148–59.

4. T. Metzinger, *Being No One: The Self-Model Theory of Subjectivity*, Cambridge, MA, MIT Press, 2003; T. Metzinger, *The Ego Tunnel*, New York, NY, Basic Books, 2009.

5. J. Hohwy, *The Predictive Mind*, Oxford, Oxford University Press, 2013; A. Clark, *Surfing Uncertainty: Prediction, Action, and the Embodied Mind*, New York, NY, Oxford University Press, 2016; T. Metzinger & W. Wiese (eds.), *Philosophy and Predictive Processing*, Frankfurt am Main, MIND Group, 2017; T. Metzinger & J.M. Windt (eds.), *Open MIND*, Frankfurt am Main: MIND Group, 2015; K. Friston, 'The Free-Energy Principle: A Unified Brain Theory?', *Nature Reviews Neuroscience*, vol. 11, no. 2, 2010, pp. 127–38; T. Metzinger, 'The Myth of Cognitive Agency: Subpersonal Thinking as a Cyclically Recurring Loss of Mental Autonomy', *Frontiers in Psychology*, no. 4, 2013, p. 931; T. Metzinger, 'M-Autonomy', *Journal of Consciousness Studies*, vol. 22, nos. 11–12, 2015, pp. 270–302.

6. See N. Grahek, *Feeling Pain and Being in Pain*, 2nd edn., Cambridge, MA, Bradford Books, MIT Press, 2007, for a notable exception.

7. S.B. Fink, 'Independence and Connections of Pain and Suffering', *Journal of Consciousness Studies*, vol. 18, nos. 9–10, 2011, p. 62.

8. M.A. Killingsworth & D.T. Gilbert, 'A Wandering Mind is an Unhappy Mind', *Science*, vol. 330, no. 6006, 2010, p. 932; A.M. Perkins et al., 'Thinking Too Much: Self-Generated Thought as the Engine of Neuroticism', *Trends in Cognitive Sciences*, vol. 19, no. 9, 2015, pp. 492–8; Metzinger, 'The Myth of Cognitive Agency'; Metzinger, 'M-Autonomy'.

9. B. Lenggenhager et al., 'Video Ergo Sum: Manipulating Bodily Self-consciousness', *Science*, vol. 317, no. 5841, 2007, pp. 1096–9; Metzinger, 'Empirical Perspectives from the Self-Model Theory of Subjectivity'; T. Metzinger, 'Why are Out-of-Body Experiences Interesting for Philosophers? The Theoretical Relevance of OBE Research', *Cortex*, vol. 45, no. 2, 2009, pp. 256–8; O. Blanke & T. Metzinger, 'Full-Body Illusions and Minimal Phenomenal Selfhood', *Trends in Cognitive Sciences*, vol. 13, no. 1, 2009, pp. 7–13.

10. K. Friston, 'The Free-Energy Principle', p. 128; J. Hohwy, 'The Self-Evidencing Brain', *Noûs*, 2014.

11. S. Eidelman, C.S. Crandall & J. Pattershall, 'The Existence Bias', *Journal of Personality and Social Psychology*, vol. 97, no. 5, 2009, pp. 765–75; S. Eidelman & C.S. Crandall, 'Bias in Favor of the Status Quo', *Social and Personality Psychology Compass*, vol. 6, no. 3, 2012, pp. 270–81.

12. See T. Pyszczynski, S. Solomon & J. Greenberg, 'Thirty Years of Terror Management Theory', *Advances in Experimental Social Psychology*, no. 52, 2015, pp. 1–70, for a recent review.

13. F. Nietzsche, *Beyond Good and Evil*, ed. R.-P. Horstmann & J. Norman, Cambridge, Cambridge University Press, 2002, aphorism 146, p. 69.

14. Quantitatively speaking, and under practically every conceivable metric, wild-animal suffering exceeds human suffering and the suffering inflicted by humans on other animals by factory farming and so on by many orders of magnitude. See, eg, B. Tomasik, 'The Importance of Wild Animal Suffering', *Relations: Beyond Anthropocentrism*, vol. 3, no. 2, 2015, pp. 133–52.

15. Metzinger, *Being No One*; T. Metzinger, 'Précis: Being No One', *Psyche*, vol. 11, no. 5, 2006, pp. 1–35; Metzinger, 'Empirical Perspectives from the Self-Model Theory of Subjectivity'.

16. Perkins et al., 'Thinking Too Much'; J. Smallwood & J.W. Schooler, 'The Science of Mind Wandering: Empirically Navigating the Stream of Consciousness', *Annual Review of Psychology*, no. 66, 2015, pp. 487–518; Metzinger, 'The Myth of Cognitive Agency'; Metzinger, 'M-Autonomy'.

17. R.E. Schmidt & M. van der Linden, 'The Aftermath of Rash Action: Sleep-Interfering Counterfactual Thoughts and Emotions', *Emotion*, vol. 9, no. 4, 2009, pp. 549–53; P. Gay, R.E. Schmidt & M. van der Linden, 'Impulsivity and Intrusive Thoughts: Related Manifestations of Self-Control Difficulties?', *Cognitive Therapy and Research*, vol. 35, no. 4, 2011, pp. 293–303; R.E. Schmidt, A.G. Harvey & M. van der Linden, 'Cognitive and Affective Control in Insomnia', *Frontiers in Psychology*, no. 2, 2011, p. 349.

18. A. Seth, 'Models of Consciousness', *Scholarpedia*, vol. 2, no. 1, 2007, p. 1328; Metzinger (ed.), *Conscious Experience*; Metzinger (ed.), *Neural Correlates of Consciousness*.

19. A.K. Seth, B.J. Baars & D.B. Edelman, 'Criteria for Consciousness in Humans and Other Mammals', *Consciousness and Cognition*, vol. 14, no. 1, 2005, pp. 119–39; P. Low et al., 'The Cambridge Declaration on Consciousness', 2012, http://fcmconference.org/img/CambridgeDeclarationOnConsciousness.pdf (accessed 6 January 2016); T. Metzinger, 'Two Principles for Robot Ethics', in E. Hilgendorf & J.-P. Günther (eds.), *Robotik und Gesetzgebung*, Baden-Baden, Nomos, 2013, pp. 263–302.

20. Metzinger, 'Two Principles for Robot Ethics'.

21. Metzinger, *Being No One*.

22. N. Bostrom, *Superintelligence: Paths, Dangers, Strategies*, Oxford, Oxford University Press, 2014.

23. See T. Metzinger, 'Phenomenal Transparency and Cognitive Self-Reference', *Phenomenology and the Cognitive Sciences*, vol. 2, no. 4, 2003, pp. 353–93, for a concise introduction.

24. See T. Metzinger, 'The No-Self Alternative', in S. Gallagher (ed.), *The Oxford Handbook of the Self*, Oxford, Oxford University Press, 2011, pp. 279–96.

25. See the thought experiment in Metzinger, *The Ego Tunnel*, p. 194.

26. See F. Fricke, 'Verschiedene Versionen des Negativen Utilitarismus', *Kriterion*, no. 15, 2002, pp. 13–27, for introductory references. An interesting discussion is B. Contestabile, 'Negative Utilitarianism and Buddhist Intuition', *Contemporary Buddhism*, vol. 15, no. 2, 2014, pp. 298–311.

27. D. Benatar, *Better Never to Have Been: The Harm of Coming into Existence*, Oxford & New York, Clarendon Press, Oxford University Press, 2006.

28. A. Mannino et al., 'Künstliche Intelligenz: Chancen und Risiken', *Diskussionspapiere der Stiftung für Effektiven Altruismus*, no. 2, 2015, pp. 1–17.

29. Fricke, 'Verschiedene Versionen des Negativen Utilitarismus'; B. Contestabile, 'Negative Utilitarianism and Buddhist Intuition'.

30. M. Siderits, *Buddhism as Philosophy: An Introduction*, Indianapolis, IN, Hackett Publishing, 2007; M. Siderits, 'Buddhist Non-Self: The No-Owner's Manual', in S. Gallagher (ed.), *The Oxford Handbook of the Self*, Oxford, Oxford University Press, 2011, pp. 296–315.

31. Metzinger, 'The Myth of Cognitive Agency'; T. Metzinger, 'Why are Dreams Interesting for Philosophers? The Example of Minimal Phenomenal Selfhood, plus an Agenda for Future Research', *Frontiers in Psychology*, no. 4, 2013, p. 746.

32. Metzinger, *Being No One*; Metzinger, 'Phenomenal Transparency and Cognitive Self-Reference'; Metzinger, 'Précis'; Metzinger, 'Empirical Perspectives from the Self-Model Theory of Subjectivity'.

ALTERED STATES OF CONSCIOUSNESS

THE RETURN OF DREAMING
AND CONSCIOUSNESS

Antti Revonsuo

The loss of consciousness and dreaming

The study of consciousness has gone through roughly three stages in the history of psychological science: the first golden age, during the introspectionist era at the end of the 19th century; the following dark ages, during the behaviourist and functionalist era, covering most of the 20th century; and the present, second golden age of consciousness science, which started to emerge during the 1990s.

The scientific study of dreaming followed a somewhat similar historical pathway.[1] There was an early interest in systematic studies of the contents of dreaming during the introspectionist era. For example, a student of William James, Mary Calkins, published descriptive statistics of the perceptual contents of dreaming. The figures she arrived at were in fact rather accurate in the light of modern studies.

The promising early start for dream science did not last long. It was replaced by two influential approaches, behaviourism and psychoanalysis, which halted the development of dream science for about the first half of the 20th century.

Behaviourism discouraged the study of any mental phenomena with a subjective component. Thus, dreaming as a purely subjective experience, lacking any objective behavioural index or criteria for external observation, was among the mental phenomena that had to be excluded from behaviouristic psychological science. Behaviourism, the dominating paradigm in academic psychology from the 1930s to the 1960s, had no place for a science of dreaming.

In the philosophy of mind, the behaviourist approach was called "logical behaviourism". Philosophers attempted to define "mind" and other concepts in an objective manner. Famously, Norman Malcolm tried to analyse the concept of "dreaming" in the logical-behaviourist spirit, in his eponymously titled text of 1959.[2] He concluded that "dreaming" could not refer to subjective experiences or states of consciousness that happen during sleep. Instead, "dreaming" referred to dream-reporting behaviours that take place during wakefulness. Thus, dreams were not experiences happening during sleep; they were storytelling events that happen after sleep, during wakefulness. With this move, Malcolm was able to preserve the everyday concept that people use, but without assuming that any subjective, unobservable phenomenon really happens during sleep.

As late as the 1970s, another philosopher of mind, Daniel Dennett, returned to Malcolm's question: "Are dreams experiences?"[3] Although Dennett did not entirely agree with Malcolm's denial of dreaming, he nevertheless argued that it is quite possible that dreams are *not* experiences happening during sleep. Dennett presented an alternative explanation: perhaps dreams happen in a few seconds just as we wake up, and they consist of the unconscious uploading of a (false) memory, to which we gain access after waking up, being thereby fooled to believe that the events depicted in the false memory actually were experienced during sleep as dreams. Dennett, like behaviourists before him, thus resisted the idea that there could be fully-formed, intense, colourful, subjective experiences going on in our mind during sleep, when an external observer could not see any evidence for them while viewing the behaviour of a sleeping person.

Overall, Malcolm's and Dennett's behaviourist interpretations of the nature of dreaming denied any connection to consciousness. As we will see, dreaming is now seen, on the contrary, as an important state of consciousness – even as the paradigm of the purest form of conscious experience.

Sigmund Freud and his psychoanalysis, of course, were most influential in 20th-century psychiatry and clinical psychology and, famously, very interested in dreaming. Dreaming plays a central role both in Freud's theory of the structure of the (conscious and unconscious) mind and in the practice of psychoanalysis, in the form of dream interpretation.

Psychoanalysis however failed to promote any systematic scientific approach to the study of the contents of dreaming. Instead, it was interested in the symbolic interpretation of the hidden meaning of dreams, a pursuit that was both theoretically and methodologically far from scientific.

The idea that manifest dreams – the events, objects, people, emotions, actions and so on which we directly experience in our dreams – are in fact symbols that stand for something else is an old and traditional one. In almost every ancient culture, dreams are seen as symbolic messages from gods, dead ancestors or the spirit world, or as warnings or other signs about the future. Freud did not reject the traditional idea of dreams as symbolic messages but, instead of having supernatural or other-worldly origins, for him symbols in dreams were coded messages from the unconscious, the deep realm of our own mind which we can never directly experience. To uncover and interpret the true meaning of dream symbolism, a psychoanalyst, an expert in dream interpretation, was required, much as in ancient cultures, where an oracle, prophet, shaman or some other special person played this role.

Modern scientific dream research has rejected the idea that there are two different dreams, the manifest and the latent, and the idea that dream contents contain hidden messages or symbolic meanings that require interpretation. That idea cannot be formulated as a credible scientific theory, and there is no objective manner to interpret the supposedly hidden messages in dreams. Any interpretation is as credible as any other; thus, the hidden "message" the dream supposedly contains is not there in the dream but only in the eye of the beholder, or in that of the dream interpreter with a dream-symbol dictionary. We have no objective scientific reason to believe that dreams carry symbols or messages from anywhere for us to read, any more than the shapes of clouds in the sky carry messages to us.

Modern research thus studies dream experiences exactly as they manifest themselves to us, without assuming that they include any hidden messages. Dreams are simply what they seem to be, and we need to describe and explain their contents and features as they are revealed to us in our dream experiences.

Because of the dominating (and detrimental) influences of behaviourism and psychoanalysis, the systematic scientific study of dreaming as a conscious experience came to a halt for more than half a century, parallelling the fate of consciousness in science. New developments in dream science started to take place in the 1950s and they eventually led to the current science of dreaming and consciousness.

Dreaming: A neurophysiological or a cognitive phenomenon?
The scientific study of dreaming started all over again during the 1950s and 1960s. Two theoretically different, and opposing, approaches developed: one inspired by the (then new) neurophysiology of sleep, the other by the (also new) cognitive science of the mind.

The first research programme was inspired by, and anchored to, new discoveries about rapid-eye-movement (REM) sleep psychophysiology and neurophysiology. Once a strong association between dreaming and the REM stage of sleep had been found in 1953, it sparked the theoretical idea that dreaming could be fully explained by and, consequently, reduced to the brain activations of REM sleep neurophysiology.

This line of theorising developed in the 1970s and produced the neurophysiological theory of REM sleep, in which dreaming was seen as a byproduct of random neural activity reaching the cortex during such periods.[4] The contents of dreaming were also, according to this theory, supposed to be random, disorganised, bizarre and possibly similar to psychosis or delirium.[5]

This characterisation of dreaming was perhaps in accordance with our everyday intuitive notion and spontaneous recollections of dreaming, as a crazy and hazy mixture of all things possible and impossible. The disorganised, random contents of dreaming that we experience during sleep, according to the neurophysiological approach, are not in any way useful or functional: they are mere epiphenomena arising as side effects from lower-level neurophysiological activity.[6]

A similar theoretical idea was that the neural-level random activity has a memory-cleaning function in overloaded neuronal networks, and the disorganised, random dream contents we experience reflect this low-level cleaning in action.[7] These ideas were promoted mostly by researchers with a strong background in REM sleep neurophysiology but little familiarity with studies of dream-content analysis.

Thus, after Freud's symbolism was discarded, dream research made a turn to neurophysiology. Dreaming, previously thought to be the royal road to the human unconscious mind, was suddenly no more than a neurophysiological trash can. But that idea came from a field, neurophysiology, uninterested in the contents of the human mind. Within psychology, the science of the mind, there was however growing opposition to the idea that dreaming could be reduced to REM neurophysiology.

The competing research programme was represented by cognitive psychologists (such as David Foulkes), who paid much more attention to the actual data on dreaming as a subjective experience, as revealed by carefully conducted dream-content analysis. The supporters of the cognitive approach argued that dreaming, as indicated in thousands of dream reports systematically collected and analysed by content, was an organised psychological and cognitive phenomenon, not a random, disorganised, neurophysiological one. Indeed, to understand dreaming, it was not necessary to descend to the lower neurophysiological level of description at all, they contended. Dreaming should be explained at the cognitive-psychological level, in terms of memory functions and mental information processing during sleep.[8]

This controversy reflected the great gap between the study of the mind (psychology and cognitive science) and of the brain (neurophysiology and neuroscience) in the 1970s and 1980s. Cognitive science took psychology as an independent, higher-level science of the mind, treating the cognitive mind as detached from and independent of biological foundations. Cognitive scientists opposed any attempt to reduce the mind to brain activity, or to reduce psychology to neuroscience. By contrast, neuroscientists took psychology to be so reducible to neurophysiology.

When it came to dreaming, there was, on the one hand, a tendency to see it as a purely cognitive phenomenon and, on the other, as purely neurophysiological. The two viewpoints seemed fundamentally incompatible. The controversy however gradually dissolved in the 1990s, when the new, cross-disciplinary cognitive neuroscience emerged. It showed that psychological or cognitive, mental-level phenomena could be described and explained in the context of a biological and neuroscientific approach, without flatly reducing psychology to neuroscience.

So theories of dreaming can keep their psychological-level descriptions and explanations, yet still connect them with the neural correlates and the underlying biological mechanisms of dreaming. In this cross-disciplinary approach, instead of the isolation or reduction of the psychological level, the ultimate aim is a multilevel theoretical model of dreaming, in which the psychological level is seen as emerging from the underlying biological level but yet is irreducible to it.[9]

Dreaming and consciousness as phenomenal consciousness
For empirical dream science to have a credible philosophical foundation, one fundamental metaphysical question remained to be resolved. This is also the most crucial one when it comes to the ontological relationship between dreaming and consciousness: does dreaming as a (mental) phenomenon belong to the same metaphysical category as (waking) consciousness? Are dreams phenomena of subjective consciousness occurring during sleep?

In other words: are dreams experiences?[10] To elaborate: is the question about dreaming being a conscious experience a logically coherent question, and is it empirically meaningful? And, if dreams are experiences, is it possible to collect valid, empirically verifiable, objective data about them?

These questions were similar in spirit to those which had originally led behaviourists to eliminate consciousness from psychological science. A totally subjective phenomenon whose nature or existence cannot be verified in any objective, public manner does not seem to fulfil the requirements of a "real" phenomenon for science to study. It surely cannot be an object of observation or theorising.

This problem needed to be solved before dreaming could be incorporated into the science of consciousness. Many philosophers however resisted the idea that dreams are phenomena of consciousness. As mentioned, Malcolm had argued that "dreaming" did not refer to any mental phenomenon which happened, unobservably, during sleep but, rather, to the impressions we have and the verbal reports we give after we wake up: dream-recall and dream-reporting behaviour. Beyond those objective behaviours during wakefulness, there was for him no subjective phenomenon called dreaming.

In the 1970s, Dennett returned to the question: are dreams subjective phenomena of consciousness? According to him, no empirical evidence forced us to make that assumption. Dreams might as well be false memories and impressions of having dreamt, experienced and reported after awakening.

Thus, in philosophy, as before in behaviouristic psychology, there was much opposition to the idea that a subjective experience without any means of objective verification could exist during sleep. But, with the rise of cognitive neuroscience in the 1990s, the philosophical landscape changed. Much more empirical evidence about dreaming became available, which needed to be taken into account where the metaphysics of dreaming was concerned.

I have argued that, in the light of the best empirical evidence, Malcom's and Dennett's philosophical scepticism about dreaming had become implausible and outdated.[11] The new evidence from dream research showed, beyond reasonable doubt, that dreaming was a subjective state of altered consciousness going on in the internally activated but sleeping brain. We have subjective experiences when we dream, even though these are (mostly) unreportable and unobservable at the time when they take place. Dream experiences are phenomenologically similar to waking consciousness. A similar line of argument has recently been advanced by other consciousness philosophers, such as Metzinger and Windt.[12]

Many philosophical theories of mind are in difficulties with dreaming, because dreaming shows that the existence of conscious experiences with *qualia* and subjectivity does not directly depend on external behaviours: verbal reports, language, online sensory input or stimulation, or direct perception of the external world. I argue that dreaming presents an insurmountable problem for externalist, embodied theories of consciousness, such as that advocated by Noë.[13]

The minimal difference between the presence and absence of phenomenal consciousness is the contrast between dreamless sleep and vivid dreaming – and that difference is a difference inside the brain. No differences outside the brain are required to bring consciousness to the world in this minimal-contrast case; therefore, consciousness cannot be constituted by anything external to the brain. Sebastian argues that dreaming might help to resolve the current debate between "phenomenal" and "access" consciousness,[14] because dreaming presents a convincing empirical case for vivid phenomenology occurring within the brain without concurrent access to behaviour or other cognitive mechanisms.[15]

The question "are dreams experiences?" has been settled for good, and answered in the affirmative.[16] Dreaming is phenomenal consciousness generated by the sleeping brain. Other questions follow. What *kind* of experiences are dreams? What are the defining features of dreaming? What is it *like* to dream? And what kind of theory do we need to explain dreaming and its relationship to waking consciousness?

Dreaming as virtual reality or world simulation
While philosophers struggled long with the question of whether dreams were experiences or not, empirical dream researchers struggled with the definition of dreaming as a phenomenon. What kinds of experience count as dreams? Does the concept of dreaming encompass *all* types of experience during sleep? Or do only some *types* of experience fulfil the definition of dreaming, whereas other sleep-related experiences should not count?

Although there has been much disagreement about the precise definition of dreaming in the research literature, recently significant conceptual unification has taken place. First, dream researchers now agree that not all types of experience during sleep should be included in the definition of dreaming. There are sleep experiences that are too simple, too isolated or too stagnant to count as genuine dreams. The crucial features that make an experience dreaming (as opposed to simple sleep mentation) are its organisation, complexity and temporal evolution.

How can dream researchers carry out scientific observations of dreams, to get an objective understanding of what dreams are like? Dreams pose a particularly challenging case for science, because they are subjective experiences and are not coupled with external behaviour which would reveal them to outsiders while they happen. Still, it is not impossible to get objective scientific data about dreaming.

Typically, dream researchers first give very detailed instructions to study participants, so that they recall and report their dreams immediately after awakening. The greatest problem with dream experiences is that we tend to forget them quickly, unless we pay attention to them before they disappear from our short-term memory. Participants in dream studies are thus trained to focus on their dreams as soon as they wake up, recall and go through what they can remember dreaming about, and then as quickly as possible make a permanent record of the dream, in as much detail as possible: simply describing everything they can remember, without adding or taking away and without trying to interpret the dream experience in any way.

These verbal dream reports constitute the data for researchers to study dream contents. Dream reports can be collected from participants who sleep at home or they can sleep in the laboratory, in which case the researchers will wake them up and ask for the dream report immediately. Sometimes dream contents are also studied by asking people about their dreams in interviews or questionnaires, but such data reflect only what people happen to remember about their dreams. Detailed dream reports, collected immediately after awakening, from well-trained, motivated subjects with good dream recall are the best-quality data researchers can come up with to study the dream world.

The verbal dream reports can then be subjected to content analysis. Different types of content – colours, persons, dangerous events etc – are identified and the researchers pick every instance of a particular type from the dream report. Then it is possible to quantify the different contents of dreams, and to answer questions about the types of experiences they contain and their incidence. The dream reports are turned into data sets for statistical analyses of the occurrence and frequency of, and relationships between, different dream contents. It is also possible to test theories that include claims about dream contents. Thus, it is possible to adopt a similar scientific approach to dream data as to any other type of data in science.

What have such data revealed about the nature of dreams? Dreams are, in their basic form, well organised. The universal *form* of dreams is spatio-temporal and centred: there is a sensory-perceptual space, organised around an observer's first-person perspective or around a dream self. Almost all dreams have a dream self; that is, we feel that we are personally present inside the dream world while we have the dream experience.

The dream space depicts the general context or the type of place in which dream events occur. The dream place typically includes many perceptual (especially visual) objects as well as living (human) characters. The place may be familiar or it may be a place that we do not recognise from our waking life (although it might feel familiar in the dream). The people we meet in our dreams may also be familiar or unfamiliar; both kinds exist abundantly in our dream world. Most of the objects and people also appear relatively normal, although deviations from our waking world occur.

Surprising, unlikely or impossible objects, people and events in dreams are referred to by the term *bizarreness*. Mild forms of bizarreness occur very commonly in dreams, physically impossible and fantastic forms only rarely. Some common types of bizarreness include the place of the dream suddenly changing, a person suddenly changing to another, a person appearing in a place where that person would never appear or a dead person appearing alive. While we are dreaming, we rarely notice that such things are highly unlikely or impossible, but after we wake up we can recognise weird occurrences for what they were.

A typical feature of ourselves in dreams is that we lack the capacity for critical thinking and reflection, which makes us gullible and accepting of even the craziest events as if they were really happening. It is very difficult to recognise a dream for what it is while it is going on. Sometimes this happens however, in a *lucid* dream.

Dream experiences are temporally evolving events where physical and social interactions take place. Dreams are complex sensory-perceptual experiences. Studies have shown that practically every dream

involves visual sensations and percepts, and that often the visual world
we experience in dreams is in colour, though black-and-white dreams do
occur. Most dreams include sounds and voices that we can hear; very
often this takes the form of conversations with other dream characters.
Often other sensory qualities also appear: we can feel touch, heat, cold,
bodily movement, smells and tastes and sometimes even pain in our
dreams, although this does not happen often.

Dream events evolve and unfold in time. There is temporal continuity
within a dream, a connected chain of events or a theme around which the
events are organised. Dreams thus resemble videoclips or movies, not
photographs.

This universal form of dream experiences has led several researchers
to define dreaming as an *analogue* of the waking world. Based on decades
of research on dream contents, David Foulkes first came up with the conception that dreams *simulate* waking life in a realistic manner.[17]
Subsequently, I defined dreaming as a virtual reality or world simulation.[18] Dreams imitate our waking experiences, as if dreaming were an
internal virtual-reality generator which becomes active during sleep
every night. The philosopher Jennifer Windt expresses a similar idea in
her definition of dreaming as "an immersive spatio-temporal hallucination".[19] And many leading dream researchers, who previously adopted
widely differing definitions, now seem to accept the basic characterisation of dreaming as a simulation of the waking world or virtual reality.[20]

This unification around the notion of simulation is a remarkable conceptual step forward in a field which used to be torn apart by definitional
differences and obscurities. Now there is a concept of dreaming on which
most researchers agree.

Towards unified theories of dreaming and consciousness
The science of dreaming is thus converging on the concept of dreaming
as an off-line simulation of the perceptual world. In their ontology and
fundamental form, waking and dreaming consciousness are identical:
they are phenomenal consciousness. Consciousness presents itself in a
globally unified form, as a temporally progressing "being-in-the-world"
experience, during both dreaming and wakefulness.

The crucial difference is that dreaming is generated by the internal
activities of the brain. Waking consciousness is guided by the senses, and
the brain's simulation of the world corresponds to the world around us

and helps to guide our behaviour. During dreaming, however, the world simulation does not correspond to the reality around the sleeping person: it is isolated from perception and behaviour.

This shared conception of the fundamental form of dreaming as world simulation still leaves a lot of room for different, competing, even conflicting, theories of the *functions* of dreaming. But the shared ground about the nature and definition of dreaming allows different theories to be compared and empirically tested against one another. Thus, dream science seems to have matured to a stage where genuine progress is possible.

Without going into the details of the different theories, I will briefly mention four, which differ as to the functions they propose dreaming to have.[21] First, there are two theories that focus on the universal *form* of dreaming as a dynamic, simulated world with an active dream self. These propose that the universal, general form of dreaming is functional for the organism, but that the particular, idiosyncratic, unpredictable contents of dreams are not functional as such.

One of these theories is Protoconsciousness, formulated by Hobson.[22] According to this theory, the universal form of dreaming is functional in that it prepares the foetal and the newborn brain for conscious perception of, and bodily interaction with, the "real" waking world and use of the "real" physical body. During the last trimester, foetal REM sleep is more abundant than at any time later in life; indeed, most of the time is spent in REM sleep. Protoconsciousness theory interprets this peak in REM sleep as the first emergence of consciousness: the internally generated activation of the foetal brain in REM sleep brings about a basic form of phenomenal consciousness. It is a virtual-reality simulation of the self-in-the-world, a template that will be refined when sensory-perceptual interaction with the real physical world becomes possible after birth.

Protoconsciousness theory also explains why people who have had sensory or motor deficits from birth can have dreams in which they have experiences that are for them impossible during wakefulness (such as walking or running in paralysed patients, hearing and talking in deafmute subjects). Those experiences can be simulated on the basis of the protoconscious templates of universal human experiences, independently of ever having had those experiences personally during wakefulness.[23]

According to Protoconsciousness theory, the function of dreaming is to be predictive of, and preparatory for, future waking consciousness. It is primarily developmental and genetically coded. Protoconsciousness is the hard-wired, virtual-reality program that prepares the brain for conscious interactions with the world. Thus, the basic form of dreaming as a simulated world has a function in early brain maturation and in the emergence of waking consciousness, but the particular contents of dreaming in adulthood do not necessarily have any functions.

Protoconsciousness theory is difficult to test directly, as it seems nearly impossible to verify or falsify the statement that foetal REM is associated with basic forms of dream experience or being in the world. Newborn babies are unable to report the experiences they have had in the womb. Only if neuroscientists develop an objective measurement of consciousness will it be possible to test whether a conscious state simulating the world emerges in REM sleep in the developing brain.

The Continuity Hypothesis (CH) also suggests that the general form of dreaming as world simulation has a function but the particular contents do not.[24] This theory however focuses on adults and it rejects the idea that dreaming occurs at all in babies or very small children. According to CH, the function of dreaming is related to long-term memory processing, perhaps to memory-consolidation processes. Those processes require random activation of, and sampling from, recent memory in unique recombinations. Thus, particular dream contents are unpredictable in their details but not in their overall statistical properties: they will always reflect continuity with previous waking experiences (in so far as those are represented in memory).

This theory can be tested empirically, as it predicts that dream contents represent the results of random sampling and recombination of memorised experiences. If dream contents turn out to be non-random, selective or reflecting contents never (or rarely) experienced in the waking world, CH predictions would not hold. At least in some cases, the data do go against such predictions: what we dream about cannot be directly based on a random sample of our previous experiences.

Theories about the relationship between sleep and memory consolidation have received strong support from studies, but these studies say nothing about the role of dream contents, only that sleeping as such is important for memory. If we are deprived of sleep (or of REM sleep only), our new memories are not consolidated into long-term memory as well as when we get normal amounts of sleep.

Two further simulation theories of dreaming propose that its function is to simulate particular contents and events that are important for future survival, to prepare the organism to deal with such events efficiently in the real world.

Threat Simulation Theory (TST) proposes that, during our evolutionary history, dreaming was selected because it made it possible to simulate, safely and repeatedly, dangerous and even life-threatening events.[25] Thus, threat perception and avoidance mechanisms would have been well-rehearsed when real threats were encountered. This theory has been widely tested, and its predictions have received support from many empirical studies on the contents of dreams and nightmares in various populations.[26] The studies have shown that threatening situations are common in dreams, that they occur more often in dreams than in waking life, that real-life threats get incorporated into dreams and that people who live in threatening environments have more threat-simulation dreams. All these results from different types of dreams are well in accordance with the predictions of TST: we dream about threats to survive threatening situations in real life.

Some of the most convincing evidence comes from universal dreams – bad dreams, nightmares, recurrent and post-traumatic dreams – in which threats to the well-being and even survival of the dream self and other personally important people are ubiquitous. The dream self is typically attacked or chased by criminals, wild animals, bad guys, monsters and evil characters from horror movies, wartime enemies, or bullies from work or school. The dream self encounters natural catastrophies, traffic accidents, dysfunctional machines, losing valuables, being late for important events, getting lost in dangerous or unfamiliar places and so on.

Such universal threat simulations appear to reflect evolutionary programs that are deeply embedded in the human dream consciousness. Perhaps we could even go so far as to say that they are "evolutionary archetypes", prototypes of dangerous and threatening situations that humans have simulated throughout the ages, to be better prepared to survive them during their waking lives.

Finally there is Social Simulation Theory (SST), recently formulated in such a way as to be testable. It is similar to TST but accounts for a different type of dream content.[27] SST proposes that one original evolutionary function of dreaming is to simulate social perception, social bonding and social interactions, to support and strengthen those social bonds most important for the survival and reproductive success of an individual.

Dream contents seem to support the idea: dreams are intensely social. In almost every dream, there are several other human characters, apart from the dream self, and frequent social interactions take place among them. We are almost never alone in our dreams.

However, SST has not yet been properly tested to show that these social contents really serve a simulation function. It is possible that they are merely a passive reflection of the social contents of our waking life – this is what CH would say. Or it is possible that the social contents of dreams are merely a reflection of social threats: threat simulations in dreams involve human enemies, as well as our families and loved ones, being threatened. In that case, TST would be able to explain the social nature of dreams too, as a way to depict many kinds of social threat.

Although social perception and interaction are abundant in dreams, taking place in almost every dream, it is too early to tell whether SST as a whole correctly predicts some important features of social dream contents and events, or whether TST and CH turn out to be better supported. Studies directly testing the predictions of SST will be under way in the near future.

Conclusions

The science of dreaming and the science of consciousness have both made a spectacular return, and now go hand in hand. Both fields went through their dark ages, when the scientific study of dreaming and consciousness was halted in the early 20th century. Both also went through a lengthy revival, when they were ill-defined and controversial topics in psychology and neuroscience. But today the new paradigm of cross-disciplinary consciousness science includes both of them.

The major current conception of dreaming, as phenomenal consciousness in the form of an internal world simulation or a virtual reality in the brain, now marries dreaming and consciousness both metaphysically and empirically. Dreaming and wakeful consciousness are manifestations of the same, phenomenal level of organisation in the brain.

Phenomenal consciousness is the mechanism which grants us the feeling of our first-person presence, of being in the world. The world in which we experience our presence is usually the waking world that we consciously perceive around us, but we also spend a significant amount of time in the dream world, a credible simulation of the waking reality.

The challenge for dream science is to formulate empirical predictions, derived from testable theories that explain how and why the brain simulates worlds during sleep, and then run studies that test these predictions. In that way, dream science will become a productive and progressive field, which can eventually answer fundamental questions, such as "why do we dream?", and contribute to the overall explanation of consciousness.

1. For an illuminating account of this history, see S. Schwartz, 'A Historical Loop of One Hundred Years: Similarities between 19th Century and Contemporary Dream Research', *Dreaming*, no. 10, 2000, pp. 55–66.
2. N. Malcolm, *Dreaming*, London, Routledge & Kegan Paul, 1959.
3. D.C. Dennett, 'Are Dreams Experiences?', *Philosophical Review*, no. 73, 1976, pp. 151–71.
4. J.A. Hobson & R.W. McCarley, 'The Brain as a Dream State Generator: An Activation-Synthesis Hypothesis of the Dream Process', *American Journal of Psychiatry*, no. 134, 1977, pp. 1335–48.
5. J.A. Hobson, 'Dreaming as Delirium: A Mental Status Exam of our Nightly Madness', *Seminars in Neurology*, no. 17, 1997, pp. 121–28.
6. Hobson & McCarley, 'The Brain as a Dream State Generator'.
7. F. Crick & G. Mitchinson, 'The Function of Dream Sleep', *Nature*, no. 304, 1983, pp. 111–14.
8. D. Foulkes, *Dreaming: A Cognitive-Psychological Analysis*, Hillsdale, NJ, Lawrence Erlbaum, 1985; C. Cavallero & D. Foulkes (eds.), *Dreaming as Cognition*, New York, NY, Harvester Wheatsheaf, 1993.
9. A. Revonsuo, *Inner Presence: Consciousness as a Biological Phenomenon*, Cambridge, MA, MIT Press, 2006; K. Valli, 'Dreaming in the Multilevel Framework', *Consciousness and Cognition*, vol. 20, no. 4, 2011, pp. 1084–90.
10. Dennett, 'Are Dreams Experiences?'.
11. A. Revonsuo, 'Consciousness, Dreams, and Virtual Realities', *Philosophical Psychology*, vol. 8, no. 1, 1995, pp. 35–58.
12. T. Metzinger, *Being No One: The Self-Model Theory of Subjectivity*, Cambridge, MA, MIT Press, 2003; J.M. Windt, *Dreaming: A Conceptual Framework for Philosophy of Mind and Empirical Research*, Cambridge, MA, MIT Press, 2015.
13. A. Revonsuo, 'Hard to See the Problem?', *Journal of Consciousness Studies*, vol. 22, nos. 3–4, 2015, pp. 52–67; A. Noë, *Out of Our Heads*, New York, NY, Hill & Wang, 2009.
14. See the essay by Seth in this volume.
15. M.A. Sebastian, 'Dreams: An Empirical Way to Settle the Discussion between Cognitive and Non-Cognitive Theories of Consciousness', *Synthese*, no. 191, 2014, pp. 263–85.
16. A. Revonsuo, *Inner Presence: Consciousness as a Biological Phenomenon*, Cambridge, MA, MIT Press, 2006; Windt, *Dreaming*.
17. Foulkes, *Dreaming*.
18. Revonsuo, 'Consciousness, Dreams, and Virtual Realities'; Revonsuo, *Inner Presence*.
19. J.M. Windt, 'The Immersive Spatio-temporal Hallucination Model of Dreaming', *Phenomenology and Cognitive Science*, vol. 9, no. 2, 2010, pp. 295–316.
20. G.W. Domhoff, 'Realistic Simulation and Bizarreness in Dream Content: Past Findings and Suggestions for Future Research', in D. Barrett & P. McNamara (eds.), *The New Science of Dreaming*, vol. II, Westport, CT, Praeger, 2007, pp. 1–27; J.A.

Hobson, 'REM Sleep and Dreaming: Towards a Theory of Protoconsciousness', *Nature Reviews Neuroscience*, vol. 10, no. 11, 2009, pp. 803–13; T.A. Nielsen, 'Dream Analysis and Classification: The Reality Simulation Perspective', in M. Kryeger, T. Roth & W.C. Dement (eds.), *Principles and Practice of Sleep Medicine*, New York, NY, Elsevier, 2010, pp. 595–603; A. Revonsuo, J. Tuominen & K. Valli, 'The Avatars in the Machine: Dreaming as a Simulation of Social Reality', in T. Metzinger & J.M. Windt (eds.), *Open MIND:* 32(T), Frankfurt a.M., MIND Group, 2015.

21. For a more detailed presentation and analysis of these theories, see Revonsuo, Tuominen & Valli, 'The Avatars in the Machine: Dreaming as a Simulation of Social Reality'; A. Revonsuo, J. Tuominen & K. Valli, 'The Simulation Theories of Dreaming: How to Make Theoretical Progress in Dream Science – A Reply to Martin Dresler', in T. Metzinger & J.M. Windt (eds.), *Open MIND:* 32(T), Frankfurt a.M., MIND Group, 2015.

22. Hobson, 'REM Sleep and Dreaming'.

23. U. Voss et al., 'Waking and Dreaming: Related but Structurally Independent. Dream Reports of Congenitally Paraplegic and Deaf-Mute Persons', *Consciousness and Cognition*, vol. 20, no. 3, 2011, pp. 673–87.

24. See, eg, Foulkes, *Dreaming: A Cognitive-Psychological Analysis*; M. Schredl & F. Hofmann, 'Continuity Between Waking Activities and Dream Activities', *Consciousness and Cognition*, vol. 12, no. 2, 2003, pp. 298–308.

25. A. Revonsuo, 'The Reinterpretation of Dreams: An Evolutionary Hypothesis of the Function of Dreaming', *Behavioral and Brain Sciences*, vol. 23, no. 6, 2000, pp. 877–901.

26. Eg, A. Zadra, S. Desjardins & E. Marcotte, 'Evolutionary Function of Dreams: A Test of the Threat Simulation Theory in Recurrent Dreams', *Consciousness and Cognition*, no. 15, 2006, pp. 450–63; for reviews, see K. Valli & A. Revonsuo, 'The Threat Simulation Theory in Light of Recent Empirical Evidence: A Review', *American Journal of Psychology*, vol. 122, no. 1, 2009, pp. 17–38; Revonsuo, Tuominen & Valli, 'The Avatars in the Machine'.

27. Revonsuo, Tuominen & Valli, 'The Avatars in the Machine'.

THE RETURN OF HYPNOSIS AS AN ALTERED STATE OF CONSCIOUSNESS

Sakari Kallio

Hypnosis is a concept familiar to most of us. There seems to be no end to scientific theorising, however, about what really causes hypnotic behaviour or experiences. The hypnosis research community has struggled for more than 200 years to formulate a universally-agreed definition of hypnosis that could be shared with the public and utilised in guiding scientific research and clinical practice.

Modern notions of hypnosis can be traced to the work of Franz Anton Mesmer, who purportedly cured people by using "animal magnetism". A French royal commission discredited his theory in 1784, under the direction of the American ambassador, Benjamin Franklin. Theoretical debate was renewed in the 1880s, when two neurologists, Jean Martin Charcot and Professor Hippolyte Bernheim, disputed whether hypnosis was a neurophysiological or a psychological phenomenon. Indeed, since the French commission's investigation, a number of theoretical accounts of hypnotic phenomena have been offered.[1] These vary from Mesmerism[2] to trance states[3] to compliance and belief.[4]

Chaves has listed three notions that have almost always been axiomatic in the history of hypnosis. First, the term "hypnosis" refers to a denotable state or condition of a person, in some sense discontinuous from the person's normal waking experience. Secondly, this state can be induced (at least in susceptible individuals) by certain identifiable rituals or "hypnosis induction procedures". And, thirdly, the hypnotic state induced by these rituals possesses at least some invariant or characteristic properties, independent of the means by which the trance is elicited.[5]

This "traditional view" considers hypnosis to be an altered state of consciousness (ASC), characterised by alterations in mental processes such as perception, thought, memory and control of behaviour.[6] This view includes the notion that the hypnotic induction leads to a change in the way the brain functions and processes information. According to

Kallio and Revonsuo, it would be more logical to refer to this non-conscious brain state as an *altered background state of consciousness.*[7]

As a reaction to such traditional "state views" (SV), the social aspects of hypnotic behaviour began to interest researchers. Here the pioneer was Robert White, who conceptualised hypnotic behaviour in terms of meaningful, goal-directed striving.[8] Such social-cognitive or non-state views (NSV) of hypnosis are supported by many contemporary researchers.[9] These theorists agree that hypnosis is not any special state of consciousness but a perfectly normal waking condition, where the subjects are active, problem-solving agents using goal-directed fantasy in a special social situation.[10] The strength of NSV, according to its proponents, is that there is no need to assume any mysterious concepts like "trance" or "hypnotic state". As Lynn and others contend from a social-cognitive perspective, hypnosis might as well be defined as a situation in which people respond to imaginative suggestions, regardless of whether a formal hypnotic induction is given or even whether the word hypnosis has been used.[11]

This debate continues actively, since approximately every decade Division 30 (Society of Psychological Hypnosis) of the American Psychological Association (APA) has redefined hypnosis.[12] In their latest (2015) affirmation, the Hypnosis Definition Committee defined it as a "state of consciousness involving focused attention and reduced peripheral awareness characterized by an enhanced capacity for response to suggestion".[13] This definition was published in the *American Journal of Clinical Hypnosis* in a special issue, which included the new definition and 11 commentaries criticising or praising it. The discussion once more boiled down to the question whether it is correct to define hypnosis as a "state of consciousness".

These two types of theory assume that very different things are happening in the mind of the person who is in the social situation labelled as hypnosis. SV assumes that the hypnotic induction (hypnotising someone) automatically leads to a change in brain function, which can be referred to as a "hypnotic state". NSV assumes that the person who enters this situation already understands the rules of the "game", since the nature of hypnosis is general knowledge in society:[14] the hypnotic induction is just a ritual, which defines the situation as hypnosis and precedes suggestions that call for the use of imagination.

Responding to hypnotic suggestions also has a completely different nature depending on the theoretical view. According to SV, this happens *automatically* without conscious effort, given that the hypnotic state is present. The phenomenon is labelled as the "classical suggestion effect" and it is considered to be the crucial difference between true hypnotic responding and acting along, following requests or complying.[15] Imagine a person who receives a suggestion of seeing a kitten playing on the floor (a suggestion of a visual hallucination). Automatic hypnotic responding implies that the person would perhaps notice the "kitten" at some point and be able to follow it playing around. This should, however, feel like watching a real kitten, without any effort to imagine a kitten whatsoever. The person should be able to look away from the "kitten" and when looking back it should be there just as before.

For an NSV advocate, a hypnotic suggestion is asking the subject to engage in fantasies that lead to subjective experiences which are at variance with what one knows to be objectively true and thus are to be interpreted metaphorically.[16] Hypnotic suggestions are referred to as "imaginative suggestions", requests to experience an imaginary state of affairs as if it were real.[17] NSV proponents agree that responding is always deliberate, although the strategies and imagination may lead to an experience that things happen automatically and without effort. This means that when a hypnotic suggestion of seeing a kitten playing on a floor is given, the person knows that there is no real kitten and further understands that she has to try to imagine the kitten. According to NSV, those whith good imagination can see the kitten as if it was real (ie, hallucinate the kitten), but they could equally imagine the same kitten without hypnosis.

There is agreement that, in addition to the changes in external behaviour, suggestions presented in a hypnotic context may give rise to changes in subjective experience. But there is no general agreement about the theoretical framework within which these changes in experience and behaviour should be explained.

The theoretical controversy concerns two problems. What I will call Problem 1 is the nature of hypnosis itself: is a special brain state involved or not? Problem 2 is the nature of responding to hypnotic suggestion: is it based on voluntary, goal-directed behaviour and imagination or not?

In this essay, I describe some theoretical assumptions of the Altered State Theory (AST) of hypnosis[18] and review some experiments in which this theory has been empirically tested.

How people generally react to hypnosis

One of the most consistent findings in hypnosis research is that there are large individual differences in how people respond to hypnosis.[19] Responsiveness is scaled by giving participants different kinds of suggestion. These can be statements to *imagine* a state of affairs ("Imagine a heavy object in your outstretched hand") or they can be statements that reality *has actually changed* ("You have not noticed that there is a fly in the room, but now you can feel it buzzing around your face").

Most people experience something interesting and unusual when they imagine things (usually the imagined state of affairs feels stronger and more real in a hypnotic context than one has expected), but others may feel nothing strange or interesting during the entire procedure. And only a very small minority react to statements of actual changes in reality.

These individuals may profess to see or hear things that have no physical source and may display a curious inability to remember anything that happened during a hypnosis session – as if the whole procedure had been wiped from their memory. Persons who are able to experience practically all hypnotic phenomena known to science are in the literature typically referred to as "hypnotic virtuosos".

Hypnotic virtuosos as a model system

The history of science has shown that an efficient way to capture a phenomenon through empirical studies is to identify a "model system", in which the phenomenon of interest manifests itself in an exceptionally clear form. Model systems are widely used in biology; a good example is the use of the fruit fly (*Drosophila melanogaster*) when studying genetics. In the ideal case, the phenomenon can be clearly isolated from others with which it might otherwise be confused, and it is accessible to easy observation or manipulation by the researchers.

In hypnosis research, hypnotic virtuosos are rather rare but they possess the characteristics of hypnosis as clearly as can be. Studies using hypnotic virtuosos could thus serve the same role as studies of model systems generally. I have argued that focusing on these special cases could lead to a leap forward in hypnosis research.[20]

In the following review of experiments, I have mostly studied a hypnotic virtuoso; I call her TS-H. I will first describe experiments where the hypothesis of a hypnotic state has been tested (Problem 1). After that, I give an overview of studies which have focused on testing the automaticity of hypnotic responding (Problem 2). I have concentrated on visual hallucinations, since the visual modality gives opportunities to study visual consciousness in a precise and clear way. We have a rather good understanding of how different aspects of visual information (colour, form, movement etc) are processed, which provides numerous possibilities for manipulating the stimuli. Furthermore, with current technology it is possible to analyse non-conscious information-processing, which may offer crucial information when comparing SV and NSV theories of hypnosis.

The experimental participant, TS-H, was 34 years old when participating in a hypnosis experiment for the first time in 1999. She is a female office worker who also performs semi-professionally as a classical singer. TS-H possesses qualities that make her an ideal subject for experiments where hypnosis is being used. She displays all phenomena typically associated with highly hypnotisable individuals, such as vivid visual and acoustic hallucinations and an immediate re-entry into hypnosis when using a previously given suggestion. In her case the suggestion (consisting of one word) to "enter" a hypnotic state results in a dramatic change in her behaviour. Her eyes immediately become glazed (Figure 1, next page) and blinking is markedly reduced. This phenomenon has been reported in scientific literature several times, although never studied in detail.[21] It resembles the "trance stare" widely used in popular culture to represent a person being put under hypnosis.

In all the experiments described below, hypnosis has been induced by this one-word induction, so the process is very rapid. Between 1999 and 2014 TS-H has participated in nine experiments where hypnosis and hallucinations have been studied. She has no history of any neurological or psychiatric illnesses and has a normal psychometric profile.[22]

Experiments testing the altered state hypothesis (Problem 1)
An ideal experimental design to test the hypothesis of the existence of a hypnotic state could be something like the following. The assumed "altered state" of hypnosis should preferably be produced with a post-hypnotic suggestion about entering hypnosis (eg, uttering the word "hypno"). The cancelling of hypnosis (or "waking") should be done in the same manner (eg, uttering the word "base"). The use of these one-word suggestions to induce and cancel hypnosis would minimise the need for suggestions of focusing attention, relaxation, drowsiness and so on, which

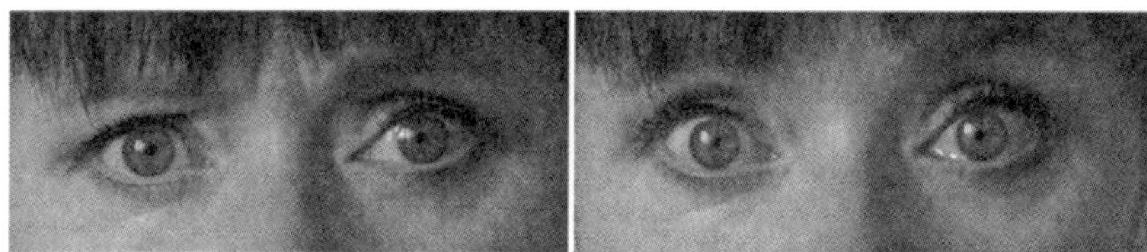

Figure 1: The hypnotically induced stare
(HIS). TS-H in normal baseline state
(left) and during hypnosis (right).

are generally used in a hypnotic induction and regularly take approximately 10–15 minutes. No additional suggestions should be given. This is often referred to as a "neutral hypnosis" and means that the hypnotic induction is the only suggestion that is given. It is also referred to as "pure hypnosis", indicating that just the assumed hypnotic state is present but nothing in addition.

In the control condition, the baseline state of consciousness should be matched as closely as possible and instead of uttering "hypno", another, entirely neutral word, is uttered (eg, "ready"). After that, the experimental and control conditions should be as close to each other as possible with identical instructions/suggestions. When looking at the neural mechanisms, the hypnosis and control condition would be varied and neural activity should be measured by such means as an electroencephalogram (EEG), functional magnetic resonance imaging (fMRI) or event-related potentials (ERP). In the ideal case, data acquisition should be continuous and the hypnosis and control conditions would be switched using the one-word induction ("hypno") and one-word "waking" suggestion ("base").

The first experiment in which TS-H participated was a study where the neural mechanisms associated with hypnosis were investigated by measuring the mismatch negativity (MMN) component of auditory ERP.[23] MMN is elicited in a passive oddball situation, where infrequent (deviant) stimuli are presented amid a sequence of frequent (standard) stimuli. MMN is calculated just by subtracting the ERP to the standard stimuli from the ERP to the deviant stimuli. This wave has been suggested to reflect the function of an automatic preconscious detector of stimulus change.[24]

In this study, TS-H received instructions to sit comfortably on a chair and watch a voiceless video-programme (a slow-tempo cartoon, *Family of the Moomins*). The stimuli were auditory: short tone pips, delivered through earphones. TS-H was instructed just to concentrate on the programme and not to pay attention to the pips. During each session, TS-H received two identical stimulus blocks: one in baseline state and one in hypnosis.

The results showed that hypnosis gave rise to an altered way of processing information in the brain. This result is very difficult to explain in social-cognitive terms, since the MMN component is considered to be a result of a pre-attentive process and peaks at about 170 milliseconds after the stimulus onset. This indicates that the process eliciting it happens prior to the time point when a stimulus becomes consciously experienced.

This experiment also led to an interesting behavioural finding. During data acquisition, the experimental participants are typically monitored by camera to see that everything is going well. TS-H's markedly diminished blink rate under hypnosis was easy to notice. Post-hoc analysis revealed that during a ten minute hypnosis block, she blinked on average of 6.8 times, compared with 86.6 blinks over the same period of baseline. This inspired us to study the phenomenon more closely (see below).

Another experiment investigated the cortex functional connectivity associated with the neutral hypnosis in TS-H, in a baseline condition and under hypnosis, during two sessions separated by a year.[25] TS-H sat in a comfortable chair during the EEG data acquisition and the hypnotist sat immediately behind her. She received instructions to sit comfortably and look at a dim LED light placed about two metres in front of her as she was subjected to three blocks of intermittent hypnosis. By the hypnotist uttering the relevant pseudo-word, implanted as a post-hypnotic suggestion, hypnosis was successively triggered and cancelled. Each block consisted of three to four periods of hypnosis (H) and non-hypnosis (NH), lasting about two minutes each.

Analysis of the data revealed that connections between different cortical areas were significantly lower during hypnosis, compared with the baseline. Especially the neuronal assemblies from the frontal areas lost active functional connections with the rest of the cortex during hypnosis. There were also significant differences between H and NH in all studied frequency bands (alpha, beta, delta, gamma) of EEG-recorded brain activity. These results were consistent and stable after one year.

An eye-movement camera was used to get a better understanding of the previously mentioned change in blink frequency and the peculiar stare in TH-S's eyes under hypnosis. We designed an experiment where we presented a well-established set of oculomotor tasks that trigger automatic eye behaviour.[26]

This experiment followed the same set-up, with hypnosis induced by the one-word hypnotic induction and cancelled accordingly. Different aspects of automatic eye behaviour were measured: the pupillary reflex, programming a saccade to a single target and the optokinetic reflex. TS-H sat in front of a 21-inch monitor and the tasks were presented twice, with identical instructions, before periods of hypnosis and non-hypnosis. All the tasks were presented during two separate sessions, across which conditions were counterbalanced and data averaged.

Control subjects were also asked to perform all the tasks twice: in a normal condition (NC) and in a hypnosis simulation condition (HSC). The control group received the task instructions in the NC exactly the same way as did TS-H. In the HSC, they were requested to attempt to simulate how a hypnotised person would perform the tasks as best they could. To be able to mimic the appropriate behavioural outcome (staring eyes and almost petrified stance), the subjects were shown a video clip of how TS-H behaved upon hearing the cue word "hypno". Then they were given a verbal description of how the eyes of TS-H moved during the specific task and, in addition, were shown a video clip of the eye movements of TS-H in the respective task during hypnosis. For the control group the same cue word "hypno" served as a sign to start simulating hypnosis.

The results showed that the hypnotically induced stare (HIS) of TS-H was accompanied by large, objective and inimitable changes in the patterns of eye movement. The amplitude, velocity and frequency of reflexive saccades were radically suppressed, and the fixation time was increased. Also the pupil size of TS-H diminished during the hypnosis condition (Figure 1).

This study provides the first demonstration of a behavioural aspect of hypnosis which should be theoretically impossible to mimic. In practice, it was clear that, even when given all information (verbal descriptions and a video) of the behaviour, the simulators were unable to imitate it.

Experiments testing the automaticity of hypnotic responding (Problem 2)
I have previously postulated that the triggering of a hypnotic hallucination happens entirely outside the subject's conscious experience or voluntary control.[27] Thus, the altered phenomenal contents of consciousness simply appear in the subject's consciousness, without any special effort on the subject's part to produce them. This is qualitatively different from mental imagery, whose production requires voluntary intention, subjective effort and focused attention.

The experiments described below were planned in such a way that managing to do the task by using any kind of mental imagery or cognitive strategy (as indicated by NSV) would be far more demanding than truly experiencing a suggested hallucination. According to NSV, suggestions given in a hypnotic context are always "imaginative suggestions", asking the subjects to engage in fantasies leading to subjective experiences which they know objectively to be not true. In these experiments the suggestions used are formulated in such a way as to claim that the external world has changed (so-called deceptive suggestions, eg, "*there is* a kitten playing on the floor"). The subjects are always interviewed concerning their subjective experience and, in addition, behavioural and/or neurophysiological data are collected. This means, in practice, that a subject who does not experience a suggested hallucination has to lie deliberately about her subjective experience, as well as to think carefully of a behavioural strategy that supports this.

In a behavioural reaction-time experiment, I studied whether a post-hypnotic suggestion to see a brief, masked target (which could be a red, blue or grey square) as always grey could change the colour experience of TS-H.[28] The task in the control condition (CC) was to press a button as quickly as possible, indicating the colour of the target stimulus. The visibility of the target was manipulated by varying the delay between the target and the mask that followed it.

In the experimental condition (EC), TS-H was given a suggestion of a visual hallucination: "Soon you will see squares on the screen and all of them will always be of grey colour." The control group were instructed to *simulate the hallucination*: "Try now as best you can to answer (ie, press a button indicating the experienced colour) in a way as though you had actually seen all the squares as grey. Try to do it so that anyone who would look at your results and reaction times would come to the conclusion that you had truly seen only grey squares."

In the control condition (CC) all the participants' response patterns were very similar (including TS-H) and no differences between reaction times or accuracy were detected. In the EC, the subjective reports of TS-H revealed that, after the hypnotic suggestion, her conscious experience of colour altered: blue and red targets were seen as grey. The response times in the task revealed that TS-H performed the experimental task by using a similar strategy in the EC as in the CC, which is consistent with her subjective reports that she did not recall receipt of any suggestions and just completed both tasks in the same way. In the EC, however, the control participants performed the task using a different strategy as compared with that in the CC. In summary, although the control participants were able to simulate TS-H's subjective reports of seeing all squares as grey, their reaction times did not reflect the visibility of the target as they should have. It would indeed be quite impossible to work out how the period of visibility of the target should affect a reaction time and consciously alter one's own reaction time accordingly.

In another experiment, the neural mechanism of this colour hallucination was studied in a colour hallucination task where both behavioural and neural data were collected.[29] The stimuli were squares, triangles and circles, presented either in red or blue colour in random order in the centre of a computer screen for 24 milliseconds. In this experiment, two highly hypnotisable participants (TS-H and RM) were studied. The task was to attend to a *certain colour* and covertly count its incidence and overtly press the button when a figure of that colour appeared.

In the experimental condition (EC) a one-word induction of hypnosis was applied for both participants and they were then given a deceptive suggestion that particular shapes were always shown in a specific colour (eg, all squares were red) when performing the task. In the control condition (CC) the participants were asked to behave as if they had received the suggestion and as if they actually saw the shape in the target colour (ie, simulate a colour hallucination).

Both TS-H and RM were interviewed about how they consciously experienced the task. The most interesting stimulus was naturally when the suggestion had been, say, that all squares are red and a blue square was presented.[30] TS-H claimed that she always saw these critical stimuli as red. Furthermore, she did not experience anything strange or different when reacting to these stimuli. RM experienced these stimuli in a very different way, however. She reported that she experienced a conflict between what she saw and what she "felt" the colour was or that "sometimes I saw the shape as blue but my brain said it was red". So for TS-H the suggestion led to a hallucination of red colour but for RM it led to a "feeling of red" yet not to a changed experience. Both participants had been given a suggestion that they would not remember things they had been told during hypnosis (suggested amnesia). Both also stated in the interview afterwards that they did not recall any suggestions whatsoever but only remembered that hypnosis was used.

Behaviourally, the two participants responded to the deceptive suggestions in different ways. This is interesting since both were highly hypnotisable and from the NSV perspective they could therefore be expected to perform rather similarly. TS-H pressed the response button in response to the stimuli presented in the suggestion-relevant shape but a non-target colour (eg, a blue square when red was the target colour that required a response, and "all squares are red" was the suggestion) more frequently after the colour change suggestion in the EC (96 per cent) than when mimicking the effects of the suggestion in the CC (44 per cent). Thus, after the hypnotic suggestions, TS-H reported subjective colour alterations in the targeted shapes (eg, seeing a blue square as red) in almost every trial, but she was less able to simulate the effects of such suggestions. The reversed pattern was true for RM, who reported fewer post-hypnotic colour alterations in the EC (31 per cent) but performed well in the CC simulation (95 per cent).

The interesting issue in this study was that EEG data were registered throughout. Thus we were able to look at the electrical activity which took place in the brain at the precise moment the stimulus was presented to the participants. We indeed found a striking difference in brain function between TS-H and RM. After just 70–120 milliseconds from the onset of the stimulus, evoked 22 hertz activity over the posterior cortex was enhanced for TS-H in response *only to the suggestion-relevant shapes.* When simulating the effects of suggestion, this modulation of beta activity was not observed. In RM, who did not experience the visual hallucination, no enhanced, evoked 22 hertz activity was observed in the CC or the EC.

These results converge with the view that evoked high-frequency oscillations reflect automatic matching of the input to memory representations,[31] in this case to that of the given deceptive suggestion. The matching must have occurred preconsciously because of the early latency of the effect and the immediacy of the colour change. TS-H's own report of not remembering receiving any suggestions reinforces this conclusion. The puzzling question is what mechanism can convert the memory representation into a changed perception, turning the memory of a hypnotic suggestion – "all squares are red" – into making them *appear* as red.

Conclusions

It is quite clear that, as long as the different theories have so diverse views on the definitions of basic concepts (such as the "state of consciousness"), it is very difficult to achieve fruitful discussions among different researchers. Progressive and unified research programmes in science can only be based on a clear conceptual foundation widely shared in the research community. If hypnosis and states of consciousness exist, then the research community should aim to develop an internally coherent and widely shared theoretical vocabulary to make genuine progress in their scientific explanation. The crucial problem in defining hypnosis is that the definition is supposed to cover a wide range of phenomena, to embrace both SV and NSV theories. This includes everything from simply imagining things to true hallucinations and cognitive distortions. The root of this praxis is the recommendation by Ernest Hilgard, who presented the idea of a *domain of hypnosis*.[32] The constructive idea was to have a broad definition and end the fruitless debates between SV and NSV, instead focusing on common topics.

Due to rapid technological development, it is now possible to solve the long-lasting debates by using empirical methods. I suggest that "the domain of hypnosis" as it is currently understood is too wide and therefore lacks explanatory power. There is a continuum of imaginative phenomena that can be well explained without any mysterious concepts. Genuine cognitive distortions like hallucinations, however, *necessarily* involve another type of explanation. In this essay, I have presented examples of experiments where the focus has been to test empirically if these most extraordinary phenomena truly exist. These experiments also serve as examples of how the crucial unsolved issues can be empirically approached.

The way to proceed may first be to find enough evidence to be able to answer Problem 2 (the question regarding the automaticity of hypnotic responding). If we can find enough empirical evidence that, for example, true automatic visual hallucinations can be produced by hypnosis, then we can already conclude that some change in brain function *has to* take place. Then Problem 1 (is there a special state of consciousness during hypnosis?) will become a question of searching for the neural mechanisms that can explain those phenomena.

Our most convincing empirical evidence has so far been found to manifest itself in only one individual: TS-H. There are several experiments showing that a pure hypnotic induction leads to a change in brain function. Also, several experiments support the view that her responding to hypnotic suggestions happens automatically and cannot be produced by purposeful strategies or using mere mental imagery. It is evident that this evidence is not enough to conclude that the 200-year-old scientific debate concerning the nature of hypnosis is now resolved. More persons like TS-H must be found before we can conclude anything about the brain mechanisms of hypnosis. Though we should remember, that many phenomena in cognitive neuroscience (blindsight, for instance) were initially detected in a single individual.

The results presented here can also be explained from a social-cognitive perspective, assuming that some kinds of cognitive strategy are used throughout these experiments. In that case the first assumption would be that TS-H is perhaps trying to please the experimenter and therefore consistently reports her subjective experiences and behaves in a way that she believes is required in these experiments. To be able to succeed, however, she must have a capability to manipulate her reaction times in a way that simulators cannot imitate. Also, she has to be capable of affecting her automatic eye reflexes and electrical activity of the brain (measured by EEG) in such a way that the hypnosis condition appears to be somehow special, compared with a normal baseline. Furthermore, she must be capable of affecting auditory and visual stimuli at a stage that is generally regarded to consist of only non-conscious or preconscious information-processing.

The dilemma here concerns how we should use Occam's razor regarding these results. Do our current scientific concepts, such as imagination, expectations and social compliance, provide fewer assumptions than postulating a hypnotic state or altered state of consciousness? Nevertheless, I believe that, at this point, the results are sufficiently compelling to warrant further research – and to integrate hypnosis with the developing multidisciplinary research on other phenomena of consciousness.

1. A. Gauld, *A History of Hypnotism*, Cambridge, MA, Cambridge University Press, 1992.
2. F.A. Mesmer, *The Discovery of Animal Magnetism*, Edmonds, WA, Holmes Publishing Group, 1998 [1779].
3. W. James, *The Principles of Psychology*, Cambridge, MA, Harvard University Press, 1983 [1890].
4. G.F. Wagstaff, *Hypnosis, Compliance and Belief*, New York, NY, St. Martin's Press, 1981.
5. J.F. Chaves, 'The State of the "State" Debate in Hypnosis: A View from the Cognitive-Behavioral Perspective', *International Journal of Clinical and Experimental Hypnosis*, vol. 45, no. 3, 1997, p. 251.
6. K.S. Bowers, *Hypnosis for the Seriously Curious*, Monterey, CA, Brooks/Cole, 1976.
7. S. Kallio & A. Revonsuo, 'Hypnotic Phenomena and Altered States of Consciousness: A Multilevel Framework of Description and Explanation', *Contemporary Hypnosis*, vol. 20, no. 3, 2003, pp. 111–64. See also D. Chalmers, 'What is a Neural Correlate of Consciousness?', in T. Metzinger (ed.), *Neural Correlates of Consciousness: Empirical and Conceptual Questions*, Cambridge, MA, MIT Press, 2000, pp. 17–39.
8. R.W. White, 'A Preface to a Theory of Hypnotism', *Journal of Abnormal and Social Psychology*, vol. 36, no. 4, 1941, pp. 477–505.
9. See, eg, S.J. Lynn, I. Kirsch & M.N. Hallquist, 'Social Cognitive Theories of Hypnosis', in A. Barnier & M. Nash (eds.), *The Oxford Handbook of Hypnosis: Theory, Research and Practice*, New York, NY, Oxford University Press, 2008, pp. 111-40.
10. I. Kirsch & J.R. Council, 'Situational and Personality Correlates of Hypnotic Responsiveness', in E. Fromm & M. Nash (eds.), *Contemporary Hypnosis Research*, New York, NY, Guilford Press, 1992, pp. 267–91.
11. Lynn, Kirsch & Hallquist, 'Social Cognitive Theories of Hypnosis'.
12. G.R. Elkins et al., 'Advancing Research and Practice: The Revised APA Division 30 Definition of Hypnosis', *American Journal of Clinical Hypnosis*, vol. 57, no. 4, 2015, pp. 378–85; J.P. Green et al., 'Forging Ahead: The 2003 APA Division 30 Definition of Hypnosis', *International Journal of Clinical and Experimental Hypnosis*, vol. 53, no. 3, 2005, pp. 259–64; I. Kirsch, 'Defining Hypnosis for the Public', *Contemporary Hypnosis*, vol. 11, no. 3, 1994, pp. 142–43.
13. Elkins et al., 'Advancing Research and Practice', p. 6.
14. Lynn, Kirsch & Hallquist, 'Social Cognitive Theories of Hypnosis'.
15. See, eg, A.M. Weitzenhoffer, *The Practice of Hypnotism*, New York, NY, Wiley, 2000.
16. Lynn, Kirsch & Hallquist, 'Social Cognitive Theories of Hypnosis'.
17. I. Kirsch & W. Braffman, 'Imaginative Suggestibility and Hypnotizability', *Current Directions in Psychological Science*, vol. 4, no. 2, 2001, pp. 57–61.
18. Kallio & Revonsuo, 'Hypnotic Phenomena and Altered States of Consciousness'; 'Altering the State of the Altered State Debate: Reply to Commentaries', *Contemporary Hypnosis*, vol. 22, no. 1, 2005, pp. 46–55.

19. E.R. Hilgard, *Hypnotic Susceptibility*, New York, NY, Harcourt, Brace & World, 1965.

20. Kallio & Revonsuo, 'Hypnotic Phenomena and Altered States of Consciousness'.

21. See, eg, Weitzenhoffer, *The Practice of Hypnotism*.

22. S. Kallio et al., 'The Existence of a Hypnotic State is Revealed by Eye Movements', *PLOS ONE*, vol. 6, no. 10, 2011, http://journals.plos.org/plosone/article?id= 10.1371/ journal.pone.0026374 (accessed 25 August 2015).

23. S. Kallio et al., 'The MMN Amplitude Increases in Hypnosis: A Case Study', *NeuroReport*, vol. 10, no. 17, 1999, pp. 3579–82.

24. R. Näätänen, *Attention and Brain Function*, Hilsdale, NJ, Lawrence Erlbaum, 1992.

25. A. Fingelkurts et al., 'Cortex Functional Connectivity as a Neurophysiological Correlate of Hypnosis: An EEG Case Study', *Neuropsychologia*, vol. 45, no. 7, 2007, pp. 1452–62.

26. Kallio et al., 'The Existence of a Hypnotic State is Revealed by Eye Movements'.

27. Kallio & Revonsuo, 'Hypnotic Phenomena and Altered States of Consciousness'.

28. S. Kallio & M. Koivisto, 'Posthypnotic Suggestion Alters Conscious Color Perception in an Automatic Manner', *International Journal of Clinical and Experimental Hypnosis*, vol. 61, no. 4, 2013, pp. 371–87.

29. M. Koivisto et al., 'A Preconscious Neural Mechanism of Hypnotically Altered Colors: A Double Case Study', *PLOS ONE*, vol. 8, no. 8, 2013, http://journals.plos. org/plosone/article?id=10.1371/journal.pone.0070900 (accessed 25 August 2015).

30. In the experiment, each shape was targeted by the suggestion (ie, was the suggestion-relevant shape) equally frequently across the conditions as well as both red and blue as suggested colours.

31. C.S. Herrmann, I. Fründ & D. Lenz, 'Human Gamma-Band Activity: A Review on Cognitive and Behavioral Correlates and Network Models', *Neuroscience & Biobehavioral Reviews*, vol. 34, no. 7, 2010, pp. 981–92.

32. E.R. Hilgard, 'The Domain of Hypnosis, With Some Comments on Alternative Paradigms', *American Psychologist*, vol. 28, no. 11, 1973, pp. 972–82.

CHANGING YOUR MIND
THROUGH MEDITATION

Marieke van Vugt

What are the cognitive mechanisms?

Meditation, frequently defined as "a practice of paying attention in a particular way to one's experience and one's mind, non-judgmentally", has become more and more popular in recent years. While there are many types of meditation, most instruct the meditator to bring their attention gently to an object of focus and observe where their attention is ("bringing attention to experience"). When the attention strays from the object, the meditator is asked, kindly and non-judgmentally, to bring it back to the object again.

Meditation is the basis of many clinical interventions and is used widely in hospitals under the name of mindfulness-based stress reduction and mindfulness-based cognitive therapy. In fact, mindfulness-based cognitive therapy has become so popular that it is now the treatment of choice for depression recommended by the National Health Service in the United Kingdom, and has been shown to be as good in preventing depressive relapse as medication.[1] Meditation has been associated with many mental, emotional and health benefits.[2]

At the same time, a comprehensive theory of meditation is missing.[3] Sometimes meditation is thought of as some mystical technique that results in altered states of consciousness that are difficult to understand. I want to approach it from a different angle, and examine how much we can learn about what meditation is from using what we know about cognition in general. For example, the meditative state, which many people report as feeling "spacious", could in the language of cognitive science be associated with an increase in the time between the stimulus and the response.

To work out this idea, that meditation can be understood using our tools of cognitive science, I will first discuss how meditation affects cognitive function; specifically, how it is associated with enhanced mental flexibility, clarity of perception and executive monitoring, as well as a change in the structure of thinking. Then I will propose a computational model that can account for some of these cognitive effects, which could provide this missing comprehensive theory. Of course it should be kept in mind that, as with any scientific model, this is merely a model that does not capture every aspect of meditation practice. Nevertheless, it provides at least a useful simplification.

Effects of meditation on cognitive function
The first studies of the cognitive effects of meditation have focused on attention. This is not surprising given that the instructions for meditation emphasise it. The meditator is typically asked to bring their attention to their breath or another object of focus and, as soon as they realise it has wandered, to bring it back.[4] In bringing it back, the meditator trains him/herself to remain non-judgmental; in other words, to not become too upset about having lost focus again and to not become too proud if they can maintain focus for a long time. Whatever happens is fine. In fact this non-judgmentalness (in Buddhist psychology referred to as "equanimity") may be an important active ingredient of the intervention.[5]

Closely related to non-judgmentalness, meditation has also been shown to affect *how* people are paying attention, in particular their mental flexibility. This flexibility of attention can be measured in laboratory tasks, in which participants are shown stimuli about which they have to make judgments, and where their response time is measured.

A very influential class of tasks in the study of attention are "flanker tasks", in which people have to decide whether the middle arrow in an array like >><>> is pointing left or right. By manipulating the location of the array on the screen, the timing of its appearance and the direction of the centre arrow relative to its flankers, different components of attention can be indexed.

It was found that meditators have an increased ability to deal with conflicting information, which is shown by comparing conditions in which the arrows all point in the same direction (eg, >>>>>) with conditions in which the centre arrow points in a different direction (eg, >><>>). Meditators are also able to move their attention more efficiently to the part of space where a cue indicates that the array will appear (a phenomenon labelled "attentional orienting").[6]

In different tasks, the agility of attention can be measured. For example, in an "attentional blink paradigm", participants see a very rapid stream (ie, about 90 milliseconds per stimulus) of presented letters; within that stream they have to detect two digits and report them in order. The trick is that when two of these digits appear in close succession, with only about 200–300 milliseconds between them, people tend to miss the second digit. This phenomenon is referred to as the attentional blink, because it is as if attention "blinks", even though the eyes stay open. It is thought that the attentional blink is caused by investing too many mental resources in processing the first stimulus, such that the second is overlooked. In terms relevant to meditation, one could say that people get stuck on processing the first stimulus, and thereby fail to see the second one.

Now, meditation is thought to reduce the amount of clinging to perceptions. Indeed, when meditators are given this attentional blink task, after an intensive meditation retreat of three months in which people practise ten hours per day, the magnitude of the attentional blink is reduced.[7] One may wonder whether that is a permanent change or depends more on temporary effects of meditation.

In a follow-up study, we showed that the effect was dependent on the type of meditation practice people did. In the literature, two types of meditation have been distinguished: open monitoring and focused attention. While focused attention involves focusing on a chosen meditation object, and returning attention whenever it gets distracted, open monitoring involves a more global sense of awareness, not focused on anything in particular and not "attached" to any particular thought. Consequently, open-monitoring meditation cultivates a sense of non-judging and open awareness. We showed that the attentional blink, reflecting the lingering on target stimuli, was reduced for open-monitoring relative to focused-attention meditation, although only for people who had extensive meditation experience.[8]

Meditation has also been shown to improve the clarity of perception. In a study of meditators taking part in a one-month, focused-attention meditation retreat, we examined memory for detailed visual stimuli.[9] The stimuli were synthetic faces, which were all very similar to each other. Participants were asked to commit three faces to memory, and a few seconds later were asked whether a fourth face was identical to one of the three they had had to remember. We know that performance on this task is affected by the similarity of these stimuli, such that stimuli that are very similar are difficult to distinguish. In other words, when the fourth (probe) item is very similar to one or more of the stimuli to be remembered, people frequently mistakenly claim to have seen it. We found that, after a month-long retreat, meditators were able to respond to the probes more quickly and with less variability. Importantly, we showed using computational modelling that people were more clearly able to distinguish between probe and similar memorised stimuli after the retreat. This means that the clarity of participants' perception improved, such that they could see the stimuli with more detail and keep them in mind better.

The process of meditation, in which one needs continuously to monitor whether one gets distracted from the object of meditation, has also been shown to affect executive monitoring. This is the monitoring, and if necessary adjustment, of cognitive processes. With another cognitive task, the flanker task, we can assess executive monitoring.

We can conceptualise performance of this task in terms of decision-making. The speed and accuracy of a decision are governed by three main factors: the quality of the information on which the decision is based, one's degree of caution (decisions are slower but more accurate when caution is greater) and (fixed) delays in the perceptual and motor systems.[10] In this context, one can assess executive monitoring through looking at how much a person adapts the decision threshold in response to changing circumstances. We found that, relative to a control group, meditators better adjusted their decision threshold to the level of conflict in a stimulus.[11]

Meditation has been shown to improve working-memory capacity, which is the ability to keep in mind multiple pieces of information and manipulate them. Clearly, manipulating and keeping in mind information is crucial for executive monitoring and, experimentally, those faculties are closely related.

Working-memory capacity is measured by giving people a task in which they see a sequence of letters that they have to memorise and reproduce in order. But, between each of the letters, people have to do another task, such as solving mathematical equations. The in-between task ensures that people cannot rely on verbal rehearsal to maintain these stimuli, and actually have to keep the memorised items active by carefully monitoring where attention is at each moment in time. Working-memory capacity was measured in soldiers preparing for deployment, some of whom were given a version of mindfulness training.[12] While the stress caused a decline in working-memory capacity for those who did not follow this training, it did not do so for the people trained with mindfulness, as if the mindfulness had a protective effect on being able to remember things.

While up to now we have primarily considered how meditation practice affects attentional faculties and cognitive control, we can turn our attention to the structure of thought, which is really the mental trajectory we move through when we are distracted. An important claim made by meditators is that, by repeatedly monitoring one's thoughts and emotions, moving attention non-judgmentally back to the object of focus tends also to alter the structure of the distracting thought itself.

Normally, the structure of our thoughts is such that we automatically repeat mental habits, often of a negative valence – such as, upon receiving a nasty e-mail, we may think that we are worthless, we will never make it in life, nobody likes us and so on. Every time we go through such a thinking pattern, it is reinforced. In meditation, by not following these trains of thought to their end, but instead by returning to the meditation object, the claim is that the thinking patterns are not reinforced, thereby allowing for a sense of openness and, again, mental flexibility.

We tested this hypothesis with patients involved in mindfulness-based cognitive therapy. Mindfulness-based cognitive therapy primarily involves open-monitoring meditation. We asked the participants in this intervention, all suffering from clinical depression, to memorise lists of positive, negative and neutral words. It is known that people with depression have a bias towards remembering negative words and are less good at remembering positive words. We therefore compared performance on this task before and after the intervention, and compared that with a control group that did not undergo the mindfulness-based cognitive therapy. We did not find a difference in the average number of positive or negative items that people recalled between the groups and between the two points in time. But we showed that the mindfulness-based cognitive therapy increased participants' tendency to recall positive items and to stick with doing so, while it decreased participants' tendency to recall negative items.[13] In other words, the structure of their thoughts had changed, such that they were able to get out of cycles of remembering negative things more quickly than before the intervention. Summarising, there is some evidence that meditation practice affects various aspects of cognition, such as perceptual clarity, mental flexibility, executive monitoring and the structure of trains of thought. How exactly does it do that? To address this question, I propose a more detailed computational model of what people are doing during meditation practice, and what it means to be distracted.

Computational modelling of meditation

While the studies described above seem to indicate that meditation affects the cognitive system, there is no theory about how it does so. To come to such a mechanistic understanding, we need process models of different types of meditation practice that describe in great detail what cognitive processes are involved in performing these practices. Once there is such a computational process model, it will be possible to make a priori predictions about how the meditation "task" would change performance on other cognitive tasks.[14] Basically, if meditation trains strategies that can be reused in other cognitive tasks, then performance on those other tasks should improve as well.

Verbal models (which are not computational) do not allow us to make such specific predictions. Before launching into the computational cognitive model of meditation (in some sense a meditating computer), let us discuss the logic and method of this approach. The main idea underlying cognitive modelling (the term used to describe this computational-modelling approach to cognition) is that one understands a system by building it. In other words, if we can build a system that has attention, memory and other cognitive functions, then we start to understand those functions.[15] We can test these models by giving them the same tasks as humans and simulating the responses. If the model can reproduce the human's behaviour, and if it can make testable predictions that are subsequently borne out, then the model is thought to be accurate.

In this case, I have created a model in the ACT-R (adaptive control of thought – rational) cognitive architecture.[16] ACT-R could be conceived of as a programming language of cognition, in which the modeller develops rules that manipulate its different cognitive resources. Specifically, ACT-R consists of modules corresponding to perceptual input (visual and aural), motor output and cognitive processing (working memory, long-term memory and cognitive control). The rules consist of statements of the form "if in such a state, then do that". The long-term memory module consists of a series of mechanisms that implement what is known about long-term memory from psychological experiments, such as a specific rate of memory decay and a retrieval duration for each memory (which depends on how frequently it is used). These tools can be used to create a model of what people do when they sit down to meditate.

The core of my model of meditation is a process of mind-wandering,[17] which is the cognitive process that takes place while one is meditating but one's attention is not on the meditation object. As mentioned above, by repeatedly going through the cycle of focusing on an object, becoming distracted and returning gently back to focus, the structure of thought is modified. The distraction or mind-wandering process is in competition with a "paying-attention" process. When one brings one's attention to the object of one's meditation, at first it is very strong but it slowly weakens over time, due to decay that is natural to all memories. The weaker it gets, the stronger the chance that the mind-wandering process can take over. Mind-wandering is conceived of as a process of repeated memory retrievals, in line with thinking that states that mind-wandering relies on activation in brain areas associated with episodic memory retrieval, planning and simulation. The mind-wandering process continues until the person retrieves the memory that reminds them of intending to meditate. When that happens, the person returns to the focus of attention.

This model did not only arise from my own reflections on the topic but also from a cross-cultural collaboration with meditation teachers and Tibetan Buddhist teachers and practitioners. Some of the structure of the model was informed by a basic scripture in Buddhist thought called the *Abhidharma*, which posits that thought has a discrete nature. The ACT-R cognitive architecture also posits that cognition proceeds in steps, of approximately 50 milliseconds. The way the model gets distracted, by a loss of goal focus, is consistent with the Buddhist idea that one loses focus by either laxity or excitation.[18] Laxity could be conceived of as the "attention" goal becoming too weak, while excitation could mean that a "distraction" goal becomes too strong.

I further tested this model in a series of workshops I gave to Tibetan Buddhist monks in the Science for Monks project in Dharamsala, India.[19] In this project, Tibetan Buddhist monastic scholars learn for a month about Western science (neuroscience and physics). We discussed the mechanisms of this model of focused-attention meditation practice and refined it. The interactions resulted in a consideration of the intention to meditate or frameset, which I will discuss at the end of this chapter. This approach of computational modelling allows for connections to be drawn between Western experimental psychology on the one hand and Buddhist psychology on the other. I hope that more direct translation dictionaries or ontologies can be created to aid this cross-cultural and cross-scientific interaction.

Even though the model does not derive from thin air, it is crucial to test a model's predictions against empirical data. By definition, however, typically meditators do not exhibit behaviour, since the practice is about not reacting to stimuli. How, then, can we verify this computational model of meditation?

The emerging field of investigating the neural and behavioural mechanisms underlying mind-wandering may provide a way out. If we can test the distraction component of the model, then at least that part will have been verified. Mind-wandering is typically studied by giving a person a very boring behavioural task and observing how task performance declines. Crucially, every now and then the task contains probes in which participants report whether they have been distracted or are on task. It then becomes possible to assess how behaviour changes just prior to a report of being off-task, when presumably the person is distracted. It has been found that behaviour becomes worse and more variable just prior to reports of being off-task.[20] This is accompanied by specific neural and physiological signatures reflecting being disconnected from what happens in the outside world.

One task frequently used to study mind-wandering is the sustained attention to response task. Participants see a series of stimuli, presented roughly every two seconds. Their task is to press a button whenever the stimulus appears, except when it is an infrequent target stimulus. For example, the stimuli could be the numbers 1–9, where responses should be withheld for the stimulus 3. When people become distracted, their responses become more variable, and they will be more likely to respond (incorrectly) to the stimulus 3.

We model performance on this task by assuming that when people are on-task they perceive the stimulus as soon as it appears, retrieve the response that is desired for that stimulus and implement that response. After the response is done, they keep checking whether they are still focusing their attention correctly, until the next stimulus appears (the same mechanism as the meditation model). When, however, the model is distracted, involved in retrieving memories, then it may take a little while before it notices the stimulus, because it first needs to finish memory retrieval. This results in the observed increase in response-time variability. Once the model sees the stimulus, it just implements the default response, irrespective of the stimulus' identity. Consequently, it will often be wrong.

We have shown that this model of mind-wandering can reproduce the behaviour reported in two published studies of the phenomenon.[21] Moreover, it gives as estimate of how often and how long people tend to be distracted. We showed that the model gets more distracted as the task progresses and it is typically distracted for 1–20 seconds.

Importantly, we can also give the model the same thought probes (ie, "Were you on-task or off-task?") that are given to humans doing the task. We have shown that we can reproduce the appropriate fraction of reports being off-task (approximately 30–40 per cent of the time). This is the first model that can respond to thought probes and that can actually introspect. The modelling exercise also led me to an interesting follow-up question: what are people really doing to make up their responses to the thought probes? Response times to thought probes had not yet been reported in the literature, but we found upon inspecting the data that these are of the order of 3–6 seconds. For experimental psychologists, this is a really long time, which therefore our model cannot reproduce. The reason that we cannot do so is that we do not know what drives these long response times.

There are several possible explanations. One option is that people never know for certain whether they are on-task or off-task, and always have to engage in a slow evidence-accumulation process to adjudicate between these competing options.[22] Alternatively, people may not base their decision on what is happening just then, but also on what happened in the preceding seconds. In other words, before responding, they may engage in mental time travel to find out what they were thinking in the recent past and decide on the basis of that whether they were on-task.[23] Future studies should decide which of these options is more likely. Without the detailed behavioural analyses that were prompted by the modelling exercise, however, we would have never considered those questions.

With the model thus validated, how would meditation practice affect the modelled mind-wandering process? As mentioned above, our working hypothesis is that meditation affects the structure of distraction. Mental habits get loosened up, which is how we conceptualise the report of many people that they feel more spacious when they start practising meditation. What does that mean? Normally it is very easy to get lost in almost claustrophobic circles of thinking, especially when they involve "sticky memories", such as self-related hopes and fears. We either get lost in negative associative elaboration, which in an extreme case is called rumination,[24] or more positive-valence associative elaboration, which in an extreme case is called craving.[25] While rumination and craving are more pathological states, their milder forms are present in every human being.

Now meditation is a practice of disengaging from these cycles of associative elaboration through a process of decentring,[26] which means that, instead of being absorbed in the thought, a distance is placed between oneself and the thought. This decentring could be implemented in our model as a decrease in associative strength between one thought and the next. When the associative strength decreases, it is easier for other memories, and in particular for the memory of "paying attention", to interrupt the elaboration process. When that happens, the connection strength between the sticky memories is further reduced, because memory strength is use-dependent, such that associations between memories that are retrieved in sequence are strengthened while others decay. By mentally travelling through alternative thought networks, slowly the sticky patterns of memories are resolved and the meditator starts to feel more spacious. As the number of different mental pathways increases in this way, and the connections between sticky memories are loosened, there is a larger space between the stimulus and response, and there is a smaller probability of getting stuck in habits.[27]

Meditation is typically also associated with a feeling of fewer thoughts or a more open mind, an experience traditionally referred to as "absence of thought".[28] This feeling could be explained as a smaller reservoir of memories capable of being retrieved. As the number of memories decreases, there are fewer competitors for the memory that is a reminder of returning to focus, making it easy to retrieve that memory and thereby returning to the main task. One is therefore less likely to be distracted for a long period of time. Subsequent work with this model showed that conversely, when the mind becomes more sticky during depressive rumination, it could predict performance declines that are observed in depression.[29]

This theory of guidance of thought processes by available memories could also explain why the motivation or intention with which one starts the practice is thought to be such an important component of meditation. When Buddhists practice meditation, they first invoke a motivation of helping all sentient beings. Even in the more secular mindfulness-based stress-reduction practice, intention is important enough to be part of its operational definition.[30] Such a focus on others and on positivity could serve to activate a memory context in which sticky memories involving self-related hopes and fears are less available, while other-related, non-sticky memories are more available. This should then change the contents of the thoughts that are being experienced when one is distracted. Moreover, it could make the memory of attending or meditating more available, such that it is easier to come back from a distracted episode.

Up to now, the model I have presented has been primarily describing focused-attention meditation, in which there is a single meditation object to which one returns again and again. Future work should elaborate how other types of meditation work, but I shall offer some suggestions. Many forms of meditation involve the repetition of a mantra, which should involve the recruitment of speech resources, but also should activate a set of memories associated with its meaning. Again, this activation of specific memories guides the specific trajectories that one follows in the process of being distracted. Meditation types more similar to open monitoring are a bit of a challenge for this model, since there is not a single object on which the model focuses. In an ideal state, the model would be simply aware of whatever happens internally and externally, but not react in any way. After every memory retrieval, it should go back to a state of simply monitoring whatever occurs in the internal and external environment. At this point, it is not clear whether the checking process occurring in this type of meditation is the same as, or different from, that involved in focused-attention meditation. Future modelling studies will address these questions.

Conclusion

As more studies develop on the effect of meditation on cognition, we need better theories to explain how this comes about. Instead of describing meditation as an altered state of consciousness, thereby effectively placing it outside the scientific realm, we attempt to connect it to existing cognitive theories. Computational modelling helps to make such theories more precise, and in the future will allow us to make predictions for how specific types of meditation affect cognition and emotion. This in turn could have important implications for working out how individual differences in emotional and cognitive make-up make different types of meditation more or less helpful for a particular person.

In summary: a meditating computer is in itself not so interesting. But the mental exercise and cross-cultural thinking it requires definitely is.

1. W. Kuyken et al., 'Effectiveness and Cost-Effectiveness of Mindfulness-Based Cognitive Therapy Compared with Maintenance Antidepressant Treatment in the Prevention of Depressive Relapse or Recurrence (PREVENT): A Randomised Controlled Trial', *The Lancet*, no. 386, 2015, pp. 63–73.

2. A. Chiesa & A. Serretti, 'A Systematic Review of Neurobiological and Clinical Features of Mindfulness Meditations', *Psychological Medicine*, no. 40, 2010, pp. 1239–52; B. Holzel et al., 'How Does Mindfulness Meditation Work? Proposing Mechanisms of Action from a Conceptual and Neural Perspective', *Perspectives on Psychological Science*, no. 6, 2011, pp. 537–59.

3. But see D.R. Vago & D.A. Silbersweig, 'Self-Awareness, Self-Regulation, and Self-Transcendence (S-ART): A Framework for Understanding the Neurobiological Mechanisms of Mindfulness', *Frontiers in Human Neuroscience*, no. 6, 2012, p. 296.

4. B.A. Wallace, 'The Buddhist Tradition of Samatha: Methods for Refining and Examining Consciousness', *Journal of Consciousness Studies*, no. 6, 1999, pp. 175–87; B.A. Wallace, *The Attention Revolution*, Somerville, MA, Wisdom Publications, 2008.

5. G. Desbordes et al., 'Moving beyond Mindfulness: Defining Equanimity as an Outcome Measure in Meditation and Contemplative Research', *Mindfulness*, no. 1, 2014.

6. A.P. Jha, J. Krompinger & M.J. Baime, 'Mindfulness Training Modifies Subsystems of Attention', *Cognitive, Affective & Behavioral Neuroscience*, no. 7, 2007, pp. 109–19.

7. H.A. Slagter et al., 'Mental Training Affects Distribution of Limited Brain Resources', *PLOS Biology*, vol. 5, no. 6, 2007, p. e138.

8. M.K. van Vugt & H.A. Slagter, 'Control over Experience? Magnitude of the Attentional Blink Depends on Meditative State', *Consciousness and Cognition*, no. 23, 2014, pp. 32–9.

9. M.K. van Vugt & A.P. Jha, 'Investigating the Impact of Mindfulness Meditation Training on Working Memory: A Mathematical Modeling Approach', *Cognitive, Affective, & Behavioral Neuroscience*, no. 11, 2011, pp. 344–53.

10. E.-J. Wagenmakers, H.L.J. Van Der Maas & R.P.P.P. Grasman, 'An EZ-Diffusion Model for Response Time and Accuracy', *Psychonomic Bulletin & Review*, no. 14, 2007, pp. 3–22.

11. M.K. van Vugt & P.M. van den Hurk, 'Modeling the Effects of Attention Cueing on Mediators', *Mindfulness*, 2016.

12. A.P. Jha et al., 'Examining the Protective Effects of Mindfulness Training on Working Memory Capacity and Affective Experience', *Emotion*, no. 10, 2010, pp. 54–64; F. Zeidan et al., 'Mindfulness Meditation Improves Cognition: Evidence of Brief Mental Training', *Consciousness and Cognition*, no. 19, 2010, pp. 597–605.

13. M.K. van Vugt et al., 'The Effects of Mindfulness-Based Cognitive Therapy on Affective Memory Associations in Depression: A Mechanistic Model of Rumination', *Frontiers in Human Neuroscience*, no. 6, 2012, p. 257.

14. N.A. Taatgen, 'The Nature and Transfer of Cognitive Skills', *Psychological Review*, no. 120, 2013, pp. 439–71.

15. C. Eliasmith et al., 'A Large-Scale Model of the Functioning Brain', *Science*, no. 338, 2012, pp. 1202–05.

16. J.R. Anderson, *How Can the Human Mind Occur in the Physical Universe?*, Oxford, Oxford University Press, 2007.

17. M.K. Van Vugt et al., 'Modeling Mind-Wandering: A Tool to Better Understand Distraction', in N. Taatgen et al. (eds.), *Proceedings of the International Conference in Cognitive Modeling*, Groningen, University of Groningen, 2015, pp. 252–57.

18. G. Dreyfus, 'Is Mindfulness Present-Centred and Non-Judgmental? A Discussion of the Cognitive Dimensions of Mindfulness', *Contemporary Buddhism*, no. 12, 2011, pp. 41–54.

19. See http://www.scienceformonks.org.

20. J. Smallwood & J.W. Schooler, 'The Science of Mind Wandering: Empirically Navigating the Stream of Consciousness', *Annual Review of Psychology*, no. 66, 2015, pp. 487–518; M. Bastian & J. Sackur, 'Mind Wandering at the Fingertips: Automatic Parsing of Subjective States Based on Response Time Variability', *Frontiers in Psychology*, no. 4, 2013, p. 573.

21. Bastian & Sackur, 'Mind Wandering at the Fingertips'; M.D. Mrazek, J. Smallwood & J.W. Schooler, 'Mindfulness and Mind-Wandering: Finding Convergence through Opposing Constructs', *Emotion*, no. 12, 2012, pp. 442–48.

22. R. Ratcliff & P.L. Smith, 'A Comparison of Sequential Sampling Models for Two-Choice Reaction Time', *Psychological Review*, no. 111, 2004, pp. 333–67.

23. E. Tulving, 'Episodic Memory: From Mind to Brain', *Annual Review of Psychology*, no. 53, 2002, pp. 1–25.

24. S. Nolen-Hoeksema & J. Morrow, 'A Prospective Study of Depression and Posttraumatic Stress Symptoms after a Natural Disaster: The 1989 Loma Prieta Earthquake', *Journal of Personality and Social Psychology*, no. 61, 1991, pp. 115–21; W. Treynor, R. Gonzalez & S. Nolen-Hoeksema, 'Rumination Reconsidered: A Psychometric Analysis', *Cognitive Therapy and Research*, no. 27, 2003, pp. 247–59.

25. D.J. Kavanagh, J. Andrade & J. May, 'Imaginary Relish and Exquisite Torture: The Elaborated Intrusion Theory of Desire', *Psychological Review*, no. 112, 2005, pp. 446–67.

26. Vago & Silbersweig, 'Self-Awareness, Self-Regulation, and Self-Transcendence'.

27. D.T. Neal et al., 'How Do Habits Guide Behavior? Perceived and Actual Triggers of Habits in Daily Life', *Journal of Experimental Social Psychology*, no. 48, 2012, pp. 492–98.

28. S. Rinpoche, *The Tibetan Book of Living and Dying*, San Francisco, CA, HarperOne, 1994.

29. M.K. van Vugt & M. van der Velde, 2018, https://onlinelibrary.wiley.com/doi/full/10.1111/tops.12318 (accessed 7 june 2022).

30. S.R. Bishop et al., 'Mindfulness: A Proposed Operational Definition', *Clinical Psychology: Science and Practice*, no. 11, 2004, pp. 230–41.

THE NEW SCIENCE OF OUT-OF-BODY EXPERIENCES

Susan Blackmore

Out of the body?

I was just 19, and a first-year psychology student at Oxford, when a brief experience changed my life. Indeed what happened in those two or three hours subsequently drove both my intellectual and spiritual lives. I do not, to this day, know what caused it. Perhaps it was extreme tiredness from having too much late-night fun and getting up for early lectures, perhaps it was the Ouija board session we had just finished, perhaps it was the small amount of cannabis we were smoking or perhaps it was something else altogether.

Whatever the cause, I was sitting on the floor listening to music with my friends, Kevin and Victoria, when I found myself rushing down an imaginary tunnel of trees towards a bright light. I was beginning to drift and float, wondering what was happening, when Kevin asked: "Where are you, Sue?" As I struggled to reply, my vision cleared and there I was, looking down on the room, seeing myself and my two friends from above. "I'm on the ceiling," I said, as I watched my own mouth open and close below me.

From what I know now, I guess the experience would have ended as quickly as it had begun had it not been for Kevin continually asking me questions: "What can you see now? ... Have you got a silver cord? ... Can you go further?" I had no time to panic or worry; I just tried to answer. I zoomed up through the ceiling, out into the night and began to fly across Oxford, across the countryside, over the sea and to many other wonderful places. The scenes were vivid and glorious, the light exceptionally clear and bright. I felt vividly alive and well.

Twice I tried to come back, but it was hard. The first time, I was dismayed to find the room looking far from normal and my own body now headless and distorted. So I set off again into more adventures in ever stranger seeming worlds. The second time, I tried to get back to normal and to go inside the body, but found it impossible. First I was too small, then too large. Then I began expanding and expanding until space and time themselves seemed to lose all meaning. I was no longer a separate "me". Indeed "I" and the vivid, glowing universe were one. There was just this and this was perfect and right and there was nothing to be done ever.

There seemed to be a decision to be made: to stay in this bliss forever or to go back to "normal" life. I came back. Eventually, and with a great struggle, I emerged from oneness into separation again. I persuaded myself that I had to go back inside the body and take it with me wherever I went, which seemed a horrible thing to have to do. But I eventually succeeded and after another two days felt relatively normal again.

So what happened to me? Kevin said I had experienced "astral projection": that my astral body had left its physical shell and gone travelling on the astral planes. It was the only idea we had. I had never heard of tunnel experiences or out-of-body experiences and although I had been through almost every aspect of the now classic "near-death experience", that term was not invented until five years later.[1]

It is not surprising, then, that I jumped to false conclusions. As Thomas Metzinger puts it, after such an experience "it is almost impossible not to become an ontological dualist"[2] – and I did. I immediately became convinced of the existence of spirits or souls that can leave the body and survive death, even though my body was clearly alive and well during the whole experience. Despite this conviction, I could see that this kind of dualism made no sense in the context of the physiology and psychology I was learning in my course. So the experience created a great challenge and I grasped it. Quite illogically (it now seems) I became convinced of such paranormal powers as telepathy, clairvoyance and precognition. So I decided to become a parapsychologist and prove all my closed-minded, materialistic lecturers wrong.

A body of evidence
That decision led to a PhD documenting years of fruitless research. I did dozens of lab experiments, investigated local poltergeists and slept in haunted houses, trained as a witch and sat with mediums, learned to read Tarot cards and throw the I-Ching. But I never found the slightest evidence of any paranormal powers.

So what about that experience? If there were no paranormal powers or ghosts or spirits, how was I to explain it? I could still remember the visions and feelings vividly but could still not understand what had happened. By then I had learned that it was called an out-of-body experience (OBE) and was related to, though different from, "autoscopy" – a usually pathological experience in which people see a duplicate self, or *Doppelganger*, but remain within their own physical body. Pulling together what I could of the classic astral-projection literature and the small amount of available research, I wrote *Beyond the Body* and later *Seeing Myself: What out-of-body experiences tell us about life, death and the mind*.[3] From the 1960s to the 1980s very few parapsychologists were researching OBEs from a scientific rather than an occult or theosophical perspective. Celia Green, John Palmer and Harvey Irwin studied the phenomenology and psychology of the experience and defined it purely as an experience.[4] My preferred definition is "an experience in which you seem to see the world from a location outside of your physical body". As Palmer pointed out, this means that if someone describes such an experience, then, by definition, they have had an OBE. The question of whether anything actually leaves the body or not remains open for investigation. And that is, indeed, the big question.

If something leaves, then this soul, spirit or astral body ought to be able to see at a distance and some, including the parapsychologists Charles Tart and Karlis Osis, tried to find evidence of such paranormal vision during OBEs but their results were far from convincing. I tried myself. For several years I kept a target word, object and five-digit number on my kitchen wall so that people who claimed to have frequent OBEs could visit at their leisure and send me the answers. No one succeeded. I became ever more sceptical and, along with others, including Palmer and Irwin, developed a psychological theory of the OBE.[5] But none of us had sufficient knowledge to make this work.

Then finally, in 2002, everything changed when, quite by accident, the Swiss neurosurgeon Olaf Blanke discovered a spot in the brain which, when stimulated, produced an OBE. He had inserted subdural electrodes on the brain of a patient with severe epilepsy, so that by stimulating different areas very precisely he could locate the epileptic focus. When he tried a spot in the right temporoparietal junction (TPJ), she reported seeming to leave her body, and by increasing or decreasing the stimulation he could control the OBEs and create various bodily distortions of size or shape. The critical brain area had been found.

The relevance of the TPJ to OBEs has been confirmed in many other ways.[6] For example, Blanke and his colleagues scanned six neurological patients who had experiences of OBEs or autoscopy, as well as floating, flying or bodily distortions. In five of the six patients the brain damage was located in the TPJ. Another Swiss group studied patients with brain damage or epilepsy, comparing the precise location of the damage or lesions in nine patients who reported OBEs, compared with eight others who did not. In eight out of the nine OBE patients the damage was in the right temporal and/or parietal cortex and most often at the TPJ.[7]

An OBE was even captured as it happened to a ten-year old boy with epilepsy who had a seizure in hospital. He described flying up to the ceiling and looking down on the room and his mother from above.[8] Throughout the seizure, his brain activity was measured in several ways. The EEG (electroencephalogram) suggested a focus in the right temporal lobe and an MRI scan revealed a lesion in the right angular gyrus – the same place that Blanke had identified before.

For many scientists this discovery was enough. If stimulating a particular spot on the brain could induce an OBE, this proved that it was a perfectly natural, brain-based phenomenon and they did not need to know any more. But believers in an astral world or an afterlife were not convinced.

The arguments are reminiscent of those over the so-called God spot. When brain scans were used to show that spiritual experiences have a basis in brain activity, the media were quick to proclaim that the "God spot" had been found, but opinion quickly polarised into two opposing interpretations of the same evidence. One group took the findings to show that there is no God while others claimed quite the opposite: that there is a God and he uses this spot in the brain to make his presence felt. The latter claimed, for example, that we use our brains to contact the divine, that God works through this special part of the brain to inspire us, that the seat of the soul has been found or that this is the place where the material and spiritual worlds meet.

Returning to OBEs, finding the spot that induces the experience is clearly not sufficient. Against those happy to have discovered a natural foundation, others could just as easily argue that this is the special spot that when stimulated releases the soul from its prison in the brain or causes the astral body to separate from its physical home. If we are to find out which interpretation is correct, we need to understand why stimulating the TPJ induces the sense of leaving the body rather than any other experience.

The answer lies in the functions of the TPJ, one of which is to construct the body schema. This is a detailed, accurate and constantly updated model that keeps track, all the time, of where our body is and what it is doing. This is needed for all animals, not just us, to control movements accurately and the TPJ is ideally placed for this task, as it can bring together information from many neighbouring areas of the brain. This includes information from the emotions, memory and the senses via the thalamus and limbic system, and from the visual, auditory and somatosensory systems.

Among experiments to explore this further are some that have used the "own body transformation task", which involves mentally rotating a drawing of a body as it might be rotated during an OBE. When people are monitored while doing this task it is found that the TPJ is selectively activated. Also, their ability to carry out the rotation task is disrupted by applying TMS (transcranial magnetic stimulation) to the TPJ to interfere with its normal operation.

It has also been found that the TPJ, with its central position between the temporal and parietal lobes, brings together further information to construct our body image (the way we imagine ourselves to look) and our self-image (including our memories and all the stories we tell about ourselves). In other words, what goes on in the TPJ and all its associated connections makes up our sense of self. We are not a separate conscious agent living inside a physical body but a *model* of a conscious agent living inside a physical body.

The body self-model
All this suggests that our "self" is not the unified, thinking and acting entity we often assume it to be. Indeed there are at least four distinct aspects to our model of self:[9]

1 Embodiment or self-location: the position where I seem to be.
2 Body ownership or self-identification: the knowledge that this body is mine.
3 First-person perspective: the position from which I am seeing the world.
4 Agency: the sense that I am in control of the body's actions.

These four aspects of self are normally coincident. We feel ourselves to be inside our own body, looking out through our eyes and in control of what we do. But this is only a useful illusion. There is no simple soul, spirit or astral body to account for this sense of unity. Instead there are complex integrative processes inside a brain that bring diverse aspects of self together to provide the convincing model of a unified, conscious "me".

Some simple tricks can tease these aspects of self apart. For example, in the well-known "rubber hand illusion" a person sits with one hand concealed in a box or behind a screen while looking at a rubber hand lying to one side of their hidden real hand. The experimenter then strokes both the real and rubber hands in precise synchrony. After some time, many people come to feel the touch as though it is on the rubber hand and even to feel that their own hand has moved towards the rubber hand – an effect called proprioceptive drift. In other words, the senses of both self-location and ownership can be moved for just one part of the body while the first-person perspective remains unchanged. In this multisensory conflict between vision and proprioception, between where the brushing is seen to happen and where it is felt to be, vision wins and a small part of the sense of self shifts.[10]

Could a similar trick produce a full-body illusion, one in which the whole body seems to move to a different position? With modern virtual-reality technology, it can. The neuropsychologist Bigna Lenggenhager and her colleagues in Zurich[11] asked volunteers to stand two metres in front of a video camera. The view from the camera was then projected onto a 3D video, head-mounted display (HMD). You can try to imagine what you would see in this situation – that is, you would see your own back standing two metres in front of you. Now imagine that someone strokes your back up and down. You would feel the sensation on your back but see the stroking happening to the back projected in front of you. So what would happen?

The volunteers had the strange impression that the touch they felt was on the virtual body rather than on their own back. When asked to pinpoint their own position they chose a spot closer to the virtual body and this happened only when the stroking was synchronous, and not when a block of wood was filmed instead of their own back. Once again the multisensory conflict led to vision overruling touch, which is why the authors called their paper 'Video ergo sum': "I see, therefore I am".

This is certainly a dramatic demonstration. Yet none of the participants actually had an OBE or even reported feeling disembodied. They did not fly around the room or float above themselves. But another experiment brought the illusions closer to a real OBE.

Henrik Ehrsson and his team at the Brain, Body and Self Laboratory at the Karolinska Institute in Sweden[12] claim to be able to induce OBEs using virtual reality but with a method different from Lenggenhager's. In their first experiment, the volunteer sat in a chair wearing a pair of head-mounted displays. Two metres behind the chair were two video cameras which sent images that would appear as though he was looking at himself from behind his own back. But this time the experimenter did not stroke his back. Instead he stroked the person's chest with a plastic rod and at the same time stroked the air just below the cameras.

If you look straight ahead and stroke your own chest with a pen or pencil, you can imagine what this looks like. You see the pen going up and down, in and out of your lower field of vision. In a similar way, the display showed what the person would see if he were looking from the camera's position. After just two minutes the participants began to feel they were not inside their own body but were sitting at the position of the camera, behind their own body and looking at its back – a convincing "out-of-body illusion".

As a next step, Lenggenhager's team tried to produce both effects in one go. They designed a special table for participants to lie on, with a slot through which their chest could be automatically stroked. In this way either their back or chest could be touched. Cameras were fixed two metres above the table and projected images to the HMD as before. In both cases powerful illusions were created. When the men's backs were stroked, they seemed to remain lying on the table looking down at a body beneath them, and with synchronous stroking they seemed to move down closer to the seen body and to identify with it. When their chest was stroked, they seemed to be up nearer the cameras, looking down on their physical body and feeling the stroking on an imaginary, floating body. As one volunteer reported, it was "as if the self and the body were in different locations".[13]

Many further studies have followed. For example, to test how far people had really disidentified with their physical bodies, the experi-menters threatened their real body with a knife, making a slow stabbing motion towards their upper back. The stress reaction was measured using electrodes on the skin and this was found to be reduced when the out-of-body illusion was created. Other studies have shown that body temperature can drop during synchronous stroking and pain is less strongly felt when people identify with a virtual body rather than their real body. This all suggests that when embodiment shifts to an imagined body, this is not just a high-level cognitive impression but feels real and involves physiological changes throughout the body. This is important because we know that OBEs are sometimes experienced by abused children, rape victims and people in traffic accidents. These results suggest that having an OBE may really be a way of escaping, or at least reducing, intolerable pain.

Is there still a link to the TPJ? Yes. In technically demanding experiments, Silvio Ionta and his colleagues in Switzerland induced illusions in more than twenty volunteers who lay on their backs in an fMRI scanner and were stroked by a robotic device while watching a video of someone lying face down with their back being stroked.[14] As before, many reported that the stroking seemed to be happening to the virtual body rather than to their own and some found themselves flipping over and looking down on the other body, which is much more like a typical OBE. One said: "I felt as if I were 'rising' in a strange way towards the roof." Another "had the impression of being in two places at the same time as if I had two bodies". Some sounded very much like OBEs: "I was 'watching' myself, 'my real me', from above."; "I had the impression of being two people at the same time. One myself was flying, and was watching the other (real) myself being touched by the stick." Data from the scanner revealed that seven different cortical regions were involved but only one showed changes in activity that reflected the changes in self-location. That was once again the TPJ.

Many questions remain. In these illusions, the world as seen is created by video, whereas in an OBE it is not. Where does the realistic and convincing OB world come from? Presumably it has to come from the person's own imagination and there are various theories of how this comes about. For example, I long ago proposed a psychological theory of the OBE, in which a bird's-eye view takes over when sensory input is reduced or absent and the brain is struggling to find an adequate model of reality. Evidence to back this up includes the finding that people who regularly dream in bird's-eye views are more likely to have had an OBE.[15]

The Australian psychologist Harvey Irwin proposed that synaesthesia accounts for the creation of the OB world. Synaesthesia is the tendency to mix up the senses, for example, hearing shapes as sounds or seeing particular letters or numerals as a certain colour. It has been found that being mildly synaesthetic correlates with having OBEs. But why can the OB world seem even more real than ordinary life and what accounts for the various positions people take up, the way they seem to leave their bodies and all the other little details we know about typical OBEs? Now that serious research has started, we will surely find the answers.

Science and spirituality

For the moment, these experiments have given us an entirely new way of understanding the nature of the OBE. Blanke concludes that OBEs reflect a "failure by the brain to integrate complex somatosensory and vestibular information",[16] "disturbed self-processing at the TPJ" or "discrepant central representations by the different sensory systems".[17] Such descriptions sound so dismissive! And sometimes I look back on my own dramatic experience and am a little sad that it wasn't an excursion of my soul into another realm but an example of "deviant phenomenal self-modeling"[18] or "impressive transient deviations of intact bodily self-integration".[19]

Yet, realistically, it is far better to understand the truth about the experience than to cling to the unworkable dualist notion of a soul or spirit that leaves the body. Indeed, when I throw off that slight feeling of disappointment, I find the recent research thrilling in two completely different ways. The first concerns science and the second spirituality.

Back in the 1970s, the OBE was barely accepted by scientists as happening at all and if any research was done it was by a handful of parapsychologists. Now the OBE seems to interest both scientists and philosophers because it is helping us to understand the nature of our very self and consciousness – those big mysteries of our times.[20]

Great thinkers have long doubted the validity of our ordinary, unitary sense of self. These include mystics and meditators from the Hindu tradition of Advaita Vedanta, the Christian mystical tradition and the Buddhist notion of *Annata* or "no-self", as well as philosophers and psychologists. One of my great heroes, the "founding father of American psychology", William James, claimed that "thought is itself the thinker, and psychology need not look beyond" and that "[t]he same brain may subserve many conscious selves".[21]

In *Buddha's Brain*, the American psychologist and meditation teacher Rick Hanson brings these insights together with the modern idea that the powerful experience of being a self exists only as patterns in the mind and brain. So the question we should ask is not whether those patterns exist.

Rather, "does that which those patterns seem to stand for – an 'I' who is the unified, ongoing owner of experiences and agent of actions – truly exist? Or is the self like a unicorn, a mythical being whose representations exist but who is actually imaginary?"[22] In this sense the self is an illusion. It does exist, but is not the way it seems.

Science, including the study of OBEs, is now throwing light on how this illusion is created and maintained, and philosophers, such as Daniel Dennett and Thomas Metzinger, are exploring the implications. Popular books are appearing with such titles as *The Self Illusion: Why There is No 'You' Inside Your Head*.[23]

Metzinger asserts: "Nobody ever was or had a self."[24] He argues that selves just seem to be real and continuous because we confuse our "phenomenal self-model" (PSM) with what it represents. No wonder we so easily fall into believing in spirits and souls, and OBEs just add to the illusion. The soul, he says, is the OBE-PSM. His "self-model theory of subjectivity" comes close to my own conclusions about the self and consciousness: that it is not physical human beings or cats, dogs or bats that have subjective experiences, but only the models they create of themselves. It is models of selves that are conscious. It is models of self that experience being out of the body.

So does something leave the body during an OBE? No, because there is not and never was anything that could leave.

The second exciting implication of recent research concerns spirituality. This might seem odd if one thinks these scientific ideas imply the very opposite of a "spiritual" view of the self. Indeed, a popular attitude seems to be that being "spiritual" requires believing in a conscious, independent spirit which dwells temporarily in a gross physical body and can leave it during an OBE and then go on to survive after death. By contrast, I believe that any true spirituality has to accept what science tells us about human nature, even if it is not what we would like to believe. What this new research on OBEs tells us is that our model of self can be split into its constituent parts, giving rise to OBEs, autoscopy and many other illusions. So we are not a spirit or soul or astral body or any kind of persisting self. We are a model or representation of a persisting self.

Once we see this, we have a completely different idea of our self as an ephemeral construction which arises and falls away. This self, like everything else, is impermanent and seeing this makes it easier to let go.[25] This, I believe, is a better foundation for a spiritual life. It means throwing off our self-centred illusions and learning, however difficult it is, to accept our true nature.

I am grateful for having had that extraordinary experience in the first place, grateful that I was able to work on trying to understand it, and especially grateful to all the recent researchers who are finally beginning to make sense of the out-of-body experience.

1. See R.A. Moody, *Life after Life*, Atlanta, GA, Mockingbird, 1975.
2. T. Metzinger, 'Out-of-Body Experiences as the Origin of the Concept of a "Soul"', *Mind and Matter*, vol. 3, no. 1, 2005, p. 78.
3. S.J. Blackmore, *Beyond the Body: An Investigation into Out-of-Body Experiences*, 2nd edn., Chicago, IL, Academy Chicago, 1992 [1982]. S. Blackmore, *Seeing Myself: What Out-of-body Experiences Tell Us About Life, Death & the Mind*, London. Little, Brown Book Group. 2020.
4. C.E. Green, *Out-of-the-Body Experiences*, London, Hamish Hamilton, 1968; J. Palmer, 'The Out-of-Body Experience: A Psychological Theory', *Parapsychology Review*, no. 9, 1978, pp. 19–22; H.J. Irwin, *Flight of Mind: A Psychological Study of the Out-of-Body Experience*, Metuchen, NJ, Scarecrow Press, 1985.
5. S.J. Blackmore, 'A Psychological Theory of the OBE', *Journal of Parapsychology*, no. 48, 1984, pp. 201–18; Irwin, *Flight of Mind*; Palmer, 'The Out-of-Body Experience'.
6. O. Blanke & S. Arzy, 'The Out-of-Body Experience: Disturbed Self-Processing at the Temporo-Parietal Junction', *The Neuroscientist*, vol. 11, no. 1, 2005, pp. 16–24.
7. S. Ionta et al., 'Multisensory Mechanisms in Temporo-Parietal Cortex Support Self-Location and First-Person Perspective', *Neuron*, vol. 70, no. 2, 2011, pp. 363–74.
8. L. Heydrich et al., 'Partial and Full Own-Body Illusions of Epileptic Origin in a Child with Right Temporoparietal Epilepsy', *Epilepsy & Behavior*, vol. 20, no. 3, 2011, pp. 583–6.
9. O. Blanke, 'Multisensory Brain Mechanisms of Bodily Self-Consciousness', *Nature Reviews Neuroscience*, vol. 13, no. 8, 2012, pp. 556–71; Blanke & Arzy, 'The Out-of-Body Experience'.
10. M. Botvinick & J. Cohen, 'Rubber Hands "Feel" Touch that Eyes See', *Nature*, vol. 391, no. 6669, 1998, p. 756.
11. B. Lenggenhager et al., 'Video Ergo Sum: Manipulating Bodily Self-Consciousness', *Science*, vol. 317, no. 5841, 2007, 1096–9.
12. H.H. Ehrsson, 'The Experimental Induction of Out-of-Body Experiences', *Science*, vol. 317, no. 5841, 2007, p. 1048.
13. B. Lenggenhager, M. Mouthon & O. Blanke, 'Spatial Aspects of Bodily Self-Consciousness', *Consciousness and Cognition*, vol. 18, no. 1, 2009, p. 114.
14. Ionta et al., 'Multisensory Mechanisms in Temporo-Parietal Cortex Support Self-Location and First-Person Perspective'.
15. S.J. Blackmore, 'Where am I? Perspectives in Imagery, and the Out-of-Body Experience', *Journal of Mental Imagery*, no. 11, 1987, pp. 53–66.
16. O. Blanke et al., 'Neuropsychology: Stimulating Illusory Own-Body Perceptions', *Nature*, vol. 419, no. 6904, 2002, p. 269.
17. Blanke & Arzy, 'The Out-of-Body Experience', p. 20.
18. Metzinger, 'Out-of-Body Experiences as the Origin of the Concept of a "Soul"', p. 81.
19. S. Easton, O. Blanke & C. Mohr, 'A Putative Implication for Fronto-Parietal Connectivity in Out-of-Body Experiences', *Cortex*, vol. 45, no. 2, 2009, p. 216.

20. Metzinger, 'Out-of-Body Experiences as the Origin of the Concept of a "Soul"'.
21. W. James, *The Principles of Psychology,* vol. 1, London, Macmillan, 1890, pp. i, 401.
22. R. Hanson, *Buddha's Brain: The Practical Neuroscience of Happiness, Love, and Wisdom,* Oakland, CA, New Harbinger Publications, 2009, pp. 208–9.
23. B. Hood, *The Self Illusion: Why There is No 'You' Inside Your Head,* London, Hachette, 2012.
24. Metzinger, 'Out-of-Body Experiences as the Origin of the Concept of a "Soul"'.
25. S. Blackmore, *Zen and the Art of Consciousness,* Oxford, Oneworld Publications, 2011.

CONTEMPORARY THEORIES OF CONSCIOUSNESS

CONSCIOUSNESS AND THE MORAL SCIENCES: POSITIVE METAPHYSICAL HALLUCINATIONS

Owen Flanagan

Mind, morals and the meaning(s) of lives

This chapter is a meditation on two questions. First, what are the prospects for the science of consciousness? Specifically, can we reasonably expect to have a unified science of consciousness? Secondly, how will the science of consciousness, in whatever form it takes, connect with theorising about the place of consciousness in a life well lived? Once we understand better what makes humans tick, how conscious mental life figures in the overall economy of life and mind, what implications, if any, will this have for what conscious mental states we judge to be good for us, existentially or in terms of moral health? On almost every view, what matters in human life depends essentially on what conscious experiences we have.

I discuss a variety of hallucinatory experience, a kind of conscious mental state that involves an "altered state" which is existentially meaningful, morally motivating and also likely to be false; or, if not false, not supported by any other evidence than that the hallucinatory experience seems self-certifying, or beautiful or good. Thus, it seems like a good idea to continue to see things that way after the hallucination proper is over. And doing this, carrying the hallucination forward, as if the way things seem while hallucinating is the way things are, is not so hard once the right kind of hallucination has occurred.

Thus a conscious mental state exists that is long-lasting, experientially profound and hence significant in the morals and meaning-of-life departments, yet also epistemically dubious. The consensus is that if consciousness is good for us, and if it evolved to enhance fitness, it is because normally it accurately reveals the way things are: "this is a cliff edge, so stay away"; "that is a ferocious tiger, so move away". The hallucinations I have in mind produce feelings of awe, experiences that all is one and that I am not really a separate thing but a relational node in a larger cosmic unfolding.

Since this might all sound a bit weird, I begin with a few remarks about how I see the study of consciousness proceeding as a science, and then address the question of whether and how the science can or does contribute to various normative projects that philosophers are typically interested in: questions about what makes for a good human life and what kinds of conscious experience contribute to flourishing, goodness and their ilk.

It might be thought odd that I want to explore the connection between a mature descriptive and explanatory science of the mind, including the conscious mind, and normative issues like mental health, ethics and wellbeing, since we have been taught that facts and values should be kept apart. Yet that division is not honoured, for sensible reasons I cannot rehearse here. And the entire field of psychiatry is devoted to making judgments about what kinds of experience are good: good for us and good for those we are in relations with.

Varieties of experience
In *Consciousness Reconsidered,* I said there were three great mysteries: why is there something rather than nothing; why is there life and how did life come to be; and why and how did some life, some living things, come to be conscious?[1] All three questions are diachronic. They ask how something, the universe, life and conscious life emerged over time, over the last 14 billion years or so. I proposed that we work towards a theory of consciousness that was fully naturalistic, assuming that consciousness, like the impersonal cosmos and like vegetative and animal life, was fully natural. We have some decent explanatory sketches of how each phenomenon might have happened, might have come to be, but nothing like a full explanation.

Besides the diachronic question of how consciousness emerged over time, there is also the synchronic question of how consciousness is in you and me, and in our dogs and cats, right now. How is it, where is it, what if anything does it do and what is it good for? What realises the taste of the tea I am drinking and the sight of the pine trees outside my office window? There are also questions about what consciousness does for me, for you and for our pets, right now. The function question can be asked diachronically: how did experience come to enhance fitness if it does (it could be a free rider), such that all mammals are conscious now? And synchronically: how does my experience of the tea cup in front of me help with my drinking the tea (easy), how does my anxiety in meeting the deadline help with my finishing this paper (harder) and how does

my worry that sentient life might end in several million or billion years
help with anything (hard)?

The natural method

I proposed that if consciousness was to become an object of scientific
study, we would need to run three kinds of enquiry at the same time: phenomenology, behavioural psychology and neuroscience. Phenomenology,
conceived as enquiry into "what-it-is-likeness", is the best and still the only
known method for getting at the first-person side of conscious experience.
So the blindsighted person says she sees no dots to her left but five to her
right. We then ask her to guess how many there might be on the left side.
Whatever number she guesses comprises data for and from psychology.
Then, if we have the technology, we look at what the brain is doing in areas
where we think seeing happens: conscious seeing on the right side, blindsight on the left. We tell a story about how the way things seem connects to
the behaviour and to the brain. In this way we build a science of the mind,
a science of consciousness and a science of the interaction between what is
conscious and what is non-conscious but nonetheless mental.

Figure 1 shows the method for studying consciousness synchronically.
The diachronic phylogeny and ontogeny of consciousness will also
involve these three elements, but it will require in addition the genea-
logical sciences, evolutionary biology, anthropology and cultural history,
among others. This requires what I called the expanded natural method.
It involves more resources but is still fully naturalistic in spirit. I have only
used it myself to think through the question of the evolution and function
of dreams.

I proposed the idea that dreaming was a spandrel.[2] Daytime consciousness evolved because it was immensely helpful at tracking things
through the five senses by the light of day. I see my tea cup, want it and
reach for it without spilling. Consciousness tunes down but does not turn
off when we sleep. Brain and bodily activity of certain useful sorts, such
as replenishing neurotransmitters, refilling various depleted tanks
(androgens, oestrogens, cortisol) and memory consolidation (trashing
what is not needed) take place and arouse endogenous brain activity –
that is the stuff dreams are made of. Since the brain activation is of our
individual brain, it has some personally meaningful aspects, which can
perhaps be used in the project of self-understanding. But dreams did not
evolve for that purpose.

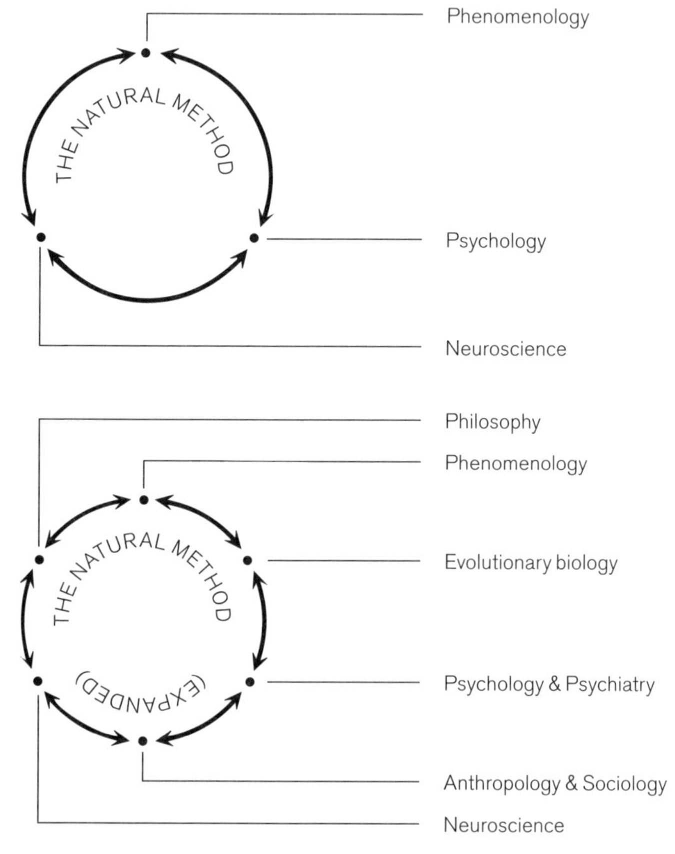

Figure 1. The natural method. Adapted from Flanagan, "Deconstructing Dreams," p. 9

Figure 2. The natural method, expanded. Adapted from Flanagan, "Deconstructing Dreams," p. 9

The natural method and the expanded natural method together re-commend using any science, any body of disciplined theorising, which is or might be useful for answering any diachronic or synchronic question about consciousness. Figure 2 shows what the expanded method looks like.

Is consciousness a unified thing?
The natural method and the expanded natural method are procedures for studying consciousness; they do not say what one will find once one does so. One question is whether consciousness is a unified thing or kind of thing. There are a lot of different ways that a natural phenomenon could be such. It might be a kind that "carves nature at its joints" – the way, for instance, the 118 elements on the periodic table seem to do. The elements are sorted on the basis of how many protons they have in their nuclei. There are however kinds that we would not say carve nature at its joints, yet nonetheless classify some set of entities in ways we all under-stand. Nation-states constitute such a kind, which we understand and which political scientists use to make generalisations. But precise phys-ical features do not fix them. The nation-states in Europe now are not made up of the same landmasses as 150 years ago: some are gone, some new ones exist. But at any given time (with some temporarily contested, indeterminate cases), one could name which nation-states there are.

An open question in consciousness studies is whether the property of being an experience, a conscious experience, a phenomenal experience, of what-it-is-likeness, is the right property to define the kind, or whether what-it-is-likeness is just a reliable marker of some deeper property that is the real kind marker, the way DNA is for life. One possibility is that con-sciousness is more of a hodgepodge than a unified kind. Superficially at least, consciousness contains multitudes. Here is a picture of some of its varieties organised by phenomenal type:

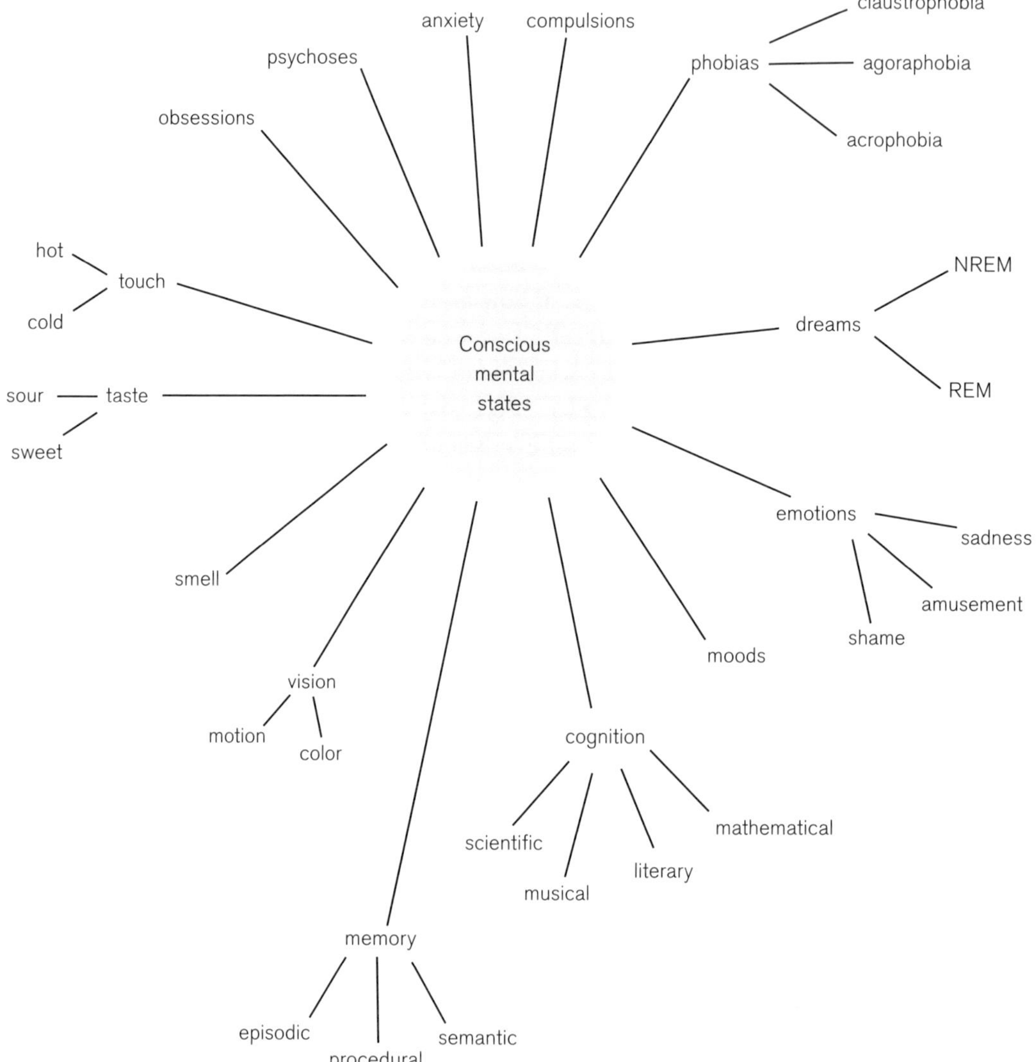

Figure 3. Heterogeneity of conscious states.

The diagram invites the observation that the kinds of mental states (processes or events) that we say are conscious come in varieties:

- multifarious phenomenal kinds: seeing colour seems very different from being sad and both seem very different from thinking that Antarctica is a continent;
- multifarious functional kinds: seeing something tasty, smelling something tasty and reaching for something that is tasty are different activities, and serve different functions;
- multifarious biological kinds: awake consciousness (adaptation) is different from rapid-eye-movement or REM dreaming (spandrel);
- multifarious neurobiological kinds: seeing involves area V1 (in the visual cortex) but smelling does not;
- multiple ecological kinds: one's sense of gender, ethnic or national identity, that one is a daughter, son, cousin, partner or employee, is different in each case and each helps one function in various ecologies.

Whether there is any unified marker of experience, as DNA is said to be for life, is a purely scientific question. In the late 1980s and early 90s there was some hope that there was a marker for all experience, possibly a certain 40 hertz oscillation pattern. Since then such hope has waxed and waned. But everyone pretty much accepts that even if there were such a marker, a property, which if it existed would be a necessary condition for conscious experience, it would not be sufficient for each kind of conscious experience. Suppose that Ω hertz turned out to be the invariant frequency that all and only conscious states came in. Knowing that some brain activity or experience was Ω hertz would not tell one by itself, without a phenomenological report or other very specific neural information, why this particular Ω oscillation was visual as opposed to an olfactory or a fear experience.

My own guess is that, as the sciences of the mind continue to develop, there will be surmises about the ways in which different kinds of consciousness, access and phenomenal, are realised, in each of the varieties and regions of the heterogeneous space they come in or occupy. The story of conscious mental life will be woven into a general science of the mind that blends knowledge about consciousness, the unmotivated computational unconscious (which does language processing, for example) and the motivated, depth psychological unconscious, altogether explaining why we do some of the things we do, experience what we do, feel as we do and so on.

Normative consciousness studies
So far I have been talking about the science of consciousness as a descriptive, explanatory science. Science describes and explains. But what relevance, if any, does a science of consciousness have for normative life? Humans have ends or goals that go beyond fitness. These include being good and living a meaningful life, a life that matters. If one is cultured in a certain way, the ends can be positively Platonic. One may aspire to live at the intersection of what is true, good and beautiful. *Eudaimonia* was Aristotle's term for the mode of being that goes beyond just being and staying alive and having pleasant experiences. *Eudaimonia* involves, in addition to being and staying alive – indeed sometimes possibly choosing not to stay alive if the cause is worthy – fulfillment, flourishing, what we think of as a life well lived.

Thinking about flourishing, fulfillment and meaning involves normative enquiry. Consciousness comes in because these things involve conscious states. Some say whether one is fulfilled or lives meaningfully is an entirely subjective matter. But we do not need to think anything so strong to think that there are normally some conscious components to living well: self-esteem, proper self-respect, a sense of doing one's best and so on.

Metaphysical hallucinations
But there is a problem: there are conscious mental states that can contribute to counterfeit flourishing, perhaps even constitute counterfeit flourishing. The study of positive illusions reveals the theoretical possibility. This is an area where the science of the mind, consciousness studies and normative enquiry meet.

Positive illusions are consciously held (or, at least, consciously accessible) false beliefs that have beneficial features.[3] People who are taught that the average person has a certain objective chance of getting a certain disease, being in a bad accident or being involved in a painful betrayal, yet who think that the poor odds do not apply to them, are generally happier and more pleasant to be around, possibly morally kinder, than people who think that the poor odds do apply to them. The people who believe that the bad objective probabilities apply to them tend be moderately depressed and self-centred. Positive illusions are thus epistemically negative but existentially positive. Most philosophers worry somewhat about positive illusions but do not lose sleep over them. We are protectors of the true, but a little false belief mixed in is a small price to pay for a mood booster.

What I call metaphysical hallucinations are more global and systematic than ordinary positive illusions, and they are considerably more interesting and puzzling. A metaphysical hallucination consists of, or at least involves, false beliefs or, what is very different, highly unwarranted beliefs about Being, about What There Is, which have positive existential and moral effects.

Experiencing no-self
Most biologists and psychologists, like most ordinary people, think that humans are individual, biologically autonomous organisms (just look), endowed with a strong sense of self and its boundaries, and lots of skills at self-protection and self-advancement. Most will say that conscious experience supports this view: each of us has our own and only our experiences.

Some philosophical traditions say there is a mistake here: there are no selves and thus one is not a self. And there are techniques that some say can disabuse one of the illusion that there are separate conscious selves. But why would one want to overcome the illusion that one is a self, assuming for a moment that it is such? One answer on offer is that it enables one – such as one is – to see things as they really are, and to be a morally better person. "No-selves" are compassionate and "loving-kind" in a way that autonomous individuals (although there really are no such things, despite appearances) are selfish.

Two standard ways to produce metaphysical hallucinations are hallucinogens (eg, peyote, ayahuasca, LSD and psilocybin) and meditative or yogic absorption (*jhanas*). In a *New Yorker* article, Michael Pollan reported on renewed research on hallucinogens at top medical centres like Johns Hopkins and NYU.[4] R.R. Griffiths and colleagues have investigated psilocybin, the key ingredient in "magic" mushrooms.[5] Psilocybin is now being given to patients with terminal illnesses and the results so far reveal that the well-controlled, day-long "trips" are normally pleasant, interesting and enjoyable – not at all like the bad trips of days of yore with unpleasant flashbacks.

Unlike dreams during REM sleep, the trips are well remembered, and thus are susceptible to revisitation and fine-grained analysis. Most importantly, as far as the patients go, the trips reduce fear and anxiety about dying and produce a kind of acceptance, even contentment, about impending death. Even for individuals at death's door, the experience is judged as in the very top group of the existentially meaningful ones in their lives.

A common feature of the phenomenology is a sense of completeness: feelings of unity, sacredness, ineffability, peace and joy, as well as the impression of having transcended space and time and the "noetic sense" that the experience has disclosed some deep truth about reality. A "complete" metaphysical experience is one that exhibits all six characteristics.

The "astronaut effect" of seeing the world from above, where one feels extremely small and experiences awe, ego-dissolution, oneness and expansive love, is similar. Interestingly, around the same time as the *New Yorker* article, Oliver Sacks wrote a moving op-ed in the *New York Times* about receiving news that he was terminally ill. He wrote: "[O]ver the last few days, I have been able to see my life as from a great altitude, as a sort of landscape, and with a deepening sense of the connection of all its parts."[6]

Buddhists, among others, think that well-being requires getting over a certain view (perhaps several views) about the self: that each one of us possesses a permanent, eternal essence that is our self and that the main project of life is to feed this self. There is a metaphysical and a moral mistake involved in believing in the self of a certain sort, in this view: it engenders egoism. One route to getting over incorrect views about the self is to meditate, to achieve an altered state of consciousness (*jhanas*), in which one sees that metaphysically one really is "no-self".

This metaphysical insight, it is said, will reduce radically moral egoism and seed compassion and loving-kindness. Ideally, the meditator thus enlightened is existentially compelled to follow the *bodhisattva* path, bringing compassion and loving-kindness to all sentient beings. She has experienced her own maximally compassionate selfless personhood, and she is committed to enacting her Buddha nature for the sake of all.

The philosopher Miri Albahari describes the relevant phenomenology of achieving "insight" this way:

[Her] theoretical understanding of the proposition that "there is no self" (and by implication that she is not such a self) is being coupled with the overcoming of a powerful and pervasive delusion – the delusion that she is a self. Overcoming this delusion imbues her with a genuinely accurate feeling of noetic resonance: of having dispelled a cognitive error – analogous, it is sometimes said, to awakening from a dream. The depth and pervasiveness of the error overcome explains and grounds her feeling that the insight is profound and irreversible, resulting in a more accurate mode of cognition.[7]

The sort of confidence that Alhabari describes in terms of "noetic resonance" is remarkably similar to the way the psilocybin patients speak of possessing unshakeable insight into the way things really are or, what is different, the way they ought to be, when they experience ego-dissolution and a sense of oneness.

Now here is the rub: Buddhists will say that no-self is true but there is vast controversy among them about what no-self means and how to express it, and thus numerous distinctive projects of providing evidence for its truth. Others will say that no-self is not true, at least not in any form stronger than the notion of psychobiological continuity familiar from thinkers who deny that humans possess eternal Platonic or immortal Hindu (*atman*) or Abrahamic souls, and claim instead that humans are finite, sentient, gregarious animals.[8] One and done – and all that.

Believing that no-self is false is however compatible with thinking it good to believe (or should we say "make-believe") in no-self – and, even better, morally good to hallucinate no-self, and then to live as if the hallucination were true. If hallucinating no-self, when no-self is false, is good, then it is an example of one kind of metaphysical hallucination, a false metaphysical belief – or, better, a complex way of envisioning things that does not mirror or represent the way things are, that can be inculcated and that has good effects.[9]

One might think that various confirmation biases overdetermine the drug-induced hallucinatory experience or meditative insight, and thus that noetic confidence is best explained in terms of leading the witness or self-hypnosis. But this is entirely acceptable on the interpretation that what is happening does not require that the relevant insights be true, but rather that they inspire uplifting experiences, positive imagination and good effects, some of which may foster good action and good being-in-the-world.

Pollan asks:

How are we to judge the veracity of the insights gleaned during a psychedelic tour? It's one thing to conclude that love is all that matters, but quite another to come away from a therapy convinced that "there is another reality awaiting us after death", as one volunteer put it, or that there is more to the universe – and consciousness – than a purely materialistic view of the world would have us believe. Is psychedelic therapy simply foisting a comforting delusion on the sick and dying?[10]

Why would Pollan let the psilocybin-induced thought that "love is all that matters" slide, yet worry about people who claim to see what heaven is like? His response likely reflects our epistemic permissiveness towards good-producing false beliefs or, better, unrealistic or perfectionist imaginings. In fact, Pollan goes on to tentatively endorse William James's view that we can judge mystical experiences not by their objective truth value but by their fruits, by whether they have positive effects.

Bertrand Russell wrote this about overcoming the fear of death:

The best way to overcome it … is to make your interests gradually wider and more impersonal, until bit by bit the walls of the ego recede, and your life becomes increasingly merged in the universal life. An individual human existence should be like a river: small at first, narrowly contained within its banks, and rushing passionately past rocks and over waterfalls. Gradually the river grows wider, the banks recede, the waters flow more quietly, and in the end, without any visible break, they become merged in the sea, and painlessly lose their individual being.[11]

This seems like good advice. But note that Russell is not speaking about adopting a particular belief or set of beliefs, but rather about adopting a certain attitude, an image, a picture that helps one accept that death, in all likelihood, is the end of one for eternity but that makes this feel fitting: I am the kind of creature who is made of stardust and will return to stardust; the cosmos is my mother and I return soon to her bosom. Russell may also be understood, not incompatibly, as speaking about what it feels or seems like to adopt that attitude, and thus in a certain sense as a careful phenomenologist. Is he saying anything about the way consciousness normally is or the way the world is, the way the metaphysical facts line up? I do not think so.

One might worry that the attitude of "make-believe" a genuine metaphysical hallucination demands is familiar in children but unusual for grown-ups, and frowned upon for good reason. It involves a credulousness towards propositions that are logically possible but, as with the tooth fairy or Santa Claus, highly implausible. For example, a metaphysical hallucinator might say that "all is love", when it is obvious, at least right now, that all is not love.

This is another reason why it is probably best not to conceive of the hallucinatory state(s) as involving primarily belief but something more like full-on imagination and a powerful desire to make real something that is not yet real. So the hallucinator who says that "all is love" might be most charitably interpreted as thinking that "all is love deep-down-inside", in the sense that reality has love as its *telos*, or that "love is the answer", in the sense that everything would be better if there were love everywhere.

Metaphysical hallucinations involve having certain experiences, embracing how things seem while having those experiences and then trying to project oneself imaginatively into a world in which the relevant experiences or thoughts seem as real as can be, as worthwhile as can be and thus spirit-constituting and action-guiding. They involve working one's way into a strong noetic confidence that reveals itself in how one experiences and lives one's life. One comes to think that a hallucinated attitude towards reality is worth adopting and then one tries to make reality – the way things seem while hallucinating – so. The noetic confidence attaches perhaps not to believing that things are in fact such (although it might involve some of that), but wanting the world to be a certain way, a way one experiences as good, better, excellent.

Most religions and most philosophies one could live by, philosophies that attempt to provide a genuine way of life, a comprehensive way of being in the world (thus not most contemporary philosophy), link a metaphysics, a story about what there is, how it is and what things would be at their best, with endorsement of an ethical vision, a picture of a good person and an excellent human life. Once in place, the typical relationship between the metaphysic and the morals is one of mutual support.

Imagine someone who hallucinates that "all is one" in some way that motivates her to want to bring love, compassion and forgiveness whenever and wherever there is hate, resentment and desire for revenge. Or imagine someone who hallucinates that everything is alive or living (vitalism) or that everything is sentient (panpsychism) and that this motivates an ethic of maximal love. Is this bad? Is there a mistake? If the hallucination is understood as a set of beliefs and vitalism and panpsychism are false, then there is a mistake. But if we understand the hallucination proper and then the orientation towards reality it engenders, not as a set of beliefs that mirror or are intended to mirror the ways things in fact are (now), it is hard to see what the mistake is.

One last remark: there is evidence in both the psilocybin cases and in the case of meditators who experience themselves as no-selves that the "default brain network" lets its guard down. This network is associated with ordinary mental alertness and serves to watch out for "number one" or, if I am not "number one", at least for "this one that is me". But the magic mushrooms tune that ego-protective network down, so I am less attuned to be self-focused, self-absorbed and self-protective. This much, the change in brain chemistry, might account for the phenomenology of ego-dissolution and blending. So one answer to the question about what there is not to like is that the altered state is weird and, even worse, it is weird and not true.

But what exactly is the truth here? Just because Mother Nature attuned organisms to see themselves as possessed of ego, as concerned with its survival and maintenance, does not remotely show that there really is any such thing.

Acknowledgment: I wrote this chapter while I was Rockefeller Fellow at the National Humanities Center, Research Triangle Park, NC 2015–16; revised while Berggruen Fellow at the Center for Advanced Study in the Behavioural Sciences, Stanford, CA 2016–17 with support from the John Templeton Foundation/Saint Louis University project on Happiness & Well-Being.

1. O. Flanagan, *Consciousness Reconsidered*, Cambridge, MA, MIT Press, 1992.
2. O. Flanagan, 'Deconstructing Dreams: The Spandrels of Sleep', *Journal of Philosophy*, no. 92, 1996, pp. 5–27.
3. S. Taylor & J. Brown, 'Illusion and Well-Being: A Social Psychological Perspective on Mental Health', *Psychological Bulletin*, vol. 103, no. 2, pp. 193–210.
4. M. Pollan, 'The Trip Treatment', *New Yorker*, 9 February 2015.
5. R.R. Griffiths et al., 'Psilocybin can Occasion Mystical-type Experiences having Substantial and Sustained Personal Meaning and Spiritual Significance', *Psychopharmacology*, vol. 187, no. 3, 2006, pp. 284–92.
6. O. Sacks, 'My Own Life', *New York Times*, 19 February 2015.
7. M. Alhabari, 'Insight Knowledge of No Self in Buddhism: An Epistemic Analysis', *Philosophers' Imprint*, vol. 14, no. 21, 2014, p. 14.
8. O. Flanagan, *The Bodhisattva's Brain*, Cambridge, MA, MIT Press, 2011.
9. There are strong veins inside the Abrahamic traditions, as well as Hinduism, Jainism and neo-Confucianism, which are not as deconstructive about the self as some varieties of Buddhism, but go directly for altering normal states of ego consciousness by prayer and meditation, thinking that my weal and woe is most important.
10. Pollan, 'The Trip Treatment'.
11. B. Russell, *Portraits from Memory and Other Essays*, New York, NY, Simon & Schuster, 1950.

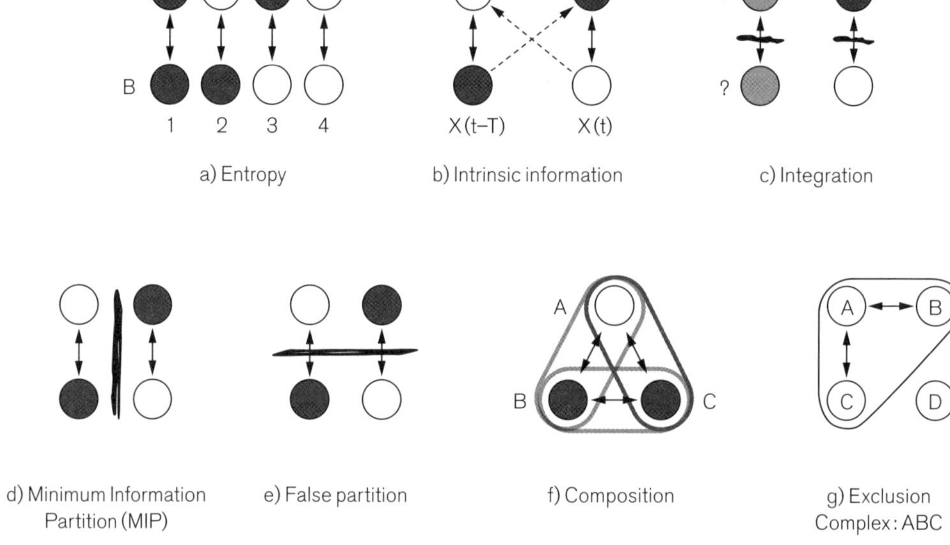

a) Entropy

b) Intrinsic information

c) Integration

d) Minimum Information
Partition (MIP)

e) False partition

f) Composition

g) Exclusion
Complex: ABC

Figure 1. Integrated information theory in a nutshell.

EMPIRICAL TESTS OF THE INTEGRATED INFORMATION THEORY OF CONSCIOUSNESS

Naotsugu Tsuchiya, Andrew Haun, Dror Cohen & Masafumi Oizumi

Consciousness science and integrated information theory

The long-standing mind–body problem is all about the relationship between the domain of the physical, biological brain and that of mental, subjective consciousness. The integrated information theory (IIT) of consciousness[1] offers a mathematical, computational or informational bridge between the two domains, which has attracted strong attention in the field. IIT has strong explanatory power with regard to many enigmatic features of consciousness and their neural correlates.

Some doubt has however been expressed as to IIT's scientific utility: the proposed mathematical analyses seem intractable for real neural systems and thus the theory seems untestable. This doubt is misplaced. In this chapter, we review recent successful empirical tests of IIT. The most successful is the TMS-EEG paradigm, where transcranial magnetic stimulation (TMS) perturbs brain activity and electroencephalography (EEG) monitors how the perturbed activity evolves. The pattern of evoked activity in the conscious and unconscious state is consistent with IIT predictions. Recently, our group and others have developed methods for computing integrated information directly from real neural data. Applying these methods to electrocorticography (ECoG) recordings, we have tested IIT predictions regarding both levels and contents of consciousness.

While the results from these tests are promising, they are just the beginning. It is becoming clear that there are many ways to test IIT despite the theoretical and empirical challenges, some of which can be resolved in the near future. In closing, we discuss potential consequences of the empirical validations of IIT in the study of the physical basis of consciousness. The empirical investigation of IIT may one day serve to comprehend the nature of consciousness in difficult cases such as severe brain injury and animals such as bats,[2] and even in the construction of artificial consciousness.

The theory

IIT starts from identifying fundamental properties common to all conscious experience.[3] Conscious experience 1) *intrinsically exists* and it is 2) *informative*, 3) *integrated*, 4) *compositional* and 5) *exclusive*.

To elaborate, consciousness is an *intrinsic* property of the system and independent of any external observer. Conscious experience is highly informative – each experience is so unique that all other possible experiences are excluded. Any moment of consciousness is experienced in an integrated and unified manner by the subject. It is composed of different modalities, such as vision and audition, with each having various aspects. Even a simple experience, such as seeing a blue ball on the left side of a room, requires integration and composition of its colour, shape, location and semantic relationships with all other objects in the room. Such a complex relational structure is central to our conscious phenomenology. This compositional character of experience further supports its informativeness, excluding any other possible experience. Further, any conscious phenomenology is experienced exclusively at a particular spatial and temporal scale. For example, consciousness flows at a certain speed (with a grain of around 100 milliseconds), not as a superposition of slow (eg, minute-scale) and fast (eg, nanosecond-scale) consciousnesses.

The above five properties of consciousness are considered fundamental in IIT and regarded as phenomenological *axioms*. From these five axioms, IIT makes five corresponding postulates,[4] which specify what types of physical substrates can possibly support each fundamental aspect of phenomenology. The postulates jointly specify how much (or what level) and what kind (or what content) of consciousness is associated with the causal structure of particular physical systems, such as connected neurons or logic gates. IIT claims that consciousness is identical to the intrinsic informational relationships between elements of a system, not to a particular physical substrate. Given a system composed of mechanisms in some state (eg, a network of neurons, some of which are firing, some not), the five postulates allow us to compute the system's intrinsic informational structure.[5]

Figure 1 (p. 346) shows a simplified illustration of the derivation of an integrated information structure. The procedure from a) to g) explains how the five phenomenological axioms are translated into the five postulates to obtain the integrated information structure.[6] The sub-figure (a) shows a system composed of two neurons (A and B). We represent the state of this system at time t as $X(t)$. The state of each neuron can be either on (white) or off (black). Both A and B copy the state of the other with a time delay. There are four possible states in this system (indicated by numbers 1 to 4). If all states are equally likely, the system state is maximally uncertain. The degree of uncertainty can be quantified by the *entropy* (H), where $H = log_2$ (possible number of equally likely states). In this case, $H = log2(4) = 2$. Sub-figure (b) shows a way to consider the intrinsic information in this system (the information postulate). If the present state (at time t) of the system $X(t)$ is 'on-off', it completely specifies its past state as 'off-on' because A and B copy the state of each other. Knowledge of the present state removes all uncertainty about the past. If we denote the remaining uncertainty about the past as H*, in this case, $H^* = log_2(1) = 0$. The reduction of uncertainty is quantified as *mutual information*: $I = H - H^* = 2.$[7]

Sub-figure (c) explains how IIT considers integration (the integration postulate). Integrated information builds upon the concept of intrinsic information. What we want to quantify is how much more information a whole system generates above and beyond its parts. In IIT, to quantify integration we make use of a concept of *disconnection*. The degree of integration can be quantified by how much loss of information there would be if one were to disconnect the system. In our example, each neuron considered separately cannot specify its past state. For example, knowing only the state of A at the present does not tell us anything about the past state of A. The intrinsic information obtained in this hypothetical scenario where the system is disconnected is expressed as I^*. Here, $I^* = 0$. Integrated information, termed Φ (*phi*), is the loss of information (I) when the whole system is cut into parts (I^*). In this case, $\Phi = I - I^* = 2$, meaning that this system *does* possess a degree of integrated information.

Sub-figure (d) illustrates how IIT considers integration when there are more than three neurons in the system, through *the minimum information partition* (MIP). The MIP is the "cut" or disconnection of the system that *least* affects its information. The information lost through the MIP is integrated information. Consider a system that is completely disconnected into two subsets on the left and on the right, as in (d) and (e). If the system is cut as in (d), there is no loss of information, making this an easy MIP – no information is generated by the whole above and beyond the parts.[8] If the MIP is not identified properly, however, and an inappropriate cut is used instead, as in (e), there is information loss $(I > I^*)$, and the integrated information is overestimated ($\Phi > 0$). Thus, identification of the true MIP is important for an accurate measure of integrated information (see below).

Sub-figure (f) illustrates how the *structure* of integrated information can be obtained by considering all possible subsets of a system – here composed of neurons A, B and C (the composition postulate). For this system, how all these subsets interact describes its integrated information structure: $[\Phi_{AB}, \Phi_{BC}, \Phi_{CA}, \Phi_{ABC}]$. The above procedure allows us to identify the core of the system, which generates a local maximum of integrated information – *a complex* (the exclusion postulate states that a complex exists *exclusively*: no part of it can belong to any other complex). If AB and AC are strongly interacting, Φ_{ABC} will be above zero (> 0). If non-interacting part D is considered together with ABC, the MIP among ABCD will be identified as ABC versus D, correctly identifying $\Phi_{ABCD} = 0$. Thus, in this case, the complex is ABC. The structure of integrated information in the complex ABC is determined by the way all *subsets* of ABC (AB, BC, AC and ABC) affect the complex as a *whole*. The integrated information structure describes the kind of experience the system has – the *content* of its consciousness.

The IIT approach is quite unlike other neuroscientific approaches to consciousness, where one observes neural activity and tries to obtain some correlation between the neural activity and reported subjective conscious experience. This process, going from the neural to the conscious, arrives at an explanatory gap – what Chalmers termed the Hard Problem of consciousness.[9] This *extrinsic* approach cannot give satisfactory explanation for why and how some types of neuronal activity in the brain *have to* give rise to specific conscious experiences – why an object reflecting light at c.700 nanometres has to be *experienced* as this particular red quality. IIT reverses the direction of explanation, starting from one's own conscious experience and arriving at a predicted neural basis of consciousness.

Empirical tests of IIT through the TMS-EEG paradigm
One way to test IIT predictions is to perturb the state of the brain and assess the information and integration in the resulting neural activity. This serves as a proxy for neural information integration in the brain. In humans, non-specific perturbation can be achieved using TMS and an estimate of neural activity can be obtained using EEG. A series of studies

has examined the pattern of TMS-evoked EEG in low levels of consciousness during sleep, under anaesthesia and in brain-damaged patients.[10] The complexity of the EEG pattern is quantified by the perturbational complexity index (PCI). The PCI captures both information and integration by quantifying the degree of variability and the degree of propagation in the TMS-evoked EEG activation. A recent study found that levels of consciousness strongly correlated with the PCI.[11] The PCI is high during alert wakefulness but low during deep general anaesthesia and in vegetative patients. The PCI is also high during REM sleep, usually accompanied by vivid dreams, and lower during non-REM sleep, which is often dreamless.[12] The anaesthetic drug ketamine is known to induce a dreamlike state, accompanied by post-anaesthesia reports of dream-like phenomenology. Recent research found that the PCI is high during ketamine anaesthesia, lending physiological support to the phenomenological reports by the subjects.[13]

The PCI was originally motivated by IIT's prediction: high levels of consciousness should be supported by highly differentiated (informative) and integrated brain states.

A closer consideration of the TMS-EEG paradigm and its relationship with IIT reveals several remarkable aspects. First, it is surprising that a combination of rather coarse and large-scale techniques has resulted in successful discrimination of levels of consciousness. TMS affects millions of neurons in an area of the brain of several square centimetres. EEG recordings reflect neural activity over an even larger extent. This level of spatial resolution in perturbation and measurement has a tenuous link with the specificity of what has been considered in IIT which considers perturbation and measurement at the level of single neuron or a few neurons.[14] Another remarkable aspect of the TMS-EEG paradigm is that the PCI, a proxy for integrated information, is based on the *observed* neural responses triggered by a TMS pulse. This paradigm is distinct from the computational requirements of IIT, which quantifies intrinsic information via the perturbation of the system into *all possible states*, and assesses integration by examining *all possible partitions* of the system (the MIP in Figure 1d and e). The success of an "observational metric" like the PCI suggests that even if some ideal empirical constructs from IIT (eg, complete perturbation and exhaustive MIP search) are practically inaccessible, the theory leads to meaningful and empirically testable predictions.[15]

The success of the TMS-EEG paradigm suggests that directly computing integrated information from real neural data may be a profitable approach. In the next section, we review recent such attempts by our group.

Computing the approximation of integrated information
from real neuronal data

Using empirical neural data to compute integrated information is very difficult for several reasons.[16] First, the theory requires perturbation of all neurons in the system in each and every possible combination of states, to elucidate completely the system's intrinsic causal structure (ie, what states are possible causes or effects of what *other* states). The perturbational approach is experimentally demanding, to say the least – it is far easier to record neural activity that is evoked by certain events or observed without any external stimulus (eg, spontaneous activity). Several means have been proposed to approximate integrated information, so that it can be computed from spontaneous or evoked neural data.[17] Recently, our group has proposed an improved approximation, using the concept of "mismatched decoding" from information theory.[18] The rest of this section summarises some of our recent attempts to test IIT empirically, based on real neuronal data.[19]

By computing integrated information, our group has tested a specific prediction from IIT: integrated information should be higher for the awake than the anaesthetised brain. In testing levels of consciousness, we focused on *information* and *integration*: IIT predicts that the intrinsic capacity of a system for differentiating various states should correlate with the level of consciousness.

We computed the amount of integrated information from neural activity recorded on the surface of the brain as an electrocorticogram (ECoG). ECoG recordings have traditionally been used to monitor epilepsy in drug-resistant patients. Recently, however, the excellent resolution, spatially (about a millimetre) and temporally (less than one millisecond), combined with the wide spatial coverage and temporal stability of such recordings (over months), have also attracted wide interest from animal electrophysiologists for various purposes. To test the IIT prediction on levels of consciousness, we used 128 channels of ECoG data recorded from monkeys implanted with electrodes in one entire brain hemisphere.

Unlike the theoretical integrated information, which requires perturbation of electrodes in all possible states, our approximated measure of integrated information, called Φ^*, is computed directly from the observed data.[20] For the analysis, we assumed that spontaneous ECoG voltage fluctuations could be approximated as Gaussian distributions,[21] allowing us to compute entropy, mutual information and integrated information (Φ^*) from observed correlations (or covariance) among the ECoG signals. The primary computational burden here is the search for the minimum information partition (the MIP, Figure 1d and e), across which Φ^* should be computed. For a system of 128 channels, the search space is inconceivably vast, and thus some strategy must be used to approximate the MIP. We used several plausible strategies to do so but, regardless of the approximation, our results indicated that the amount of integrated information in the alpha-beta range (8 to 24 hertz) of the ECoG signal was higher during the awake state and lower during anaesthesia. This conclusion was consistent across 16 experiments performed on four monkeys, with two different kinds of anaesthetic drug combination.[22]

In another study, we tested a prediction from IIT that the structure of integrated information should reflect the contents of consciousness. In testing the contents, in addition to information and integration, we also focused on compositionality: IIT predicts that the way a subset of mechanisms interacts should distinguish various states of the system and this should correspond to various contents of consciousness.

As a test case, we used ECoG data recorded from six human epilepsy patients during the monitoring period for epilepsy localisation. We focused on the high-order visual areas, such as the fusiform gyrus and superior temporal sulcus, which have been suggested as neural correlates of conscious object perception – of faces in particular.[23]

In one experiment, we showed subjects various categories of object, including faces, tools and houses. In other experiments, we showed a picture of a face whose perceptibility was manipulated by visual illusions, such as backward masking[24] and continuous flash suppression.[25] Before explaining the experimental results, it is necessary to recapitulate briefly the known neural responses in the recorded areas, the difference between extrinsic and intrinsic information, and the expected results based on IIT.

Consistent with the literature,[26] we confirmed that raw ECoG data contain information about the presented stimuli (eg, evoked responses distinguishing faces from other object categories). This extrinsic information, a familiar concept in neuroscience, quantifies how much uncertainty about

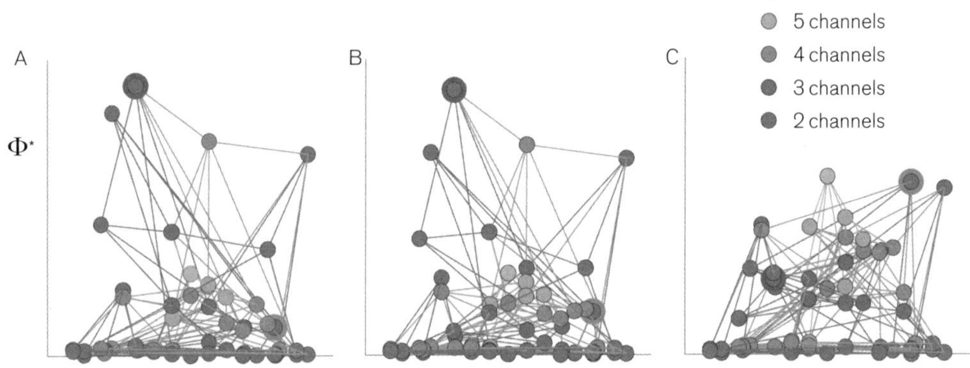

Figure 2: Testing IIT's prediction on the contents of consciousness. Φ^* structure (the structure of integrated information) reflects 55 points of integrated information (Φ^*, plotted on the y-axis), derived from all possible subsets of six ECoG channels (15 pairs, 20 trios and so on), recorded from the fusiform gyrus of one epilepsy patient. The shade of each point represents the number of channels for the subsystem. The lines between points represent addition or subtraction of one channel. The x-position of each dot is arbitrary but the same across A, B and C.

A) Φ^* structure in trials where the patient consciously saw a face in the backward-masking task.
B) Φ^* structure in trials where she consciously saw a face in the continuous flash-suppression (CFS) task. Note that backward masking and CFS differed in task demands and in stimulus properties.
C) Φ^* structure in trials where she consciously did not see a face in the CFS task. Note that physical input to the patient was identical in B and C.

the stimulus can be removed for an external experimenter who observes the brain responses. In IIT, a conscious state is intrinsically informative, in that it excludes the possibility of other conscious states for the experiencing subject. To understand intrinsic information from the system's own point of view, one has to quantify how much its current states limit its possible previous and future states.

Suppose a subject consciously sees a face at time t_1. The corresponding brain state, $X(t_1)$, is more likely to be preceded by a particular past brain state, $X(t_0)$, than other brain states. Similarly, $X(t_1)$ is more likely to precede a particular future brain state, $X(t_2)$, than other brain states. The degree of difference that $X(t_1)$ makes for the system's past and future is intrinsic information. This does not directly reflect anything in the external world, yet IIT predicts that the composition of intrinsic integrated information within a complex – that is, a pattern of integrated information formed by all possible subsets of mechanisms in the complex – is equivalent to contents of conscious experience.

To test this prediction, we focused on a pattern of integrated information that is generated by all subsets of a few selected electrodes, located in the high-order visual areas, and computed the exact MIP for each subsystem in the selected electrodes. Based on IIT, we expected that visual conscious perception of objects should be specified by the structure of integrated information across local populations of neurons in high-order visual areas.

Our results supported the IIT predictions: the structure of integrated information derived from the high-order visual areas naturally classified categories of the objects (for examples from one subject, see Figure 2). When the external stimuli were held constant in backward masking and continuous flash suppression, the shape of the integrated information structure naturally mirrored the experience of seeing faces.

In deriving these patterns of integrated information, the number of variables involved grows very rapidly as the number of the channels increases. Considering a system of just six electrodes, we must compute integrated information in 55 subsystems. To check if the higher dimensions alone explained the results, we compared how well a dimension-matched pattern of entropy (H) and mutual information (I) derived from the same dataset would classify the presented object categories, as well as conscious perception. In all cases tested Φ^* classified the contents of consciousness better than H and I.

Entropy (H) is a measure of the randomness or uncertainty of brain states (across many trials, or many time points in a single trial) at time t_1. Mutual information (I) between times t_1 and t_0 reflects how much the uncertainty of the past state is reduced given the current state (or vice versa). Φ^* is the amount of information that is lost by cutting the system. When there is no information in the system or there are no connections between its parts, Φ^* is expected to be 0. Indeed, many dots in Figure 2 are close to zero, implying that there is only a sparse subset of 55 sub-mechanisms that maps on to the conscious percept. In contrast, entropy and mutual information structures are far from sparse: entropy and mutual information values for almost all combinations of electrodes are similar and proportional to subsystem size – this relatively static structure leads to poor perceptual classification. Meanwhile, Φ^* is highly variable, non-linear, sparse, and changes structurally depending on conscious perception. The fact that integrated information structure more closely reflects perceived object categories than either mutual information (information irrespective of integration) or entropy structure shows that integrated information is relevant for conscious perception of objects: more "basic" measures of neural variation are not sufficient to explain the contents of consciousness.

Challenges for empirical testing of IIT

We have reviewed promising results from TMS-EEG paradigms, and computation of approximated integrated information in ECoG recordings from monkeys and humans. Through these empirical studies, several key theoretical challenges became clear. In this section, we discuss three of these: first, understanding the causal structures of a neural system through observational approaches; secondly, determining the neural system variables that represent the intrinsic perspective; and, thirdly, estimating the minimum information partition (MIP), which identifies the largest subsets of strongly interacting subsystems, or complexes, within the brain (Figure 1).

In IIT, consciousness can be understood as the integrated (irreducible) set of causal constraints which a current neural state places on future and past possible neural states. To reveal these causal constraints, a system must be perturbed into every one of its possible states and allowed to make the transition naturally to the next state as determined by its causal structure. The set of all these transitions thus encompasses all the possible cause–effect relationships in the system.

In the TMS-EEG experiments, the single-pulse TMS is applied at some cortical area to perturb the thalamo-cortical system, and the evoked EEG response patterns are analysed. In the ECoG experiments, an observational approach was adopted by using spontaneous activity or activities that were evoked by various visual stimuli as the basis of integrated information computations.

In IIT, the causal interactions between neurons or logic gates are assessed by perturbation of the system into all possible states.[27] This characterises completely how the system's current state – whatever it may be – constrains its possible past and future states. While this "complete perturbation" is ideal, it is unattainable in reality. With just a small neural network in a petri dish composed of ten neurons, and with the gross simplification that neurons are either "on" or "off", there will be $2^{10} = 1,024$ possible states to explore. For a human brain with 1,011 neurons and multiple possible states per neuron, complete perturbation is impossible. Indeed, the TMS-EEG paradigm is not perturbing the system in this fine sense. This does not mean, however, that we cannot make progress with a simplified perturbational approach. The TMS-EEG paradigm is, in a sense, assessing a controlled subset of state transitions in the brain, by directly stimulating the thalamo-cortical complex (thought to be the seat of consciousness). As long as the approximated methods are constrained by the critical concepts in IIT, empirical tests should be able to address the essential predictions from IIT.

For example, a TMS-EEG-style stimulation-recording paradigm can address the question of why the cerebellum, containing four times more neurons than the thalamo-cortical system, hardly contributes to consciousness, as evidenced by lesions.[28] IIT explains that this is due to the parallel structure of the cerebellum, which should generate only small, isolated compartments of integrated information. Applying TMS to the cerebellum is difficult due to the muscles around the neck, but more focal stimulation via non-invasive ultrasound, combined with EEG, may yet be able to test this prediction in humans.[29] According to IIT, no matter which site within the cerebellum is stimulated, evoked EEG patterns should be less complex reflecting the cerebellum's pronounced compartmentalisation, resulting in a low score for the PCI. The same test can be applied to animals. Assuming the same cerebellar/thalamo-cortical consciousness dichotomy in animals, the same prediction can be tested using invasive methods, combining focal stimulation – electrical, magnetic, ultrasound or optogenetic – with high-resolution neural recordings, such as ECoG and optical imaging, to cover the entire surface of the cerebellum. The key is to assess the intrinsic information in the cerebellum by quantifying the distribution of patterns of evoked activity via perturbation.

Focal stimulation with high-resolution neural recording can address another IIT prediction: the different ways different sensory modalities of experience are felt should be reflected in how populations of neurons causally interact.[30] Subjectively, all visual experiences are alike in some way, and qualitatively different from any auditory experience. IIT predicts that this difference should be reflected in qualitative, possibly topological, differences in the structure of integrated information. By bypassing the sensory input pathways, any difference between the visual or auditory regions in terms of evoked activation patterns due to direct cortical stimulation should reflect how populations of neurons interact within each modality. Such experimentation is expected to reveal structures of integrated information that are characteristic of particular modalities. Studies such as this could be extended to motor areas, where the qualitative differences should be even larger, reflecting the qualitative difference between sensory, including visual and auditory, and motor experience. The key in revealing these structures is to probe the patterns of interactions among neurons through direct perturbation of the brain.

An approximated version of the perturbational experiments can be achieved by presenting many different kinds of sensory stimuli and indirectly perturbing a targeted area. Perturbation by sensory stimuli, however, needs to be carefully interpreted. For example, when testing predictions about differential quality of experiences across modalities, differences in input pathways may contaminate the estimate of potential differences in interaction among neural populations, potentially leading to difference in structures of integrated information. When levels of consciousness are assessed for clinical diagnosis, sensory perturbation can be susceptible to damage in the peripheral sensory pathways: some damage at the retina could mean possible patterns of cortical activation by visual stimuli being underestimated, leading to erroneous estimates of levels of consciousness.

The two ECoG studies mentioned in the previous sections applied an empirical measure of integrated information, Φ^*, to examine levels and contents of consciousness. In these studies, we assumed that the observed

ECoG recordings were distributed in a normal (Gaussian) manner. While the Gaussian assumption makes computation of Φ^* much easier, its validity needs to be examined. When such an assumption is grossly violated, different ways of approximation of Φ^*, such as via discretising the signal,[31] would be needed for a more accurate estimation. Inference of causal mechanisms from observational data is an active area of mathematical and computational neuroscience[32] and we are hopeful of breakthroughs in this line of research.

The second challenge in empirical testing of IIT relates to the spatiotemporal grain of consciousness and the corresponding grain of analysis of the system. When empirically testing IIT with real data, one needs to decide on appropriate spatial and temporal scales. According to the exclusion postulate, the appropriate scale is the one that maximises integrated information. The temporal scale of experience is thought to be in the range of 50–500 milliseconds.[33] In terms of spatial scale, it should be the one that maximises integrated information. Theoretical studies suggest that larger integrated information can be generated at the level of population of neurons than at the level of single neurons.[34]

In the empirical studies we reviewed, the unit of analysis was voltage measured at the surface of the skull (EEG) or brain (ECoG). Both electrical signals reflect the aggregate of spiking and synaptic activity over many neurons. ECoG is much finer than EEG in spatio-temporal resolution, yet still cannot resolve activity in single neurons. To date, no studies have directly computed integrated information at a single-neuron level.

Even with coarser measures, IIT predictions can be empirically tested. TMS-EEG experiments have been adequate to quantify levels of consciousness and ECoG may be sufficient to estimate structures of integrated information and to test IIT predictions on contents of consciousness. Although fMRI is too slow to resolve the rapidly changing conscious percepts, which operate on an order of 50–500 milliseconds, it may be sufficient to resolve more slowly changing levels or contents of consciousness.[35]

It is important to demonstrate empirically which scales of description of neural activity actually maximise integrated information. A theoretical study implies that, under some conditions, a system's integrated information may reach a maximum at the macroscopic rather than the microscopic scale.[36] To test this idea, it is necessary to record neural activity at different scales simultaneously and compare integrated information with various scales of coarseness of grain, in space or time. Current equipment used in electrophysiological recordings allows us to sample neural spikes and local field potentials (voltage differences associated with signals) at 10–50 kilohertz, a much higher temporal resolution than our perception. If appropriately quantified, integrated information of a perceptual system should be higher when activity is coarsely down-sampled at a rate closer to the perceptual resolution (2–20 hertz) than when estimated at a very high temporal resolution (more than 1 kilohertz) or a much slower rate (less than 0.1 hertz). This prediction can be empirically investigated.

From a physical point of view, neuronal spikes are just one kind of membrane fluctuation; there is no a priori reason for spikes to have a privileged position in giving rise to consciousness. From the IIT perspective, the real question is whether spikes or local field potentials – or some other descriptor of neural state – are crucial in constraining future and past states of the brain. Quantification of causal interactions, computed with analogue membrane potentials and digital spikes within a given small system, would be a fundamentally important project from a theoretical viewpoint.

The third challenge is the identification of the minimum information partition (MIP). To assess the integrated information of a system, we measure how much information is lost if the system is cut into its least interacting parts; this cut is the MIP. From an intrinsic viewpoint, the MIP is the natural boundary among groups of elements which minimises interactions between the groups.

To illustrate the MIP, consider a human split-brain patient, whose left and right hemispheres have been surgically disconnected.[37] If the brain is partitioned into two hemispheres, no or little information will be lost (measured Φ would be very low), since the connections have already been physically cut. But if the brain were partitioned into anterior and posterior parts (eg, frontal-parietal versus temporal-occipital), a significant amount of information would be lost across the cut (measured Φ would be very high). The between-hemisphere cut would, thus, be closer to the correct MIP for the whole system, identifying a low Φ value, while each hemisphere, taken as a local system, would have a different MIP across which significant Φ was generated. In other words, two hemispheres of a split-brain patient do not form a complex as a whole, while each hemisphere forms a complex of itself as a local maximum of integrated information. According to the exclusion principle, each hemisphere can thus contribute to one consciousness, resulting in two separate consciousnesses.[38] This is consistent with the behaviour of split-brain patients.[39]

To identify the MIP in a real system, however, requires extensive inspection of how interactions are lost with every possible way to cut the system. This is one of the current bottlenecks in the empirical application of IIT. In the TMS-EEG paradigm, partitions were not considered and integration was indirectly inferred from the way the EEG responses propagated across different cortical areas. For the ECoG study of levels of consciousness, we employed all 128 electrodes for the analysis, but did not compute the actual MIP; instead, we approximated the MIP in various ways and confirmed that the results did not depend on how it was computed. For the ECoG study of contents of consciousness, we restricted our analyses to small systems, allowing for exhaustive search for the "true" MIP.

The difficulty in identifying the MIP for a real neural system is discouraging but is no reason to give up on testing IIT. It is easy to conceive of empirical studies that work around the MIP difficulty, based on the idea of the "obvious" MIP in split-brain patients, for example. If major connections between a monkey's hemispheres (eg, corpus callosum and anterior commissure) are reversibly inactivated by some means (such as cooling[40]), then at some point the left and right hemispheres would become independent, as in those of acute split-brain patients. Visual search in each hemisphere might become independent, controlled by two independent attentional mechanisms and possibly showing some advantages over the performance before cooling.[41] Some memory association learned in one hemisphere might not transfer to the other, producing suboptimal controlled behaviours in some tasks.[42] Crucially, IIT predicts that split of consciousness should occur abruptly, where integrated information within each hemisphere becomes a separate local maximum and higher than that computed *across* the hemispheres. Assuming that the behavioural testings can tap into conscious processing, there should be drastic qualitative changes in behaviour when a single complex across two hemispheres splits into two complexes, one for each hemisphere. The amount of integrated information across and within hemispheres can be computed by some approximated measures from ECoG electrodes implanted in the monkey's brain, similar to our work with anaesthesia described above.

While exhaustive search for the MIP might be considered the "gold standard", we may also devise heuristics or algorithms that find the approximate MIP based on efficient search, such as simulated annealing or genetic algorithm. Knowledge of the anatomical and/or functional connectivity of the system can massively narrow down the search space of the MIP as well. Such techniques can be fine-tuned on simulated systems where the exact MIP is known. The development of these iterative algorithms would be a fruitful and promising project, especially in combination with the mature field of mathematical graph theory, and could deeply inform the study of large-scale brain connectivity (the "connectome").[43]

Concluding remarks

IIT is the first attempt to derive a mathematical structure based on a brain's connectivity and activity states and to claim some form of identity[44] between a mathematical structure and a specific conscious experience (Figure 3).

In this chapter, we reviewed recent attempts to test IIT predictions empirically. As to levels of consciousness, the IIT-inspired index of complexity (the PCI) computed in the TMS-EEG paradigm has been impressively successful in detecting loss of consciousness.[45] Direct computation of approximated integrated information, Φ^*, was also successful in discriminating between awake and anaesthetised conditions.[46] As to contents of consciousness, the structure of Φ^* derived from ECoG recordings in the high-order, face-responsive visual areas naturally categorises object percepts and, in particular, mirrors conscious perception of faces.[47] These promising tests suggest that, in the foreseeable future, challenges are empirically addressable, especially those around perturbational and observational approaches, definitions of mechanisms and states, and the MIP. Novel analyses from an IIT standpoint, such as of intrinsic information and the quantification of integration, will inform neuroscientists as to critical aspects of neural systems, which have been difficult to study in previous frameworks.

While IIT's concrete and quantitative proposals immediately attract strong interest in the proposed measure Φ, its starting point is easily misunderstood and forgotten. IIT's first phenomenological axiom affirms the intrinsic existence of one's own consciousness. Starting from fundamental properties of conscious experience and seeking physical substrates that can possibly support such properties is a strategy unique to

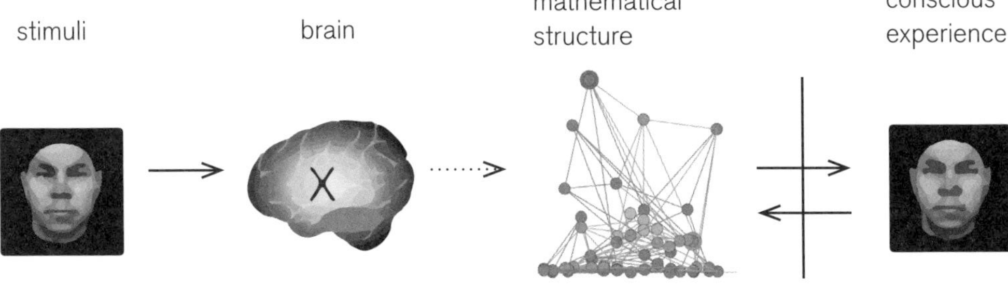

Figure 3. Potential equivalence between a mathematical structure (eg, structures of integrated information) and conscious experience, proposed by IIT.

the IIT. In theory, any of the enigmatic features of conscious phenomenology can be formulated in terms of IIT. The similarity of experiences within one modality and dissimilarity across modalities are so obvious that they often are treated as beneath notice, but these phenomena have basic correlates in IIT. Many powerful visual illusions can be vividly experienced, demonstrating that one's own conscious phenomenology can fluctuate despite constant retinal input, such as in binocular rivalry (where different images are presented to each eye)[48] and motion-induced blindness.[49] Such phenomenological characterisation from one's own experience is a critical starting point, and it is an immense advantage of IIT that it is formulated on the basis of such characterisation.

As long as IIT explains all of human consciousness, it makes sense to empirically test IIT predictions with other systems, especially animal brains with neural recording and stimulation.[50] If the theory continues to thrive after many empirical tests, we may seriously consider its predictions on seemingly non-verifiable cases – such as consciousness in babies, severely injured patients and remotely-related animals (such as octopuses and bats[51]), as well as artificial neural networks, computers and robots. It would then be critical to develop mechanical tools to allow those who cannot communicate their experience to verify the theory, such as an extended and more refined version of fMRI-based decoding.[52] Implanting artificial neuronal networks directly into a human brain and predicting what kind of experience s/he would have, based on the theory, will be another strong test.

Unexpected clinical cases can test IIT's predictions as well. A long history of clinical studies has provided unimaginable cases, such as nearly intact conscious lives in people who were born without a cerebellum[53] or had massive bilateral damage in the prefrontal cortex.[54] It is possible that some very rare patients will strongly challenge, or support, IIT's predictions. Detailed phenomenological and neuroscientific studies of conjoined twins or striking cases of multiple personality disorders may be such cases.[55]

A good, useful scientific theory guides exploration and helps generate ideas and drive progress. As we have seen, IIT has already served such a purpose, becoming empirically testable in several aspects and generating many different types of experiment and discussion. IIT drives new approaches and asks difficult questions, which used to be exclusively for philosophers, with hard science.

Empirically testing IIT predictions is challenging. These challenges are not essentially different, however, from those faced in the other scientific disciplines, especially if related to fundamental questions such as the origin of the universe or of life. Indeed, the gradual validation of extraordinary cases (eg, observation of the moving away of galaxies, of ancient fossils and so on) has pushed and refined theory on these fundamental questions. Is there any reason not to expect something similar to happen with regards to the origin of consciousness? While consciousness research lags behind research into the origin of the universe or of life, finally, we have a theory that can be tested. Though the road ahead is tough, the path is clear.

---

1. G. Tononi, 'An Information Integration Theory of Consciousness', *BMC Neuroscience*, no. 5, 2004, p. 42, DOI: 10.1186/1471-2202-5-42 (accessed 27 January 2016); M. Oizumi, L. Albantakis & G. Tononi, 'From the Phenomenology to the Mechanisms of Consciousness: Integrated Information Theory 3.0', *PLOS Computational Biology*, vol. 10, no. 5, 2014, DOI: 10.1371/journal.pcbi.1003588 (accessed 27 January 2016).
2. T. Nagel, 'What is it Like to be a Bat?', *The Philosophical Review*, vol. 83, no. 4, 1974, pp. 435–50.
3. Tononi, 'An Information Integration Theory of Consciousness'; Oizumi, Albantakis & Tononi, 'From the Phenomenology to the Mechanisms of Consciousness …'.
4. For the details of the postulates, see Oizumi, Albantakis & Tononi.
5. Oizumi, Albantakis & Tononi.
6. For an updated and more advanced treatment, see Oizumi, Albantakis & Tononi.
7. Information defined as the reduction of uncertainty is consistent with the notion of information deployed by Claude Shannon in C.E. Shannon & W. Weaver, *The Mathematical Theory of Communication*, Urbana, IL, University of Illinois Press, 1949. But the way information is defined here does not refer to anything external to the system, including any observer; thus it should be considered as "intrinsic" information. Shannon's information always assumes an external observer, who assesses the statistical relationship between the inputs and outputs across a noisy channel, and it should be distinguished as "extrinsic" information.
8. This concept can be applied to two persons. As far as we know, there is no single consciousness between two people and we can assume there is no integrated information between two people. This is equivalent to saying that there is no loss of information if one considers each person separately, because they are independent entities.
9. D.J. Chalmers, *The Conscious Mind* (Philosophy of Mind series), New York, NY, Oxford University Press, 1996.
10. F. Ferrarelli et al., 'Breakdown in Cortical Effective Connectivity During

Midazolam-induced Loss of Consciousness', *Proceedings of the National Academy of Sciences of the United States of America*, vol. 107, no. 6, 2010, pp. 2681–6; M. Massimini et al., 'Breakdown of Cortical Effective Connectivity During Sleep', *Science*, vol. 309, no. 5744, 2005, pp. 2228–32; M. Rosanova et al., 'Recovery of Cortical Effective Connectivity and Recovery of Consciousness in Vegetative Patients', *Brain*, no. 135 (pt. 4), 2012, pp. 1308–20.

11. A. G. Casali et al., 'A Theoretically Based Index of Consciousness Independent of Sensory Processing and Behavior', *Science Translational Medicine*, vol. 5, no. 198, 2013, 198ra05 (accessed 20 December 2015).

12. Y. Nir & G. Tononi, 'Dreaming and the Brain: From Phenomenology to Neurophysiology', *Trends in Cognitive Sciences*, vol. 14, no. 2, 2010, pp. 88–100.

13. S. Sarasso et al., 'Consciousness and Complexity during Unresponsiveness Induced by Propofol, Xenon, and Ketamine', *Current Biology*, no. 25, pp. 3099–105.

14. Oizumi, Albantakis & Tononi, 'From the Phenomenology to the Mechanisms of Consciousness …'; Tononi, 'An Information Integration Theory of Consciousness'.

15. In general, empirical tests of any theory can be valid even if exact constructs are not directly available; these are as valid as the experiments conducted to test the theories on the origin of the universe or of life. The theory, however, has to provide a strong and meaningful constraint on the approximation. In the case of the origin of the universe, a theory has to be consistent with everything observed now. As to the origin of life, a theory has to reconcile any observed (or to be observed) fossils and all the features of biochemistry.

16. D. Balduzzi & G. Tononi, 'Integrated Information in Discrete Dynamical Systems: Motivation and Theoretical Framework', *PLOS Computational Biology*, vol. 4, no. 6, 2008, e1000091 (accessed 20 December 2015); Oizumi, Albantakis & Tononi, 'From the Phenomenology to the Mechanisms of Consciousness …'.

17. A.B. Barrett & A.K. Seth, 'Practical Measures of Integrated Information for Time-series Data', *PLOS Computational Biology*, vol. 7, no. 1, 2011, e1001052 (accessed 20 December 2015).

18. M. Oizumi et al., 'Measuring Integrated Information from the Decoding Perspective', *PLOS Computational Biology*, 2016, DOI: 10.1371/journal.pcbi.1004654 (accessed 27 January 2016).

19. For other attempts, see J.Y. Chang et al., 'Multivariate Autoregressive Models with Exogenous Inputs for Intracerebral Responses to Direct Electrical Stimulation of the Human Brain', *Frontiers in Human Neuroscience*, vol. 6, no. 317, 2012, DOI: 10.3389/fnhum.2012.00317 (accessed 20 December 2015); U. Lee et al., 'Propofol Induction Reduces the Capacity for Neural Information Integration: Implications for the Mechanism of Consciousness and General Anesthesia', *Consciousness and Cognition*, vol. 18, no. 1, 2009, pp. 56–64; S. Sasai, M. Bol, A. Mensen & G., Tononi, 'Functional split brain in a driving/listening paradigm,' *Proceedings of the National Academy of Sciences*, 2016, p. 13200.

20. Oizumi et al., 'Measuring Integrated Information from the Decoding Perspective'.

21. Barrett & Seth, 'Practical Measures of Integrated Information for Time-series Data'.

22. M. Oizumi et al., 'Modified Measure for Integrated Information Theory and its Application to 128-Channel Electrocorticogram Data Recorded in Macaque Monkeys', paper presented at the annual conference of the Association for the Scientific Study of Consciousness, Kyoto, 2011.

23. F. Tong et al., 'Binocular Rivalry and Visual Awareness in Human Extrastriate Cortex', *Neuron*, vol. 21, no. 4, 1998, pp. 753–9; J. Parvizi et al., 'Electrical Stimulation of Human Fusiform Face-Selective Regions Distorts Face Perception', *Journal of Neuroscience*, vol. 32, no. 43, 2012, pp. 14915–20.

24. B.G. Breitmeyer & H. Ogmen, 'Visual Masking', *Scholarpedia*, vol. 2, no. 7, 2007, p. 3330.

25. N. Tsuchiya & C. Koch, 'Continuous Flash Suppression Reduces Negative Afterimages', *Nature Neuroscience*, vol. 8, no. 8, 2005, 1096–101.

26. T. Allison et al., 'Electrophysiological Studies of Human Face Perception. I: Potentials Generated in Occipitotemporal Cortex by Face and Non-Face Stimuli', *Cerebral Cortex*, vol. 9, no.5, 1999, pp. 415–30; H. Kawasaki et al., 'Processing of Facial Emotion in the Human Fusiform Gyrus', *Journal of Cognitive Neuroscience*, vol. 24, no. 6, 2012, pp. 1358–70; N. Tsuchiya et al., 'Decoding Face Information in Time, Frequency and Space from Direct Intracranial Recordings of the Human Brain', *PLOS One*, vol. 3, no. 12, 2008, e3892 (accessed 21 December 2015).

27. Balduzzi & Tononi, 'Integrated Information in Discrete Dynamical Systems ...'; D. Balduzzi & G. Tononi, 'Qualia: The Geometry of Integrated Information', *PLOS Computational Biology*, vol. 5, no. 8, 2009, e1000462 (accessed 20 December 2015); Oizumi, Albantakis & Tononi, 'From the Phenomenology to the Mechanisms of Consciousness ...'; Tononi, 'An Information Integration Theory of Consciousness'.

28. R.N. Lemon & S.A. Edgley, 'Life Without a Cerebellum', *Brain,* no. 133 (Pt 3), 2010, pp. 652–4; G. Tononi & C. Koch, 'Consciousness: Here, There and Everywhere?', *Philosophical Transactions of the Royal Society B: Biological Sciences*, vol. 370, no. 1668, 2015, DOI: 10.1098/rstb.2014.0167 (accessed 21 December 2015).

29. W. Legon et al., 'Transcranial Focused Ultrasound Modulates the Activity of Primary Somatosensory Cortex in Humans', *Nature Neuroscience*, vol. 17, no. 2, 2014, pp. 322–9.

30. Balduzzi & Tononi, 'Qualia: The Geometry of Integrated Information'.

31. King et al., 'Information Sharing in the Brain Indexes Consciousness in Noncommunicative Patients'.

32. K.Friston, R. Moran & A.K. Seth, 'Analysing Connectivity with Granger Causality and Dynamic Causal Modelling', *Current Opinion in Neurobiology*, vol. 23, no. 2, 2013, pp. 172–8.

33. T. Bachmann, *Microgenetic Approach to the Conscious Mind,* Amsterdam, John Benjamins Publishing, 2000.

34. E.P. Hoel, L. Albantakis & G. Tononi, 'Quantifying Causal Emergence Shows that

Macro can Beat Micro', *Proceedings of the Nationall Academy of Sciences of the United States of America*, vol. 110, no. 49, 2013, pp. 19790–5. E.P. Hoel, L. Albantakis, W. Marshall & G. Tononi, 'Can the macro beat the micro? Integrated information across spatio-temporal scales', *Neuroscience of Consciousness*, 2016 (1), pp. niwo12.

35. M. Boly et al., 'Stimulus Set Meaningfulness and Neurophysiological Differentiation: A Functional Magnetic Resonance Imaging Study', *PLOS One*, vol. 10, no. 5, 2015, e0125337 (accessed 21 December 2015); S. Sasai, M. Boly, A. Mensen & G. Tononi, 'Functional split brain in a driving/listening paradigm', *Proceedings of the National Academy of Sciences*, 2016, p. 13200.

36. Hoel, Albantakis & Tononi, 'Quantifying Causal Emergence Shows that Macro can Beat Micro'; Hoel, Albantakis, Marshall & Tononi, 'Can the macro beat the micro? Integrated information across spatio-temporal scales', *Neuroscience of Consciousness*, 2016 (1), pp. niwo12.

37. M.S. Gazzaniga, 'Forty-Five Years of Split-Brain Research and Still Going Strong', *Nature Reviews Neuroscience*, vol. 6, no. 8, 2005, pp. 653–9.

38. G. Tononi, 'Consciousness as Integrated Information: A Provisional Manifesto', *Biological Bulletin*, vol. 215, no. 3, 2008, pp. 216–42.

39. Gazzaniga, 'Forty-Five Years of Split-Brain Research and Still Going Strong'.

40. J.M. Hupe et al., 'Cortical Feedback Improves Discrimination Between Figure and Background by V1, V2 and V3 neurons', *Nature*, vol. 394, no. 6695, 1998, pp. 784–7.

41. S.J. Luck et al., 'Independent Hemispheric Attentional Systems Mediate Visual Search in Split-brain Patients', *Nature*, vol. 342, no. 6249, 1989, pp. 543–5.

42. H. Tomita et al., 'Top–down Signal from Prefrontal Cortex in Executive Control of Memory Retrieval', *Nature*, vol. 401, no. 6754, 1999, pp. 699–703.

43. Bullmore, Ed, & Olaf Sporns. 'Complex brain networks: graph theoretical analysis of structural and functional systems.', *Nature Reviews Neuroscience*, vol. 10, no. 3 (2009): pp. 186–98.

44. As a general mathematical approach to evaluate the claimed "identity" between a mathematical structure and conscious experience, we advocate a use of mathematical formalism, called category theory – see N. Tsuchiya, S. Taguchi and H. Saigo, 'Using Category Theory to Assess the Relationship between Consciousness and Integrated Information Theory', *Neuroscience Research*, 2016 (in press), DOI: 10.1016/j.neures.2015.12.007 (accessed 27 January 2016).

45. Casali et al., 'A Theoretically Based Index of Consciousness Independent of Sensory Processing and Behavior'.

46. Oizumi et al., 'Modified Measure for Integrated Information Theory …'.

47. A. M. Haun, M. Oizumi, C. K. Kovach, H. Kawasaki, H. Oya, M. A. Howard, R. Adolphs & N. Tsuchiya, Contents of Consciousness Investigated as Integrated Information in Direct Human Brain Recordings, *bioRxiv*, 2016, pp. 039032, DOI: https://doi.org/10.1101/039032.

48. R. Blake & N.K. Logothetis, 'Visual Competition', *Nature Reviews Neuroscience*, vol. 3, no. 1, 2002, pp. 13–21.

49. Y. S. Bonneh, A. Cooperman & D. Sagi, 'Motion-Induced Blindness in Normal Observers', *Nature*, vol. 411, no. 6839, 2001, pp. 798–801.

50. G. Doron & M. Brecht, 'What Single-Cell Stimulation has told us about Neural Coding', *Philosophical Transactions of the Royal Society of London B: Biological Sciences*, vol. 370, no. 1677, 2015, DOI: 10.1098/rstb.2014.0204 (accessed 27 January 2016).

51. T. Nagel, 'What is it like to be a bat?' *The Philosophical Reveiw*, vol. 83(no. 4), pp. 435–50; N. Tsuchiya, '"What is it like to be a bat?" – a pathway to the answer from the integrated information theory', *Philosophy Compas*, 2017, e12407, DOI: 10.1111/phc3.12407.

52. J.D. Haynes & G. Rees, 'Decoding Mental States from Brain Activity in Humans', *Nature Reviews Neuroscience*, vol. 7, no. 7, 2006, pp. 523–34; T. Horikawa et al., 'Neural Decoding of Visual Imagery During Sleep', *Science,* vol. 340, no. 6132, 2013, pp. 639–42; A.M. Owen, 'Detecting Consciousness: A Unique Role for Neuroimaging', *Annual Review of Psychology,* no. 64, 2013, pp. 109–33.

53. Lemon and Edgley, 'Life Without a Cerebellum'.

54. M. Mataro et al., 'Long-term Effects of Bilateral Frontal Brain Lesion: 60 Years after Injury with an Iron Bar', *Archives of Neurology*, vol. 58, no. 7, 2001, pp. 1139–42.

55. S. Dominus, 'Could Conjoined Twins Share a Mind?', *New York Times Magazine*, 25 May 2011; H. Strasburger & B. Waldvogel, 'Sight and Blindness in the Same Person: Gating in the Visual System', *PsyCh Journal*, vol. 4, no. 4, 2015, pp. 178–85.

REFERENCES

Adam, M.T., 'No Self, No Free Will, No Problem: Implications of the Anatta-lakkhana Sutta for a Perennial Philosophical Issue', *Journal of the International Association of Buddhist Studies*, no. 33, 2011, pp. 239–65.

Adams, D., *The Hitchhiker's Guide to the Galaxy*, Basingstoke, Pan Books, 1979.

Adams, J.H., D.I. Graham & B. Jennett, 'The Neuropathology of the Vegetative State after Acute Insult', *Brain*, no. 123, 2000, pp. 1327–38.

Alhabari, M., 'Insight Knowledge of No Self in Buddhism: An Epistemic Analysis', *Philosophers' Imprint*, vol. 14, no.21, 2014, pp. 1–30.

Allison, T., et al., 'Electrophysiological Studies of Human Face Perception. I: Potentials Generated in Occipitotemporal Cortex by Face and Non-Face Stimuli', *Cerebral Cortex*, vol. 9, no. 5, 1999, pp. 415–30.

Allman, J., *Evolving Brains*, New York. NY, Scientific American Library, 1999.

American Academy of Neurology, 'Position of the American Academy of Neurology on Certain Aspects of the Care and Management of the Persistent Vegetative State Patient', *Neurology*, no. 39, 1989, pp. 125–6.

Anderson, J.R., *How Can the Human Mind Occur in the Physical Universe?*, Oxford, Oxford University Press, 2007.

Apps, M.A. & M. Tsakiris, 'The Free-Energy Self: A Predictive Coding Account of Self-Recognition', *Neuroscience & Biobehavioral Reviews*, vol. 41C, 2014, pp. 85–97, DOI: 10.1016/j.neubiorev.2013.01.029.

Aru, J. et al., 'Distilling the Neural Correlates of Consciousness', *Neuroscience & Biobehavioral Reviews*, vol. 36, no. 2, 2012, pp. 737–46, DOI: 10.1016/j.neubiorev.2011.12.003.

Atlas, L.Y. & T.D. Wager, 'How Expectations Shape Pain, *Neuroscience Letters*, no. 520, 2012, pp. 140–8, DOI: 10.1016/j.neulet.2012.03.039 (accessed 13 January 2016).

Baars, B.J. & N.M. Gage, *Cognition, Brain and Consciousness*, San Diego, CA, Academic Press, 2007.

Baars, B.J., 'The Conscious Access Hypothesis: Origins and Recent Evidence', *Trends in Cognitive Sciences*, vol. 6, no. 1, 2002, pp. 47–52.

Baars, B.J., *A Cognitive Theory of Consciousness*, New York, NY, Cambridge University Press, 1988.

Bachmann, T., *Microgenetic Approach to the Conscious Mind*, Amsterdam, John Benjamins Publishing, 2000.

Bacon, F., *The New Organon*, trans. L. Jardine & M. Silverthorne, Cambridge, Cambridge University Press, 2000 [1620].

Balduzzi, D. & G. Tononi, 'Integrated Information in Discrete Dynamical Systems: Motivation and Theoretical Framework', *PLOS Computational Biology*, vol. 4, no. 6, 2008, e1000091 (accessed 20 December 2015).

Balduzzi, D. & G. Tononi, 'Qualia: The Geometry of Integrated Information', *PLOS Computational Biology*, vol. 5, no. 8, 2009, e1000462 (accessed 20 December 2015).

Bardin, J.C. et al., 'Dissociations Between Behavioural and Functional Magnetic Resonance Imaging-Based Evaluations of Cognitive Function after Brain Injury', *Brain*, no. 134 (pt. 3), 2011, pp. 769–82.

Barnes, J., *The Presocratics*, London, Routledge & Kegan Paul, 1979.

Barrett, A.B. & A.K. Seth, 'Practical Measures of Integrated Information for Time-Series Data', *PLOS Computational Biology*, vol. 7, no. 1, 2011, e1001052 (accessed 20 December 2015).

Barrett, D., *New Science of Dreaming*, vol. II, Westport, CT, Praeger., 2007, pp. 1–27.

Barrett, L.F. & W.K. Simmons, 'Interoceptive Predictions in the Brain', *Nature Reviews Neuroscience*, vol. 16, no. 7, 2015, pp. 419–29, DOI: 10.1038/nrn3950.

Bastian, M. & J. Sackur, 'Mind Wandering at the Fingertips: Automatic Parsing of Subjective States Based on Response Time Variability', *Frontiers in Psychology*, no. 4, 2013, p. 573, DOI: 10.3389/fpsyg.2013.00573.

Bastos, A.M. et al., 'Visual Areas Exert Feedforward and Feedback Influences Through Distinct Frequency Channels', *Neuron*, vol. 85, no. 2, 2015, pp. 390–401, DOI: 10.1016/j.neuron.2014.12.018.

Bateson, M. et al., 'Agitated Honeybees Exhibit Pessimistic Cognitive Biases', *Current Biology*, vol. 21, no. 12, 2011, pp. 1070–3.

Baum, W.M., *Understanding Behaviorism: Behavior, Culture, and Evolution*, 2nd edn., Hoboken, NJ, Wiley-Blackwell, 2004.

Benatar, D., *Better Never to Have Been: The Harm of Coming into Existence*, Oxford & New York, Clarendon Press, Oxford University Press, 2006.

Bergouignan, L., L. Nyberg & H.H. Ehrsson, 'Out-of-Body-Induced Hippocampal Amnesia', *Proceedings of the National Academy of Sciences of the USA*, vol. 111, no. 12, 2014, pp. 4421–6, DOI: 10.1073/pnas.1318801111.

Bhalla, M. & D.R. Proffitt, 'Visual-Motor Recalibration in Geographical Slant Perception', *Journal of Experimental Psychology: Human Perception and Performance*, vol. 25, no. 4, 1999, pp. 1076–96.

Bishop, S.R. et al., 'Mindfulness: A Proposed Operational Definition', *Clinical Psychology: Science and Practice*, no. 11, 2004, pp. 230–41, DOI: 10.1093/clipsy. bph077.

Blackmore, S., *Zen and the Art of Consciousness*, Oxford, Oneworld Publications, 2011.

Blackmore, S.J., 'Where am I? Perspectives in Imagery, and the Out-of-Body Experience', *Journal of Mental Imagery*, no. 11, 1987, pp. 53–66.

Blackmore, S.J., *Beyond the Body: An Investigation into Out-of-Body Experiences*, 2nd edn., Chicago, IL, Academy Chicago, 1992 [1982].

Blackmore, S.J., 'A Psychological Theory of the OBE', *Journal of Parapsychology*, no. 48, 1984, pp. 201–18.

Blackmore, S., *Seeing Myself: What Out-of-body Experiences Tell Us About Life, Death & the Mind*, London. Little, Brown Book Group. 2020.

Blake, R. & N.K. Logothetis, 'Visual Competition', *Nature Reviews Neuroscience*, vol. 3, no. 1, 2002, pp. 13–21.

Blake, R., J. Brascamp & D.J. Heeger, 'Can Binocular Rivalry Reveal Neural Correlates of Consciousness?', *Philosophical Transactions of the Royal Society of London B: Biological Sciences*, vol. 369, no. 1641, 2014, DOI: 10.1098/rstb.2013.0211 (accessed 19 January 2016).

Blanke, O. & S. Arzy, 'The Out-of-Body Experience: Disturbed Self-Processing at the Temporo-Parietal Junction', *The Neuroscientist*, vol. 11, no. 1, 2005, pp. 16–24.

Blanke, O. & T. Metzinger, 'Full-Body Illusions and Minimal Phenomenal Selfhood', *Trends in Cognitive Sciences*, vol. 13, no. 1, 2009, pp. 7–13, DOI: 10.1016/j.tics.2008.10.003.

Blanke, O. et al., 'Neuropsychology: Stimulating Illusory Own-Body Perceptions', *Nature*, vol. 419, no. 6904, 2002, pp. 269–70.

Blanke, O., 'Multisensory Brain Mechanisms of Bodily Self-Consciousness', *Nature Reviews Neuroscience*, vol. 13, no. 8, 2012, pp. 556–71.

Blanke, O., M. Slater & A. Serino, 'Behavioral, Neural, and Computational Principles of Bodily Self-Consciousness', *Neuron*, vol. 88, no. 1, 2015, pp. 145–66, DOI: 10.1016/j. neuron.2015.09.029.

Block, N., 'On a Confusion about a Function of Consciousness', *Behavioral and Brain Sciences*, vol. 18, no. 2, 1995, pp. 227–47.

Block, N., 'Two Neural Correlates of Consciousness', *Trends in Cognitive Sciences*, vol. 9, no. 2, 2005, pp. 46–52.

Boden, M., *Mind as Machine: A History of Cognitive Science*, Oxford, Oxford University Press, 2008.

Bodhi, B. & B. Nanamoli, *The Middle Length Discourses of the Buddha*, Boston, MA, Wisdom Publications, 1995.

Bodhi, B., *The Connected Discourses of the Buddha*, Boston, MA, Wisdom Publications, 2000.

Boly, M. et al., 'Consciousness in Humans and Non-Human Animals: Recent Advances and Future Directions', *Frontiers in Psychology*, no. 4, 2013, p. 625, DOI: 10.3389/ fpsyg.2013.00625.

Boly, M. et al., 'Stimulus Set Meaningfulness and Neurophysiological Differentiation: A Functional Magnetic Resonance Imaging Study', *PLOS One*, vol. 10, no. 5, 2015, e0125337 (accessed 20 December 2015).

Boly, M. et al., 'When Thoughts Become Action: An fMRI Paradigm to Study Volitional Brain Activity in Non-Communicative Brain Injured Patients', *Neuroimage*, no. 36, 2007, pp. 979–92.

Bonneh, Y.S., A. Cooperman & D. Sagi, 'Motion-induced Blindness in Normal Observers', *Nature*, vol. 411, no. 6839, 2001, pp. 798–801.

Boring, E.G., 'The Nature of Psychology', in E.G. Boring, H.S. Langfeld & H.P. Weld (eds.), *Foundations of Psychology*, New York, NY, Wiley, 1948.

Bostrom, N., *Superintelligence: Paths, Dangers, Strategies*, Oxford, Oxford University Press, 2014.

Botvinick, M. & J. Cohen, 'Rubber Hands "Feel" Touch that Eyes See', *Nature*, vol. 391, no. 6669, 1998, p. 756.

Bowers, J.S. & C.J. Davis, 'Bayesian Just-so Stories in Psychology and Neuroscience', *Psychological Bulletin*, vol. 138, no. 3, 2012, pp. 389–414, DOI: 10.1037/ a0026450.

Bowers, K.S., *Hypnosis for the Seriously Curious*, Monterey, CA, Brooks/Cole, 1976.

Brascamp, J., R. Blake & T. Knapen, 'Negligible Fronto-Parietal BOLD Activity Accompanying Unreportable Switches in Bistable Perception', *Nature Neuroscience*, no. 18, 2015, pp. 1672–78, DOI: 10.1038/nn.4130.

Breitmeyer, B.G. & H. Ogmen, 'Visual Masking', *Scholarpedia*, vol. 2, no. 7, 2007, p. 3330.

Broad, C.D., *The Mind and Its Place in Nature,* London, Kegan Paul, 1925.

Brown, E.N., R. Lydic & N.D. Schiff, 'General Anesthesia, Sleep and Coma', *New England Journal of Medicine*, no. 363, 2010, pp. 2638–50.

Büchel, C. et al., 'Placebo Analgesia: A Predictive Coding Perspective, *Neuron*, no. 81, 2014, pp. 1223–39, DOI: 10.1016/j.neuron.2014.02.042 (accessed 13 January 2016).

Bullmore, Ed & Olaf Sporns. 'Complex Brain Networks: Graph Theoretical Analysis of Structural and Functional Systems', *Nature Reviews Neuroscience*, vol. 10, no. 3.

Carpenter, A., 'Persons Keeping Their Karma Together: On the Philosophical Motivations for the Pudgalavāda', in K. Tanaka, Y. Deguchi, J. Garfield & G. Priest (eds.), *The Moon Points Back*, New York, NY, Oxford University Press, 2015, pp. 1–44.

Carpenter, A., *Indian Buddhist Philosophy*, London, Routledge-Acumen, 2014.

Carpenter, A. 'Ethics Without Justice', in Jake Davis (ed.), *A Mirror is For Reflection*, New York, NY, Oxford University Press, 2017.

Casali, A.G. et al., 'A Theoretically Based Index of Consciousness Independent of Sensory Processing and Behavior', *Science Translational Medicine*, vol. 5, no. 198, 2013, pp. 198ra105, DOI: 10.1126/scitranslmed.3006294 (accessed 19 January 2016).

Chalmers, D., 'Consciousness and its Place in Nature', in S. Stich & T. Warfield (eds.), *Blackwell Guide to Philosophy of Mind*, Oxford, Blackwell, 2003, pp. 102– 42.

Chalmers, D., 'What is a Neural Correlate of Consciousness?', in T. Metzinger (ed.), *Neural Correlates of Consciousness: Empirical and Conceptual Questions*, Cambridge, MA, MIT Press, 2000, pp. 17–39.

Chalmers, D., *The Conscious Mind: In Search of a Fundamental Theory*, New York & Oxford, Oxford University Press, 1996.

Chalmers, D.J., 'How Can we Construct a Science of Consciousness?', *Annals of the New York Academy of Sciences,* no. 1303, 2013, pp. 25–35, DOI: 10.1111/nyas. 12166.

Chalmers, D.J., 'The Puzzle of Conscious Experience', *Scientific American*, vol. 273, no. 6, 1995, pp. 80–86.

Chang, H., *Inventing Temperature: Measurement and Scientific Progress*, New York, NY, Oxford University Press, 2004.

Chang, J.Y. et al., 'Multivariate Autoregressive Models with Exogenous Inputs for Intracerebral Responses to Direct Electrical Stimulation of the Human Brain', *Frontiers in Human Neuroscience*, vol. 6, no. 317, 2012, DOI: 10.3389/fnhum.2012.00317 (accessed 20 December 2015).

Charland-Verville, V. et al., 'Brain Dead yet Mind Alive: A Positron Emission

Tomography Case Study of Brain Metabolism in Cotard's Syndrome', *Cortex*, vol. 49, 2013, pp. 1997–99.

Châu, T.T., *The Literature of the Personalists of Early Buddhism*, trans. S. Boin-Webb, Delhi, Motilal Banarsidass, 1999.

Chaves, J.F., 'The State of the "State" Debate in Hypnosis: A View from the Cognitive-Behavioral Perspective', *International Journal of Clinical and Experimental Hypnosis*, vol. 45, no. 3, 1997, pp. 251–65.

Chemero, A., *Radical Embodied Cognitive Science*, Cambridge, MA, MIT Press, 2009.

Chennu, S. et al., 'Spectral Signatures of Reorganised Brain Networks in Disorders of Consciousness', *PLOS Computational Biology*, vol. 10, no. 10, 2014, e1003887, DOI: 10.1371/journal.pcbi.1003887 (accessed 19 January 2016).

Chiesa, A. & A. Serretti, 'A Systematic Review of Neurobiological and Clinical Features of Mindfulness Meditations', *Psychological Medicine*, no. 40, 2010, pp. 1239–52.

Churchland, P.M., 'The Rediscovery of Light', *Journal of Philosophy*, vol. 93, no. 5, 1996, pp. 211–28.

Churchland, P.M., *A Neurocomputational Perspective: The Nature of Mind and the Structure of Science*, Massachusetts, MA, MIT Press, 1989.

Churchland, P.M., *Philosophy at Work*, Cambridge, Cambridge University Press, 2007.

Churchland, P.M., *Scientific Realism and the Plasticity of Mind*, New York, NY, Cambridge University Press, 1979.

Churchland, P.M., *The Engine of Reason, The Seat of the Soul*, Massachusetts, MA, MIT Press, 1996.

Churchland, P.S., 'Exploring the Causal Underpinning of Determination, Resolve and Will', *Neuron*, vol. 80, no. 6, 2013, pp. 1337–8, DOI: 10.1016/j.neuron.2013.12.005.

Churchland, P.S., *Brainwise: Studies in Neurophilosophy*, Massachusetts, MA, MIT Press, 2002.

Churchland, P.S., *Neurophilosophy: Toward a Unified Science of the Mind-Brain*, Cambridge, MA, MIT Press, 1986.

Churchland, P.S., *Touching a Nerve*, New York, NY, Norton, 2013.

Cicero, M.T., *De senectute de amicitia de divinatione*, trans. W. Falconer, London, Heinemann, 1923 [44BC].

Clark, A., *Surfing Uncertainty: Prediction, Action, and the Embodied Mind*, New York, NY, Oxford University Press, 2016.

Collins, S., 'A Buddhist Debate About the Self; and Remarks on Buddhism in the Works of Derek Parfit and Galen Strawson', *Journal of Indian Philosophy*, no. 25, 1997, pp. 467–93.

Collins, S., 'What are Buddhists *Doing* When They Deny the Self?', in F.E. Reynolds & D. Tracy (eds.), *Religion and Practical Reason*, New York, NY, State University of New York Press, 1994, pp. 59–86.

Contestabile, B., 'Negative Utilitarianism and Buddhist Intuition', *Contemporary Buddhism*, vol. 15, no. 2, 2014, pp. 298–311.

The Cowherds, *Moonshadows*, New York, NY, Oxford University Press, 2011.

Craig, A.D., 'Interoception: The Sense of the Physiological Condition of the Body', *Current Opinion in Neurobiology*, no. 13, 2003, pp. 500–5.

Crick, F. & C. Koch, 'A Framework for Consciousness', *Nature Neuroscience*, vol. 6, no. 2, 2003, pp. 119–26.

Crick, F. & C. Koch, 'Towards a Neurobiological Theory of Consciousness', *Seminars in the Neurosciences*, no. 2, 1990, pp. 263–75.

Crick, F. & G. Mitchinson, 'The Function of Dream Sleep', *Nature*, no. 304, 1983, pp. 111–14.

Crick, F., *The Astonishing Hypothesis: Scientific Search for the Soul*, New York, NY, Simon & Schuster, 1994.

Critchley, H.D., 'Neural Mechanisms of Autonomic, Affective and Cognitive Integration', *Journal of Comparative Neurology*, vol. 493, no. 1, 2005, pp. 154–66, DOI: 10.1002/cne.20749 (accessed 13 January 2016).

Damasio, A., *Self Comes to Mind: Constructing the Conscious Brain*, New York, NY, Pantheon, 2010.

Damasio, A., *The Feeling of What Happens: Body and Emotion in the Making of Consciousness*, San Diego, CA, Harcourt, 1999.

Danks, D., *Unifying the Mind: Cognitive Representations as Graphical Models*, Massachusetts, MA, MIT Press, 2014.

Darwin, C., *On the Origin of Species by Means of Natural Selection*, London, Penguin Classics, 1967 [1859].

Dasti, M., 'Nyaya's Self as Agent and Knower', in M.R. Dasti & E.F. Bryant (eds.), *Free Will, Agency and Selfhood in Indian Philosophy*, New York, NY, Oxford University Press, 2014, pp. 112–36.

Dehaene, S. & J.P. Changeux, 'Experimental and Theoretical Approaches to Conscious Processing', *Neuron*, vol. 70, no. 2, 2011, pp. 200–27, DOI: S0896-6273(11)00258-3 [pii] 10.1016/j.neuron.2011.03.018.

Dehaene, S. & L. Naccache, 'Towards a Cognitive Neuroscience of Consciousness: Basic Evidence and a Workspace Framework', *Cognition*, vol. 79, nos. 1–2, 2001, pp. 1–37.

Dehaene, S. et al., 'Toward a Computational Theory of Conscious Processing', *Current Opinion in Neurobiology*, no. 25, 2014, pp. 76–84.

Dennett, D., 'Expecting Ourselves to Expect', *Behavioral and Brain Sciences*, vol. 36, no. 3, 2013, pp. 29–30.

Dennett, D., *Consciousness Explained*, Boston, MA, Little Brown, 1991.

Dennett, D.C., 'Are Dreams Experiences?', *Philosophical Review*, no. 73, 1976, pp. 151–71.

Dennett, D.C., 'Why and How Does Consciousness Seem the Way it Seems?', in T. Metzinger & J.M. Windt (eds.), *Open MIND:* 10(T), Frankfurt a.M., MIND Group, 2015, DOI: 10.15502/9783958570245 (accessed 13 January 2016).

Desbordes, G. et al., 'Moving Beyond Mindfulness: Defining Equanimity as an Outcome Measure in Meditation and Contemplative Research', *Mindfulness*, no. 1, 2014, DOI: 10.1007/s12671-013-0269-8.

Descartes, R. *Meditations* and *Objections and Replies*, in *The Philosophical Writings of Descartes*, vol. 2, trans. J. Cottingham et al., Cambridge, Cambridge University Press, 1985 [1641].

Domhoff, G.W., 'Realistic Simulation and Bizarreness in Dream Content: Past Findings and Suggestions for Future Research, in D. Barrett & P. McNamara (eds.), The New Science of Dreaming, vol. II, Westport, CT, Praeger, 2007, pp. 1–27.

Dominus, S., 'Could Conjoined Twins Share a Mind?', *New York Times Magazine*, 25 May 2011.

Doron, G. & M. Brecht, 'What Single-Cell Stimulation has told us about Neural Coding', *Philosophical Transactions of the Royal Society of London B: Biological Sciences*, vol. 370, no. 1677, 2015, DOI: 10.1098/rstb.2014.0204 (accessed 27 January 2016).

Doyle, J.C. & M. Csete, 'Architecture, Constraints and Behavior', *Proceedings of the National Academy of Sciences*, vol. 108, supp. 3, 2011, pp. 15624–30.

Dreyfus, G., 'Is Mindfulness Present-Centred and Non-Judgmental? A Discussion of the Cognitive Dimensions of Mindfulness', *Contemporary Buddhism*, no. 12, 2011, pp. 41–54, DOI: 10.1080/14639947.2011.564815.

Du Bois-Reymond, E., 'On the Limits of Scientific Knowledge', *Popular Science Monthly*, vol. 5, 1874 [1872].

Dugas-Ford, J., J. Rowell & C. Ragsdale, 'Cell-type Homologies and the Origins of the Neo-cortex', *Proceedings of the National Academy of Sciences*, vol. 149, no. 42, 2012, pp. 16974–9.

Dupuy, J.-P., *On the Origins of Cognitive Science: The Mechanization of Mind*, 2nd edn., Cambridge, MA, MIT Press, 2009.

Easton, S., O. Blanke & C. Mohr, 'A Putative Implication for Fronto-Parietal Connectivity in Out-of-Body Experiences', *Cortex*, vol. 45, no. 2, 2009, pp. 216–27.

Eccles, J. & W. Feindel, 'Wilder Graves Penfield. 26 January 1891–5 April 1976', *Biographical Memoirs of Fellows of the Royal Society*, no. 24, 1978, pp. 472–513.

Eccles, J.C. (ed.), *Brain and Conscious Experience*, New York, NY, Springer-Verlag, 1966.

Edelman, D.B. & A.K. Seth, 'Animal Consciousness: A Synthetic Approach', *Trends in Neuroscience*, vol. 32, no. 9, 2009, pp. 476–84.

Edelman, G.M., 'Naturalizing Consciousness: A Theoretical Framework', *Proceedings of the National Academy of Sciences of the USA*, vol. 100, no. 9, 2003, pp. 5520–4.

Edelman, G.M., *Neural Darwinism: The Theory of Neuronal Group Selection*, New York, NY, Basic Books, 1987.

Edelman, G.M., *The Remembered Present*, New York, NY, Basic Books, 1989.

Ehrsson, H.H., 'The Experimental Induction of Out-of-Body Experiences', *Science*, vol. 317, no. 5841, 2007, p. 1048.

Eidelman, S. & C.S. Crandall, 'Bias in Favor of the Status Quo', *Social and Personality Psychology Compass*, vol. 6, no. 3, 2012, pp. 270–81.

Eidelman, S., C.S. Crandall & J. Pattershall, 'The Existence Bias', *Journal of Personality and Social Psychology*, vol. 97, no. 5, 2009, pp. 765–75.

Eisemann, C.H. et al., 'Do Insects Feel Pain? A Biological View', *Experientia*, no. 40, 1984, pp. 164–7.

Eliasmith, C. et al., 'A Large-scale Model of the Functioning Brain', *Science*, no. 338, 2012, pp. 1202–5, DOI: 10.1126/science.1225266.

Elkins, G.R. et al., 'Advancing Research and Practice: The Revised APA Division 30 Definition of Hypnosis', *American Journal of Clinical Hypnosis*, vol. 57, no. 4, 2015, pp. 378–85.

Farrell, B., 'Experience', *Mind*, no. 59, 1950, pp. 170–98.

Fechner, G.T., *Elemente der Psychophysik*, Leipzig, Breitkopf und Härtel, 1860.

Feinberg, T., *Altered Egos: How the Brain Creates the Self*, New York, NY, Oxford University Press, 2001.

Fernandez-Espejo, D. et al., 'Role for the Default Mode Network in the Bases of Disorders of Consciousness', *Annals of Neurology*, no. 72, 2012, pp. 335–43.

Ferrarelli, F. et al., 'Breakdown in Cortical Effective Connectivity During Midazolam-Induced Loss of Consciousness', *Proceedings of the National Academy of Sciences of the United States of America*, vol. 107, no. 6, 2010, pp. 2681–6.

Feyerabend, P., 'Explanation, Reduction and Empiricism', in *Realism, Rationalism and Scientific Method*, Cambridge, Cambridge University Press, 1981 [1962].

Feyerabend, P., 'Mental Events and the Brain', *Journal of Philosophy*, vol. 60, no. 11, 1963, pp. 295–6.

Fields, H., 'Pain: An Unpleasant Topic', *Pain Supplement*, no. 6, 1999, pp. S61– S69.

Fingelkurts, A.A., 'Cortex Functional Connectivity as a Neurophysiological Correlate of Hypnosis: An EEG Case Study', *Neuropsychologia*, vol. 45, no. 7, 2007, pp. 1452–62.

Fink, S.B., 'Independence and Connections of Pain and Suffering', *Journal of Consciousness Studies*, vol. 18, nos. 9–10, 2011, pp. 46–66.

Fins, J.J., *Rights Come to Mind: Brain Injury, Ethics and the Struggle for Consciousness*, New York, NY, Cambridge University Press, 2015.

Flanagan O., 'Hallucinating Oneness', paper delivered at Oneness Conference, City University, Hong Kong, April 2015.

Flanagan, O. & G. Graham, 'Truth and Sanity: Positive Illusions, Spiritual Delusions and Metaphysical Hallucinations', in S. Tekin & J. Poland (eds.), *Extraordinary Science: Responding to the Crisis in Psychiatric Research*, Cambridge, MA, MIT Press, 2016.

Flanagan, O., 'Deconstructing Dreams: The Spandrels of Sleep', *Journal of Philosophy*, no. 92, 1996, pp. 5–27.

Flanagan, O., *Consciousness Reconsidered*, Cambridge, MA, MIT Press, 1992.

Flanagan, O., *The Bodhisattva's Brain*, Cambridge, MA, MIT Press, 2011.

Flanagan, O., *The Problem of the Soul*, New York, NY, Basic Books, 2003.

Flanagan, O., *The Really Hard Problem: Meaning in the Material World*, Cambridge, MA, MIT Press, 2007.

Fleming, S.M., R.J. Dolan & C.D. Frith, 'Metacognition: Computation, Biology and Function', *Philosophical Transactions of the Royal Society of London B: Biological Sciences*, vol. 367, no. 1594, 2012, pp. 1280–86, DOI: 10.1098/rstb.2012.0021.

Fletcher, P.C. & C.D. Frith, 'Perceiving is Believing: A Bayesian Approach to Explaining the Positive Symptoms of Schizophrenia', *Nature Reviews Neuroscience*, vol. 10, no. 1, pp. 48–58, DOI: nrn2536 [pii] 10.1038/nrn2536.

Fodor, J.A., 'Methodological Solipsism Considered as a Research Strategy in Cognitive Psychology', *Behavioral and Brain Sciences*, vol. 3, no. 1, 1980, pp. 63–73.

Fodor, J.A., *In Critical Condition: Polemical Essays on Cognitive Science and Philosophy of Mind*, Massachusetts, MA, MIT Press, 1998.

Fodor, J.A., *The Language of Thought*, Cambridge, MA, Harvard University Press, 1975.

Forgacs, P.B. et al., 'Preservation of Electroencephalographic Organization in Patients with Impaired Consciousness and Imaging-Based Evidence of Command-Following', *Annals of Neurology*, vol. 76, no. 6, 2014, pp. 869–79.

Foulkes, D. & C. Cavallero, 'Introduction', in C. Cavallero & D. Foulkes (eds.), *Dreaming as Cognition*, New York, NY, Harvester Wheatsheaf, 1993, pp. 1–17.

Foulkes, D., *Dreaming: A Cognitive-Psychological Analysis*, Hillsdale, NJ, Lawrence Erlbaum, 1985.

Frassle, S. et al., 'Binocular Rivalry: Frontal Activity Relates to Introspection and Action but not to Perception', *Journal of Neuroscience*, vol. 34, no. 5, 2014, pp. 1738–47, DOI: 10.1523/JNEUROSCI.4403-13.2014.

Frede, M., *A Free Will: Origins of the Notion in Ancient Thought*, ed. A.A. Long, with an introduction by D. Sedley, Berkeley, CA, University of California Press, 2012.

Freud, S., *The Ego and the Id*, Vienna, Internationaler Psychoanalytischer Verlag, 1923.

Fricke, F., 'Verschiedene Versionen des negativen Utilitarismus', *Kriterion*, no. 15, 2002, pp. 13–27.

Fridman, E.A. & N.D. Schiff, 'Neuromodulation of the Conscious State Following Severe Brain Injuries', *Current Opinion in Neurobiology*, no. 29C, 2014, pp. 172–7.

Fridman, E.A. et al., 'Regional Cerebral Metabolic Patterns Demonstrate the Role of Anterior Forebrain Mesocircuit Dysfunction in the Severely Injured Brain', *Proceedings of the National Academy of Sciences of the United States of America*, vol. 111, no. 17, 2014, pp. 6473–8.

Friston, K., 'The Free-Energy Principle: A Unified Brain Theory?', *Nature Reviews Neuroscience*, vol. 11, no. 2, 2010, pp. 127–38.

Friston, K., R. Moran & A.K. Seth, 'Analysing Connectivity with Granger Causality and Dynamic Causal Modelling', *Current Opinion in Neurobiology*, vol. 23, no. 2, 2013, pp. 172–78.

Friston, K.J., 'The Free-Energy Principle: A Unified Brain Theory?', *Nature Reviews Neuroscience*, vol. 11, no. 2, 2010, pp. 127–38, DOI: nrn2787 [pii] 10.1038/nrn2787.

Friston, K.J., J. Kilner & L. Harrison, 'A Free Energy Principle for the Brain', *Journal of Physiology – Paris*, vol. 100, nos. 1–3, 2006, pp. 70–87, DOI: S0928-4257(06)00060-X [pii] 10.1016/j.jphysparis.2006.10.001.

Frith, C. & U. Frith, 'Mechanisms of Social Cognition', *Annual Review of Psychology*, no. 63, 2012, pp. 287–313.

Frith, C., *Making Up the Mind: How the Brain Creates our Mental World*, Oxford, Blackwell's, 2007.

van Gaal, S. & V.A. Lamme, 'Unconscious High-Level Information Processing: Implication for Neurobiological Theories of Consciousness', *Neuroscientist*, vol, 18, no. 3, 2012, pp. 287–301, DOI: 10.1177/1073858411404079.

Galarza, M. et al., 'Jazz Guitar and Neurosurgery: The Pat Martino Case Report', *World Neurosurgery*, vol. 81, nos. 3–4, 2014, pp. 508–10.

Galileo, G., 'The Assayer: A Letter to the Illustrious and very Reverend Don Virginio Cesarini', repr. in *Discoveries and Opinions of Galileo*, trans. S. Drake, New York, NY, Doubleday & Co., 1957 [1623].

Gallagher, S., 'Philosophical Conceptions of the Self: Implications for Cognitive

Science', *Trends in Cognitive Sciences*, vol. 4, no. 1, 2000, pp. 14–21.

Ganeri, J., *The Concealed Art of the Soul*, Oxford, Oxford University Press, 2007.

Garfield, J., 'Just Another Word for Nothing Left to Lose: Freedom, Agency and Ethics for Madhyamikas', in M.R. Dasti & E.F. Bryant (eds.), *Free Will, Agency and Selfhood in Indian Philosophy*, New York, NY, Oxford University Press, 2014, pp. 164–85.

Garfield, J., *Engaging Buddhism*, New York, NY, Oxford University Press, 2015.

Garfinkel, S.N. et al., 'Fear from the Heart: Sensitivity to Fear Stimuli Depends on Individual Heartbeats', *Journal of Neuroscience*, vol. 34, no. 19, 2014, pp. 6573–82, DOI: 10.1523/JNEUROSCI.3507-13.2014.

Gauld, A., *A History of Hypnotism*, Cambridge, MA, Cambridge University Press, 1992.

Gay, P., R.E. Schmidt & M. van der Linden, 'Impulsivity and Intrusive Thoughts: Related Manifestations of Self-Control Difficulties?', *Cognitive Therapy and Research*, vol. 35, no. 4, 2011, pp. 293–303.

Gazzaniga M. & J. LeDoux, *The Integrated Mind*, New York, NY, Plenum Press, 1978.

Gazzaniga, M.S., 'Forty-five Years of Split-Brain Research and Still Going Strong', *Nature Reviews Neuroscience*, vol. 6, no. 8, 2005, pp. 653–59.

Gazzaniga, M.S., J.E. Bogen & R.W. Sperry, 'Some Functional Effects of Sectioning the Cerebral Commissures in Man', *Proceedings of the National Academy of Sciences of the USA*, no. 48, 1962, pp. 1765–9.

Gazzaniga, M.S., *Tales from Both Sides of the Brain: A Life in Neuroscience*, New York, NY, HarperCollins, 2015.

Gazzaniga, M.S., *Who's in Charge? Free Will and the Science of the Brain*, New York, NY, Ecco, HarperCollins, 2011.

Giacino, J.T. et al., 'Central Thalamic Deep Brain Stimulation to Promote Recovery from Chronic Posttraumatic Minimally Conscious State: Challenges and Opportunities', *Neuromodulation*, vol. 15, no. 4, 2012, pp. 339–49.

Giacino, J.T. et al., 'Disorders of Consciousness after Acquired Brain Injury: The State of the Science', *Nature Review Neurology*, vol. 10, no. 2, 2014, pp. 99–114.

Giacino, J.T. et al., 'Placebo-Controlled Trial of Amantadine for Severe Traumatic Brain Injury', *New England Journal of Medicine*, No. 366, 2012, pp. 819–26.

Gibson, J.J., *The Ecological Approach to Visual Perception*, Mahwah, NJ, Lawrence Erlbaum, 1979.

Glimcher P. & E. Fehr, *Neuroeconomics: Decision Making and the Brain*, 2nd edn., San Diego, CA, Academic Press, 2013.

Goldfine, A.M. et al, 'Determination of Awareness in Patients with Severe Brain Injury using EEG Power Spectral Analysis', *Clinical Neurophysiology*, vol. 122, no. 11, 2011, pp. 2157–68.

de Graaf, T.A. & A.T. Sack, 'Using Brain Stimulation to Disentangle Neural Correlates of Conscious Vision', *Frontiers in Psychology*, no. 5, 2014, 1019, DOI: 10.3389/fpsyg.2014.01019 (accessed 19 January 2016).

de Graaf, T.A., P.J. Hsieh & A.T. Sack, 'The "Correlates" in Neural Correlates of Consciousness', *Neuroscience & Biobehavioral Reviews*, vol. 36, no. 1, 2012, pp. 191–7, DOI: 10.1016/j.neubiorev.2011.05.012.

Grahek, N., *Feeling Pain and Being in Pain*, 2nd edn., Cambridge, MA, Bradford Books, MIT Press, 2007.

Gray, J., *Consciousness: Creeping up on the Hard Problem*, Oxford, Oxford University Press, 2004.

Graziano, M., *Consciousness and the Social Brain*, New York, NY, Oxford University Press, 2013.

Green, J.P. et al., 'Forging Ahead: The 2003 APA Division 30 Definition of Hypnosis', *International Journal of Clinical and Experimental Hypnosis*, vol. 53, no. 3, 2005, pp. 259–64.

Grens, K., 'The Rainbow Connection', *The Scientist*, 1 October 2014, http:/thescientist. com/?articles.view/articleNo/41055/title/The-Rainbow-Connection/(accessed 27 December 2015).

Griffiths, R.R. et al., 'Psilocybin can Occasion Mystical-type Experiences having Substantial and Sustained Personal Meaning and Spiritual Significance', *Psychopharmacology*, vol. 187, no. 3, 2006, pp. 284–92.

Grillner, S. et al., 'Mechanisms for Selection of Basic Motor Programs: Roles for the Striatum and Pallidum', *Trends in Neurosciences*, no. 28, 2005, pp. 364–70.

Haggard, P., 'Human Volition: Towards a Neuroscience of Will', *Nature Reviews Neuroscience*, vol. 9, no. 12, 2008, pp. 934–46.

Hall, C.S. & R.L. Van de Castle, *The Content Analysis of Dreams*, New York, NY, Appleton-Century-Crofts, 1966.

Hamilton, S., *The 'I' of the Beholder*, London, Routledge, 2000.

Hanson, R., *Buddha's Brain: The Practical Neuroscience of Happiness, Love, and Wisdom*, Oakland, CA, New Harbinger Publications, 2009.

Harvey, P., 'Freedom of the Will in Light of Theravāda Teachings', *Journal of Buddhist Ethics*, no. 14, 2007, pp. 35–98.

Haun, A. M., M. Oizumi, C. K. Kovach, H. Kawasaki, H. Oya, M. A. Howard, R. Adolphs & N. Tsuchiya, 'Contents of Consciousness Investigated as Integrated Information in Direct Human Brain Recordings', *bioRxiv*, 2016, pp. 039032+. DOI: https://doi.org/10.1101/039032

Hawking, S., *A Brief History of Time*, New York, NY, Bantam Books, 1988.

Haynes, J.D. & G. Rees, 'Decoding Mental States from Brain Activity in Humans', *Nature Reviews Neuroscience*, vol. 7, no. 7, 2006, pp. 523–34.

Heidegger, M., 'The Origin of the Work of Art', trans. D.F. Krell, in *Martin Heidegger: Basic Writings*, New York, NY, Harper & Row, 1977.

Herrmann, C.S., I. Fründ & D. Lenz, 'Human Gamma-band Activity: A Review on Cognitive and Behavioral Correlates and Network Models', *Neuroscience & Biobehavioral Reviews*, vol. 34, no. 7, 2010, pp. 981–92.

Heydrich, L. et al., 'Partial and Full Own-Body Illusions of Epileptic Origin in a Child with Right Temporoparietal Epilepsy', *Epilepsy & Behavior*, vol. 20, no. 3, 2011, pp. 583–6.

Hilgard, E.R., 'The Domain of Hypnosis, With Some Comments on Alternative Paradigms', *American Psychologist*, vol. 28, no. 11, 1973, pp. 972–82.

Hilgard, E.R., *Hypnotic Susceptibility*, New York, NY, Harcourt, Brace & World, 1965.

Hilgendorf, E. & J.-P. Günther (eds.), *Robotik und Gesetzgebung*, Baden-Baden, Nomos, 2013.

von Hippel, W. & R. Trivers, 'The Evolution and Psychology of Self-Deception', *Behavioral and Brain Sciences*, vol. 34, no. 1, 2011, pp. 1–56.

Hobson, J.A. & R.W. McCarley, 'The Brain as a Dream State Generator: An Activation-Synthesis Hypothesis of the Dream Process', *American Journal of Psychiatry*, no. 134, 1977, pp. 1335–48.

Hobson, J.A., 'Dreaming as Delirium: A Mental Status Exam of our Nightly Madness', *Seminars in Neurology*, no. 17, 1997, pp. 121–8.

Hobson, J.A., 'REM Sleep and Dreaming: Towards a Theory of Protoconsciousness', *Nature Reviews Neuroscience*, vol. 10, no. 11, 2009, pp. 803–13.

Hobson, J.A., E.F. Pace-Schott & R. Stickgold, 'Dream Science 2000: A Response to Commentaries on Dreaming and the Brain', *Behavioral and Brain Sciences*, vol. 23, no. 6, 2000, pp. 1019–35.

Hobson, J.A., E.F. Pace-Schott & R. Stickgold, 'Dreaming and the Brain: Toward a Cognitive Neuroscience of Conscious States', *Behavioral and Brain Sciences*, vol. 23, no. 6, 2000, pp. 793–842, discussion pp. 904–1121.

Hoel, E.P., L. Albantakis and G. Tononi, 'Quantifying Causal Emergence Shows that Macro can Beat Micro', *Proceedings of the Nationall Academy of Sciences of the United States of America*, vol. 110, no. 49, 2013, pp. 19790–5.

Hoel, E.P., L. Albantakis, W. Marshall & G. Tononi, 'Can the Macro Beat the Micro? Integrated Information Across Spatio-temporal Scales', *Neuroscience of Consciousness*, 2016 (1), pp. niw012.

Hohwy, J., 'The Self-Evidencing Brain', *Noûs*, vol. 50, no. 2, 2016, pp. 259–285, DOI: 10.1111/nous.12062 (accessed 10 January 2016).

Hohwy, J., *The Predictive Mind*, Oxford, Oxford University Press, 2013.

Holzel, B. et al., 'How Does Mindfulness Meditation Work? Proposing Mechanisms of Action from a Conceptual and Neural Perspective', *Perspectives on Psychological Science*, no. 6, 2011, pp. 537–59.

Hood, B., *The Self Illusion: Why There is No 'You' Inside Your Head*, London, Hachette, 2012.

Horikawa, T. et al., 'Neural Decoding of Visual Imagery During Sleep', *Science*, vol. 340, no. 6132, 2013, pp. 639–42.

Hume, D., *A Treatise of Human Nature*, London, Penguin, 1985 [1738].

Hume, D., *Enquiry Concerning Human Understanding*, Oxford, Oxford University Press, 2008 [1748].

Hupe, J.M. et al., 'Cortical Feedback Improves Discrimination Between Figure and Background by V1, V2 and V3 neurons', *Nature*, vol. 394, no. 6695, 1998, pp. 784–7.

Hurlburt, R.T. & C.L. Heavey, 'Investigating Pristine Inner Experience: Implications for Experience Sampling and Questionnaires', *Consciousness and Cognition*, no. 31, 2015, pp. 148–59.

Hurlburt, R.T., *Investigating Pristine Inner Experience: Moments of Truth*, Cambridge, Cambridge University Press, 2011.

Husserl, E., *Ideas Pertaining to a Pure Phenomenology and to a Phenomenological Philosophy*, vol. 1, *General Introduction to a Pure Phenomenology*, The Hague, Springer, 1982 [1913].

Husserl, E., *Ideas Pertaining to a Pure Phenomenology and to a Phenomenological Philosophy*, vol. 2, trans. R. Rojcewicz & A. Schuwer, Dordrecht, Kluwer, 1989 [1913].

Husserl, E., *The Crisis of the European Sciences and Transcendental Phenomenology: An Introduction to Phenomenological Philosophy*, trans. D. Carr, Evanston, IL, Northwestern University Press, 1970 [1954].

Huxley, T., *Lessons in Elementary Physiology*, London, Macmillan, 1866.

Ionta, S. et al., 'Multisensory Mechanisms in Temporo-Parietal Cortex Support Self-Location and First-Person Perspective', *Neuron*, vol. 70, no. 2, 2011, pp. 363–74.

Irvine, L., *Consciousness as a Scientific Concept: A Philosophy of Science Perspective*, Dordrecht, Springer, 2012.

Irwin, H.J., *Flight of Mind: A Psychological Study of the Out-of-Body Experience*, Metuchen, NJ, Scarecrow Press, 1985.

Ito, H. & N. Yamamoto, 'Non-Laminar Cerebral Cortex in Teleost Fish?', *Biological Letters*, no. 5, 2009, pp. 117–21.

Jackson, F., 'Epiphenomenal Qualia', *Philosophical Quarterly*, vol. 32, no. 127, 1982, pp. 127–36.

James, W., 'The Stream of Consciousness', in *Psychology*, Cleveland & New York, World, 1892.

James, W., *The Principles of Psychology*, Cambridge, MA, Harvard University Press, 1983 [1890].

James, W., *The Varieties of Religious Experience*, London, Longmans, Green & Co, 1902.

Jennett, B. et al., 'Neuropathology in Vegetative and Severely Disabled Patients after Head Injury, *Neurology*, no. 56, 2001, pp. 486–90.

Jha, A.P. et al., 'Examining the Protective Effects of Mindfulness Training on Working Memory Capacity and Affective Experience', *Emotion*, no. 10, 2010, pp. 54–64.

Jha, A.P., J. Krompinger & M.J. Baime, 'Mindfulness Training Modifies Subsystems of Attention', *Cognitive, Affective & Behavioral Neuroscience*, no. 7, 2007, pp. 109–19.

Kahneman, D., *Thinking, Fast and Slow*, New York, Farrar, Strauss, Giroux, 2011.

Kallio, S. & A. Revonsuo, 'Altering the State of the Altered State Debate: Reply to Commentaries', *Contemporary Hypnosis*, vol. 22, no. 1, 2005, pp. 46–55.

Kallio, S. & A. Revonsuo, 'Hypnotic Phenomena and Altered States of Consciousness: A Multilevel Framework of Description and Explanation', *Contemporary Hypnosis*, vol. 20, no. 3, 2003, pp. 111–64.

Kallio, S. & M. Koivisto, 'Posthypnotic Suggestion Alters Conscious Color Perception in an Automatic Manner', *International Journal of Clinical and Experimental Hypnosis*, vol. 61, no. 4, 2013, pp. 371–87.

Kallio, S. et al., 'The Existence of a Hypnotic State is Revealed by Eye Movements', *PLOS ONE*, vol. 6, no. 10, 2011, http://journals.plos.org/plosone/article?id=10.1371/journal.pone.0026374 (accessed 25 August 2015).

Kallio, S. et al., 'The MMN Amplitude Increases in Hypnosis: A Case Study', *NeuroReport*, vol. 10, no. 17, 1999, pp. 3579–82.

Kanai, R. & N. Tsuchiya, 'Qualia', *Current Biology*, vol. 22, no. 10, 2012, pp. R392-96, DOI: 10.1016/j.cub.2012.03.033.

Kapstein, M., *Reason's Traces*, Boston, MA, Wisdom Publications, 2001.

Karten, K., 'Evolutionary Developmental Biology Meets the Brain: The Origins of

Mammalian Cortex', *Proceedings of the National Academy of Sciences*, no. 94, 1997, pp. 2800–4.

Kavanagh, D.J., J. Andrade & J. May, 'Imaginary Relish and Exquisite Torture: The Elaborated Intrusion Theory of Desire', *Psychological Review*, no. 112, 2005, pp. 446–67, DOI: 10.1037/0033-295X.112.2.446.

Kawasaki, H. et al., 'Processing of Facial Emotion in the Human Fusiform Gyrus', *Journal of Cognitive Neuroscience*, vol. 24, no. 6, 2012, pp. 1358–70.

van Kerkoerle, T. et al., 'Alpha and Gamma Oscillations Characterize Feedback and Feedforward Processing in Monkey Visual Cortex', *Proceedings of the National Academy of Sciences of the USA*, vol. 111, no. 40, 2014, pp. 14332–41, DOI: 10.1073/ pnas.1402773111.

Khaligh-Razavi, S.M. et al., 'The Effects of Recurrent Dynamics on Ventral-Stream Representational Geometry', *Journal of Vision*, vol. 15, no. 12, 2015, 1089, DOI: 10.1167/15.12.1089 (accessed 19 January 2016).

Killingsworth, M.A. & D.T. Gilbert, 'A Wandering Mind is an Unhappy Mind', *Science*, vol. 330, no. 6006, 2010, p. 932.

King, J.R. et al., 'Information Sharing in the Brain Indexes Consciousness in Noncommunicative Patients', *Current Biology*, vol. 23, no. 19, 2013, pp. 1914–9.

Kirsch, I. & J.R. Council, 'Situational and Personality Correlates of Hypnotic Responsiveness', in E. Fromm & M. Nash (eds.), *Contemporary Hypnosis Research*, New York, NY, Guilford Press, 1992, pp. 267–91.

Kirsch, I. & W. Braffman, 'Imaginative Suggestibility and Hypnotizability', *Current Directions in Psychological Science*, vol. 4, no. 2, 2001, pp. 57–61.

Kirsch, I., 'Defining Hypnosis for the Public', *Contemporary Hypnosis*, vol. 11, no. 3, 1994, pp. 142–3.

Koch, C. & N. Tsuchiya, 'Attention and Consciousness: Related yet Different', *Trends in Cognitive Sciences*, vol. 16, no. 2, 2012, pp. 103–5, DOI: 10.1016/j. tics.2011.11.012.

Koivisto, M. et al., 'A Preconscious Neural Mechanism of Hypnotically Altered Colors: A Double Case Study', *PLOS ONE*, vol. 8, no. 8, 2013, http://journals.plos.org/ plosone/article?id=10.1371/journal.pone.0070900 (accessed 25 August 2015).

Kouider, S. et al., 'A Neural Marker of Perceptual Consciousness in Infants', *Science*, vol. 340, no. 6130, 2013, pp. 376–80, DOI: 10.1126/science.1232509.

Kriegel, U., *Subjective Consciousness: A Self-Representational Theory*, New York, NY, Oxford University Press, 2009.

Kuyken, W. et al., 'Effectiveness and Cost-Effectiveness of Mindfulness-Based Cognitive Therapy Compared with Maintenance Antidepressant Treatment in the Prevention of Depressive Relapse or Recurrence (PREVENT): A Randomised Controlled Trial', *The Lancet*, no. 386, 2015, pp. 63–73, DOI: 10.1016/ S0140-6736(14)62222-4.

Kveraga, K., A. Ghuman & M. Bar, 'Top–Down Predictions in the Cognitive Brain', *Brain and Cognition*, no. 65, 2007, pp. 145–68.

Lamme, V.A., 'How Neuroscience will Change our View on Consciousness', *Cognitive Neuroscience*, vol. 1, no. 3, 2010, pp. 204–40.

Lashley, K., 'The Behavioristic Interpretation of Consciousness I', *Psychological Review*, vol. 30, 1923, pp. 237–72, 329–53.

Lau, H.C. & R.E. Passingham, 'Relative Blindsight in Normal Observers and the Neural Correlate of Visual Consciousness', *Proceedings of the National Academy of Sciences of the USA*, vol. 103, no. 49, 2006, pp. 18763–8.

LeDoux, J.E., *Synaptic Self: How our Brains Become Who We Are*, New York, NY, Viking, 2002.

Lee, U. et al., 'Propofol Induction Reduces the Capacity for Neural Information Integration: Implications for the Mechanism of Consciousness and General Anesthesia', *Consciousness and Cognition*, vol. 18, no. 1, 2009, pp. 56–64.

Legon, W. et al., 'Transcranial Focused Ultrasound Modulates the Activity of Primary Somatosensory Cortex in Humans', *Nature Neuroscience*, vol. 17, no. 2, 2014, pp. 322–9.

Lehar, S., 'Gestalt Isomorphism and the Primacy of Subjective Conscious Experience: A Gestalt Bubble Model', *Behavioral and Brain Sciences*, vol. 26. no. 4, 2003, pp. 375–444.

Leibniz, G., 'Monadology', in Leibniz, *Monadology and Other Philosophical Essays*, trans. P. & A.M. Schrecker, Indianapolis, IA, Bobbs-Merrill, 1965 [1714–20].

Lemon, R.N. & S.A. Edgley, 'Life Without a Cerebellum', *Brain,* no. 133 (Pt 3), 2010, pp. 652–4.

Lenggenhager, B. et al., 'Video Ergo Sum: Manipulating Bodily Self-Consciousness', *Science*, vol. 317, no. 5841, 2007, pp. 1096–9.

Lenggenhager, B., M. Mouthon & O. Blanke, 'Spatial Aspects of Bodily Self-Consciousness', *Consciousness and Cognition*, vol. 18, no. 1, 2009, pp. 110–7.

Leopold, D.A. & N.K. Logothetis, 'Activity Changes in Early Visual Cortex Reflect Monkeys' Percepts during Binocular Rivalry', *Nature*, vol. 379, no. 6565, 1966, pp. 549–53.

Lessard, D.A., S.A. Linkenhauger & D.R. Proffitt, 'Look Before you Leap: Jumping Ability Affects Distance Perception', *Perception*, vol. 38, no. 12, 2009, pp. 1863–6.

Levine, J., 'Materialism and Qualia: The Explanatory Gap', *Pacific Philosophical Quarterly*, no. 64, 1983, pp. 35–61.

Lieberman, P., *The Unpredictable Species*, Princeton, NY, Princeton University Press, 2013.

Linkenhauger, S.A., V.C. Ramenzoni & D.R. Proffitt, 'Illusory Shrinkage and Growth: Body-based Scaling Affects the Perception of Size', *Psychological Science*, vol. 21, no. 9, 2010, pp. 1318–25.

Locke, J., *An Essay Concerning Human Understanding*, ed. P. Nidditch, Oxford, Clarendon Press, 1975 [1689–1700].

Loomis, A.L., E.N. Harvey & G. Hobart, 'Potential Rhythms of the Cerebral Cortex during Sleep', *Science*, vol. 81, no. 2111, 1935, pp. 597–8, DOI: 10.1126/science.81.2111.597.

Low, P. et al., 'The Cambridge Declaration on Consciousness', 2012, http://fcmconference.org/img/CambridgeDeclarationOnConsciousness.pdf (accessed 6 January 2016).

Luck, S.J. et al., 'Independent Hemispheric Attentional Systems Mediate Visual Search in Split-Brain Patients', *Nature*, vol. 342, no. 6249, 1989, pp. 543–5.

Lutkenhoff, E.S. et al., 'Thalamic and Extrathalamic Mechanisms of Consciousness after Severe Brain Injury', *Annals of Neurology*, vol. 78, no. 1, 2015, pp. 68–76.

Lynn, S.J., I. Kirsch & M.N. Hallquist, 'Social Cognitive Theories of Hypnosis', in A.

Barnier & M. Nash (eds.), *The Oxford Handbook of Hypnosis: Theory, Research and Practice*, New York, NY, Oxford University Press, 2008, pp. 111–40.

MacKay, D.M., *Behind the Eye*, ed. V. MacKay (based on the 1986 Gifford Lectures), Oxford, Basil Blackwell, 1991.

Maier, A. et al., 'Introduction to Research Topic – Binocular Rivalry: A Gateway to Consciousness', *Frontiers in Human Neuroscience*, no. 6, 2012, p. 263, DOI: 10.3389/fnhum.2012.00263 (accessed 31 January 2016).

Malcolm, N., *Dreaming*, London, Routledge & Kegan Paul, 1959.

Mannino, A. et al., 'Künstliche Intelligenz: Chancen und Risiken', *Diskussionspapiere der Stiftung für Effektiven Altruismus*, no. 2, 2015, pp. 1–17, http://ea-stiftung.org/ s/Kunstliche-Intelligenz-Chancen-und-Risiken.pdf (accessed 11 January 2016)

Margulis, L. & D. Sagan, *What is Life? The Eternal Enigma*, London, Weidenfield & Nicolson, 1995.

Martino, P. & B. Milkowski, *Here and Now! The Autobiography of Pat Martino*, Milwaukee, IL, Backbeat Books, 2011.

Massimini, M. et al., 'Breakdown of Cortical Effective Connectivity During Sleep', *Science*, vol. 309, no. 5744, 2005, pp. 2228–32.

Mataro, M. et al., 'Long-term Effects of Bilateral Frontal Brain Lesion: 60 Years after Injury with an Iron Bar', *Archives of Neurology*, vol. 58, no. 7, 2001, pp. 1139–42.

Maxwell, W.L. et al., 'Thalamic Nuclei after Human Blunt Head Injury', *Journal of Neuropathology and Experimental Neurology*, vol. 65, no. 5, 2006, pp. 478–88.

McGinn, C., 'All Machine and no Ghost', *New Statesman*, 20 February 2012, http://www.newstatesman.com/ideas/2012/02/consciousness-mind-brain (accessed 27 December 2015).

McGinn, C., 'Consciousness and Cosmology: Hyperdualism Ventilated', in M. Davies & G.W. Humphreys (eds.), *Consciousness*, Oxford, Blackwell, 1993, pp. 155–77.

McGinn, C., 'Storm over the Brain', review of P.S. Churchland, *Touching a Nerve, New York Review of Books*, 24 April 2014.

McGinn, C., *The Mysterious Flame: Consciousness in a Material World*, New York, NY, Basic Books, 1999.

Melloni, L. et al., 'Expectations Change the Signatures and Timing of Electrophysiological Correlates of Perceptual Awareness', *Journal of Neuroscience*, vol. 31, no. 4, 2011, pp. 1386–96, DOI: 31/4/1386 [pii] 10.1523/JNEUROSCI.4570-10.2011.

Merker, B., 'Consciousness Without a Cerebral Cortex: A Challenge for Neuroscience and Medicine', with commentaries, *Behavioral and Brain Sciences*, no. 30, 2007, pp. 63–134.

Merleau-Ponty, M., *Phenomenology of Perception*, London, Routledge & Kegan Paul, 1962.

Mesmer, F.A., *The Discovery of Animal Magnetism,* Edmonds, WA, Holmes Publishing Group, 1998 [1779].

Metzinger T. & Wiese W. (eds.), *Philosophy and Predictive Processing*, Frankfurt am Main, MIND Group, 2017, http://predictive-mind.net.

Metzinger T. & J. M. Windt (eds.), *Open MIND*, Frankfurt am Main: MIND Group, 2015, http://open-mind.net.

Metzinger, T. (ed.), *Conscious Experience*, Thorverton, Imprint Academic, 1995.

Metzinger, T. (ed.), *Neural Correlates of Consciousness: Empirical and Conceptual Questions*, Cambridge, MA, MIT Press, 2000.

Metzinger, T., 'Empirical Perspectives from the Self-Model Theory of Subjectivity: A Brief Summary with Examples', *Progress in Brain Research*, no. 168, 2008, pp. 215–78.

Metzinger, T., 'Faster than Thought', in T. Metzinger (ed.), *Conscious Experience*, Thorverton, Imprint Academic, 1995, pp. 425–61.

Metzinger, T., 'Out-of-Body Experiences as the Origin of the Concept of a "Soul"', *Mind and Matter*, vol. 3, no. 1, 2005, pp. 57–84.

Metzinger, T., 'Phenomenal Transparency and Cognitive Self-Reference', *Phenomenology and the Cognitive Sciences*, vol. 2, no. 4, 2003, pp. 353–93.

Metzinger, T., 'Précis: Being No One', *Psyche*, vol. 11, no. 5, 2006, pp. 1–35.

Metzinger, T., 'The Myth of Cognitive Agency: Subpersonal Thinking as a Cyclically Recurring Loss of Mental Autonomy', *Frontiers in Psychology*, no. 4, 2013, p. 931, DOI: 10.3389/fpsyg.2013.00931 (accessed 6 January 2016).

Metzinger, T., 'The No-Self Alternative', in S. Gallagher (ed.), *The Oxford Handbook of the Self*, Oxford, Oxford University Press, 2011, pp. 279–96.

Metzinger, T., 'Two Principles for Robot Ethics', in E. Hilgendorf & J.-P. Günther (eds.), *Robotik und Gesetzgebung*, Baden-Baden, Nomos, 2013, pp. 263–302.

Metzinger, T., 'Why are Dreams Interesting for Philosophers? The Example of Minimal Phenomenal Selfhood, plus an Agenda for Future Research', *Frontiers in Psychology*, no. 4, 2013, p. 746, DOI: 10.3389/fpsyg.2013.00746 (accessed 6 January 2016).

Metzinger, T., 'Why are Out-of-Body Experiences Interesting for Philosophers? The Theoretical Relevance of OBE Research', *Cortex*, vol. 45, no. 2, 2009, pp. 256–8.

Metzinger, T., *Being No One: The Self-Model Theory of Subjectivity*, Cambridge, MA, MIT Press, 2003.

Metzinger, T., *The Ego Tunnel*, New York, NY, Basic Books, 2009.

Meyers, K., 'Free Persons, Empty Selves: Freedom and Agency in Light of the Two Truths', in M.R. Dasti & E.F. Bryant (eds.), *Free Will, Agency and Selfhood in Indian Philosophy*, New York, NY, Oxford University Press, 2014.

Meyers, K.L., 'Freedom and Self-Control: Free Will in South Asian Buddhism', PhD dissertation, University of Chicago, 2010.

Miller, G.A., 'Computation, Consciousness, and Cognition', *Behavioral and Brain Sciences*, vol. 3, no. 1, 1980, p. 146.

Miller, G.A., *Psychology: The Science of Mental Life*, New York, NY, Harper & Row, 1962.

Mnih, V. et al., 'Human-level Control through Deep Reinforcement Learning', *Nature*, vol. 518, no. 7540, 2015, pp. 529–33, DOI: 10.1038/nature14236.

Monti, M.M. et al., 'Willful Modulation of Brain Activity in Disorders of Consciousness', *New England Journal of Medicine*, no. 362, 2010, pp. 579–89.

Moody, R.A., *Life after Life*, Atlanta, GA, Mockingbird, 1975.

Moser, E.I. et al., 'Grid Cells and Cortical Representation', *Nature Reviews Neuroscience*, no. 15, 2014, pp. 466–81.

Mountcastle, V., 'Dean's Lecture', *Johns Hopkins Medical Journal*, no. 136, 1974, pp. 109–31.

Mrazek, M.D., J. Smallwood & J.W. Schooler, 'Mindfulness and Mind-Wandering:

Finding Convergence through Opposing Constructs', *Emotion*, no. 12, 2012, pp. 442–8, DOI: 10.1037/a0026678.

Muckli, L. et al., 'Contextual Feedback to Superficial Layers of V1', *Current Biology*, vol. 25, no. 20, 2015, pp. 2690–95, DOI: 10.1016/j.cub.2015.08.057.

Näätänen, R., *Attention and Brain Function*, Hilsdale, NJ, Lawrence Erlbaum, 1992.

Nagel, T., 'What is it Like to be a Bat?' *Philosophical Review*, vol. 83, no. 4, 1974, pp. 435–50.

Nagel, T., *Concealment and Exposure*, New York, NY, Oxford University Press, 2002.

Nagel, T., *Mind and Cosmos: Why the Materialist Neo-Darwinian Conception of Nature is Almost Certainly False*, Oxford, Oxford University Press, 2012.

Neal, D.T. et al., 'How Do Habits Guide Behavior? Perceived and Actual Triggers of Habits in Daily Life', *Journal of Experimental Social Psychology*, no. 48, 2012, pp. 492–8, DOI: 10.1016/j.jesp.2011.10.011.

Neisser, U., *Cognition and Reality: Principles and Implications of Cognitive Psychology*, New York, NY, Freeman, 1976.

Newton, I., *Principia Mathematica*, London, 1687.

Nielsen, T.A., 'Dream Analysis and Classification: The Reality Simulation Perspective', in M. Kryeger, T. Roth & W.C. Dement (eds.), *Principles and Practice of Sleep Medicine*, New York, NY, Elsevier, 2010, pp. 595–603.

Nietzsche, F., *Beyond Good and Evil*, ed. R.-P. Horstmann & J. Norman, Cambridge, Cambridge University Press, 2002.

Nir, Y. & G. Tononi, 'Dreaming and the Brain: From Phenomenology to Neurophysiology', *Trends in Cognitive Sciences*, vol. 14, no. 2, 2010, pp. 88–100.

Noë, A., *Out of our Heads*, New York, NY, Hill & Wang, 2009.

Nolen-Hoeksema, S. & J. Morrow, 'A Prospective Study of Depression and Posttraumatic Stress Symptoms after a Natural Disaster: The 1989 Loma Prieta Earthquake', *Journal of Personality and Social Psychology*, no. 61, 1991, pp. 115–21.

Oizumi, M. et al., 'Measuring Integrated Information from the Decoding Perspective', *PLOS Computational Biology*, 2016, DOI: 10.1371/journal.pcbi.1004654 (accessed 27 January 2016).

Oizumi, M. et al., 'Modified Measure for Integrated Information Theory and its Application to 128-channel Electrocorticogram Data Recorded in Macaque Monkeys', paper presented at the annual conference of the Association for the Scientific Study of Consciousness, Kyoto, 2011.

Oizumi, M., L. Albantakis & G. Tononi, 'From the Phenomenology to the Mechanisms of Consciousness: Integrated Information Theory 3.0', *PLOS Computational Biology*, vol. 10, no. 5, 2014, DOI: 10.1371/journal.pcbi.1003588 (accessed 27 January 2016).

Owen, A.M. et al., 'Detecting Awareness in the Vegetative State', *Science*, vol. 313, no. 5792, 2006, p. 1402.

Owen, A.M., 'Detecting Consciousness: A Unique Role for Neuroimaging', *Annual Review of Psychology*, no. 64, 2013, pp. 109–33.

Owen, A.M., N.D. Schiff & S. Laureys, 'A New Era of Coma and Consciousness Science', *Progress in Brain Research*, no. 177, 2009, pp. 399–411, DOI: 10.1016/ S0079-6123(09)17728-2.

Pääbo, S., *Neanderthal Man: In Search of the Lost Genomes*, New York, Basic Books, 2014.

Pace-Schott, E.F. & J.A. Hobson, 'The Neurobiology of Sleep: Genetics, Cellular Physiology and Subcortical Networks', Nature Reviews Neuroscience, no. 3, 2002, pp. 591–600, DOI: 10.1038/nrn895.

Palmer, C.J., A.K. Seth & J. Hohwy, 'The Felt Presence of other Minds: Predictive Processing, Counterfactual Predictions and Mentalising in Autism', *Consciousness and Cognition*, no. 36, 2015, pp. 376–89, DOI:10.1016/j.concog.2015.04.007 (accessed 13 January 2016).

Palmer, J., 'The Out-of-Body Experience: A Psychological Theory', *Parapsychology Review*, no. 9, 1978, pp. 19–22.

Parfit, D., 'Divided Minds and the Nature of Persons', in C. Blakemore & S. Greenfield (eds.), *Mindwaves*, Oxford, Blackwell, 1987, pp. 19–26.

Parvizi, J. et al., 'Electrical Stimulation of Human Fusiform Face-selective Regions Distorts Face Perception', *Journal of Neuroscience*, vol. 32, no. 43, 2012, pp. 14915–20.

Parvizi, J. et al., 'The Will to Persevere Induced by Electrical Stimulation of the Human Cingulate Gyrus', *Neuron*, vol. 80, no. 6, 2013, pp. 1359–67, DOI: 10. 1016/j. neuron.2013.10.057.

Pascual-Leone, A. & V. Walsh, 'Fast Backprojections from the Motion to the Primary Visual Area Necessary for Visual Awareness', *Science*, vol. 292, no. 5516, 2001, pp. 510–12, DOI: 10.1126/science.1057099.

Perkins, A.M. et al., 'Thinking Too Much: Self-Generated Thought as the Engine of Neuroticism', *Trends in Cognitive Sciences*, vol. 19, no. 9, 2015, pp. 492–8.

Petersen, S.E. & M.I. Posner, 'The Attention System of the Human Brain: 20 Years After', *Annual Review of Neuroscience*, no. 35, 2012, pp. 73–89, DOI: 10.1146/annurev-neuro-062111-150525.

Pezzulo, G., F. Rigoli & K. Friston, 'Active Inference, Homeostatic Regulation and Adaptive Behavioural Control', *Progress in Neurobiology*, no. 134, 2015, pp. 17–35, DOI:10.1016/j.pneurobio.2015.09.001 (accessed 13 January 2016).

Pinto, Y. et al., 'Expectations Accelerate Entry of Visual Stimuli into Awareness', *Journal of Vision*, vol. 15, no. 8, 2015, p. 13, DOI: 10.1167/15.8.13.

Place, U.T., 'Is Consciousness a Brain Process?', *British Journal of Psychology*, vol. 47, no. 1, 1956, pp. 44–50.

Posner J. et al., *Plum and Posner's Diagnosis of Stupor and Coma*, 4th edn., New York, NY, Oxford University Press, 2007.

Pribram, K., 'Consciousness Reassessed', *Mind and Matter*, vol. 2, no. 1, 2004, pp. 7–35.

Pribram, K.H., 'Behaviorism, Phenomenology and Holism in Psychology: A Scientific Analysis', *Journal of Social and Biological Structures*, no. 2. 1979, pp. 65–72.

Pribram, K.H., 'How is it that Sensing so Much can do so Little?', in F.O. Schmitt & F.G. Worden (eds.), *The Neurosciences Third Study Program*, Cambridge, MA, MIT Press, 1974.

Pribram, K.H., *Languages of the Brain: Experimental Paradoxes and Principles in Neuropsychology*, Englewood Cliffs, NJ, Prentice-Hall, 1971.

Priestley, L., *Pudgalavada Buddhism: The Reality of the Indeterminate Self*, Toronto, Centre for South Asian Studies, University of Toronto, 1999.

Prinz, J., *Gut Reactions*, Oxford, Oxford University Press, 2004.

Proffitt, D.R. & S.A. Linkenhauger, 'Perception Viewed as a Phenotypic Expression', in W. Prinz, M. Biesert & A. Herwig (eds.), *Action Science: Foundations of an Emerging Discipline*, Cambridge, MA, MIT Press, 2013.

Pyszczynski, T., S. Solomon & J. Greenberg, 'Thirty Years of Terror Management Theory', *Advances in Experimental Social Psychology*, no. 52, 2015, pp. 1–70.

Quine, W.V., *Theories and Things*, Cambridge, MA, Harvard University Press, 1981.

Ratcliff, R. & P.L. Smith, 'A Comparison of Sequential Sampling Models for Two-Choice Reaction Time', *Psychological Review*, no. 111, 2004, pp. 333–67.

Repetti, R., 'Buddhist Hard Determinism: No Self, No Free Will, No Responsibility', *Journal of Buddhist Ethics*, no. 19, 2012, pp. 130–97.

Repetti, R., 'Buddhist Reductionism and Free Will: Palaeo-compatibilism', *Journal of Buddhist Ethics*, no. 19, 2012, pp. 33–95.

Repetti, R., 'Buddhist Theories of Free Will: Compatibilism', *Journal of Buddhist Ethics*, no. 17, 2010, pp. 279–310.

Repetti, R., 'Recent Buddhist Theories of Free Will: Compatibilism, Incompatibilism, and Beyond', *Journal of Buddhist Ethics*, no. 21, 2014, pp. 279–352.

Revonsuo A., 'Hard to See the Problem?', *Journal of Consciousness Studies*, vol. 22, nos. 3–4, 2015, pp. 52–67.

Revonsuo, A., 'Consciousness, Dreams and Virtual Realities', *Philosophical Psychology*, vol. 8, no. 1, 1995, pp. 35–58.

Revonsuo, A., 'The Reinterpretation of Dreams: An Evolutionary Hypothesis of the Function of Dreaming', *Behavioral and Brain Sciences*, vol. 23, no. 6, 2000, pp. 877–901.

Revonsuo, A., *Inner Presence: Consciousness as a Biological Phenomenon*, Cambridge, MA, MIT Press, 2006.

Revonsuo, A., J. Tuominen & K. Valli, 'The Avatars in the Machine: Dreaming as a Simulation of Social Reality', in T. Metzinger & J.M. Windt (eds.), *Open MIND:* 32(T), Frankfurt a.M., MIND Group, 2015.

Revonsuo, A., J. Tuominen & K. Valli, 'The Simulation Theories of Dreaming: How to Make Theoretical Progress in Dream Science – A Reply to Martin Dresler', in T. Metzinger & J.M. Windt (eds.), *Open MIND:* 32(T), Frankfurt a.M., MIND Group, 2015.

Rock, I., *Indirect Perception*, Cambridge, MA, MIT Press, 1997.

Roepstorff, A., J. Niewöhner & S. Beck, 'Enculturing Brains through Patterned Practices', *Neural Networks*, vol. 23, nos. 8–9, pp. 1051–9, DOI: 10.1016/j.neunet.2010.08.002 (accessed 13 January 2016).

Rorty, R., 'Mind–Body Identity, Privacy, and Categories', *Review of Metaphysics*, no. 19, 1965, pp. 24–54.

Rosanova, M. et al., 'Recovery of Cortical Effective Connectivity and Recovery of Consciousness in Vegetative Patients', *Brain*, no. 135 (pt. 4), 2012, pp. 1308–20.

Rosenthal, D.M., *Consciousness and Mind*, Oxford, Clarendon Press, 2005.

Russell, B., 'Mind and Matter', in Russell, *Portraits from Memory*, Nottingham, Spokesman, 1995 [1956].

Russell, B., *An Inquiry into Meaning and Truth*, London, George Allen and Unwin, 1940.

Russell, B., *An Outline of Philosophy*, London, Routledge, 1992 [1927].

Russell, B., *Portraits from Memory and Other Essays*, New York. NY, Simon & Schuster, 1950.

Russell, B., *The Analysis of Matter*, London, Routledge, 1992 [1927].

Russell, B., *The Analysis of Mind*, London, George Allen and Unwin, 1921.

Ryle, G., *The Concept of Mind*, Chicago, IL, University of Chicago Press, 1949.

Ryle, G., *The Concept of Mind*, London, Hutchinson, 1949.

Ryvlin, R., J.H. Cross & S. Rheims, 'Epilepsy Surgery in Children and Adults', *The Lancet Neurology*, vol. 13, no. 11, 2014, pp. 1114–26, DOI: 10.1016/S1474-4422(14)70156-5.

S. Rinpoche, *The Tibetan Book of Living and Dying*, San Francisco, CA, HarperOne, 1994.

S. Sarasso et al., 'Consciousness and Complexity during Unresponsiveness Induced by Propofol, Xenon, and Ketamine', *Current Biology*, no. 25, pp. 3099–105.

Salti, M. et al., 'Distinct Cortical Codes and Temporal Dynamics for Conscious and Unconscious Percepts', *eLife*, 2015, DOI: 10.7554/eLife.05652.

Sasai, S., M. Boly, A. Mensen, & G. Tononi, 'Functional Split Brain in a Driving/Listening Paradigm', *Proceedings of the National Academy of Sciences*, 2016, p. 13200.

Schachter, S. & J.E. Singer, 'Cognitive, Social, and Physiological determinants of Emotional State', *Psychological Review*, no. 69, 1962, pp. 379–99.

Schartner, M. et al., 'Complexity of Multi-Dimensional Spontaneous EEG Decreases during Propofol Induced General Anaesthesia', *PLOS One*, vol. 10, no 8, 2015, e0133532, DOI: 10.1371/journal.pone.0133532 (accessed 31 January 2016).

Schiff, N.D. & J.B. Posner, 'Another "Awakenings"', *Annals of Neurology*, no. 62, 2007, pp. 5–7.

Schiff, N.D., 'Central Thalamic Contributions to Arousal Regulation and Neurological Disorders of Consciousness', *Annals of the New York Academy of Sciences*, no. 1129, 2008, pp. 105–18.

Schiff, N.D., 'Cognitive Motor Dissociation Following Severe Brain Injuries', *JAMA Neurology*, no. 19, 2015, pp. 1–3.

Schiff, N.D., 'Mesocircuit Mechanisms Underlying Recovery of Consciousness Following Severe Brain Injuries: Models and Predictions', in M.M. Monti & W.G. Sannita (eds.), *Brain Function and Responsiveness in Disorders of Consciousness*, Cham, Springer International Publishing, 2016.

Schiff, N.D., 'Recovery of Consciousness after Brain Injury: A Mesocircuit Hypothesis', *Trends in Neurosciences*, no. 33, 2010, pp. 1–9.

Schmidt, R.E. & M. van der Linden, 'The Aftermath of Rash Action: Sleep-Interfering Counterfactual Thoughts and Emotions', *Emotion*, vol. 9, no. 4, 2009, pp. 549–53.

Schmidt, R.E., A.G. Harvey & M. van der Linden, 'Cognitive and Affective Control in Insomnia', *Frontiers in Psychology*, no. 2, 2011, p. 349, DOI: 10.3389/fpsyg. 2011.00349 (accessed January 6, 2016).

Schnakers, C. et al., 'Measuring the Effect of Amantadine in Chronic Anoxic Minimally Conscious State', *Journal of Neurology, Neurosurgery & Psychiatry*, vol. 79, no. 2, 2008, pp. 225–7.

Schopenhauer, A., *Prize Essay on the Freedom of the Will*, Cambridge, Cambridge University Press, 1999.

Schredl, M. & F. Hofmann, 'Continuity Between Waking Activities and Dream Activities', *Consciousness and Cognition*, vol. 12, no. 2, 2003, pp. 298–308.

Schwartz, S., 'A Historical Loop of One Hundred Years: Similarities between 19th Century and Contemporary Dream Research', *Dreaming*, no. 10, 2000, pp. 55–66.

Scoville, W.B. & B. Milner, 'Loss of Recent Memory after Bilateral Hippocampal Lesions. 1957', *Journal of Neuropsychiatry & Clinical Neurosciences*, vol. 12, no. 1, 2000, pp. 103–13.

Searle, J., 'Minds, Brains, and Programs', *Behavioral and Brain Sciences*, vol. 3, no. 3, 1980, pp. 417–57.

Sebastian, M.A., 'Dreams: An Empirical Way to Settle the Discussion between Cognitive and Non-Cognitive Theories of Consciousness', *Synthese*, no. 191, 2014, pp. 263–85.

Sellars, W., 'Philosophy and the Scientific Image of Man', in R. Colodny (ed.), *Frontiers of Science and Philosophy*, Pittsburgh, PA, University of Pittsburgh Press, 1963, pp. 35–78.

Seth, A. et al., 'Measuring Consciousness: Relating Behavioural and Neurophysiological Approaches', *Trends in Cognitive Science*, vol. 12, no. 8, 2008, pp. 314–21.

Seth, A., 'Models of Consciousness', *Scholarpedia*, vol. 2, no. 1, 2007, p. 1328, DOI:10.4249/scholarpedia.1328 (accessed 6 January 2016).

Seth, A.K., 'A Predictive Processing Theory of Sensorimotor Contingencies: Explaining the Puzzle of Perceptual Presence and its Absence in Synesthesia', *Cognitive Neuroscience*, vol. 5, no. 2, 2014, pp. 97–118, DOI: 10.1080/17588928.2013.877880.

Seth, A.K., 'Darwin's Neuroscientist: Gerald M. Edelman, 1929–2014', *Frontiers in Psychology*, vol. 5, 2014, p. 896, DOI: 10.3389/fpsyg.2014.00896.

Seth, A.K., 'Editorial', *Neuroscience of Consciousness*, no. 1, 2015, pp. 1–3.

Seth, A.K., 'Explanatory Correlates of Consciousness: Theoretical and Computational Challenges', *Cognitive Computation*, vol. 1, no. 1, 2009, pp. 50–63.

Seth, A.K., 'Interoceptive Inference, Emotion, and the Embodied Self ', *Trends in Cognitive Sciences*, vol. 17, no. 11, 2013, pp. 565–73, DOI: 10.1016/j.tics.2013.09.007.

Seth, A.K., 'The Cybernetic Bayesian Brain: From Interoceptive Inference to Sensorimotor Contingencies', in J.M. Windt & T. Metzinger (eds.), *Open MIND*, Frankfurt am Main, MIND Group, 2015, pp. 1–24.

Seth, A.K., 'The Grand Challenge of Consciousness', *Frontiers in Psychology*, vol. 1, no. 5, 2010, pp. 1–2.

Seth, A.K., 'The Strength of Weak Artificial Consciousness', *Journal of Machine Consciousness*, vol. 1, no. 1, 2009, pp. 71–82.

Seth, A.K., A.B. Barrett & L. Barnett, 'Causal Density and Integrated Information as Measures of Conscious Level', *Philosophical Transactions of the Royal Society A: Mathematical, Physical, and Engineering Sciences*, vol. 369, no. 1952, 2011, pp. 3748–67, DOI: 10.1098/rsta.2011.0079.

Seth, A.K., B.J. Baars & D.B. Edelman, 'Criteria for Consciousness in Humans and Other Mammals', *Consciousness and Cognition*, vol. 14, no. 1, 2005, pp. 119–39.

Shannon, C.E. & W. Weaver, *The Mathematical Theory of Communication*, Urbana, IL, University of Illinois Press, 1949.

Sheldrake, R., 'The Sense of Being Stared at. Part 2: Its Implications for Theories of Vision', *Journal of Consciousness Studies*, vol. 12, no. 6, 2005, pp. 32–49.

Shewmon, A., G. Holmes & P. Byrne, 'Consciousness in Congenitally Decorticate Children: Developmental Vegetative State as Self-Fulfilling Prophecy', *Developmental Medicine and Child Neurology*, no. 41, 1999, pp. 364–74.

Siderits, M., 'Beyond Compatibilism: A Buddhist Approach to Freedom and Determinism', *American Philosophical Quarterly*, no. 24, 1987, pp. 149–59.

Siderits, M., 'Buddhist Non-Self: The No-Owner's Manual', in S. Gallagher (ed.), *The Oxford Handbook of the Self*, Oxford, Oxford University Press, 2011, pp. 296–315.

Siderits, M., *Buddhism as Philosophy: An Introduction*, Indianapolis, IN, Hackett Publishing, 2007.

Sierra, M. & A.S. David, 'Depersonalization: A Selective Impairment of Selfawareness', *Consciousness and Cognition*, vol. 20, no. 1, 2011, pp. 99–108, DOI: 10.1016/j. concog.2010.10.018.

Silberstein, M. & A. Chemero, 'Complexity and Extended Phenomenological Cognitive Systems', *Topics in Cognitive Science*, vol. 4, no. 1, 2012, pp. 1–16.

Singer, E.A., 'Mind as an Observable Object', *Journal of Philosophy, Psychology, and Scientific Methods*, vol. 8, 1911, pp. 180–6.

Singer, W., 'Conscious Processing: Unity in Time rather than in Space', in S. Schneider & M. Velmans (eds.), *The Blackwell Companion to Consciousness*, 2nd edn. (in press), Chichester, Sussex, John Wiley & Sons.

Singer, W., 'Neuronal Synchrony: A Versatile Code for the Definition of Relations?', *Neuron*, no. 24, 1999, pp. 49–65.

Sitt, J.D. et al., 'Large Scale Screening of Neural Signatures of Consciousness in Patients in a Vegetative or Minimally Conscious State', *Brain*, vol. 137, pt. 8, 2014, pp. 2258–70, DOI: 10.1093/brain/awu141.

Slagter, H.A. et al., 'Mental Training Affects Distribution of Limited Brain Resources', *PLOS Biology*, vol. 5, no. 6, 2007, p. e138, DOI: 10.1371/journal.pbio. 0050138.

Slater, M. et al., 'First Person Experience of Body Transfer in Virtual Reality', *PLOS One*, vol. 5, no. 5, 2010, p. e10564, DOI: 10.1371/journal.pone.0010564.

Smallwood, J. & J.W. Schooler, 'The Science of Mind Wandering: Empirically Navigating the Stream of Consciousness', *Annual Review of Psychology*, vol. 66, 2015, pp. 487–518.

Smallwood, J. & J.W. Schooler, 'The Science of Mind Wandering: Empirically Navigating the Stream of Consciousness', *Annual Review of Psychology*, no. 66, 2015, pp. 487–518, DOI: 10.1146/annurev-psych-010814-015331.

Smart, J.J.C., 'Sensations and Brain Processes', *Philosophical Review*, vol. 68, no. 2, 1959, pp. 141–56.

Sneddon, L., 'Pain Perception in Fish: Evidence and Implications for the Use of Fish', *Journal of Consciousness Studies*, no. 18, 2012, pp. 209–29.

Sneddon, L.U., 'The Evidence for Pain in Fish: The Use of Morphine as an Analgesic', *Applied Animal Behaviour Science*, vol. 83, no. 2, 2003, pp. 153–62.

Sneddon, L.U., V.A. Braithwaite & M.J. Gentle, 'Do Fishes have Nociceptors? Evidence for the Evolution of a Vertebrate Sensory System', *Proceedings of the Royal Society B: Biological Sciences*, no. 270, 2003, pp. 1115–21.

Solomon, S.G. & P. Lennie, 'The Machinery of Colour Vision', *Nature Reviews Neuroscience*, no. 8, 2007, pp. 276–78.

Sperry, R.W., 'Toward a Theory of Mind', *Proceedings of the National Academy of Sciences*, no. 63, 1969, pp. 230–1.

Squire, L.R. et al., *Fundamental Neuroscience*, 4th edn., San Diego, CA, Academic Press, 2012.

Squire, L.R., C.E. Stark & R.E. Clark, 'The Medial Temporal Lobe', *Annual Review of Neuroscience*, no. 27, 2004, pp. 279–306.

Stender, J. et al, 'Diagnostic Precision of PET Imaging and Functional MRI in Disorders of Consciousness: A Clinical Validation Study', *The Lancet*, vol. 384, no. 9942, 2014, pp. 514–22.

Strasburger, H. & B. Waldvogel, 'Sight and blindness in the same person: Gating in the visual system', *PsyCh Journal*, vol. 4, no. 4, 2015, pp. 178–85.

Strawson, G., 'The Mind's I', review of D. Lodge, *Consciousness and the Novel*, *Guardian*, 23 November 2002, http://www.theguardian.com/books/2002/nov/23/fiction.higher-education (accessed 2 January 2016).

Strawson, G., *Freedom and Belief*, 2nd edn., Oxford, Oxford University Press, 2010.

Strawson, G., *Selves*, Oxford, Clarendon Press, 2009.

Strawson, P., 'Freedom and Resentment', *Proceedings of the British Academy*, no. 48, 1962, pp. 187–211.

Striedter, G.F. et al., 'NSF Workshop Report: Discovering General Principles of Nervous System Organization by Comparing Brain Maps Across Species', *Brain, Behavior and Evolution*, vol. 83, no. 1, 2014, pp. 1–8, DOI: 10.1159/000360152.

Summerfield, C. & F.P. de Lange, 'Expectation in Perceptual Decision Making: Neural and Computational Mechanisms', *Nature Reviews Neuroscience*, vol. 15, no. 11, 2014, pp. 745–56, DOI: 10.1038/nrn3838.

Super, H., H. Spekreijse & V.A. Lamme, 'Two Distinct Modes of Sensory Processing Observed in Monkey Primary Visual Cortex (V1)', *Nature Neuroscience*, vol. 4, no. 3, 2001, pp. 304–10, DOI: 10.1038/85170.

Sutherland, S., *International Dictionary of Psychology*, New York, NY, Crossroad Classic, 1989.

Taatgen, N.A., 'The Nature and Transfer of Cognitive Skills', *Psychological Review*, no. 120, 2013, pp. 439–71.

Taylor, S. & J. Brown, 'Illusion and Well-Being: A Social Psychological Perspective on Mental Health', *Psychological Bulletin*, vol. 103, no. 2, pp. 193–210.

Thagard, P., 'Explanatory Identities and Conceptual Change', *Science & Education*, vol. 23, no. 7, 2014, pp. 1531–48, DOI: 10.1007/s11191-014-9682-1.

Thompson, E., 'Life and Mind: From Autopoeisis to Neurophenomenology: A Tribute to Francisco Varela', *Phenomenology and the Cognitive Sciences*, no. 3, 2004, pp. 381–98.

Thompson, E., *Waking, Dreaming, Being: Self and Consciousness in Neuroscience, Meditation and Philosophy*, New York, NY, Columbia University Press, 2015.

Thomson, H., 'The Man who Believes he is Dead', *New Scientist*, 1 June 2013, p. 12.

Tomasik, B., 'The Importance of Wild Animal Suffering', *Relations: Beyond Anthropocentrism*, vol. 3, no. 2, 2015, pp. 133–52. DOI: http://dx.doi.org/10.7358/rela-2015-002-toma.

Tomita, H. et al., 'Top–Down Signal from Prefrontal Cortex in Executive Control of Memory Retrieval', *Nature*, vol. 401, no. 6754, 1999, pp. 699–703.

Tong, F. et al., 'Binocular Rivalry and Visual Awareness in Human Extrastriate Cortex', *Neuron*, vol. 21, no. 4, 1998, pp. 753–59.

Tononi, G. & C. Koch, 'Consciousness: Here, There and Everywhere?', *Philosophical Transactions of the Royal Society B: Biological Sciences*, vol. 370, no. 1668, 2015, DOI: 10.1098/rstb.2014.0167 (accessed 21 December 2015).

Tononi, G. & C. Koch, 'The Neural Correlates of Consciousness: An Update', *Annals of the New York Academy of Sciences*, no. 1124, 2008, pp. 239–61.

Tononi, G. & G.M. Edelman, 'Consciousness and Complexity', *Science*, vol. 282, no. 5395, 1998, pp. 1846–51.

Tononi, G., 'An Information Integration Theory of Consciousness', *BMC Neuroscience*, no. 5, 2004, p. 42, DOI: 10.1186/1471-2202-5-42 (accessed 27 January 2016).

Tononi, G., 'Consciousness as Integrated Information: A Provisional Manifesto', *Biological Bulletin*, vol. 215, no. 3, 2008, pp. 216–42.

Treynor, W., R. Gonzalez & S. Nolen-Hoeksema, 'Rumination Reconsidered: A Psychometric Analysis', *Cognitive Therapy and Research*, no. 27, 2003, pp. 247–59, DOI: 10.1023/A:1023910315561.

Tsuchiya, N. '"What is it like to be a bat?" A Pathway to the Answer from the Integrated Information Theory', *Philosophy Compass*, 2017, p. e12407, DOI: 10.1111/ phc3.12407.

Tsuchiya, N. & C. Koch, 'Continuous Flash Suppression Reduces Negative Afterimages', *Nature Neuroscience*, vol. 8, no. 8, 2005, pp. 1096–101.

Tsuchiya, N. et al., 'Decoding Face Information in Time, Frequency and Space from Direct Intracranial Recordings of the Human Brain', *PLOS One*, vol. 3, no. 12, 2008, p. e3892 (accessed 21 December 2015).

Tsuchiya, N. et al., 'No-Report Paradigms: Extracting the True Neural Correlates of Consciousness', *Trends in Cognitive Sciences*, vol. 19, no. 12, 2015, pp. 757–70, DOI: 10.1016/j.tics.2015.10.002.

Tulving, E. 'Episodic Memory: From Mind to Brain', *Annual Review of Psychology*, no. 53, 2002, pp. 1–25, DOI: 10.1146/annurev.psych.53.100901.135114.

Twain, M., *Autobiography of Mark Twain*, vol. 2, Berkeley, CA, University of California Press, 2013 [1906–07].

Tye, M. & A. Byrne, 'Qualia Ain't in the Head', *Noûs*, vol. 40, no. 2, 2006, pp. 241–55.

Tye, M., 'Philosophical Problems of Consciousness', in M. Velmans & S. Schneider (eds.), *The Blackwell Companion to Consciousness*, Oxford, Blackwell, 2007, pp. 23–35.

Tye, M., *Consciousness, Color and Content*, Cambridge, MA, Bradford Books, MIT Press, 2000.

Tye, M., *Ten Problems of Consciousness: A Representational Theory of the Phenomenal Mind*, Cambridge, MA, MIT Press, 1997.

Tye, M., *Tense Bees and Shell-Shocked Crabs: Consciousness in the Animal World*, Oxford, Oxford University Press, forthcoming.

Vago, D.R. & D.A. Silbersweig, 'Self-Awareness, Self-Regulation, and Self-Transcendence (S-ART): A Framework for Understanding the Neurobiological Mechanisms of Mindfulness', *Frontiers in Human Neuroscience*, no. 6, 2012, p. 296, DOI: 10.3389/fnhum.2012.00296.

Valli, K. & A. Revonsuo, 'The Threat Simulation Theory in Light of Recent Empirical Evidence: A Review', *American Journal of Psychology*, vol. 122, no. 1, 2009, pp. 17–38.

Valli, K., 'Dreaming in the Multilevel Framework', *Consciousness and Cognition*, vol. 20, no. 4, 2011, pp. 1084–90.

Velmans, M. & Y. Nagasawa, 'Introduction to Monist Alternatives to Physicalism, *Journal of Consciousness Studies*, vol. 19, nos. 9-10, 2012, pp. 7–18.

Velmans, M., 'A Reflexive Science of Consciousness', in G.R. Bock & J. Marsh (eds.), *Experimental and Theoretical Studies of Consciousness (CIBA Foundation Symposium 174)*, Chichester, Wiley, 1993, pp. 81–99.

Velmans, M., 'Consciousness from a First-Person Perspective', *Behavioral and Brain Sciences*, vol. 14, no. 4, 1991, pp. 702–26.

Velmans, M., 'Consciousness, Brain and the Physical World', *Philosophical Psychology*, no. 3, 1990, pp. 77–99.

Velmans, M., 'How to Arrive at an Eastern Place from a Western Direction: Convergences and Divergences among Samkya Yoga, Advaita Vedanta, the Body–Mind-Consciousness (Trident) Model and Reflexive Monism', in B.S. Prasad (ed.), *Consciousness, Gandhi and Yoga: Interdisciplinary, East–West Odyssey of K. Ramakrishna Rao*, New Delhi, D.K. Printworld, 2013, pp. 107–39.

Velmans, M., 'Reflexive Monism: Psychophysical Relations Among Mind, Matter and Consciousness', *Journal of Consciousness Studies*, vol. 19, nos. 9–10, 2012, pp. 143–65.

Velmans, M., review of Stanislas Dehaene, *Consciousness and the Brain: Deciphering how the Brain Codes our Thoughts*, *Journal of Consciousness Studies*, vol. 21, nos. 11–12, 2014, pp. 178–96.

Velmans, M., *Understanding Consciousness*, London, Routledge, 2000; 2nd edn., London, Routledge, 2009.

Voss, U. et al., 'Waking and Dreaming: Related but Structurally Independent. Dream Reports of Congenitally Paraplegic and Deaf-Mute Persons', *Consciousness and Cognition*, vol. 20, no. 3, 2011, pp. 673–87.

van Vugt, M.K. & A.P. Jha, 'Investigating the Impact of Mindfulness Meditation Training on Working Memory: A Mathematical Modeling Approach', *Cognitive, Affective, & Behavioral Neuroscience*, no. 11, 2011, pp. 344–53.

van Vugt, M.K. & H.A. Slagter, 'Control over Experience? Magnitude of the Attentional Blink Depends on Meditative State', *Consciousness and Cognition*, no. 23, 2014, pp. 32–9, DOI: 10.1016/j.concog.2013.11.001.

van Vugt, M.K. & P.M. van den Hurk, 'Modeling the Effects of Attention Cueing on Mediators', *Mindfulness*, 2016, DOI: 10.1007/s12671-015-0464-x.

van Vugt, M.K. et al., 'Modeling Mind-Wandering: A Tool to Better Understand

Distraction', in N. Taatgen et al. (eds.), *Proceedings of the International Conference in Cognitive Modeling*, Groningen, University of Groningen, 2015, pp. 252–7.

van Vugt, M.K. et al., 'The Effects of Mindfulness-Based Cognitive Therapy on Affective Memory Associations in Depression: A Mechanistic Model of Rumination', *Frontiers in Human Neuroscience*, no. 6, 2012, p. 257, DOI: 10.3389/ fnhum.2012.00257.

Varela, F., E. Thompson & E. Rosch, *The Embodied Mind: Cognitive Science and Human Experience*, Cambridge, MA, MIT Press, 1993.

Wagenmakers, E.-J., H.L.J. Van Der Maas & R.P.P.P. Grasman, 'An EZ-Diffusion Model for Response Time and Accuracy', *Psychonomic Bulletin & Review*, no. 14, 2007, pp. 3–22, DOI: 10.3758/BF03194023.

Wagstaff, G.F., *Hypnosis, Compliance and Belief*, New York, NY, St. Martin's Press, 1981.

Wallace, B.A., 'The Buddhist Tradition of Samatha: Methods for Refining and Examining Consciousness', *Journal of Consciousness Studies*, no. 6, 1999, pp. 175–87.

Wallace, B.A., *The Attention Revolution*, Somerville, MA, Wisdom Publications, 2008.

Walsh, D.M., 'The Struggle for Life and the Conditions of Existence: Two Interpretations of Darwinian Evolution', in F. Brinkworth & F. Weinert (eds.), *Evolution 2.0: Implications of Darwinism in Philosophy and the Social and Natural Sciences*, Dordrecht, Springer, 2012.

Watson, J.B., 'Psychology as the Behaviorist Views it', *Psychological Review*, no. 20, 1913, pp. 158–77.

Weinberger, J., 'William James and the Unconscious: Redressing a Century-old Misunderstanding', *Psychological Science*, vol. 11, no. 6, 2000, pp. 439–45.

Weitzenhoffer, A.M., *The Practice of Hypnotism*, New York, NY, Wiley, 2000.

Werfel, J., K. Petersen & Radhika Nagpal, 'Designing Collective Behavior in a Termite-inspired Robot Construction Team', *Science*, vol. 343, no. 6172, 2014, pp. 754–8.

White, R.W., 'A Preface to a Theory of Hypnotism', *Journal of Abnormal and Social Psychology*, vol. 36, no. 4, 1941, pp. 477–505.

Williams, P., *Altruism and Reality: Studies in the Philosophy of the Bodhicaryavatara*, London, Routledge, 1997.

Williams, S.T. et al., 'Common Resting Brain Dynamics Indicate a Possible Mechanism Underlying Zolpidem Response in Severely Brain-Injured Subjects', *eLife*, no. 2, p. e01157, 2013, http://elifesciences.org/content/elife/2/e01157.full.pdf (accessed 14 December 2015).

Windt, J.M., 'The Immersive Spatio-temporal Hallucination Model of Dreaming', *Phenomenology and Cognitive Science*, vol. 9, no. 2, 2010, pp. 295–316.

Windt, J.M., *Dreaming: A Conceptual Framework for Philosophy of Mind and Empirical Research*, Cambridge, MA, MIT Press, 2015.

Witt, J.K., 'Putting to a Bigger Hole: Golf Performance Relates to Perceived Size', *Psychonomic Bulletin Review*, vol. 15, no. 3, pp. 581–5.

Witt, J.K., D.R. Proffitt & W. Epstein, 'Perceiving Distance: A Role of Effort and Intent', *Perception*, vol. 33, no. 5, 2004, pp. 570–90.

Wittgenstein, L., *Philosophical Investigations*, London, Macmillan, 1953.

Young, R.M., *Mind, Brain, and Adaptation in the Nineteenth Century*, New York, NY, Oxford University Press, 1991.

Zadra, A., S. Desjardins & E. Marcotte, 'Evolutionary Function of Dreams: A Test of the Threat Simulation Theory in Recurrent Dreams', *Consciousness and Cognition*, no. 15, 2006, pp. 450–63.

Zahavi, D., 'The Experiential Self: Objections and Clarifications', in M. Siderits, E. Thompson & D. Zahavi (eds.), *Self, No-Self?*, Oxford, Oxford University Press, 2011, pp. 56–78.

Zeidan, F. et al., 'Mindfulness Meditation Improves Cognition: Evidence of Brief Mental Training', *Consciousness and Cognition*, no. 19, 2010, pp. 597–605.

CONTRIBUTORS

SUSAN BLACKMORE is a freelance writer, lecturer and broadcaster, a TED lecturer, and Visiting Professor at the University of Plymouth. She has a degree in psychology and physiology from Oxford University (1973), and an MSc and PhD in parapsychology from the University of Surrey (1980). Her research interests include memes, evolution, consciousness and AI. She practises Zen and plays in a samba band. She is author of over 60 academic articles, 80 book contributions and many book reviews. *The Meme Machine* (1999) has been translated into nearly twenty other languages. Her most recent books are *Seeing Myself: What Out-of-body Experiences Tell Us About Life, Death & the Mind* (2017) and *Consciousness: An Introduction* (3rd edition with Emily Troscianko) (2018).

PAUL BROKS is a clinical neuropsychologist-turned-writer. He gained recognition as a writer with his first book *Into the Silent Land* (2003), which mixed neurological case stories, fiction and memoir in an extended meditation on selfhood and the brain. Dr Broks has written for theatre, radio and film, and his journalistic output includes columns for *The Times* and *Prospect magazine*. He wrote and presented several episodes in the major BBC radio series *A History of Ideas* and, also for BBC, fronted *Dr. Broks's Casebook*. His latest book is, *The Darker the Night, The Brighter the Stars: A Neuropsychologist's Odyssey* (Allen Lane, 2018).

AMBER D. CARPENTER (Yale-NUS College) has published widely in ancient Greek philosophy (focus on Plato) and Indian Buddhist philosophy, both separately and increasingly by creating philosophical conversations between the two. She currently leads an international research project on Buddhist–Platonist Dialogues (buddhistplatonistdialogues.com). Having pursued questions in metaphysics, epistemology and mind, as they connect to ethical questions, she is currently elaborating a distinctive ethical perspective, found in Plato and in Indian Buddhists, which sees ethical transformation as effected by knowing impersonal reality. She has held research fellowships at Yale, Melbourne and York, and with the Einstein Forum (Potsdam) and the Templeton Religious Trust ('Ethical Ambitions and Their Formations of Character', part of the *Moral Beacon* project). Her co-edited collection of *Portraits of Integrity*, emerging from the Integrity Project (integrityproject.org), appeared in 2020.

PATRICIA SMITH CHURCHLAND is Professor Emerita of Philosophy at the University of California, San Diego, and an adjunct professor at the Salk Institute. Her research focuses on the interface between neuroscience and philosophy. She is author of the pioneering book *Neurophilosophy* (1986) and co-author with T.J. Sejnowski of *The Computational Brain* (1992). Her current work focuses on morality and the social brain: *Braintrust: What Neuroscience Tells us About Morality* (2011). *Touching a Nerve* (2013) portrays how to get comfortable with this fact: "I am what I am because my brain is as it is". She has been president of the American Philosophical Association and the Society for Philosophy and Psychology, and won a MacArthur Prize in 1991, the Rossi Prize for neuroscience in 2008, and the Prose Prize for science for the book *Braintrust*. She was chair of the Philosophy Department at the University of California San Diego from 2000 to 2007.

ANDY CLARK is Professor of Cognitive Philosophy at the University of Sussex, previously professor of logic and metaphysics at the University of Edinburgh 2004–21, where he was head of Philosophy Subject Area 2008–11. He has also had tenure at Indiana University and Washington University. Dr Clark is the author of eight monographs including *Being There: Putting Brain, Body And World Together Again* (1997), *Supersizing the Mind* (2008) and *Surfing Uncertainty: Prediction, Action, and the Embodied Mind* (2016), as well as over 120 refereed journal articles. Dr Clark is committed to public engagement and has participated in over 60 such events, appearing on both the Opinionator and The Stone blogs of *The New York Times*, and contributing to dozens of radio shows and a few television broadcasts. In 2007, he was elected fellow of the Royal Society of Edinburgh, in 2011 he was distinguished visiting fellow at the Sage Center for the Study of the Mind, University of California, Santa Barbara. In 2013, he was invited senior scholar at the Positive Neuroscience Retreat, University of Pennsylvania. In 2015, he was elected fellow of the British

Academy of Humanities and Social Sciences, and in 2016 he delivered the Chandaria Lecture Series at the University of London. He is currently PI on an ERC Synergy Grant, XScape. Material Minds: Exploring the Interactions between Predictive Brains, Cultural Artifacts, and Embodied Visual Search. EUROPEAN UNION1 Nov 2021–31 Oct 2027.

OWEN FLANAGAN is James B. Duke University Professor of Philosophy at Duke University, Durham, NC, USA, where he is co-director of the Center for Comparative Philosophy. His work is in philosophy of mind, moral psychology and comparative philosophy. He is the author of *Varieties of Moral Personality* (1991), *Consciousness Reconsidered* (1992) and many other books; his most recent books are *The Geography of Morals: Varieties of Moral Possibility* (2017) and *How to do Things with Emotions: The Morality of Anger and Shame Across Cultures* (2021). He has been a Rockefeller Fellow at the National Humanities Center (2014–15) and a Berggruen Fellow at the Center for Advanced Study in the Behavioral Sciences at Stanford (2016–17).

MICHAEL S. GAZZANIGA is the director of the Sage Center for the Study of Mind at the University of California, Santa Barbara. He received a PhD from the California Institute of Technology in 1964/65, where he worked with Roger Sperry, and had primary responsibility for initiating human split-brain research. He has carried out extensive studies on both sub-human primate and human behavior and cognition. He is the founding editor of the *Journal of Cognitive Neuroscience* and also a founder of the Cognitive Neuroscience Society. For 20 years he directed the Summer Institute in Cognitive Neuroscience and serves as editor-in-chief of the major reference text *The Cognitive Neurosciences* (2009). He was a member of the President's Council on Bioethics 2001–09. He is a member of the American Academy of Arts and Science, the Institute of Medicine and the National Academy of Sciences.

SAKARI KALLIO, PhD, is a professor of cognitive neuroscience and the head of the Department of Cognitive Neuroscience and Philosophy, University of Skövde, Sweden. After earning his doctorate at the University of Turku, Finland (2003), he moved to Skövde, where he has since been working. His research has focused on understanding the neural mechanisms of hypnosis and hypnotic response. He has, together with

Dr Revonsuo, created a theory of hypnosis (published in *Contemporary Hypnosis*, 2013), which proposes how hypnosis research could be integrated into consciousness research more generally. In Dr Kallio's recent research, his main interest has been in studying the nature of hypnotic colour hallucinations and automaticity in responding to hypnotic suggestions. Kallio serves on the editorial board of *International Journal of Clinical and Experimental Hypnosis, Psychology of Consciousness* and *Contemporary Hypnosis & Integrative Therapy*. In 2007, he received the Henry Guze Award for the best experimental article published on hypnosis that year.

JULIAN KIVERSTEIN is senior researcher at the Department of Psychiatry, Amsterdam University Medical Research. Previously he held the position of assistant professor in neurophilosophy at the University of Amsterdam. Dr Kiverstein has published extensively in the broad field of the philosophy of enactive and embodied cognition, arguing for the significance of the phenomenological tradition in philosophy for cognitive science. He is co-author (with Michael Kirchhoff) of the monograph *Extended Consciousness and Predictive Processing: A Third Wave View* (Routledge, 2019) and the editor of the *Routledge Handbook of the Philosophy of the Social Mind* (2016).

CHRISTOF KOCH is a scholar and scientist best known for experiments and writings exploring the physical basis of consciousness in humans, animals and machines. As a child, he lived in many cities in America, Africa, and Europe. After obtaining a MS and a PhD in theoretical physics at the University of Tübingen in Germany, he worked for four years as a post-doctoral fellow at the Massachusetts Institute of Technology (MIT) in Boston, before becoming a professor of biology and engineering at the California Institute of Technology (Caltech) in Pasadena, directing a laboratory studying the physical basis of computation in the brain, with a particular focus on neocortex, thalamus and claustrum, on visual perception, attention and consciousness and the underlying brain circuits. After more than a quarter of a century in Caltech's ivory tower, Dr. Koch became the Chief Scientist at the Allen Institute for Brain Science in Seattle in 2011, leading a ten-year effort in systems neuroscience funded by the Microsoft co-founder and philanthropist Paul Allen. In 2015, he became the president of the *Allen Institute for Brain Science*, overseeing the institute's growth to more than 300 scientists, engineers, and staff, focused on two large-scale programs – cataloguing the thousand or more distinct types of brain cells in mice and humans and building Brain Observatories to record the flickering activity of tens of thousands of neurons in behaving animals. Since 2021, Dr. Koch is the Chief Scientist of the MindScope Program at the Allen Institute as well as the Chief Scientist of the *Tiny Blue Dot* Foundation, in Santa Monica, seeking to understand how the physical substrate of consciousness determines and constrains how we perceive the world, that is our *Perception Box*, and developing techniques to expand the walls and borders of the Perception Box.

THOMAS METZINGER was Full Professor of Theoretical Philosophy at the Johannes Gutenberg-Universität Mainz until 2019. He is past president of the German Cognitive Science Society (2005–7) and of the Association for the Scientific Study of Consciousness (2009–11). As of 2011, he is an adjunct fellow at the Frankfurt Institute for Advanced Studies, a co-founder of the German Effective Altruism Foundation, president of the Barbara Wengeler Foundation, and on the advisory board of the Giordano Bruno Foundation. From 2008 to 2009 he served as a fellow at the Berlin Institute for Advanced Study; from 2014 to 2019 he was a fellow at the Gutenberg Research College; from 2019 to 2021 he was awarded a *Senior-Forschungsprofessur* by the Ministry of Science, Education and Culture. From 2018 to 2020 Metzinger worked as a member of the European Commission's High-Level Expert Group on Artificial Intelligence.

In the English language, he has edited two collections on consciousness (*Conscious Experience*, Imprint Academic, 1995; *Neural Correlates of Consciousness*, MIT Press, 2000) and published one major scientific monograph (*Being No One – The Self-Model Theory of Subjectivity*, MIT Press, 2003). In 2009, he published a popular book, which addresses a wider audience and discusses the ethical, cultural and social consequences of consciousness research (*The Ego Tunnel – The Science of the Mind and the Myth of the Self*). Important recent Open Access collections are Open MIND at http://www.open-mind.net (2015, with Jennifer Windt), Philosophy and Predictive Processing at http://predictive-mind.net (2017, with Wanja Wiese), and Radical Disruptions of Self-Consciousness (2020, with Raphaël Millière).

THOMAS NAGEL is Professor Emeritus at New York University. He studied at Cornell, Oxford, and Harvard, and taught at Berkeley and Princeton before moving to N.Y.U. His work falls into several fields, including ethics, epistemology, political theory and philosophy of mind. Among his books are *The Possibility of Altruism* (1970), *Mortal Questions* (1979), *The View from Nowhere* (1986), *What Does It All Mean?* (1987), *The Last Word*, and *Mind and Cosmos* (2012).

ANTTI REVONSUO is Professor of Cognitive Neuroscience at the University of Skövde, Sweden, and Professor of Psychology at the University of Turku, Finland. He has been conducting research on consciousness and the philosophical mind–brain problem since the early 1990s. Revonsuo's research has focused especially on dreaming and consciousness and on the neural correlates of visual consciousness. He has written three books on consciousness: *Inner Presence: Consciousness as a Biological Phenomenon* (2006), *Consciousness: The Science of Subjectivity* (2010) and *Foundations of Consciousness* (2018). In these books, he lays out his overall view of the fundamental nature of consciousness and how philosophy and science would best be able to approach it. Revonsuo is also known for his evolutionary-psychological theory of the function of dreaming, the Threat-Simulation Theory (published in *Behavioural and Brain Sciences*, 2000). Revonsuo and his research group have recently started to work on some new lines of research, focusing on the neural mechanisms of consciousness as revealed by general anaesthesia and on new theories of the function of dreaming (especially the Social Simulation Theory) that treat dreaming as a virtual-reality simulation of the waking world.

NICHOLAS D. SCHIFF is a physician-scientist with an internationally recognised expertise in neurological disorders of consciousness. He is the Jerold B. Katz Professor of Neurology and Neuroscience in the Feil Family Brain and Mind Research Institute at Weill Cornell Medical College. Dr Schiff's research efforts bridge basic neuroscience and clinical investigative studies of the pathophysiology of impaired consciousness using state-of-the-art neuroimaging and neurophysiological measurements. This research programme has provided several landmark contributions to the understanding of cerebral activity in severely brain-injured patients. Most notably, Dr Schiff and colleagues have taken insights into the neurophysiological mechanisms of arousal regulation and of deep brain electrical stimulation techniques to demonstrate evidence that long-lasting, severe cognitive disability may be influenced by electrical stimulation of the central thalamus. Based on extensive and long-range longitudinal human subject studies of recovery of consciousness, Dr Schiff has formulated a testable hypothesis for the contribution of the anterior forebrain mesocircuit to recovery of consciousness that organises the findings from work in central thalamic deep brain stimulation into a wider context. This work is an important foundation for developing further understanding of both the mechanisms of recovery of consciousness and basic mechanisms underlying consciousness in the human brain.

ANIL K. SETH is Professor of Cognitive and Computational Neuroscience at the University of Sussex. He is also co-director of the Canadian Institute for Advanced Research (CIFAR) Program on Brain, Mind and Consciousness, a European Research Council advanced investigator, and editor-in-chief of the journal *Neuroscience of Consciousness* (Oxford University Press). He holds degrees in natural sciences (MA, Cambridge, 1996), knowledge-based systems (MSc, Sussex, 1996), and computer science and artificial intelligence (Ph.D., Sussex, 2001). He has published more than 180 papers, is a Web of Science Highly Cited Researcher (2019–21), which places him in the top 1 per cent of researchers in his field worldwide.

Anil is the author of *Being You: A New Science of Consciousness* (Faber, 2021) – an instant *Sunday Times* bestseller and a 2021 Book of the Year for *The Economist, New Statesman, Bloomberg Business, Guardian, Financial Times* and elsewhere. His 2017 TED talk on consciousness has more than 12 million views and features in the 'Top 15' TED science talks of all time. A former Wellcome Trust Engagement Fellow, he has appeared on high-profile podcasts including *Making Sense with Sam Harris* and *Under The Skin* with Russell Brand. He has appeared in several films (*The Most Unknown, The Search*), appears regularly on BBC Radio, and has written for *Aeon*, the *Guardian, Granta, New Scientist* and *Scientific American*, among others. He was the 2017 president of the British Science Association (Psychology Section) and the 2019 winner of the KidSpirit Perspectives award.

GALEN STRAWSON holds the president's chair in philosophy at the University of Texas at Austin. He taught at the University of Oxford from

1979 until 2000 and at Reading University from 2001 until 2013. From 2004 to 2007 he was Distinguished Professor of Philosophy at the Graduate Center of the City University of New York. His publications include *Freedom and Belief* (1986, 2nd edn. 2009), *The Secret Connexion: Realism, Causation, and David Hume* (1989, 2nd edn. 2014), *Mental Reality* (1994, 2nd edn. 2009), *Selves: An Essay in Revisionary Metaphysics* (2009), *The Evident Connexion: Hume on Personal Identity* (2011), *Locke on Personal Identity: Consciousness and Concernment* (2011), *The Subject of Experience* (2017) and *Things That Bother Me* (2018). He has held visiting positions at the Research School of Social Sciences, Australian National University, New York University, Rutgers University, Massachusetts Institute of Technology, Princeton University and the École des hautes études en sciences sociales in Paris.

NAO TSUCHIYA was awarded a PhD at California Institute of Technology in 2006 and underwent postdoctoral training there until 2010. Receiving a JST grant from Japan, he went back to Japan in 2010. In 2012, he joined the School of Psychological Sciences at Monash University as an associate professor and was then promoted to a professor in 2020. His contribution to consciousness research includes development of continuous flash suppression (CFS), for which he received the William James Prize from the Association of Scientific Studies of Consciousness (ASSC) in 2008, examination of the relationship between consciousness and attention, and the analysis of neural recordings using multivariate decoding and integrated information measures. His current research focuses on the relationship between structures of consciousness and information.

MICHAEL TYE encountered philosophy at Oxford University and taught at King's College London, St Andrews and Temple University before coming to the University of Texas at Austin, where he is currently the Dallas TACA Centennial Professor in Liberal Arts. His work has focused on the philosophy of mind and, within that, consciousness in particular. He is known for elaborating and defending the representationalist approach to consciousness. He is the author of nine books, including *Ten Problems of Consciousness* (1995), *Seven Puzzles of Thought* (with Mark Sainsbury, 2011), *Tense Bees and Shell-Shocked Crabs: Are Animals Conscious?* (2016) and *Vagueness and the Evolution of Consciousness* (2021).

MAX VELMANS is Professor Emeritus of Psychology at Goldsmiths, University of London, and is a fellow of the British Psychological Society, a fellow of the Academy of the Social Sciences and has been involved in consciousness studies for around 50 years. His main research focus is on integrating work on the philosophy, cognitive psychology and neuropsychology of consciousness, and, more recently, on East–West integrative approaches. He has over 120 publications on these topics. His book *Understanding Consciousness* (2000, 2nd ed. 2009) develops "reflexive monism", a distinct analysis of consciousness. Other publications include *Consciousness* (2018) (a four-volume collection of major works), *Towards a Deeper Understanding of Consciousness* (2017), the co-edited *Blackwell Companion to Consciousness* (2007, 2nd ed. 2017), *How Could Conscious Experiences Affect Brains?* (2003), *Investigating Phenomenal Consciousness: New Methodologies and Maps* (2000) and *The Science of Consciousness: Psychological, Neuropsychological and Clinical Reviews* (1996). He was a co-founder and 2004–6 chair of the Consciousness and Experiential Psychology Section of the British Psychological Society, and an Indian Council of Philosophical Research National Visiting Professor for 2010–11.

MARIEKE VAN VUGT is Assistant Professor at the Bernoulli Institute of Mathematics, Computer Science and Artificial Intelligence at the University of Groningen (Netherlands). She obtained her PhD in neuroscience focusing on the role of brain oscillations in recognition memory with Dr Michael Kahana at the University of Pennsylvania in 2008. She then went on to do postdoctoral research on the neural correlates of decision making with Dr Jonathan Cohen at Princeton University before starting her own group as a tenure-track assistant professor in Groningen in 2010. The research in Dr van Vugt's lab focuses on how, when and why we mind-wander, and what the fundamental cognitive operations are that underlie meditation and mindfulness. She investigates these questions using a combination of computational modelling, neuroscience and experimental psychology tools. In addition, she ventures into social neuroscience, investigating inter-brain sycnrhony in challenging situations such as dance performances and debating Tibetan monks.

THE RETURN OF CONSCIOUSNESS
A New Science on Old Questions

Re-issue published by Bokförlaget Stolpe, Stockholm, Sweden, 2022

© The authors and Bokförlaget Stolpe 2022,
in association with Axel and Margaret Ax:son Johnson Foundation for Public Benefit

The essays are based on The Return of Consciousness – A New Science on Old Questions seminar held at Avesta Manor in Dalarna, Sweden in 2015. All essays, apart from *The Return of Consciousness – Redux*, were originally published in 2016. No substantial changes have been made for this edition.

Edited by
Kurt Almqvist, President, Axel and Margaret Ax:son Johnson Foundation
Anders Haag, author, journalist and lecturer

Design: Patric Leo
Cover image: Tomus secundus ... de supernaturali,
naturali, praeternaturali et contranaturali microcosmi historia,
in tractatus tres distributa. [Tomi secundi tractatus primi, sectio secunda,
de technica microcosmi historia. Tomi secundi tractatus secundus,
de praeternaturali utriusque mundi historia] / [Robert Fludd].
© Wellcome Collection / CC BY 4.0
Layout: Pontus Dahlström
Prepress and print coordinator: Italgraf Media AB, Sweden
Print: Printon, Estonia, via Italgraf Media, 2022
Second edition, first printing
ISBN: 978-91-89425-83-5

BOKFÖRLAGET STOLPE

AXEL AND MARGARET AX:SON JOHNSON
FOUNDATION FOR PUBLIC BENEFIT